AF566704

Customer Relationship Management (CRM)

Customer Relationship Management (CRM)

P.P. SINGH
M.Sc., MBA, B.Ed.
Reader and Head
Department of Business Management
Punjab College of Technical Education, Ludhiana

and

N. JINENDER KUMAR
M.Com., LL.B., C.A.(I)

REGAL PUBLICATIONS
New Delhi - 110 027

CUSTOMER RELATIONSHIP MANAGEMENT (CRM)

ISBN 978-81-8484-039-1

Printed in India at
MAYUR ENTERPRISES
WZ Plot No. 3, Gujjar Market, Tihar Village, New Delhi - 110 018

Published by
REGAL PUBLICATIONS
F-159, Rajouri Garden, New Delhi - 110 027
Phone : 45546396
E-mail : regalbookspub@yahoo.com

Contents

PREFACE

Customer Relationship Management (CRM) is one of the hot topics in marketing and information systems today. Customer relationship management is a business strategy that provides the enterprise with a complete, dependable, and integrated view of its customer base. A CRM system brings together lots of pieces of information about customers, sales, market trends, marketing effectiveness and responsiveness. CRM helps companies improve the profitability of their interactions with customers while at the same time making those interactions appear friendlier through individualisation. CRM's purpose is to enhance customer satisfaction and retention by alignment of customer business processes with technology integration. This book offers the promise of maximized profits for today's highly competitive businesses. This innovative book provides readers with the tools and techniques to effectively use CRM. It emphasizes the utilization of database marketing in order to build strong and profitable customer relationships.

Over the last decade, too many organizations have assumed that their products or services were so superior that customers would automatically keep coming back for more. But in order to compete effectively in today's marketplace, organizations must change their strategy to become more customer focused, not product focused. Customer Relationship Management (CRM) is the best way to integrate this customer-facing approach throughout an organization. Aimed at understanding and anticipating the needs of an organization's current and potential customers, this innovative book shows how CRM links people, process, and technology to optimize an enterprise's revenue and profits by first providing maximum customer satisfaction.

Completion of this work would not have been possible without reference to the authentic publications on the subject—Indian and Foreign. We shall, therefore, like to record our sincerest thank to the authors and publication houses of those publication. Although every effort has been made to offer the most authentic position on the subject, claiming hundred per cent accuracy will be too tall a claim. Any error, omission and suggestions for the improvement of the book brought to our notice shall be thankfully acknowledged and incorporated in the next edition.

First of all, we heartily thankful to Almighty God. We acknowledge the inspiration and blessings of our parents from the core of our heart and extend thanks to our family members for their moral support which helped us in successful completion of this book.

At last, we extend our sincere thanks to Mr. R.D.S. Bhatia of Regal Publications for his motivating guidance during preparation of this book on several aspects.

P.P. SINGH
N. JINENDER KUMAR

1

An Introduction to Customer Relationship Management (CRM)

INTRODUCTION

The dynamics of the business ecosystem have changed the way in which companies do business both in relationship management and the streamlining of their operations. Relationship marketing is emerging as the core marketing activity for businesses operating in fiercely competitive environments. On an average, businesses spend six times more to acquire new customers than to keep them. Therefore, many firms are now paying more attention to their relationships with existing customers to retain them and increase their share of customer's purchases. The practice of relationship marketing also has the potential to improve marketing productivity through improved marketing efficiencies and effectiveness. Retaining and developing customers has long been a critical success factor for businesses. In that sense, Customer Relationship Management is not new, previously falling under the guise of customer satisfaction. Worldwide, service organisations have been pioneers in developing customer retention strategies. Banks have relationship managers for select customers, airlines have frequent flyer programs to reward loyal customers, credit card companies offer redeemable bonus points for increased card usage, telecom service operators provide customised services to their heavy users, and hotels have personalised services for their regular guests. It is, however, with the rapid rise of new entrants into the market place and increased competition that companies in other sectors have recognised the business potential within a captured base.

"CRM is the business strategy that aims to understand, anticipate, manage and personalize the needs of an organization's current and potential customers".

From this we can learn that CRM is more than just a piece of software; CRM is a business strategy, one that puts the customer at the heart of the business.

"That's nothing new" I hear you say, and you would be right. Good business people have always understood the relationship between happy customers that come back again and again and creating long term, sustainable profitability.

You just have to think of the local shop owner who knew everyone of his customer's names, birthdays and particular ailments to prove that point. What is new is that there now exists the technology to enable this customer-centricity on a much larger scale.

It is said that a successful CRM implementation will allow your Customer Service, Sales and Marketing people (and anyone else in your organization) to have a holistic view of each and everyone of your customers. In theory this will enable them to make quick, informed decisions, create cross selling and up selling opportunities, measure marketing effectiveness and deliver personalized Customer Care. Sound's great doesn't it!

THE HISTORY OF CRM

Following on from Enterprise Resource Planning or ERP (the business strategy that promised to automate the "back-office"), the term CRM was first coined in the mid-1990s. CRM in those days referred to the software used to help businesses manage their customer relationships. From sales force automation software (SFA) that focused on customer contact management to integrated knowledge management solutions, these were the early foundations of CRM.

The last couple of years have seen the term broaden to encompass a more strategic approach and the investment of billions of dollars worldwide into CRM solutions and services has followed.

First Things First

Successful CRM always starts with a business strategy, which drives change in the organization and work processes, enabled by technology. The reverse rarely works.

The key here is to create a truly Customer-Centric philosophy that touches every point and more importantly every person in the company. From CSR to CEO everyone must live and breathe customer focus for all of this to work.

At the same time you should look at your which processes could be re-engineered to make them more effective for your customers. Until you have done this, put away your chequebook!

The Right Technology

It is estimated that the global market for CRM services and solutions is currently worth $148 billion. That means a lot of choice when selecting your technology - from web-based solutions aimed at small businesses with less than 10 employees to solutions suitable for multinational enterprises with millions of customers.

We have taken at look at the most widely used solutions and services and listed them in our CRM Application Guide. Although this is certainly not an exhaustive list, it will give you a good idea of what's out there.

MEANING AND DEFINITIONS OF CRM

CRM is a term that can refer to a range of things from the 'management of the relationship with customers' all the way to 'the software and hardware that allow one to manage [his or her] relationship with a customer.' It has become a catchall term. CRM generally is an enterprise-focused endeavour encompassing all departments in a business. For example, in addition to customer service, CRM would also include operations — manufacturing, assembly, product testing — as well as other areas like purchasing, billing, HR, engineering, marketing and sales. When the full company spectrum of departments is focused on building, maintaining, and constantly improving not only the product but also the relationship with the customer, this is what is meant by CRM. This requires a deep look at the goals and objects of the entire business and how those goals at the executive level are carried out in the sublevels of management and employees.

Practitioners and consultants use Customer Relationship Management (CRM) to refer to technology enabled processes for customer interactions and relationship building while marketing academicians prefer the term "relationship marketing". So there are three words that mean many things to many people when linked together, Customer Relationship Management has become something of an enigma. There is little doubt, it would seem, about what a customer is, though the term CRM is applied to "things done" to non-customers as well. The key that makes CRM different from other forms of strategy or marketing is that it is about relationship management. That pair of words has two implications that may or may not be true that the firm can identify the type or types of relationships it wishes to have with customers and that the customer will allow the firm to manage those relationships. There are a number of dreams to which CRM software can contribute, dreams such as seamless customer interaction across multiple channels, one-to-one marketing, 360-degree knowledge of the customer, and so forth. The reality is that CRM often devolves into an endless stream of campaigns that may take advantage of better customer data, but do not really build or contribute to a relationship. The most important step is to define what is meant, then, by relationship. Consumer package goods manufacturers, like Kraft or M&Ms, are not going to have the same types of relationships with their buyers as are business-to-business companies such as BASF or SAP Moreover, Karr-Hunter Pontiac/GMC has different and more direct relationships with its customers than does the Pontiac division of GM. How each of those organisations defines relationship categories is going to be different. But what many pundits and experts fail to recognise is that simply dividing customers into "bins" (or whatever terminology they use) based on recency and frequency of purchase doesn't define the relationship. Having sex every night with the same person does not guarantee marriage-knowing that information might make for a useful prediction as to what will happen tomorrow night, but it won't predict what will happen next year, nor will it predict any other aspect of the relationship. Why is it so important to define the type of ıelationship? Because what is left out of CRM, especially when defined operationally as campaign management, is the future. We are forecasting the future entirely based on yesterday's information. We are not building into our forecast anything about the buyer's commitment (or lack of) to us, nor anything about how much the buyer likes doing business with us or any other relational input. As such, we can't forecast our buyer's behaviour any further than tomorrow night. That's why we lose important opportunities for product development, channel development, and more. The dark side of how CRM is made operational in many organisations is how we train customers to play us. Years ago, the grocers complained about "deal-prone" consumers. The prevalence of couponing meant that grocers couldn't sell anything at regular price — coupons had trained buyers to look for deals and eroded brand and store loyalty. Now we are training consumers to use our "loyalty" programs in much the same way. What we are finding is that light users become stuck in loyalty programs, but they aren't the ones we really want anyway. Few vendors get all of the business of the heaviest users because we don't have a relationship with them; we sell loyalty as just another feature of the product/service mix. With too much emphasis on customer management, we lose sight of what the CRM revolution is really about.

Definitions of CRM

According to various scholars and experts CRM may be defined as below:

(i) "CRM deals with long term mutually beneficial relationship among consumers, companies and other stakeholder."

(ii) CRM is a new technology enabled way to do business that revives a simple, old-fashioned notion: keep pleasing customers and they will keep coming back."

(iii) "CRM is a well defined series of functions, skills, processes and technologies which together will allow companies to more profitable manage customer as tangible assets."

So at the last, CRM (customer relationship management) is an information industry term for methodologies, software, and usually Internet capabilities that help an enterprise manage customer relationships in an organised way. For example, an enterprise might build a database about its customers that described relationships in sufficient detail so that management, salespeople, people providing service, and perhaps the customer directly could access information, match customer needs with product plans and offerings, remind customers of service requirements, know what other products a customer had purchased, and so forth. According to one industry view, CRM consists of:

(i) Allowing the formation of individualised relationships with customers, with the aim of improving customer satisfaction and maximizing profits; identifying the most profitable customers and providing them the highest level of service.

(ii) Providing employees with the information and processes necessary to know their customers, understand their needs, and effectively build relationships between the company, its customer base, and distribution partners.

(iii) Helping an enterprise to enable its marketing departments to identify and target their best customers, manage marketing campaigns with clear goals and objectives, and generate quality leads for the sales team.

(iv) Assisting the organisation to improve telesales, account, and sales management by optimising information shared by multiple employees, and streamlining existing processes (for example, taking orders using mobile devices).

VIEWS OF DIFFERENT SCHOLARS ON CRM

As per Culbert, "In today's global market that usually means some form of currency or debt instrument, however, a customer transaction could also include barter and service in kind in consideration for the value received." So with this definition of the customer, CRM is then a customer-focused business strategy designed to optimise customer satisfaction, revenue, and profitability. These strategies and tactics shape a company's people, business process, and technology infrastructure around identifying acquiring, retaining and growing profitable customer relationships. In today's customer driven economy, it is important to recognise that a consistent plan for continuing your relevance to your customer is paramount.

For CRM strategies to be effective they require an enterprise-wide commitment to understanding your customers' wants and needs, creating compelling and relevant value propositions to offer them and delivering these value propositions profitably to the customer in their channel of preference (the Web, in store, through a distributor, and so on). Much has been accomplished in the past 5-10 years in leveraging advancements in process and technology to improve the effectiveness of what is referred to as operational or functional CRM. Salesforce automation (SFA), improved marketing effectiveness, and service consolidation and automation initiatives have been deployed to some extent in every industry. Many leading companies have taken actions to integrate and synchronize one or more of these operational initiatives in an attempt to deliver a superior customer experience and increase the ROI of their investments. The customer has an increasing expectation to interact in real time or near real time. The organisation just can't react in real time, but must already be prepared to respond because they are committed to knowing their customers and anticipating their needs.

By using the data and information obtained from the integrated functional areas — marketing, sales, and service — and tactics derived from customer intelligence and business analytics, companies have significantly increased their ability to know the customer and anticipate the customer's needs in ways that reinforce a company's relevance to their customers while sustaining and building profitable relationships. Companies who are able to retain their relevance while understanding the needs of their customers and take action quicker than their competitors will be the ones that lead their industries. Keeping customers, growing market share with current customers, and adding profitable new customers are the imperatives today. It is no longer appropriate to invest blindly and disproportionately without knowing your customer's value to your business if you expect to achieve top line revenue growth. Culbert believes that we are at a fundamental paradigm shift in how companies create and sustain value for their customers. According to him moving forward, it will be imperative that companies accept the evolving nature of CRM. Opportunity can be derived from the time you start to learn the value of your customers and learn from the needs of your customers. This will provide the valuable insights needed to keep companies in front of their customer's changing needs. If you are in business and currently have customers, you want to learn as much about them as profitably possible. It may not be worth going through the expense of collecting information and knowledge of your customer if you cannot or will not use it to shape your offerings to the market, service your current clients effectively and efficiently, and build loyalty for your company's goods and services. Fortunate for today's business, the CRM market for solutions has continued to evolve just as the consumer has never been so empowered, businesses have never had so many tools and techniques available to them, enabling companies to think "customer first." Thinking "customer first" may require a cultural shift in the business from product or service strategies to customer strategies.

The impact of these changes should not be taken lightly. For most organisations, this will require a strategy and plan to change the company's focus, behaviour, organisation, compensation, training, and incentives. While this may seem to be an overwhelming task, in most cases it should not be undertaken all at once. An incremental approach incorporating lessons learned and best practices has proven to produce the best results.

According to the great American cycling giant Armstrong," in competitive cycling indeed, in life-success depends on the brains, foresight, and heart one brings to an endeavour. The equipment is secondary. As many enterprises are discovering today, the same applies to Customer Relationship Management. It is not about the software. It is about the people. Specifically, it is about sales, service, helpdesk, and marketing people sharing information about customers. Armed with more complete, timely information, these people can make better decisions and, ultimately, keep customers coming back to buy more products. Like wishful contenders obsessing over the latest cycling technology, however, too many companies have spent too much time and far too much money focusing on the software. Software vendors and analysts have convinced many that the key to CRM is to license and deploy increasingly complex and extremely expensive CRM software packages.

Unfortunately, like most licensed enterprise software packages, CRM suites have proven difficult to deploy and difficult to use. One well-known software industry analyst has estimated that between 1999 and 2002, enterprises overspent by $100 billion to $200 billion on enterprise software — much of it for CRM — that has simply gone unused. Another information technology advisory firm estimated that half of all new enterprise software system deployment projects have ended in failure.

As a result, many CEOs have concluded that CRM—or atleast CRM software—has been oversold and that returns have not justified the investments. Many are scaling back on CRM software purchases. For example, banks, insurance companies, and other financial services firms were among the most committed CRM proponents. With rich stores of customer information, various methods of reaching customers and often multiple lines of business, financial services companies saw CRM as an excellent way to retain and sell more products and services to customers. Recently, however, a prominent publication covering the financial service industry noted a profound shift in the way many banks are approaching CRM.

According to an article in The American Banker, rather than CRM centred on complex software deployments, banks are "trying to achieve the goals of a well- functioning CRM system — cross-sales and customer retention — in a more collegial and less technology-oriented way." Specifically, the article reports, many banks are focused on employee training and business processes that emphasize collaboration and shared customer information across lines of business. This is not to imply that CRM and CRM technology have no future.

Companies that are able to understand — even anticipate—customer behaviours and preferences and quickly accommodate them will enjoy a profound competitive advantage. And comprehensive, up-to-date, and easily accessed customer data along with applications that help reinforce collaborative sales, marketing, and customer support processes will continue to deliver important business advantages. But technology must support critical CRM processes, not complicate them the way packaged CRM software so often does today. At its core, CRM is an important business methodology that helps companies quickly align their products, services, marketing message, and sales approach with customer needs and expectations.

Technology should be, as much as possible, transparent in supporting that methodology. There are alternatives to software complexity. One is to avoid licensing and deploying CRM packages altogether. Growing numbers of large, medium, and small companies are beginning to buy CRM technology as if it were electricity, water, or another commodity available from a utility. Using this utility model, a service provider creates and hosts CRM applications into which business users can tap on a subscription basis. For $50 per user per month, businesses can get online access to the same type of sales force automation, marketing automation, and customer support functionality they get from licensed software. But they do not have to license software. Nor must they employee a large IT staff to customise software, test it, deploy it, support it, and upgrade it when a new release comes out. While using the Internet to deliver software as a service is a relatively new idea, it is beginning to take off, particularly as service providers prove they can keep customer data secure and private. That is particularly true in the CRM space.

The same Aberdeen report that predicted CRM software license revenue will continue to slide through 2006 also said the CRM market will "rapidly transition to a . . . subscription-oriented model." By 2006, the report predicted, subscription revenues for hosted CRM application services will have grown to $2.8 billion. There are reasons a software-as a service approach makes sense for companies launching CRM initiatives. Sales people, who have often resisted using complex CRM software, have an easier time adopting hosted CRM services that they access from their already familiar Web browser. In addition, the model supports easy and low-cost integration with other critical systems via Web services, erasing the cost, length, and risk that has characterised software integration and application development projects. But, more importantly, by tapping into hosted applications that are already up and running, companies start seeing the benefits of CRM immediately. That is particularly important to top sales, marketing, and support executives, who often have been stuck paying for under-used or even unused CRM software. And, more than anyone else, they understand that CRM is not about the software. It is about the people.

Don Peppers and Martha Rogers, Ph.D., continue to set the standards in Customer Relationship Management by demonstrating how to reap customer value in a global marketplace. At the root of the problems with the term "Customer Relationship Management" is the fact that the software vendors have used the term so much that many business practitioners equate "CRM" with "CRM software."

Technology is a very important, enabling first step, but we have seen a variety of firms spend vast amounts on the installation and integration of technology without moving the needle on their bottom line at all as a result. Usually, this is because of a "ready, fire, aim" approach which puts the technology horse before the strategy cart. We've met officers at very large companies where tens of millions of dollars have been spent on "CRM" technology who did not know how that technology was going to contribute to the value of their customer base. And that's the point. We are in business because we have customers. Those customers are variably and predictably valuable to us now and potentially. They have different needs from us, which we can fulfil in different ways. The way we can grow the company's bottom line, ultimately, is to reduce the cost of serving each customer, or to increase the revenue received from each customer, or both. That means we differentiate our customers by value (fairly common these days) as well as need (almost unheard of, effectively speaking), and then we change our behaviour toward each customer in order to encourage the customer to change his behaviour toward us. CRM is not better targeted harassment. CRM is not even the same as better customer service, because customer service doesn't have a memory. While it's a good idea to teach our frontline personnel to be more polite, there is no "relationship" until the good service a customer gets today can be replicated without his having to ask for it again.

CRM, OR ONE-TO-ONE CUSTOMER STRATEGY

(i) Recognising a customer as that customer through any channel, at any time, across product purchase and service lines, and over time;

(ii) Treating different customers differently;

(iii) Remembering things for and about customers;

(iv) Applying more resources to more valuable customers, and more resources to keeping valuable customers, rather than to acquiring new customers of unknown value;

(v) Building shareholder value by increasing the value of the customer base;

(vi) Using information from a customer to do something for that customer that no competitor can do who does not have information from that customer;

(vii) Using information about each customer to make each customer more valuable to your firm, and your firm more valuable to each customer, while decreasing the cost of servicing each customer;

(viii) Deciding what each customer needs from the firm next, based on the customer's feedback (even more than on demographics, zip code information, or other traditional third-party data-after all, your competitors can buy the same third-party data, but only your firm has the information the customer gave you herself); and

(ix) Enterprise-wide.

According to Bob Thompson, "Customer Relationship Management means taking great care of your prospects and customers, using information technology." There are over 500 CRM solutions on the market from contact managers like ACT! to enterprise-wide information systems costing hundreds of thousands of dollars. Whatever the size of these solutions, the goals are similar to improve the effectiveness and efficiency of marketing, sales, or customer care. Since then, it's become a bit of closet industry to define and debate the meaning of CRM. Is it as-old-as-business philosophy—"Customers Really Matter'— or just the latest management fad to line the pockets of high-priced consultants-"Consultants Reap Millions"? With the industry's sometimes-painful experiences of the past few years, it's clear that CRM is far more than front-office efficiency. Simply put, CRM is a business strategy to get, grow, and retain the most profitable relationships. However, making CRM work well is not quite that simple.

Can Automating Sales and Service Help?

Surely, if it focused correctly. On the other hand, sales automation can enable companies to be stupid faster by selling to even more unprofitable customers. And automated support systems won't help a surly support rep create a positive impression with a customer. Over the past few years we've put the spotlight on CRM tools when the real challenges are with people. To better understand current market perceptions, we conducted a major online survey and found the definition of CRM continues to be fragmented. Selecting from five choices, only 9 percent said CRM was "automation of customer business processes."

However, none of the other responses gained a majority. Still, looking at the two answers, "Putting customers at the heart of business" and "Business strategy to increase customer profitability," reveals that being customer-centric is part of the answer.

Why is being Customer-centric Important?

Because, Loyalty Guru Reichheld found that loyalty leaders grow at 220 percent of the industry average, at 15 percent lower operating costs. It doesn't take a mathematician to understand why loyal customers are having a positive impact on the bottom line of companies. While it's great fun to debate the meaning of life and CRM, the more critical issue is this: what determines whether CRM projects succeed or fail? First, survey-takers defined in detail the kinds of activities they performed in planning and implementing their CRM projects. Then they rated benefits received in the following areas, which collectively determined the ROI of the project.

(i) Decreasing front office staffing costs;

(ii) Improving customer satisfaction;

(iii) Increasing customer acquisition rate;

(iv) Decreasing defection rate; and

(v) Increasing share of customer.

Guru Reichheld found that about two out of three CRM projects are delivering a return on investment, from modest to outstanding. Four major factors accounted for 72 percent of CRM project success. The number one driver for achieving ROI was "customer-centric strategy," which included using customer satisfaction and attrition data and getting customers involved in the planning process.

In general, it meant driving the CRM project from an "outside-in" approach. First consider what's good for the customer, then how to make money doing so. Next, "frontline training and support" and "organisational change" were tied for the number two spot. Companies tended to get a better return on their CRM investment if they proactively explained the value of CRM, providing training on the new skills required, redesigned work processes as needed, and changed roles and responsibilities. The fourth key driver was using metrics effectively. Higher performing projects tended to invest considerable effort defining customer metrics, establishing a baseline performance, developing specific goals, and tracking against those goals. What was even more interesting was what factor didn't make the list of key drivers: technology. By and large, companies are doing a good job selecting and implementing CRM solutions, whether from major software vendors, hosted services, or in-house development. In the research conducted by the Reichheldfound no correlation between the choice of software and achieving ROI.

Does This Mean Technology Doesn't Matter, or All Software Vendors are the Same?

No. What it does mean is that there are Plenty of great CRM tools in the market. The difference between success and failure lies in the hands of people, not the tools they're using. Some companies succeed by building a better mousetrap, some by selling at lowest costs, and others by creating "better" customer relationships than their competitors. If you don't have the best product or lowest price in your industry (and not many companies do these days), odds are you're thinking about CRM and what it can do for your bottom line. If you want CRM to deliver value to your business, you'd better start by figuring out the "win" for the customer, then getting your organisation on board to make it happen. Otherwise CRM will be just another fad or software tool with unfulfilled promise.

According to CEO and president of SAP America, Inc., William R. "Bill" McDermott says that there are many ways a business responds to individual customer needs that create value for its customers and itself. They call that value creation CRM. Companies benefit from CRM when they use information about their customers to operate more efficiently or bring products to market more quickly.

For instance, a company yields value when its call centre automatically routes high-value customers to special, high-capability agents. In addition, a business may use CRM to save money by eliminating duplicate mailings or to focus on a new service or product based on customer feedback its sales force has captured. To benefit fully from such customer-specific activities, companies must identify and remember customers individually, understand customer differences, interact with them, and tailor those interactions to particular customers or customer segments. CRM thus unites a company's customer-facing side with its production or service side.

Effective CRM connects a company's demand and supply chains. The better CRM technologies is a natural result of the search by businesses for greater productivity and efficiency in customer-facing operations like sales, marketing customer service, and support. For example, in sales, companies need IT systems that provide greater control and efficiency. This means improved forecasting capability, greater visibility into sales performance across a variety of channels, increased productivity by external sales forces, and reduced sales costs.

Meanwhile, companies must meet customer demands for better quality, timeliness, and customisation in the service they deliver. Companies also need technology that helps them approach customers in a rational way. A company must, for example, remember a customer's address from one transaction to another and carefully choreograph contacts between its sales force and customers.

In addition to being wasteful and inefficient, pitching a new product to a customer who has just bought the same item makes the company look incompetent to the customer. The Internet has dramatically accelerated the focus on CRM by making customer interactions more cost-efficient. In addition, the Web has established a new, more direct sales channel that supports rapid customer interaction and short sales cycles.

Using Internet technologies, customers can interact with information from a wide variety of sources without special training. Most companies can easily document the financial benefits from CRM technology by the costs they saved from greater efficiencies in sales, marketing, and service.

More importantly, CRM can increase the true economic worth of a business by improving the total lifetime value of its customers. Successful CRM strategies encourage customers to buy more products, stay loyal for longer periods, or communicate more effectively with a company. CRM solutions with robust analytics can help companies identify and take advantage of winning business strategies. All too often, however, a CRM implementation falls short of expectations, triggering debate about the costs and benefits involved. The successful implementations must involved:

(i) Support the company's business strategy;

(ii) Integrate information and process to deliver key insights; and

(iii) Encourage adoption by users.

IMPORTANCE OF CRM

The importance of CRM are as follows:

(i) *Common growth for marketers and customers*: CRM will help customers to identify the right product that will suit them; also the marketers will know about their target audience and will not waste their time.

(ii) *Customized marketing efforts*: Much B2B marketing today is customized, in that a manufacturer will customize the offer, logistics, communications and financial terms for each major account. Computers, database, e-mail, fax, etc., permit companies to return to customized marketing. Today customers are taking more individual initiative in determining what had how to buy. CRM helps customize marketing to be more effective.

(iii) *Lower cost of marketing*: As products manufactured with the help of CRM techniques the customers will accept it and they will also be satisfied with the product. Also a good relationship will be maintained with the customers and thus more and more money will not be wasted in advertising and promotions.

(iv) *Strong customer loyalty: Today* the loyalty of customers is decreasing for any brand. So if with the help of CRM good relationship is developed with the customers than chances are less of customers not being loyal. Thus CRM develops a strong customer loyalty and also a good company image.

(v) *Improve customer satisfaction*: Companies now are trying to offer total customer satisfaction. "Xerox guarantees total customer satisfaction. As with the use of CRM firstly the customers will choose the right product offered and also if they face any problems they will be solved quickly. Thus the Level of customer satisfaction can be raised with CRM.

(vi) *Improved employee and customer retention*: With the help of CRM customer retention will improve. As the old customers will be fully satisfied they will buy the same companies products. If a person bought a colour TV of Sony and he is fully satisfied, as the company solved some problems quickly, if he has to buy a C.D. player he will buy of Sony. Thus CRM helps to retain new customers and maintain old customers.

(vii) *Decreased cost for customers*: As the marketing expenses of a firm will decrease in long run firms can offer the same product at a bit low cost, which will be in the benefit of the customers.

ADVANTAGES OF CRM

The advantages of customer relationship management are considered are abound. It allows organisations not only to retain customers, but enables more effective marketing, creates intelligent opportunities for cross selling and opens up the possibility of rapid introduction of new brands and products.

To be able to deliver these benefits, organisations must be able to customise their product offering, optimize price, integrate products and services and deliver the service as promised and demanded by the customer base. Keeping the customer happy is obviously one way of ensuring that they stay with the organisation.

However, by maintaining an overall relationship with the customer, companies are able to unlock the potential of their customer base and maximise the contribution to their business. Whilst the value of customer relationship management has been identified by the full implications organisations, and benefits are yet to be.

Those responsible for delivery are perhaps the most informed about these strategic benefits yet the transformation is a long-drawn-out process. The strategic benefits of customer relationship management allow companies to reduce the cost of customer acquisition and give established players the ability to react like a new market entrant, the very people they are battling against. Ironically these are increased and the potential of customers can be then capitalised through cross selling of other products and services. It is important to understand the key benefits of CRM for most companies.

These advantages generally fall into three categories: cost savings, revenue enhancement, and strategic impact. Based on successful CRM implementations, the following advantages seem reasonable:

(i) *Increased margins*. Increased margins resulting from knowing customers better, providing a value-sell, and discounting prices.

(ii) *Improved customer satisfaction ratings*. This increase occurs since customers find the company to be more responsive and better in touch with their specific needs.

(iii) *Increased sales revenues*. Increased sales result from spending more time with customers which results from spending less time chasing needed information (i.e., productivity improvement).

(iv) *Increased win rates*. Win rates improve since companies can withdraw from unlikely or bad deals earlier on in the sales process.

FACTORS FOR THE GROWTH OF CRM

The marvellous growth of interest and investments in CRM across the globe can be attributed to the following macro-environmental factors:

(i) Emergence of Market Economy

Market regulation was in place all over the world including the US, Europe, USSR, China and India. The 1990s witnessed acceleration in the deregulation of many large industries including banking, telecommunications, broadcasting and airlines across the world.

As a result, market-oriented firms operating in intensely competitive markets now take decisions that was once controlled by the government (Victor). The focus has shifted from capacity creation under control to the markets. Market-oriented economy necessitated a customer focus and boosted the importance of CRM.

(ii) Global Orientation of Businesses

International trade became the growth engine for the global economy. Liberalisation of markets and trade proved to be a far stronger growth engine. It has eased the entry into foreign markets. Firms need stronger customer-orientation to be able to tap opportunities in new markets while defending themselves in their home markets. National boundaries are giving way to either a borderless world or at least a regional world resulting in the emergence of trading blocks like North American Free Trade Agreement (NAFTA), European Union and the Association of South-East Asian Nations (ASEAN). The abolishment of the General Agreement on Tariffs and Trade (GATT) and the emergence of World Trade Organisation (WTO) helped create a global orientation for business establishments.

(iii) Emergence of Service Economy

The emergence of service economy is a global phenomenon. The growing importance of services resulted in greater customer orientation as services are characterised by simultaneity/inseparability/heterogeneity /perishability (Berry and Parasuraman). It implies that the production and consumption of services are inseparable. In services, one needs to be close to customers to deliver the service offering. The factory is where the customer is and service is offered in real time. The customer perceives the production process as part of the service consumption, not just the outcome of a production process as in traditional marketing of physical goods (Gronroos). Therefore, it is not surprising that service businesses like hotels, airlines, banking, financial services, telecom and retailing were the early adopters of CRM.

The service sector contributes to 60-70 per cent of the GDP of economically advanced nations of Western Europe, Canada and Japan. The increasing contribution of the service sector is not limited to developed countries. Developing economics like China, Indonesia and Thailand employ about 40 per cent of the workforce in the service sector (Wirtz). In the year 2001, the service sector contributed to 48 per cent of the GDP in India, 54 per cent in Philippines and 33 per cent in China. The average annual growth rate of the services during the decade of 1990s was 8 per cent in India, 9 per cent in China and 4.1 per cent in the Philippines (Statistical outline India, 2002-03). In the US, the service sector accounts for over 75 per cent of GNP and employs 80 per cent of the workforce (Czinkota and Ronkainen). Advanced countries progressed from agricultural to industrial and then to post-industrial economies. The shift from manufacturing to services was spread over a few decades of the last century. However, in developing countries, the growth is led by all three sectors of the economy in varying proportions.

(iv) Aging Population in Economically Developed Countries

Aging of population has been attributed to the combined effects of a slowdown in birthrate and an increase in life expectancy. The economically advanced nations are witnessing an aging of their population. In 2000, 12.6 per cent of the US population was 65 years of age or older. The comparative figures for Sweden and Japan were 17.2 per cent and 17 per cent of their respective population. This trend is visible in most parts of Europe, except in Ireland. While an aging population creates new opportunities for wellness, financial well being, safety and security and recreation, it has also slowed the markets for traditional goods .and services designed for a younger population.

Therefore, in these markets, growth is being achieved by increasing the 'share of wallet' and not through growth of markets driven by a growing population. Marketers are now forced to develop a deep understanding of their existing customers and meet their ever changing needs through suitable products and services. Indeed, most large companies, especially the services sector, wants to become one-stop-shop for the customers.

TECHNOLOGY — AN ESSENTIAL FACTOR FOR CRM

Firms can now manage every single contact with the customer from account management personnel, call centres, interactive voice response systems, on-line dial-up applications, and websites to build lasting relationships. Developments in information technology, data warehousing and data mining have made it possible for firms to maintain a one above relationship with their customers. These interactions can be used to glean information and insights about customer needs and their buying behaviour to design and develop services, which help create value for the customers as well as the firms. Although customised as well as off the shelf technological solutions are available in the marketplace, businesses need to do a lot more than just adopt these solutions to implement customer relationship management (CRM) practices. CRM offers huge potential benefits but requires a more sophisticated approach adapted to specific opportunities and circumstances. At the core of any technology enabler for CRM is the customer database. This represents the data hub that integrates the various statistical modelling, campaign management, contact history and response tracking components of the marketing campaign life-cycle. The technology layer and — its integration with emerging business processes is therefore the key to successful implementation of a data-driven customer relationship management. To take advantage of the benefits of CRM, a company must undertake a structured process that ensures the automation venture does not become the automation misadventure. For effective implementation of CRM concept, it is important to identify which process to Automate and which not to automate. Reengineering could be improved for providing complete end-to-end set of activities that together create value for a customer. It should be coupled with the complete vision of the business process — keeping customer as its base. Cross functional teams have proven to be the most successful organisations for CRM.

IMPLEMENTATION OF CRM CONCEPT

Customer relationship management is accomplishable. Top management commitment, personnel motivation, user training and prototyping the system are the other key factors for successful implementation of CRM concept. However, the following guidelines must be taken into consideration before implementing the CRM concept, which are on next page:

(i) *Evaluate and plan.* All aspects of customer relationship management, including technology solutions, must be fully explored to effectively deliver the competencies required to realize the business benefits.

(ii) Tackling any one competence alone will lead to a dysfunctional business. One competence does not make customer relationship management.

(iii) Take pragmatic steps with a clear view on delivery of all the components in the medium term, rather than adopting a piecemeal approach in the short term.

(iv) Successful mass customisation is crucial to reducing customer acquisition costs and improving the cross-selling capability.

(v) *Channels are a delivery mechanism.* The effectiveness of the mechanism can be achieved only when it is seamless.

Firms would adopt relationship marketing only if it in CRM has the potential to benefit them. The benefits come through lower costs of retention and increased profits due to lower defection rates. When customers enter into a relationship with a firm, they are willingly foregoing other options and limiting their choice. Some of the personal motivations to do so result from greater efficiency in decision- making, reduction in information processing, achieving more cognitive consistency in decisions and reduction of perceived risks with future decisions. It is generally accepted that it costs, more to acquire a customer than to retain an existing one. However, identifying valuable customers is also important. There is still a trend that a customer must be kept no matter what the cost to the organisation, even if it mean incurring a loss. It is a realisation that countless organisations have been oblivious to and in the process have experienced substantial customer churn. Successful implementation of CRM requires a strategic approach, which encompasses developing customer centric processes, selecting and implementing technology solutions, employee empowerment, customer information and knowledge generation capabilities to differentiate them, and the ability to learn from outstanding practices.

NECESSITY FOR ADOPTION OF CRM

Customer relationship management, if implemented successfully, enables companies to capitalize and grow their business. Still relationship marketing appears to be an expensive alternative to firms practising mass marketing due to the relatively high initial investment. We believe that a combination of demand and supply led factors will accelerate the adoption of CRM in the coming years. On the demand side, rising customer expectations will force businesses to: adopt CRM. And on the supply side, technological advances and the declining costs of information and communication technology will reduce the barriers to adoption of technology led CRM initiatives.

(i) Customer Expectations

Customer expectations are rising due to increasing affluence in the increasing customer diversity, emerging economies and greater awareness due to media explosion.

(a) *Customer diversity*: Many of the mass marketing practices fall with customers who are diverse in their lifestyles, age, income and ethnicity. In the last decade, more people have migrated to obtain better living standards after the economic integration of Europe. In the US, ethnic pluralism is increasing as some minority groups like the Hispanic, Afro-American and the Asian are growing rapidly (Cory). About 29 per cent of the workforce in the US are minorities. One-third of all children in the US in 1995 were Asian, African American or Hispanic (Francese). This increase in diversity will greatly increase the diversity in demand and expectations.

(b) *Increasing affluence in the emerging economies*: The economic growth in the emerging economies have created a large middle class, estimated at 250 and 300 million people in India and China, respectively. This middle class is very demanding and quality conscious. The transition of these markets from a sellers to a buyers market and the buying power of the middle class makes them attractive to all businesses. Taken together, nine developing nations — China, India, Brazil, Mexico, Russia, Indonesia, Turkey, South Africa and Thailand — have a combined GDP that is larger, in purchasing power parity, than the combined GDPs of Japan, Germany, France, UK and Italy. The middle class has a large proportion of professional class with greater global awareness and influence. For example, in India every year over 3,00,000 engineers and about 1,00,000 MBAs join the workforce. They can afford and are willing to pay for better and customised products and services. Many of them are nuclear families and have double income with the spouses employed. This has resulted in a lot of the traditional homemaking activities like cooking, cleaning and childcare being outsourced to service providers. All these will drive the service economy.

(c) *Greater awareness due to explosive media growth*: The information explosion has played a significant role in raising customer aspirations as well as expectations. Customers in the emerging markets have greater access to marketplace information about products, services and lifestyles through the explosion in the traditional media like the newspapers and television as well new media like cable television and the internet. The total number of TV homes has remained stable at about 100 million in the US in the last decade while it has exploded in the developing countries. China (341 million), India (80 million) and Brazil (44 million) have witnessed some of the fastest penetration growth of TV in homes in the last decade.

(ii) Technological Advancement

Rising customer expectations will make CRM a necessity for businesses to be able to customise all elements of marketing mix to satisfy these customers. Fortunately for businesses, advances in affordable technology will help them meet these divergent needs from demanding customers. Advancement in technology have made an impact on all stages from production to final consumption. They are allowing marketers to offer unique solutions to individual customers. We describe some of the key technology advances in production, distribution, facilitation and consumption and their impact on marketing practices as shown in Figure 1.

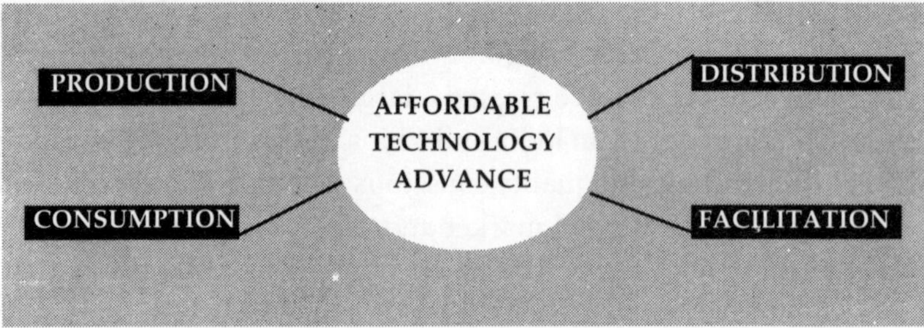

Fig:1 — *Affordable Technology Advances.*

(a) *Production*: Consumers will benefit as they are offered products and services tailored to their specific requirements through mass-customisation at prices comparable to mass-marketed products. Breakthroughs, including computer-aided design and computer-aided manufacturing (CAD-CAM) and processes like fordable manufacturing systems (FMS) and just-in-time operations (JIT), have helped improve the quality while reducing the costs across the supply chain. Production technology leaders like Toyota and Dell Computers have gained significant competitive advantage in their respective markets by being early adopters of these technologies.

(b) *Distribution*: Distribution intermediaries and third party logistics providers leverage technology to rapidly deliver products at affordable prices and increase market coverage. Distribution capabilities of firms have been enhanced due to computer-aided logistics (CALS) and scanner technology which allows faster response for replenishment with fewer stock-outs. Improvements in forecasting and database technologies allow fine tuned targeted approaches to marketing and close to real- time fulfilment in many cases, specially information intensive services.

(c) *Facilitation*: Customer shopping habits are changing with the convenience of information availability, evaluation, and purchase through the click of a mouse. The use of internet to connect enterprise within and outside with suppliers as well as customers through c-commerce technologies has resulted in major improvements in facilitating commercial as well informational exchanges. Dramatic reductions in transaction costs have allowed even small businesses to aspire for a global reach. Large businesses in the airlines, banking and financial services have leveraged the power of the internet to offer services directly to their end customers at a lower cost to them as well as to customers. In many industries the sellers as well as the buyers have benefited by this process of disintermediation, i.e. cutting down layers of intermediaries. While the inefficiencies of the traditional intermediation process were reduced through disintermediation, a new class of intermediaries, e.g. Priceline.com and Freemarkets.com have emerged to facilitate transactions between sellers and buyers.

(d) *Consumption*: In emerging countries like India, customers have started shifting to electronic channels. ICICI Bank, the second largest bank in India, has reported that 70 per cent of its transactions are conducted through electronic channels. Its 1,800 ATMs account for 48 per cent of the transactions while the remaining 22 per cent is divided equally between call centre and interact banking. Breakthroughs in consumption occurred due to the development of affordable personal IDs, e.g. individual login which helped customise the consumption experience. It allows the seller to datamine the transaction, purchase and usage history at the level of an individual to personalise the offerings. For the consumer, it has given the power to be a co-producer by intervening and providing direct inputs into the making of the product. Dell.com allows buyers to configure the computer of their choice by co-opting them as co-producers during the design stage. In addition to the personalised consumption, these technologies have allowed customers as well as marketers to overcome the limitations imposed by time and place.

Customer's desire for instant gratification will drive businesses to provide access to their products anytime and anywhere. Banks have discovered that as customers shift from a time and place restricted channel like the branch to electronic channels like ATMS, call centres and internet, they save on costs and are able to provide improved services. These technological developments are proving to be a win-win for companies as well as customers. Therefore it is not surprising that shopping on the internet is growing rapidly. According to an expending report by Goldman

Sachs & Co., Harris Interactive Inc., and Nielsen/NetRatings Online holiday shoppers spent US$ 18.5 billion during the year end 2003 holiday season, excluding travel, an increase of 35 per cent from the US$ 13.7 billion spent during the 2002 holiday season, (Linda Rosencrance, Computerworld, January 6, 2004). Retailers have reworked their supply chain so that orders could be placed even two days before Christmas. Earlier this took two weeks. Shipping is free.

Thus, the Internet has made e-commerce easy for customers as well as companies. We will witness greater adoption of these technologies as customers demand for hassle free product information, delivery, consumption and even disposal from businesses. Lowering costs of both information as well as communication technologies will attract firms to invest in these technologies.

SEVEN GUIDELINES FOR EFFECTIVE CRM

The CRM market and our collective experience have matured. Whether we are embarking on an enterprise-wide strategy or a specific functional point solution, we have learned to apply best practices and lessons learned to help ensure success from our CRM investments. As a result, I would recommend that each organisation consider the following seven tips for highly effective CRM prior to implementation and deployment of any initiative:

(i) Changes in process, people, and technology should be evaluated and the business impact should be quantified and prioritised, supported by a solid business case and tangible return on investment (ROI).

(ii) Develop an iterative and incremental approach focused on addressing the highest value opportunities first-think big, start small, and deliver results quickly.

(iii) Align to corporate strategy, ensuring that CRM initiatives are in complete alignment with the organisation's overall business goals.

(iv) Measure the effectiveness of your initiatives and create accountability for customer and business results. What is your baseline performance and what key performance indicators (KPIS) will you measure to know that you are getting results from your CRM initiatives?

(v) Create an overall CRM vision for the company. Develop and communicate the CRM vision to the organisation and key constituents, such as customers, employees, and partners.

(vi) Secure the commitment and buy-in of senior management to the overall project vision, project objectives, and measurements of success.

(vii) Recognise the organisation change and motivations required to achieve full benefits, and create the action plans to achieve and sustain the future state of organisational readiness.

Following these tips will not guarantee your CRM success. However, if your organisation has a plan to address these areas, you will improve your chances of success and reap the rewards of profitable, customer-focused business strategies.

FUTURE OF CRM

CRM has already made a big impact in the world of Customer Service and will continue to do so. As more and more companies become customer-centric those that fail to do so will lose competitive advantage. As technology increases to develop at a startling rate the key emphasis will be how we can fully utilise it within our business. However let's not lose sight of the fact that Customer Relationship Management is about people first and technology second. That's where the real value of CRM lies, harnessing the potential of people to create a greater customer experience, using the technology of CRM as the enabler. CRM may or may not prove to be the answer to providing excellent customer care, but the philosophy of putting customers at the heart of our business is definitely a step in the right direction.

CRM today is part of an extended value chain that will push itself into the broader business ecosystem. CRM, which become a visible force about a decade long ago, is now much more than it ever was anticipated to be. "It started its life viewed as a technology, then became "a system, not a technology," then became "people, processes, and technology." It is now a philosophy and business strategy that is supported by those systems and technologies. It is a science and an art:

(i) It is the art of knowing every single customer of your millions of customers without having necessarily known any of them.

(ii) It is the science of definition for increasing precision about how to effect a customer strategy using the appropriate tools and techniques.

(iii) It is the art of negotiation and managing cultures. How can you get the disparate elements that these different groups represent to collaborate without all the commensurate hurt feelings, political ramifications, and fundamental disagreements that always characterize this?

(iv) It is the science of benchmarks and measurements for customer successes and corporate performance.

(v) It is the science of planning, defining how you are going to craft a customer strategy within the realm of your own business ecology, working with your employees, partners, and suppliers- your extended value chain.

(vi) It is the art of interpreting human behaviours and conditions to continuously gain more and more insight.

An all-encompassing, multifaceted and, when well crafted, beautiful piece of art, created using scientific principles. There are practical implications of this vision of CRM's future. How is CRM going to look in the next year or two? Is it going to seize the strategic high ground and inaugurate the era of customer ubiquity or will it just be another $27 billion (2003 figures) big blip on the radar screen, because, mature or not, companies and customers just never got the idea? As every good (or bad) consultant will tell you: that depends.

CASE STUDIES

INTRODUCTION

CRM is a set of strategies, processes, metrics, organizational culture and technology solutions that enhance an organization's ability to see the differences in its customers' and prospects' behavior and needs, track new opportunities to better serve their customers and act, instantly and profitably, on those differences and opportunities. Recently CRM has taken a center stage in the business world with businesses concentrating on saving money and increasing profits by redefining internal processes and procedures. It costs a company dramatically less to retain and grow an existing client, than it does to court new ones. It is said that "It is seven times more expensive to acquire a new customer than to keep an existing one", therefore the value of customer information and management should never be underestimated. Customer relation management analysts say

CRM BUSINESS CYCLE

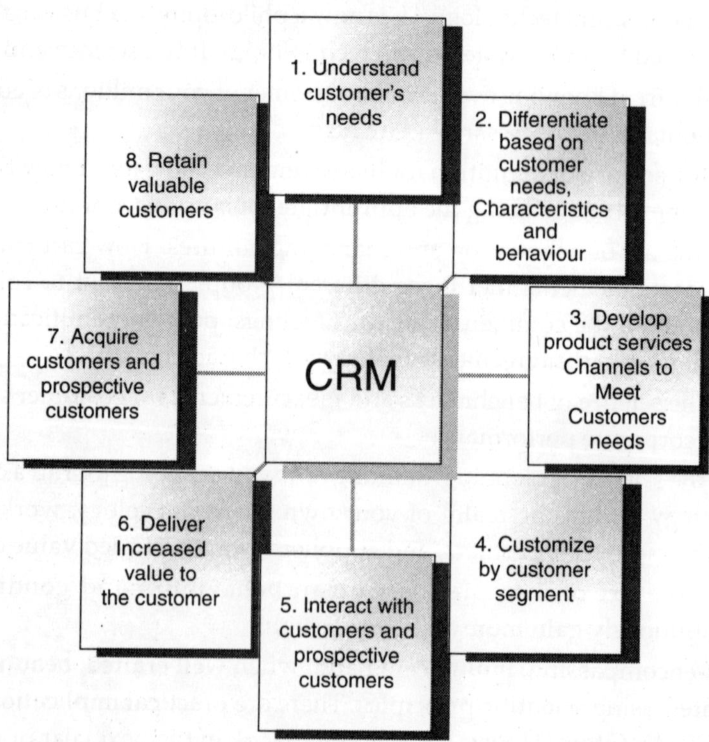

CRM is "a buzzword that's really not so new. What's new is the technology is allowing us to do what we could do at the turn of the century with the neighborhood grocer. He had few enough customers and enough brainpower to keep track of everyone's preferences. Technology has allowed us to go back to the future to this model." The aim of CRM is optimize the use of technology and human resources for the business to gain insight into the behavior of costumer. Seeing the new market (CRM) emerge, the world's leading business software vendors have reinvented themselves to focus on CRM, and there has been a fierce competition for the dominance in this market. Technology is now an essential part of CRM nowadays but buying technology before defining CRM business goals is a recipe for disaster. It is important to remember that technology used for CRM should be 'tailor-made' depending on the type of consumer base of the company and the business goals. Companies need to understand CRM in relevance to customers and customers only. Technology like call center services and softwares will prove helpful only if they improve the customer services and relation, otherwise all fancy technology is useless if it fails to benefit the customer.

IJIJI

HISTORY

To understand about this big bank, we need to understand how it became so big a force to reckon with. Industrial Credit Investment Company of India promoted the IJIJI bank in 1994 with its stake reducing to 46% after the IPO in 1998. IJIJI is a well-known name in India along with ICBI and was formed in 1955 at the initiative of the World Bank, Indian Government and Indian Industries. Both of these institutions have an exceptional brand-image and one of the highest possible ratings from CRISIL and other rating organizations. IJIJI can be considered an oligopolistic corporation along with ICBI. IJIJI listed in NYSE in 2000. In 2001 it underwent a tight marriage with Bank of Madura in a stock—only amalgamation. This was a tough marriage and they are still suffering from this hiccup, which kind of substantiates their mediocre performance today. This and the merger with the IJIJI Corporation have caused some management strain and some tough merger time.

INTRODUCTION

IJIJI Bank is India's second-largest bank, with total assets of about Rs.1,676.59 billion on 31 March 2005. IJIJI Bank began its life 1994 as a wholly-owned subsidiary of IJIJI Limited, an Indian financial institution, whose shareholding in the bank was reduced to 46 per cent through a public offering of shares in India in 1997-98, an equity offering in the form of ADRs listed on the NYSE in fiscal 1999-2000, the IJIJI Bank's acquisition of Bank of Madura in fiscal 2000-01, and secondary market sales by IJIJI to institutional investors in fiscal 2001 and fiscal 2002.

Business

IJIJI Bank offers a range of banking products and financial services to corporate and retail customers through several delivery channels and specialised subsidiaries and affiliates. The areas include: investment banking, life and non-life insurance, venture capital and asset management.

IJIJI Bank set-up its international banking group in fiscal 2002 to cater to clients' cross-border needs. It currently has subsidiaries in the UK, Canada and Russia, branches in Singapore and Bahrain, and representative offices in the US, China, UAE, Bangladesh and South Africa.

Location

IJIJI Bank has a network of about 573 branches and extension counters and over 2,000 ATMs.

RECURRING DEPOSIT ACCOUNT OF IJIJI

IJIJI Bank's Recurring Deposits are the ideal way to invest small amounts of money every month and end up with a large saving on maturity.

Features

Encourages savings without stress on your finances.

High rates of interest (identical to the fixed deposit rates).

Non-applicability of Tax Deduction at Source (TDS).

Minimum Balance

The minimum balance of deposit is Rs. 500 per month and thereafter, in multiples of Rs. 100.

PERIOD OF DEPOSIT

The minimum period is 6 months, and thereafter—in multiples of 3 months.

TDS is not applicable on recurring deposits.

Nomination

The facility of Nomination is available for relationships in the names of individuals. Unless otherwise specifically given in writing by depositors, nomination in deposit accounts will be at Customer ID level.

A depositor(s) however has/have the right to specify different nominations at account level by completing the appropriate forms.

Further, the applicant(s) is/are at liberty to change the nominee during the currency of the relationship accounts with the Bank, through a declaration to the effect in the appropriate form.

To open a recurring deposit one can approach any of the following ways:

Write to IJIJI at info@ijijibank.com

Call IJIJI at 24 hour Customer Care Centre

One can just walk into any of their branches.

Extra benefits in the form of higher interest rates to the senior citizens.

Redeeming the recurring deposit account before the original terms

In the event of the Recurring Deposit being closed before completing the original term of the deposit, interest will be paid at the rate applicable on the date of deposit, for the period for which the deposit has remained with the Bank.

In case of premature withdrawal the deposit may be subject to a penal rate of interest as prescribed by the Bank on the date of deposit.

INTEREST RATES

Interest rates (per cent per annum) w.e.f. 17.11.04*

Maturity Period	*Single Deposit of*			
	Less than Rs. 1.5 mn.	*Annualized yield at the beginning of the slab*	*Rs. 1.5 mn. and above but less than Rs. 10.0 mn.*	*Annualized yield at the beginning of the slab*
91 days and above up to 180 days	4.50%	4.50%	4.75%	4.75%
181 days and above up to 1 year	5.00%	5.03%	5.00%	5.03%
More than 1 year up to 3 years	5.50%	5.61%	5.50%	5.61%
More than 3 years upto 5 years	5.75%	6.23%	5.75%	6.23%
More than 5 years upto 10 years	6.25%	7.27%	6.25%	7.27%

* Subject to revision without prior notice.

Note : Rates for Deposits for Rs. 1 crore and above will be advised by treasury from time to time.

INTEREST RATES FOR SENIOR CITIZENS

1. Eligibility Criteria

A person who has completed the age of 60 years may be treated as a senior citizen for getting the benefit under the special deposit scheme for senior citizens.

2. Verification of Age

Opening of New Account

At the time of opening of a new deposit account of a senior citizen, the branch should satisfy about the age through verification of any of the following documents:

Secondary School Leaving Certificate indicating date of Birth

LIC Policy

Voter's Identity Card

Pension Payment Order

Birth Certificate issued by the competent authority

Passport

PAN Card

INTEREST RATES

Interest rates (per cent per annum) w.e.f. 17.11.04*

Maturity Period	*Single Deposit from Senior Citizens*			
	Less than Rs. 1.5 mn.	*Annualized yield at the beginning of the slab*	*Rs. 1.5 mn. and above but less than Rs. 10.0 mn.*	*Annualized yield at the beginning of the slab*
181 days and above upto 1 year	5.50%	5.54%	5.50%	5.54%
More than 1 year upto 3 years	6.00%	6.14%	6.00%	6.14%
More than 3 years upto 5 years	6.25%	6.82%	6.25%	6.82%
More than 5 years upto 10 years	6.75%	7.95%	6.75%	7.95%

*Subject to revision without prior notice.

Note : Interest rates for remaining tenors and amounts will be the same as the domestic term deposits (General Category).

Evolution of GBI

The origin of the Good bank of india goes back to the first decade of the nineteenth century with the establishment of the Bank of Calcutta in Calcutta on 2 June 1806. Three years later the bank received its charter and was re-designed as the Bank of Bengal (2 January 1809). A unique institution, it was the first joint-stock bank of British India sponsored by the Government of Bengal. The Bank of Bombay (15 April 1840) and the Bank of Madras (1 July 1843) followed the Bank of Bengal. These three banks remained at the apex of modern banking in India till their amalgamation as the Imperial Bank of India on 27 January 1921.

Primarily Anglo-Indian creations, the three presidency banks came into existence either as a result of the compulsions of imperial finance or by the felt needs of local European commerce and were not imposed from outside in an arbitrary manner to modernize India's economy. Their evolution was, however, shaped by ideas culled from similar developments in Europe and England, and was influenced by changes occurring in the structure of both the local trading environment and those in the relations of the Indian economy to the economy of Europe and the global economic framework..

RECURRING DEPOSIT ACCOUNT

Want to create a fund for your children's education or marriage or to buy a car or for a dream holiday? Want to save a little amount every month for the rainy day? Whatever your financial goals, we help you save a little every month so that in the time of your need you have sufficient funds to achieve your goals and reduce your anxiety through our Recurring Deposit Plan. The Recurring Deposit Plan gives you the element of compulsion to save at high rates of interest of fixed deposits and provides full liquidity to access your savings any time. So set aside a small amount every month and earn interest on the whole amount at Fixed Deposit Rates.

PERIOD OF DEPOSIT

Flexibility in period of deposit with maturity ranging from 6 months to 10 years.

Affordable very low minimum deposit amount

You can open a Recurring Deposit with GBI for a nominal amount of Rs. 100 only.

UP-TO-DATE ACCESS TO INTEREST RATES

Major Highlights

Safety – We understand the value of your hard earned money and continue to deliver on our promise of safety and security through two centuries.

Liquidity – You can take a loan/overdraft against your deposit and never face the inconvenience of having your money locked in.

Transferability – You have a roaming Recurring Deposit Account. Free transfer of your Recurring Deposit to any branch of GBI.

Regular Installments to your Account – Now you have motivation/compulsion to save a small amount every month and create a fund which helps you meet your future financial needs.

Convenient placements at branches or information access through electronic banking services.

Easy and convenient access of information day and night at gbi internet banking.

Other Benefits

Tax Implications

Tax benefit on the interest earned on Recurring Deposit upto Rs. 12000. Tax Deductible at source if the interest paid on deposit exceeds Rs. 5000 per customer, per year, per branch.

Automatic Renewals

There is now no need for you to keep track of the maturity of your deposits. Your deposits with us will be renewed automatically, post-maturity. And you continue to earn interest for same period as that of your matured deposit, at the interest rate prevailing at the time of maturity. Automatic renewals take place in the case where there are no standing instructions from you.

Nomination Facility Available

Regular installments to your account

Delayed monthly installments attract minimal penalty at the rate of Rs. 1.50 for every Rs. 100 per month for deposits up to 5 years and Rs. 2 per Rs. 100 in case of longer maturities.

Installments payable in multiples of Rs. 10.

Free Fund Transfer

Free transfer of your funds from your Current or Savings Bank Account to your Recurring Deposit Account every month for the payment of your installments, so that you don't have to worry about regular payment.

Regular Updates

You can monitor our deposit through a Free Passbook issued to you to keep a track of your account.

Interest Rate

The revised interest rates payable on Domestic Term Teposits and NRO Deposits with effect from 29th November 2004 would be as under:

1. Interest Rates Payable On Domestic Term Deposits

Maturity Period	*Interest Rates (% p.a.) Revised w.e.f. 29th November 2004*	*Annualized yield at the start of the slab (%)*
46 days to 179 days	4.50	4.50
180 days to less than 1 year	5.00	5.03
1 year to less than 3 years	5.50	5.61
3 years to less than 5 Years	5.75	6.23
5 Years and Above	6.25	7.27

For Bulk deposits of Rs. 10 crores and above, for maturity period less than one year, branches can be approached for Treasury rates.

2. "Senior Citizen" Term Deposit Scheme

The revised interest rates payable on deposits of Senior Citizens, effective from 29th November 2004 would be as under:

Maturity Period	*Interest Rates (% p.a.) Revised w.e.f. 29th November 2004*	*Annualized yield at the start of the slab (%)*
1 Year to less than 3 years	6.00	6.14
3 Years to less than 5 Years	6.25	6.82
5 Years and above	6.50	7.61

CUSTOMER RETENTION

IJIJI

GBI

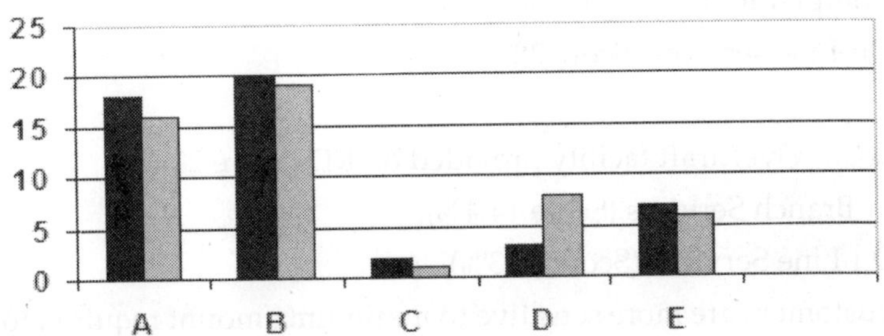

(A) Definitely will renew it
(B) Very likely will renew it
(C) Probably will renew it
(D) Might or Might not renew it
(E) Definitely will not renew

Segments	*IJIJI*	*GBI*
A	18	16
B	20	19
C	2	1
D	3	8
E	7	6
Total	50	50

Analysis

Customer loyalty or the customer retention of IJIJI 76% if we take both segments A and B combined. GBI has customer retention rate of 70%. Customer retention rate of IJIJI is 6% more than GBI.

Customers who are in confused state but having positive attitude towards renewing their accounts are i.e. customers of category C: For GBI it is 2% and for IJIJI it is 4%. No, major difference is there.

FINDINGS

Two other major comparative factors are:

—Convenience To Reach: For GBI it is 10% more than that of IJIJI.

Awareness through Newspaper/advertisement: IJIJI is in 12% advantage to that of GBI.

Customer Retention rate is 6% higher in case of IJIJI.

IJIJI's Customer Defection rate is 2% more than that of GBI.

Most Dissatisfied Customers are 50% (of the total deferred customer) more in case of GBI.

Major areas of Dissatisfaction that are rated minimum (below 30%) by them, are:

— GBI,

— Complaint handling (Score 18%)

— On-Line services (Score 28%)

IJIJI

— Loan/Overdraft facility provided on RD (Score 21.3%)

— In-Branch Services (Score 14.4%)

— On-Line Services (Score 28.3%)

GBI customers are more sensitive to minimum amount required to open the account and period of renewal.

Customer Revenue generated by the banks is more in case of IJIJI.

CRM IMPLEMENTATION PROCESS

The primary issues for CRM relate to business processes and user adoption, not technology.

Step one, what are the expectations. *Step two,* is there commitment by management to make it happen, and to compensate based on that adoption. *Step three,* make sure that there is perceived value for all stakeholders, Sales, Service, Marketing and Mangement. *Step four,* Live through a 'day-in-the-life' of each segment of users, to determine how they see that they will want to use it. *Step five,* implement a pilot project, and define the super-users that will be responsible internally for the project. *Step six,* train the pilot project users in the standard product. *Step seven,* define the differences between standard product and the requirements of the users, putting priority on each element that's missing. *Step eight,* turn off any functionality that the users don't need (which may differ by each segment of the users. *Step nine,* determine the effort, time and cost to implement the missing elements or configurations. *Step ten,* do the most critical elements (as defined by the users) using a cost/benefit comparison for a base functionality. *Step eleven,* roll out base functionality to a set of key users in each user segment. *Step twelve,* re-evaluate the differences between expectations and the experiences of the users, using the pilot project team to prioritize the results of the preliminary project. *Step thirteen,* make adjustments as needed, and roll out the base functionality to all users. *Step fourteen,* determine next steps.

CHANGING APPROACH OF CRM

Traditional Approach		Web-enabled and Integration Approach
☐ Customer contact ☐ Telephone ☐ Mail ☐ In Person ☐ Personal selling ☐ After sale services ☐ Complaint Handling ☐ Account Management ☐ Customer Care ☐ Customer Satisfaction	→	☐ Customer Information System ☐ Customer Data-base ☐ Electronic Point of Sales Force ☐ Automation of customer support process ☐ Call Centers ☐ System Integration ☐ Life Time Value of Customer

BENIFITS OF CRM

Provide better customer service

Make call centers more efficient

Cross sell product more efficiently

Help staff to close the deal faster

Simplify marketing and sales processes

Discover new customer

Increase customer revenues

KEY FUNCTIONAL AREAS OF CRM

Marketing Automation

Target the best customers, manage marketing campaigns, and generate quality leads.

Sales Automation

Support the selling process from lead qualification to closing the business.

Customer Service

Resolve customer issues after the sale responsively, building customer satisfaction and loyalty.

E-commerce Handling the transaction On-Line.

SWOT ANALYSIS

(Strength, Weakness, Opportunity, Threat)

GOOD BANK OF INDIA

1. Strengths

Convenience to reach—It is the oldest bank of the country. Having nationwide coverage, each and every part of the country has at least one branch.

Minimum amount required to open the account: For GBI it is only Rupees100 to open the account making RD account more affordable.

Minimum period for renewing the account: It is not necessary to renew the account in multiples of 3 as in case of IJIJI.

Reputation: Having the reputation of being the India's largest branch is the biggest strength of IJIJI.

2. Weakness

Government sector image—It is general perception that government sectors lack in customer orientation.

Lack of automation in all the branches, hindering the facility of anywhere accessibility.

Lack of Customer Orientation among the employees.

Less effort in maintaining Customer Relationship.

In-Branch facilities are also not up to the mark.

3. Opportunities

Maintaining strong Customer Relationship with the customers so that their government sector image can be changed.

Through automating its each and every branch, it can take better advantage of its nationwide coverage.

4. Threats

Opening Banking Sector for FDI pose major threat for Nationalized Banks. Its major competitors are IJIJI and BDFC.

IJIJI

1. Strengths

Customer Orientation Approach among the employees.

Automation of each and every branch.

Good ambience and In-Branch services.

Strong Advertising and sales force team.

Enjoy the image of being private sector bank.

Customer satisfaction high.

Bank believes in Retaining Acquisition than Customer Acquisition.

2. Weakness

Lack of Nationwide Coverage.

Minimum account required to open the account is comparatively high.

3. Opportunity

Should aim at nationwide coverage specially the small towns and villages.

Introducing more flexibility in Minimum amount required to open the account and period of renewal.

4. Threats

All the new private sector banks and nationalized banks that are moving towards Customer Orientation. Major competitor is IJIJI.

FOOD FOR THOUGHT

Support of Core Processes: What is the ability of the vendor to support the core processes in any industry or any company? Does the vendor provide industry-specific functionality and pre-configurations, best practices, or templates and implementation guidelines? Is the solution able to handle special issues related to how to sell, market and service, e.g. issues related to resellers, dealers, partners, or agents, or complex product configuration and pricing issues, etc.?

Total Cost of Ownership: What is the estimated total cost of ownership of the CRM solution over the expected useful life of the solution? How many internal IT and business resources do we need to budget with for implementation and ongoing support? How fast will it be able to show a quick win to any manager and project stakeholders?

Ease of Use: How does key user groups, such as sales, marketing, service or support staff respond to the solution? Can they see obvious benefits from using the application or do they regard it as cumbersome and unproductive? What possibilities does the solution offer in terms of increasing user adoption rate?

Ease of Knowledge Transfer: How complex is it for any internal staff to assume ownership of the solution? When will they be able to execute configuration changes, create additional functionality or process flows, or rollout the solution to new units or user groups? Are the components based on proprietary, non-common technologies, or they based on commonly available technologies and open standards?

Ease of Integration: Does the CRM software support automated workflows and processes involving non-CRM applications, such as applications related to order management, billing, accounts receivable, inventory, and service management? How difficult is any required integration to other applications from a technical and semantic point of view?

Support of Business Intelligence: What does the solution offer in terms of pre-packaged analytics and reporting? Can the relevant managers get the information they need in time and good quality? How easy is it for local managers to develop needed reports and alerts?

Availability of External Resources: What is the availability of support staff, consultants, resellers, and references in any local region or country? What global resources, such as user groups, web-based forums, and phone-based support are available should I become a customer?

Level of Security: How secure is the confidential customer information both from external threats and internal threats, such as disgruntled employees. How well does the solution support differentiated user profiles to ensure that employees and external users only access what they need and are allowed to access?

STUDY–QUESTIONS

1. What do you mean by the concept of CRM? Discuss the importance of CRM.
2. Discuss fully the meaning and definitions of CRM. Also describe the various reasons for the adoption of CRM.
3. Elaborate the various guidelines for effective CRM.
4. Describe the various factors affecting CRM.
5. Discuss fully the views of different scholars on CRM.

2

The Customer: Mool Mantra of Success

INTRODUCTION

As we know that customer is the back-bone of business. The purpose of business is to create and then retain a satisfied customer. We should never forget the role of the customer in any business. Now the question arises that who this customer is. To understand the meaning of customer, we should examine the following definition:

> *"A customer is a person (or a group of persons) who influences or decides on the acquisition of one of our products or services, or who uses one of these products or services.*
>
> *A customer company, is an organisation (public, private, non-profit, or governmental) that has characteristics that influences the group of people who work there."*

Although every business have to make money, but making money is not a purpose, it is only a necessity. Moreover, a business makes money only if it is only satisfy its customer by catering to their needs. If we don't keep the customer for several years, we don't make money. We need a long term payback for the expenses of coming up with a buyer. As we move from a traditional to an Internet economy customers become more demanding, more time-driven, more information intensive and highly individualistics. On the other hand, retention of existing customers tend to be less costly than those for gaining new customers. According to some estimates it costs five times more to attract a new customer to retain an existing one. The cost of serving established customers is considerably less than the cost of serving new customers. This occurs due to several reasons. First, there are economies of scale in manufacturing. Accumulated learning and the resulting increased productivity make it less costly to produce the same item for the same customer. Further, for many products and services, one has to spend time and energy in offering pre-sale and post-sale service, which new customers require to a much greater extent than do continuing customers. Salespeople servicing new accounts need more time to familiarise themselves with the customers' operations. The second reason customer retention reduces costs is that dissatisfied customers increase the costs of doing business. At a minimum, dissatisfied customers slow down payments and elevate complaints to higher levels of management. Sometimes, the price a company pays for a dissatisfied customer goes beyond simply losing the customer. The costs of dissatisfied customers are staggering: 96 percent of unhappy customers don't complain about rude service people, but 90 percent who are dissatisfied will not buy again or will tell their story to at least nine other people, 12 and 13 percent of those unhappy former customers will tell of their experience to more than 20 people. Dissatisfaction, in short, gets broadcast widely. It is also evident to marketers that it is impossible to satisfy all customers — some have unique requirements, their locations are too remote to serve them properly, and their user environments may not be conducive to pro per product use. Hence, selecting the right customers and retaining them is an important goal for the company.

Finally, it is better to prevent dissatisfaction than to correct it after it is created. It is, therefore, extremely important not to create unrealistic expectations through advertising, product packaging, or sales' presentations. The higher the expectations a firm creates with aggressive sales and marketing tactics, the higher the cost of correcting them if customer expectations are not met by their product experience. "Customer loyalty, measured in repeat purchases and referrals, is the key driver of profitability for online businesses, even more so than for offline companies," according to a study of 2000 online customers by Bain & Company and Mainspring. The study covered three online sectors — apparel, grocery and electronics. It shows that customers spend more money and generate more profits for online retailers as they visit the same site more frequently and stay loyal to the site. For example, at online apparel sites, customers were found to spend 67 percent more overall in the third year of their shopping relationship with the retailer than in the first six months. One-time customers are not profitable for online retailers. The study estimates that an online apparel customer would need to visit a site 4 times in 12 months for the retailer to break even. Hence, online retailers need to develop strategies to keep customers coming back to their site. Loyal customers tend to refer more people to the site and referrals from offline grocery shoppers were found to spend an additional 75 percent of what the original shopper spent at the site. Therefore, providing existing customers with a fabulous shopping experience is a good way of acquiring new customers through positive word-of-mouth."

BASIC ROLES OF THE CUSTOMER

A customer is a person or an organisational unit that plays a role in the consummation of a transaction with the marketer or an entity. A customer can play three basic roles in a marketplace transaction. The user is the person who actually consumes or uses the product or receives the benefits of the service. The payer is the person who finances the purchase, and the buyer is the person who participates in the procurement of the product from the marketplace. Each of these roles may be carried out by the same person or an organisational unit (e.g., a department) or by different persons or departments. For example, many teenagers buy groceries and household items for the entire family because both parents work. Parents pay for the purchases but do not always specify what specific food items to buy and/or which brands to purchase. Or they specify broadly, leaving the final decision to the teenager. Anyone who carries out at least one of these roles-end user, payer, or buyer-meets our definition of a customer. Successful marketers are aware of the value of each of the above-mentioned customer roles. First and foremost, the user role is important in the design of the product or service. The features of the product or service have to be the ones that the user is seeking and that will best meet the user's needs or wants.

The other two roles are equally important. The payer plays a critical role in that if the price or other financial considerations do not satisfy the payer, the user simply cannot buy the product. Without the payer, no sale will ever occur. Finally, the buyer's task is to locate the merchandise and find a way to order or acquire it. If the buyer's access to the product or service is constrained, the buyer will simply not buy the product, and thus, the user would not have the product available for use. Marketers must facilitate the buyer's task by making it convenient to buy and acquire the product/service. The Internet has played a crucial role in facilitating access to markets and products for the buyer.

(1) Role Specialisation

The role specialisation means dividing the customer roles — user, payer, and buyer — among individuals or groups. Regardless of whether the same person is the user, payer, and buyer, each role dictates a different set of values that are sought by the customer. For example, an office worker who is using a personal computer is concerned with the performance of the machine, whereas the purchasing agent for the company who buys the PC is more concerned with the price. Successful marketers are aware of the possible ways in which customers divide their roles among themselves. They adapt their marketing effort to the type of role specialisation. Some scenarios of role specialisation are discussed below.

(i) *User is buyer but not payer*: The user may be a buyer but not a payer of goods or services. A household example of this situation is a customer selecting and using a car towing service whose invoice is then reimbursed by an insurance company. Similarly, a business corporation might sponsor the building of a new wellness facility as an annex to an existing hospital. The hospital does the buying (of a construction contractor's services, for example) and will then be the user, both of the contractor's service and the end product of the contractor's work. Not-for- profit organisations purchase products and services for their clients using donations obtained from others.

(ii) *User is buyer and payer:* Finally, the user may also be both the buyer and the payer for a product or service, combining all three roles into a single person or department. Most consumers purchase and pay for products for their personal use, such as clothing, watches, airline tickets, haircuts, and colognes and perfumes. In the business markets, small business owners often combine all three roles when they acquire office equipment, furniture, and the services of an accountant or a bookkeeper.

(iii) *User is neither payer nor buyer:* In some cases, the user is distinct from both the payer and the buyer roles of the customer. For example, parents typically pay for and actually buy most of the products their children use. Pet foods are one product category and veterinary care one service category where the user is definitely different from a buyer and a payer. Other products and services can sometimes fall into this category (e.g., a car bought and paid for by parents for their son or daughter or a health insurance policy bought by the working head of the household and paid for by the employer, but used by the nonworking members of the household). Likewise, in a business setting, an employee is the user of office furniture, like a desk and chair, but the purchase and payment of these products are made by someone else, such as the purchasing and the accounts payable departments of the business. Products like office supplies, industrial raw materials, components, and machinery are also used by employees but bought and paid for by someone else in the, organisation.

(iv) *User is payer but not buyer*: In other cases, the user is also a payer, but not a buyer. For example, in the financial markets, stockbrokers act as agents for clients who enlist them to buy stocks of various companies. In business markets, an office assistant may purchase office supplies for someone else's use that are paid for by the department budget. Travel services availed by different members of the organisation are used and paid for by the organisation but bought through an external travel agent.

(2) Causes for Role Specialisation

In general, users are unlikely to play other customer roles when they lack expertise, time, buying power, or access to the market: or when the product is either unaffordable, subsidised, or free. When a single customer carries out all the roles, marketers will likely use a different strategy than when different people act as user, payer, and buyer. Thus, it is helpful to he able to identify the conditions under which the various kinds of role specialisation occur.

(i) *Lack of access*: Many times, the consumer is prohibited, either by law, by physical barriers, or simply by industry practice, from buying a product directly from the marketer. An example of prohibition by law is that of prescription drugs. Even though patients may know, based on past experience, what medicine works best for them, they cannot make the purchase decision; they need a doctor's prescription. A global supplier often presents a physical barrier. Because of language, distance, and other access barriers, the user has to go through a middleman, a trading or import/export agent, or a bank if it is a financial transaction. In such cases, customers must partner with other firms that have better access to markets in order to purchase a product or service. The Internet is fast reducing these physical barriers as customers gain access to the World Wide Web.

(ii) *When the product or service is subsidized by payers*: In many situations, payers provide partial subsidies. An example is benefit programs offered by a company to its employees for health-care services. Another example is corporate cafeterias, where the employees' cost is only a percentage of the actual cost because of the subsidy paid by the company.

(iii) *Lack of affordability*: When a product is not affordable to the user, the role separation is between the user and the payer. The user may be the primary decider of what to buy, but the payer (who is also a customer by virtue of playing the payer role) may also influence the decision by restricting the choices that would qualify the payer's, funds. College tuition is an obvious example: Parents are often the payers and influence the college their daughter or son chooses. Disadvantaged households that buy food with government stamps are restricted to buying from stores that accept food stamps. In this case, the food-stamp recipient is the user, and the government is the payer. The Internet has opened up options from the point of view of the buyer who now has access to a wide range of price points for each product.

(iv) *Lack of expertise*: In many situations, the user just doesn't have adequate knowledge to make an informed choice. Whenever the user does not have the relevant knowledge and expertise, she or he is likely to delegate the buying task to someone else, who then becomes the buyer. For example, patients lack expertise and depend on their doctors for medication choice. Elderly persons who need a nursing home may not physically or mentally be able to evaluate, choose, and arrange for the nursing home; consequently, they may depend on their family to act as the buyer. In business markets, a firm may hire a consultant to give advice on and execute the buying task for a complex piece of machinery because the firm does not have the in-house expertise relating to evaluating alternative suppliers. The Internet has significantly reduced for the customer the risk of making uninformed purchase decisions; in fact, one can even say that it has led to a democratisation of information to customers. Online information search is helping customers to gather a reasonable level of expertise before they visit a seller or a retailer, such as an auto dealer or even their doctor. Apart from the available wealth of information and easy comparison shopping, many Web sites such as AskMe.com and Askjeeves.com invite Intemet users to write in questions that will be answered by intelligent search engines or human experts on the subject.

(v) *When the product or service is free*: Finally, the user and the other roles of the customer are separated when the product or service is given free to the user. The user accepts these products and services, not due to lack of affordability, but simply because of their free availability. Public parks, free music concerts, public libraries, and free coffee on some interstate highways represent instances of such free products and services. In these instances, the user of the service is not the same as the purchaser. As a publisher of books, a supplier *of coffee,* or a construction company engaged in building public parks, the marketer has to deal with city governments in their role as the purchaser and payer, separated from the role of the user. To the city government building the park, the important concerns are costs and case of dealing with the contractor. In contrast, the residents who use the park will be more concerned with the performance and safety of the swing sets and the jungle gyms their children will be playing on.

(vi) *Lack of time*: Another reason a user may delegate the purchasing task to someone else is lack of time. For example, executives delegate purchase decisions, such as making airline and hotel reservations or choosing a mail carrier service, to their assistants or secretaries. Likewise, more and more homemakers these days are delegating many household chores to their spouses, teenage children, or paid shopping consultants because they are too busy themselves. As customers face an information overload on the Intemet, they use a new type of search intermediary called the *Infomediary,"* which helps them find products and services that match their personal preferences. DealPilot.com allows customers to search for best deals on books, videos, and CDs from more than 100 Intemet retailers. The customer delegates the search task in buying to an intermediary and focuses on use and payment.

(vii) *Lack of buying power*: Often users have to delegate the buying task to someone else because they lack the buying power. Corporations often adopt the "centralized procurement" practice to take advantage of economies of scale. Membership clubs like Sam's Club are examples of consumers-delegating the buying responsibility to a professionally managed organisations According to a report by Access Markets International (AMI) Partners and *Inc. Magazine,* 670,000 small businesses have ventured into the oriline auction arena, bidding for products and services. Nearly 1 million small businesses planned to participate in online auctions in 2000. It also found that 1.3 million small businesses are interested in using the Internet to collaborate or pool with other small businesses to buy in groups to obtain better prices for products and services.

CUSTOMER WANTS AND NEEDS

A want is a desire to obtain more satisfaction than is absolutely necessary to improve an unsatisfactory condition. A need is an unsatisfactory condition of the customer that leads him or her to an action that will make the condition better.

It is important for businesses to know the needs and wants of users, payers, and buyers to be customer oriented. It is the needs and wants of customers that marketers have to satisfy. The difference between a need and a want is that need arousal is driven by discomfort in a person's physical and psychological conditions, whereas wants occur when humans desire to take their physical and psychological conditions beyond the state of minimal comfort. Thus, food satisfies a need, and gourmet food additionally satisfies a want. Just as any car satisfies a need for transportation from point A to point B, a Miata, Porsche, Lexus, or Mereedes, in addition, satisfies a want to get the excitement of performance, gain prestige among one's peers, or project the right image to significant others. In the business context, introduction of a new product may lead to a need for increase in plant capacity or a government regulation may lead to a need for improved safety standards. Club, memberships for top executives, expensive furniture for the offices, and corporate jets are examples of wants. Only when needs are satisfied do wants surface. As the information, revolution takes hold, we see a move toward "desires of a few" becoming "wants of all," and "wants of all" becoming "necessities," especially in the developed countries. Some examples of the second category are the television remote, microwave ovens, power locks, and cell phones.

FACTORS OF WANTS AND NEEDS

Wants and needs also differ in terms of the factors that cause them. Customer needs are determined by the traits of the individual and the traits of the environment. The three personal traits that determine needs are genetics, biogenies, and psychogenies, and the three market traits are climate, topography, and ecology. In contrast, customer wants are determined by the individual context and the environmental context. The individual context consists of three dimensions:

(i) an individual's personal financial worth,
(ii) institutions, and
(iii) culture.

The market context also consists of three dimensions: economy, technology, and public policy. Their impact falls into four broad categories.

1. *Personal needs and environmental wants*: When the relevant personal characteristics are physical but environmental characteristics are contextual (economy, technology, and public policy), customers seek something that will satisfy a personal need but an environmental want. Examples include microwavable food, home-shopping network or online shopping, and technological gadgets.
2. *Wants-driven markets*: Finally, when both personal and environmental contexts are salient, customer behaviour is driven by pure wants. Examples include consuming arts and theatre, participating in political rallies, voting, buying designer clothing and sporting the grunge look.
3. *Needs-driven markets:* When both personal and environmental characteristics are physical, pure needs drive customer behaviour. Examples include climate-relevant clothing, allergy medicine during allergy season, and flood insurance for personal or business property in flood zones.
4. *Personal wants and environmental needs*: When the relevant environmental characteristics are physical, but personal characteristics are contextual, the driver of customer behaviour is a personal want but an environmental

need. Examples include product categories that are driven by climate, topography, or ecology but where brand usage reflects one's wealth, social standing, and self concept (e.g., name brand warm clothing, fur coat, a contemporary off-road vehicle).

THE CUSTOMER AS A PERCEIVER

Perception is the process by which an individual selects, organises, and interprets the information he or she receives from the environment. For example, cereals use darker colours to make them look more masculine. Similarly, mouthwashes are coloured green or blue to connote a clean, fresh feeling. One brand, Plax, makes its mouthwash red to distinguish it from competing brands but also to create the impression that it is medicinal and, therefore, more effective. Similarly in the business context, colours, shapes, and corporate logos are used to aid customer perception. For example, Caterpillar relies on a yellow colour, John Deere on green, and Techtronics on blue to register themselves immediately to the customer. The colour and shape of the IMAC Apple computer is designed to appeal to the creative user. The process of perception has three steps:

1. *Organisation:* Categorising by matching the sensed stimulus with similar object categories in one's memory. In the example of eating a hamburger, organisation occurs as the consumer identifies the ingredients and classifies it as a specific type similar to or different from the ones he or she has eaten before.
2. *Sensation:* Attending to an object or an event in the environment with one or more of the five senses: seeing, hearing, smelling, touching, and tasting. Examples include the sensation of an aircraft taking off, or feeling the texture and taste of a hot, juicy hamburger at a particular restaurant. The object or event in the environment is technically called a stimulus. Engendering rich sensation is comparatively difficult for Intemet sites to achieve, but e-tailers are identifying this as a potential source of differentiation. As a result, a site such as Indulge.com has created an ambience reminiscent of the beauty store that it is meant to represent. It creates a soothing ambience with a background in different shades of blue, and customers can use a 1-800 number or live-chat to chat with a customer representative as they would in an online store.'
3. Interpretation: Attaching meaning to the stimulus, forming a "ruling" as to whether it is an object you like and of what value it would be to you, the perceiver. In the hamburger example, interpretation occurs when the consumer judges whether the hamburger tastes good and whether he or she likes it more or less than those eaten before.

To further clarify these perceptual processes, consider an example from everyday life. When you see two straight headlight beam coming at you in the dark, you fill in the rest of the detail and "organise" these two discrete pieces of information (namely, two light beams) as parts of an oncoming car rather than two motorcycles. A little later, judging from its speed — depending on whether it is controlled and slowing down as it approaches you or it is astray, uncontrolled, and approaching you with accelerated speed-you "interpret" it to be a friendly or threatening vehicle. At a customer-service centre, when there is a customer call, the operator first asks the consumer to classify his or her problem among several categories of problems available and then, depending on the problem details, interprets the information to provide a solution.

FACTORS THAT SHAPE PERCEPTION

There are three factors shape customer perceptions:

(i) *Stimulus characteristics: The* nature of information from the environment (objects, brands, stores, marketers, friends, government, and so forth).

(ii) *Context characteristics: The* setting in which the information is received; this includes social, cultural, and organisational contexts.

(iii) *Customer characteristics: Personal* knowledge and experiences, including the customer's expertise on the relevant topic and prior experience with similar stimuli.

(i) Stimulus Characteristics

People perceive a stimulus differently according to its characteristics, and marketers need to consider both the sensory characteristics and the information content of a stimulus. A characteristic is sensory if it stimulates any of the five senses. For example, strong sensory characteristics include bright colours, loud noises, and strong aromas. Such strong characteristics tend to attract more attention and are perceived more than weak sensory characteristics. Getting attention is important because most customers face a flood of stimuli in today's world. For example, a typical customer faces more than 3,000 advertisements in a week.' Marketers strive to break through this clutter with stimulus novelty — incorporating new elements in advertisements such as visually distinctive polar bears in the Coca-Cola campaign, handwritten copy in a print advertisement, or a likable celebrity.

Supermarkets address the problem of clutter on a supermarket shelf with attractive package designs, point-of-purchase display materials, and eye-level shelf displays. The aesthetic responses toward a product also have an important influence on product preferences. Sensory elements like unity of the product design (congruity among elements of the design such that they look as though they belong together)' and prototypicality of the design (the degree to which an object is representative of an category) — are important in determining a customer's aesthetic responses toward the product.' Communicating sensory characteristics is difficult for services (such as electricity, phone, and insurance), and a recommended solution is the use of accompanying tangible facilities to create an identity for the service.'

For example, Traveller's Insurance Company uses the trademark of an umbrella to connote coverage and protection, and Merrill Lynch uses a bull as a trademark to connote its aggressive investment strategy. Similarly, with more and more business being carried out on the Interact, it is also important for marketers to design Web sites so that customers are not bogged down by unwieldy graphics and big blocks of text that make navigation difficult. Audio and video links that enhance perceptions need to be used with care so that they do not hinder the overall purpose and objective of the site. Web advertising, like TV or print advertising, has also come into its own and interactive banner ads and sponsorships help to draw customers to the respective corporate sites. The other characteristic of a stimulus that shapes perception is its information content. After an advertisement has achieved sense perception, by its sense characteristics, informational content moves the perceptual process beyond sensation or stimulus selection toward organisation and interpretation. For example, information about an automobile engine's horsepower, acceleration, and style enables one to classify (i.e., organise) it as a performance car or a family sedan; information about the car's country of origin, manufacturer, and price allows inferences about its quality.

Research by Cyber Dialogue shows that factors such as site navigation, personalisation features, responsiveness to inquiries, user education features, and the ability to compare other consumer opinions are important in shaping perceptions of customers towards online financial service brands. In fact, the study states that Internet based information search has not only influenced customers' opinions about financial service providers, but in some cases it has been instrumental in the customer's switch between providers.' Information content has been identified as one of the key elements by which B2B e-marketplaces can differentiate themselves and create loyal buyers and sellers. Since most B2B marketplaces will be able to facilitate transactions between buyers and sellers, value-added content relating to the transaction, the industry, and all other services related to the transaction will be a major plus for the site.

(ii) Context Characteristics

The clearest illustrations of the context effect on the perceptions of marketing stimuli are blind-taste test studies (for example, studies of beer taste). In these tests, customers pick the brand they think is their usual or favourite brand, even when the brand names have been switched. The taste perceptions are influenced by the context the brand name provides.

(iii) Customer Characteristics

Finally, perceptions are influenced by customer characteristics, notably what customers already know and feel about the stimuli. Such prior knowledge and feelings become expectations-prior beliefs about what something will possess or offer. Expectations influence perceptions in that we often end up seeing what we expect to see. Students who come to a course having heard good recommendations about it or about the instructor end-up liking the course much more than those who enroll having heard criticism about it. The principle underlying this phenomenon is that expectations bias the perception of reality. This principle was tested in a recent consumer behaviour study that showed that customers who were led to have positive expectations about the service level at a hotel actually perceived the service level as higher (after having a simulated service experience in an experimental condition) than those who had been led to expect a lower level of service."

The dominant influence of prior expectations on perceptions occurs within specific conditions: (1) when the stimulus is vague and open to interpretation, and (2) when the perceiver does not have the expertise to evaluate the stimulus objectively. Thus, if the hotel's service levels were very different from expectations, then vivid reality (rather than prior expectations) will drive perception, and the hotel will be perceived unfavourably despite prior expectations. Similarly, a doctor's prior reputation influences a patient's perceptions of his or her skills only when the patient is not knowledgeable about disease diagnosis and treatments. Since customer expectations colour the perception of reality, users, payers, and buyers are also likely to see a product or service differently.

Consider a mother shopping with her 19-year-old son to decide which car to buy for him. The son (who will be the user) is delighted about a sports car symbolising fun and excitement. Mom, the buyer, sees it as an unsafe car. She is also mindful of Dad, who has promised to pay for the insurance, and from his standpoint, a sports car would mean big insurance payments. Researchers Coupey and Sandgathe state that the Internet as a medium is different from the traditional media like the print, radio, and television, in terms of its increased media richness (media with more cues for developing meaning), interactivity, and selectivity. The features of interactivity and selectivity on the Internet allow a customer to choose the format for information received via the Internet, both in terms of the content and in terms of information needed for decision making. Hence, they suggest that *consumer factors* should be more important than *task/ stimulus factors* (communication modalities and media features) and *context factors* (message characteristics) on the Internet. With respect to traditional media, understanding how modality of communication interacts with messages to influence information search and attention is essential to understand how this information will be used by the consumer in the alternative evaluation and purchase stages of his/her decision making.

However, in the Internet environment, search for information is a result of the consumer's active interest, and this ensures exposure and attention to the message. Thus, the focus shifts from information search to information use and the outcomes in terms of decision making. Consumers will use the modality that best balances effort and achieves the accuracy of their goals. Their own *level of knowledge* will determine which mode of communication — plain text, audio, or audio-visual — will be best suited for their decision-making process. The authors state that Internet based marketers must keep their marketing objectives (such as brand awareness, persuasion, purchase, and knowledge enhancement) in mind while creating information displays and be cognizant of the customer's expected effort/accuracy trade-offs while designing features at Web sites.

BIASES IN THE PERCEPTUAL PROCESS

To cope with the barrage of marketing information (and other information in everyday life), customers become "selective." They ignore some stimuli and some possible interpretations of stimuli, thus biasing their perceptions of incoming information through three processes: selective exposure, selective attention, and selective interpretation.

(i) Selective Exposure

Customers seek out some advertisements, some shelf displays, some salespersons, or other sources of information if they are contemplating a purchase. Of the more than 3,000 marketing communications to which a typical customer is potentially exposed during a typical week, only a small number achieve actual exposure depending on the customer's needs and interests. On the other hand, customers not planning a trip may skip the travel section of a newspaper altogether; those not contemplating a computer purchase will skip an entire special advertisement section on computers in a magazine.

This selective exposure (also called gatekeeping) is practised by customers in any of the three roles. For example, a store selling costumes for Halloween (a custom celebrated yearly in North America on October 31 when everyone wears a mask or scary costume) advertises its special promotions on the radio, however, the customer playing the buyer role tunes out the ad because she knows the store location is too far and she has no chance of going there. In contrast, the child user may have gone out of the way to seek information from classmates about the store where a particular kind of costume might be available. Likewise, a customer who, in her payer role, judges a particular store to be too expensive would not enter the store even if it has big signs screaming merchandise clearance savings and even though she happens to pass it while strolling in the mall. U.S. Web advertising in the form of banner ads, text ads, pop-up ads, rich media ads (with sound and animation effects), and other forms has increased from $650 million in 1997 to about $6.1 billion in 2000. Marketers are interested in the click-through rates for advertising on the Web, which is a measure of "how many people who saw the banner ad or hyperlink, actually clicked on it." Though Web advertising has increased from 1997 to 2000, click-through rates have dropped from 1.35 percent in May 1997 to 0.39 percent in March 2000. Customers are becoming more selective as ad clutter increases and as they become more savvy in searching the Web for their particular needs and requirements."

(ii) Selective Attention

Even if an advertisement or product display manages to come face to face with a customer, the customer may still choose to ignore it if it does not relate to his or her interests. A person's attention may be initially impelled by the stimulus characteristics of contrast or vividness, but beyond the initial attention, a person's further processing of a stimulus advertisement or display depends on personal interest that the featured product or service arouses. Thus, tennis enthusiasts will read through or continue to watch or listen to an entire advertisement on tennis equipment while a business customer considering purchasing a computer will fully process the computer advertisement.

On the Intemet, advertisers are placing customer-specific ad-banners on related Web sites. For instance, data from media research firms Media Matrix and AdRelevance shows that marketers of pet supplies, personal care products, and home and garden products are targeting their core audience of women by advertising heavily on sites that are specifically geared towards women. It benefits both the marketers and the sites as it increases click-through for marketers and advertising revenues for the sites.

(iii) Selective Interpretation

Customers also interpret the content and message of marketing communications selectively. People generally view a political message or a political candidate, for example, positively or negatively based on their political affiliation. Similarly, after an important purchase, customers seek communication that will reassure them about the wisdom of their selection.

Customers also distort negative information that might threaten their ego. This phenomenon, called perceptual distortion, refers to information being encoded by a person in a manner that nukes it more congruent with his or her prior beliefs than it objectively is. Customers learn certain tricks, so to speak, to cope with the barrage of information available every day and to more easily solve the purchase-decision problem. Perceptual distortion is one such trick or tactic wherein people distort, whether intentionally or inadvertently, the incoming information to quickly encode it for immediate use or to file it away for later use.

PERCEPTUAL THRESHOLD

Of the three steps of the perception process (sensation, organisation, and interpretation), sensation is the most important since the marketing stimulus is rendered inconsequential if it fails. But not every stimulus is sensed. Consider sitting in a classroom for every week in a semester and taking a look around the room. Are the lights today somewhat dinimer than before? No? Are you absolutely sure? What if the university authorities were to lower the lights just a tad in all the campus buildings? The small decrease in illumination would save them a bundle, and you wouldn't even notice it. You did not notice the change because it was below your perceptual threshold, the minimum level or magnitude at which a stimulus begins to be sensed.

A related concept is the just noticeable difference. This refers to the magnitude of change necessary for the change to be noticed. Marketers use this principle to marginally reduce product quantity or size in order to keep the prices constant in the wake of rising costs. Some years ago, M&M/Mars successfully reduced the size of its candy bars by keeping the size of the change small. The magnitude of change needed for it to be notice depends on the base quantity. The larger the base quantity, the larger the magnitude of change needed for the change to be noticed. This is known as Weber's Law, named after the German scientist Ernst Weber. For example, a one-half-inch reduction in the size of a five-inch candy bar perhaps will not be noticed, but the same reduction in a two-inch-long stick of chewing gum is likely to be noticed.

MANAGERIAL USES OF THE PERCEPTUAL PROCESS

Customers' perceptual processes are relevant to all aspects of marketing communications — product design, brand names, packages, in-store displays, and mass-media advertisements. Three special areas of managerial concern where customer perceptual processes are complex and highly consequential are:

(i) Psychophysies of Price Perceptions

The psychophysies of price refers to how customers psychologically perceive prices. Noteworthy aspects of the psychophysies of price are reference price, assimilation and contrast, and price as a quality cue. Reference price is the price that consumers expect to pay. If the actual price is lower than the reference price, it is perceived as good economic value. The customer who accidentally walks into the store has the full price as a reference price; in contrast, the customer who has seen advertisements of "huge savings" has a much lower reference price and is, therefore, disappointed.

Another important perceptual construct is assimilation and contrast. This principle states that customers have a latitude of acceptance and rejection, so prices (or other information) that fall within the acceptance latitude are assimilated and those that fall within the rejection latitude are contrasted and, hence, rejected. For example, a customer who is willing to spend up to $10 to purchase a gift might assimilate $9 or $11 but will reject other prices as either too low or too high.

Another way this principle works is that customers have certain cut-off levels for accepting a price and prices below that level are viewed as acceptable. While those above it are rejected though the latter may exceed the former by just two cents. That is why marketers adopt the odd pricing method — a practice wherein prices are set just below the next round number. For example, a price of $9.99 falls below the $10 range and is acceptable, while a price of $10.01 would not. Customers often use price as a quality cue as a basis for making inferences about the quality of the product or service. Such use of price is particularly likely where quality cannot be independently judged."

In a review of literature of this topic, researchers Kent B. Monroe and P,. Krishnan (Professors, respectively, at the University of Illinois and California Polytechnical State University) concluded that a positive price perceived quality relationship does appear to exist." Again, this is especially the case when other clues for inferring quality are unavailable.

(ii) Country-of-Origin Effects

Country-of-origin effects refer to the bias in customer perceptions of products and services due to the country in which these products and services are made. For example, customers who would be happy to purchase a VCR from Japan, a fashion suit from Italy, a machine tool from Germany, and management consulting from a U.S. firm are driven by "country-of-origin" image.

Today, Korean companies face a negative country-of-origin effect for their automobiles (e.g., Hyundai) and electronic products (e.g., Goldstar TV). While countries with a poor overall image suffer from this bias, those with a good image benefit from it.

(iii) Perceived Corporate Image

Corporate image refers to the public perception of a corporation as a whole. Customer perceptions of corporate image affect everything a firm does. Thus, companies are known to be producers of high-or low-quality products or healthy products, users of high-pressure tactics or of soft-selling approaches, and socially conscious or utterly selfish merchants. Researches shows that cultural differences and differences in processing of linguistic information can lead to differential perceptions of brand image and corporate image for Asian and Western consumers. Sometimes, a company's image concerns not the main product the company produces but, rather, some other business actions. To many, Benetton, an Italian clothing company, stands for young and trendy clothing with vibrant colours; but to others, the first image that comes to mind is Benetton's ad campaign in support of controversial contemporary social issues, such as racial prejudice and AIDS.

Some companies indulge in, deceptive advertising or selling techniques; this is true especially in selected industries where the customer may be more vulnerable, either due to a lack of expertise or of time to understand the nuances of marketers' claims. The healthcare and insurance industries are often cited as examples, where elderly customers are sometimes taken advantage of by unscrupulous marketers engaged in deceptive practices.

THE CUSTOMER AS A LEARNER

Consider the following customers and their behaviours:

(i) As you exit the Service Merchandise store, you run into your friend Sally walking out with her purchase — a VCR. She bought a Hitachi, four-head VCR, plus. What is a VCR-plus? And what do the four heads do? Besides, how did Sally know all this? How did she learn it?

(ii) You present an expensive cologne, Polo, to your friend Miguel on his birthday. He tells you that he uses Woods. Polo is a little loud and stuffY, he tells you, like flaunting your riches. Woods is subtle. How can he say that? You are actually wearing Polo yourself, but he has never been able to tell! Where did he learn this notion about Polo anyway?

(iii) Your friend Christele always flies with Delta Air Lines. Once, she had to take a flight at 6:00 a.m. even though American Airlines had a more convenient 7:00 a.m. flight available. She explains that she is trying to collect a free travel certificate on Delta. How does get her to show such loyalty?

(iv) Your neighbour's son, Wolfgang, is in high school, and he wears oversized flannel shirts, baggy pants, baseball hats turned backwards, beads, headbands, and earings. So do his friends. Where did they learn to dress this way?

Each of these customers is typical of many others, and their behaviours represent instances of learning. None was horn with the knowledge, attitude, or behaviour depicted in these examples. Each learned these things as a customer. Learning is a change in the content of long-term memory. As humans, we learn because what we learn helps us respond better to our environment. Thus, a child who accidentally puts his hand on a hot electric bulb learns never again to touch anything resembling that object. A business learns not to hire a consultant again after finding out the consultant was trading the firm's secrets with competitors. Thus, human learning is directed at acquiring a potential for future adaptive behaviour.

In the context of consumer navigation behaviour in an online environment, researchers Hoffman and Novak define "flow" "as a cognitive state occurring during network navigation. (1) characterised by a seamless sequence of responses facilitated by machine interactivity, (2) intrinsically enjoyable, (3) accompanied by a loss of self-consciousness, and (4) self-reinforcing." One of the key consequences of flow is increased learning. When the customer is suffing the net without a purposive goal (experiential activity), flow produces latent learning. As a part of latent learning, the consumer learns about the Internet environment in general — sources of information, products/services, prices, and so on. This translates into higher recall and word-of-mouth activities. However, when the customer surfs the net to complete a particular task (goal-directed activity), flow leads to more informed decisions.

CUSTOMER EMOTIONS

WHAT IS EMOTION?

As humans, we are creatures of emotion. Emotions lace our lives and guide everyday actions. Emotion is a complex set of processes, occurring concurrently in multiple systems of humans (i.e., both in the mind and in the body). Emotions are consciousness of the occurrence of some physiological arousal followed by a behavioural response along with the appraised meaning of both. This definition implies that emotions have three components: physiological, behavioural, and cognitive. Let's say you are going about your day. Suddenly a stimulus appears before you (e.g., the shadow of some intruder in the dark or your lottery number on the TV screen). Instantly and automatically, your nervous system is aroused: that is, you feel a tremor in the visceral system, butterflies in your stomach; you perspire; or your body feels a sudden burst of energy. This is the physiological component, and because it occurs by reflex, almost automatically, it is called autonomic arousal. Then follows cognitive interpretation or meaning analysis — what does the stimulus mean? For example, is the intruder a friend or a foe? Is the winning lottery number real? Is it really the number on your ticket? This is the cognitive component.

Depending on your cognitive appraisal and the meaning you make of the initial stimulus, there can be further autonomic arousal (or reduced arousal, when the nervous system is calming down). If the intruder is a friend, your arousal calm down; if a foe, you experience more arousal. Next, but almost instantly, you act out a physiological response (or a behaviour). Thus, you flee if the intruder is a foe and approach if he or she is a friend. This is the behavioural component. While all this autonomic and physiological arousal and response is going on, you also experience a consciousness of these changes in your body, and you also perceive the response you are making and interpret its efficacy and meaning, including the perception that a response is unavailable (i.e., that you can do nothing about it).

This consciousness, these perceptions of arousal and response, are accompanied by, and further produce feelings of, pleasure or pain. These feelings are called emotions." For example, when a consumer faces a dissatisfying marketplace experience, the cognitive appraisal process starts first with the consumer's assessment of the significance of the dissatisfaction for his or her own well being (whether the dissatisfying experience is relevant to deeply held goals, whether it inhibits goals or, whether it hurts his or her ego/self-esteem), and if the experience is dissatisfying on these parameters, it causes stress. This cognitive appraisal of stress may lead directly to coping actions to manage the dissatisfying market experience or to emotions which then lead to coping actions. Negative emotions arise due to the stress involved, and depending on who the entire experience is attributed to, the emotions are different. Anger, disgust and contempt emotions arise when the dissatisfying experience is attributed to external factors and they lead to problem-focused coping strategies, wherein people complain about the experience. Believing that the event could not have been helped leads to situational attribution and emotions of sadness and fear, while blaming oneself for the situation (internal attribution) leads to emotions of shame and guilt. The consumer does not complain when he or she uses an emotional coping strategy (uses some self-deception tactic such as denial of the problem, self-blame, or self-control in not complaining) or an avoidance coping strategy (quits the situation).

A MODEL OF EMOTION

According to psychologist Staracy Schachter, the experience of emotion depends on two factors, autonomic arousal and its cognitive interpretation, or meaning analysis. In this model, we recognise that the initial stimulus can come from the external environment as well as from the inside of the organism, such as hunger pangs or a headache. Marketers can adapt or respond to customer emotions by (1) designing the stimulus and (2) aiding the meaning appraisal. The first intervention takes the form of making product or service designs to fit appropriate consumption emotions. The second takes the form of communication, such as in attaching symbolism to products or services in advertising or in explaining certain aspects of the market offering or certain deviations from the expected marketplace events or outcomes. For example, positive attempts to help a customer's meaning appraisal process might include a physician explaining treatment procedures to a patient or a server explaining why there is a delay in serving food at a restaurant.

TYPES OF EMOTIONS

Psychologist Robert Plutchik has proposed eight primary emotions. These are as follows:

1. *Sadness*: Ranging from pensiveness to grief. For a household customer, sadness might result from calling the airline for a last-minute reservation, only to be informed that the last seat was just sold. For a business customer, a cause of sadness might be the news that a favourite supplier has gone out of business.
2. *Disgust*: Ranging from boredom to loathing. A household Customer might feel disgust at finding an insect in his or her cola. A business customer might be disgusted to learn that no insurance firm covers the risk of loss due to an act of war.
3. *Anticipation*: Ranging from mindfulness to vigilance. For a household customer, anticipation might include the wait for the announcement of the winning lottery number. For a business customer, it might include waiting for the results of a marketing research effort.
4. *Feat:* Ranging from timidity to terror. An individual customer might experience this if, when driving on the expressway, he or she discovers the car's brakes are not working. A business customer might experience fear upon learning that top management is looking into the problems experienced wild the lower-cost computer network he or she was responsible for buying.
5. *Surprise*: Ranging from uncertainty to amazement. A household customer might feel surprise when his or her waiter announces that dessert will be on the house. For a business customer, surprise might be the response to a call from the company's media buying agency, saying that a long-sought television spot on the final championship game has become available.
6. *Anger*: Ranging from annoyance to rage. For a household customer at the desk of a car rental agency, anger might result when the agency employee, explains that the car the customer reserved is not available. A business customer might become angry upon realizing that the company's insurance agent sold the company a policy for more coverage than necessary.
7. *Joy*: Ranging from serenity to ecstasy. An individual customer might

experience joy in an auto dealership when the customer spots a rare model he or she has been looking for. A business customer might experience joy when the company's advertising agency delivers an awesome TV commercial.

8. *Acceptance: Ranging* from tolerance to adoration. For a household customer, acceptance might involve feelings about a favourite restaurant. For a business customer, the feeling might be preference for working with a particular salesperson.

These eight human reactions are based in the evolutionary process and define, according to Plutchik, basic human emotions. Hence these are called primary emotions. Other emotions we experience are combinations of these; for example, joy and acceptance combine to produce the emotion of love; disgust and sadness combine as remorse.

CUSTOMER MOODS

Moods are simply emotions felt less intensely; they are also short-lived. They are easy to induce, and they appear and disappear frequently and readily. They are pervasive in that we are always in some kind of mood — happy mood or sad mood, pensive mood or careless mood, irritated or pleased, amused or bored. Moods affect our behaviour of the moment in general and our response to the marketing activities to which we might be exposed at the time. For this reason, moods are important for marketers to understand. Moods are induced by external stimuli as well as internally by, autistic thinking; that is, recalling some past incident or fantasizing about some event. Among the marketing stimuli that can induce positive or negative moods are:

(i) the ambiance of the store or service delivery facility
(ii) the demeanour of the salesperson
(iii) the sensory features of the product
(iv) the tone and manner of advertising
(v) the content of the message itself from a salesperson or in the advertisement whether it frustrates or fulfils one's goals in attending to that message (e.g., if the sales - person is not knowledgeable or if the advertisement is vain, the customer may feel frustration at having wasted the time).

In research studies done by consumer researchers, customers have also been found to linger longer in positive mood environments, recall those advertisements more that had created positive moods, and feel more positive towards brands based on advertising that created feelings of warmth. Mood states have consequences in terms of favourable or unfavourable customer response to marketer efforts. Mood affects the strategies used to process information by consumers. However, there is one stream of research that states that positive mood reduces the processing of stimulus information, and there is another that states that positive mood enhances the learning of brand names better in comparison to a neutral mood. Brand name recall is a pre-requisite for the choice of the brand and recall depends on the process by which the brand was first encoded into memory. Researchers Lee and Stemthal state that two factors important in the encoding process are *brand rehearsal* — "how frequently and recently the brand has been exposed in the memory as a member of a particular category"— and *relational elaboration*—"the process by which consumers link the brands to the specific categories they belong to."

In a brand-learning task, they found that being in a positive mood helps consumers to cluster the brands that they are exposed to, by the categories they belong to. When the respondents are asked to recall as many brands as possible after this exposure, a positive mood helps them recall more categories and more brands as members of these categories, thus increasing the number of brands recalled compared to when they are in a neutral mood. Corroborating this finding, is the research study by Barone, Miniard, and Romeo on the effect of positive mood on brand extension evaluations. They show that a positive mood influences the perceptions of similarity between the brand extension and the core brand (particularly for extensions that are moderately similar to the core brand) and the perceived competency of the manufacturer in producing the extension. Both of these factors are important determinants of extension evaluations, and positive mood enhances evaluation of brand extensions by influencing these determinants. Thus, marketers could use advertising, point-of-sale material, celebrity endorsements, free gifts, and several other strategies to induce positive moods in consumers to enable a more positive evaluation of a brand extension, thereby influencing choice. Marketers on the Internet attempt to overcome their inability to actually bring the customer into the store by creating the mood or ambience within the web site. This might include the incorporation of store colours and background music aimed at creating a favourable mood in the customer.

HEDONIC CONSUMPTION: SEEKING EMOTIONAL VALUE

Emotions and moods drive a host of consumption behaviours. While detergents, lawn mowers, microwave ovens, chain saws, insurance policies, investment portfolios, and computers are purchased and used for some utilitarian/functional end-states, such products and services as perfumes/colognes, diamonds, and bubble baths and such activities as sports, theatre, movies, music concerts, and amusement parks are used or engaged in purely for the emotional or hedonic values they provide. *Hedonic consumption* refers to the use of products or services for the sake of intrinsic enjoyment rather than to solve some problem in the physical environment. More specifically, hedonism refers to sensory pleasure. Thus, hedonic consumption is the use *of* products and services that give pleasure through the senses, that help create fantasies, and that give emotional arousal." Here are some examples:

(i) *Fun and enjoyment — video* game arcade; playing sports; dancing; vacationing; attending a business convention; entertaining a business customer in a game of golf., attending office Christmas parties.

(ii) *Emotional* experience — watching movies or soap operas on TV; taking a roller- coaster ride; sending gifts; receiving gifts, visiting relatives; making or receiving long-distance social calls; dating; attending class reunion; celebrating silver wedding anniversary; celebrating winning a major business contract from a highly coveted client.

(iii) *Aesthetic pleasure* — reading poetry; visiting an art gallery; taking a course in Greek history; having original works of art in the corporate offices.

(iv) *Sensory pleasure — taking* a bubble bath; relaxing in a jacuzzi or sauna; using perfume and colognes., wearing exciting colours in clothing; enjoying strobe lights in a discotheque; choosing office decor; landscaping the corporate office building.

It is interesting to note that while American teenagers are enamoured by the newness and hedonic value of technological gadgets, European teenagers are concerned with their functional utility. They look at technology as a means to an end. The "end" they are interested in is social connectivity. They want to keep in touch with friends and develop relationships with peers, and they consider devices such as computers and cellphones to be a means to achieving this end."

DEEP INVOLVEMENT

One special case of hedonic consumption is deep involvement in a product, service, or activity. This describes customers' relationships with a select few products that are consumed with interest, pausing to savour their taste, smell their aroma, feel their texture, or hear their sound. We like them; we enjoy them; we love them. Everyone has a favourite activity, a favourite product, a favourite brand. Some of us are fashion experts; others, car buffs; still others, computer jocks. We are eager to get to know these products (e.g., fashions, cars, and computers) and find out everything there is to know; we get excited whenever the topic comes up, and, of course, we want to be using them whenever possible.

This relationship we develop as users with selected products and services is called deep involvement. It can be defined as a customer's extreme interest in a product or service on an ongoing basis. Involvement is a general term that can be defined as the degree of personal relevance of an object, product, or service to a customer. Furthermore, involvement is a matter of degree — how relevant or how central a product is. Involvement, defined as the degree of interest, can be viewed as having two forms: enduring involvement and situational involvement. Enduring involvement is the degree of interest a customer feels in a product or service on an ongoing basis. In contrast, situational involvement is the degree of interest in a specific situation or on a specific occasion, such as when buying a product or when consuming something in the presence of an important client or friend.

Thus, Celia Fernandez is not much interested in dishwashers; she takes the one in her kitchen for granted. But the last time she was buying one, she became extremely interested (i.e., involved) in dish- washers, attempting to learn about them, deliberating over various options, and weighing them vis-a-vis her own needs. In contrast, she is enduringly involved in gardening and in garden-related products, taking considerable interest in them and enjoying them. In a business context, a major infrastructure project in a company is an object of high situational involvement, and maximising the lifetime value of its customers would be a matter of enduring involvement. The extreme form of enduring involvement is deep involvement. Deep involvement affects customer behaviour in a number of ways. First, deeply involved consumers are knowledgeable about the product or service and, thus, can act as opinion leaders. Second, they consume a greater quantity of the product and also buy related products. Third, they are less price sensitive for that product and are willing to spend well. Fourth, they seek constant information about products and services. Fifth, they want to spend more time in related activities. It is easier to build more extended relationships with these customers. Consider, for example, Harley-Davidson motorcycle owners; there is a Harley Owners Club (HOG), and members participate in a wide range of activities, including charity work. The fanatic loyalty that favoured IBM at one time but now favours the Apple Mac shows the deep involvement that these users have for the product. Finally, deeply involved customers can act as lead users for new products; they products in innovative ways and, thus, are sources of new-product ideas.

CUSTOMER DECISION PROCESS

Customer decisions are decisions customers make in the marketplace as buyers, payers, and users. Typically, these decisions include *whether* to purchase, *what* to purchase, *when* to purchase, from *whom* to purchase, and *how* to pay for it. *Whether* to purchase something is the first level of decision that entails weighing alternative uses of money and time resources. Customers have finite amounts of money and time, and they must allocate them judiciously. Alternative demands on time, such as a deadline at work, may constrain a customer to postpone or dismiss a purchase altogether, say a vacation plan. Allocating money resources entails weighing alternative needs at the level of the product or service category.

For example, a family may have to choose between taking a cruise and investing in remodeling the house. This product/service-level choice is both a *whether* to purchase and *a what* to purchase decision. An important customer behaviour at this category-level decision is mental budgeting — how the budget customers set for a product category guides their subsequent behaviour as a customer.

The concept of mental budgeting highlights the importance of the payer role. The payer role (regardless of whether it is the customer or someone else in the payer role) imposes relatively inflexible budget limits, and in this way, imposes some self-discipline on the user, whose needs and wants can sometimes be infinitely expendable. Unfortunately, research on mental budgeting is limited, and it is based solely on Western consumers. It is entirely possible that consumers in other cultures, and/or consumers who live from hand to mouth, might not practice the concept of mental budgeting, or might implement it in a flexible way, adjusting the budget at the time of the purchase. This is an issue that needs cross-cultural research. Nevertheless, the concept of mental budgeting can guide marketers' positioning efforts; a product or service may be positioned in one category rather than the other to take advantage of the budget earmarked for each category. For example, a frozen dinner of lobster may be viewed by the customer as an expensive food item; the marketer might, in contrast, present it as a relatively economical entertainment (compared to going out to eat at a restaurant). Following the choice at the product/service level, the customer makes another "what to purchase" decision — a choice among brands. Thus, illustratively, if a product category, level decision is made — namely, "take the cruise"-the next decision is which brand to purchase (e.g., which travel destination to select and which cruise line to purchase tickets on).

These decisions at various levels of hierarchy can all be framed in a general way: these are all *alternatives,* and the customer task is to decide among alternatives. Thus, this section uses the term *alternatives* generically to refer to product and service categories, brands, stores, suppliers, and so on, and deals with customer choice decisions among alternatives.

The process of customer decision making consists of the steps shown below:

STEP — 1: PROBLEM RECOGNITION

The decision process begins with a customer recognising a problem to be solved or a need to be satisfied. The customer notices, for example, that he or she is hungry and needs get some food, that the light bulb has blown out and needs to be replaced, that the roof has begun to leak and needs to be repaired, or that the office copier has run out of paper and needs to be refilled.

As these examples illustrate, a customer problem is not necessarily a physical problem, such as a hungry stomach or dirty laundry. Rather a customer problem is any state of deprivation, discomfort, or wanting (whether physical or psychological) felt by a person. Problem recognition is a realization by the customer that he or she needs to buy something to get back to the normal state of comfort physically and psychologically.

Stimuli for Problem Recognition

Problem recognition can occur in two ways: due to an internal stimulus or an external stimulus. Internal stimuli are perceived states of discomfort and can be physical or psychological (e.g., hunger or boredom, respectively). External stimuli are marketplace information items that lead the customer to realise the problem. Thus, an advertisement about multivitamins or the sight of a Pizza Hut can serve as external stimuli to arouse the recognition of a need.

The terms external and internal stimuli are commonly used in psychology; however, more apt terms would be problem-stimuli and solution-stimuli. A problem-stimulus is one in which the problem itself is the source of information. This source could lie within the customer (as in hunger pangs) or outside the customer (as in dirty laundry). The solution-stimulus is the information emanating from a solution itself, exposure to a potential solution arouses the recognition of the need or the problem. For example, the smell of fresh-baked cinnamon rolls from a bakery might arouse your desire for cinnamon rolls. Marketing communications, product or service samples, window shopping, and so on, have their utility precisely because they serve as problem-recognition stimuli. On the Internet, broadband providers (cable and DSL) use banner advertising with messages like "You are wasting your time" and "Your Internet connection is too slow" to " to make people aware of faster alternatives to their current dial-up ISP.

As customers, you can expect to encounter solution-stimuli in three states of mind:

1. When you have already recognised the problem and are looking for a solution; for example, suppose you have dandruff and are looking for a more effective shampoo than the one you are using currently; or you find your current food service contractor for the company cafeteria unsatisfactory and are planning to find a new contractor.
2. When the problem had been recognized in the past, but it was just not salient (i.e., not in the top-of-the-mind awareness) at the moment of the exposure to the solution. An example would be that you had thought of buying some exercise equipment, but you never pursued the thought actively;. an infomercial or a product display or the fact that a friend bought exercise equipment rekindles the need you had previously recognised.

3. When you never recognised the need in the past, but exposure to the solution-product makes you realise that the product or service would solve a condition now perceived as a problem. Thus, a display of a caller-ID device in a store and the salesperson's explanation of its use might make you realise that not knowing who is calling had been a fimstrating experience all along, even though until now you never viewed it as a problem. For a health-conscious customer, information on dietary requirements obtained during exploratory browsing of the Internet could act as problem-recognition stimuli. The consumer might now perceive a problem in his or her eating habits and change them accordingly.

Life situations that cause inconvenience but have no solutions are generally not viewed as problems; they are simply viewed as life conditions, taken for granted, Only when a solution appears on the horizon does the life condition become a problem. For example, before the invention of the microwave ovens, the slow process of conventional ovens was not perceived as a problem. Or before the home delivery of pizza, going to the pizzeria was not perceived as a problem. Before e-mail and fax, the effort, cost, and delay in getting messages from one person to another was not perceived as a problem.

This distinction is important for two reasons. First, it underscores the role of what is known as educational or pioneering marketing. Pioneering marketing and communications promote a new product or a new service by educating the customer about what the product or service will do and how it can solve a hitherto unsolved or unrecognized problem. Some of these marketing efforts are intended to create primary demand rather than secondary demand. Primary demand is demand for the product or service category itself, seeking to convert nonbuyers of the product/service category into buyers.

Secondary demand (also known as selective demand), in contrast, is simply to deflect demand from one brand to the other. There is a noteworthy controversy on this issue in cigarette advertising today. The government and anti-tobacco groups claim that cigarette advertising is targeted at the youth, promoting the primary demand for smoking among new customers. If this is true, then cigarette advertising is a solution-stimulus arousing a problem recognition among youth by presenting the product as a solution to their enduring need to be perceived by their peers as being cool. The tobacco industry, on the other hand, argues that it is merely creating secondary demand for specific brands, rather than enticing and recruiting new smokers. Advertising on comparison sites like MySimon.com, Deal-time.com and Bizrate.com are attempts by advertisers to switch demand from another brand to theirs (secondary demand). To reduce the risk involved in shopping from "unknown" vendors, MySimon, Dealtime and Bizrate rate the sellers to give buyers a degree of confidence. The distinction between primary and secondary demand for products is visible in emerging versus mature markets as well. Several products like automobiles, ecuphones, and video cameras already have a secondary demand in the mature Western markets, while marketers are still trying to create primary demand for these products in the emerging markets in Asia. The second implication of solution- versus problem-stimulus goes to the heart of a basic controversy in marketing. An often-asked and hotly debated question is, "Does marketing create a need or merely satisfy one?" In arguing that it indeed *creates* needs, critics note that no one needed a VCR, a video camera, a cellular phone, a $150 pair of Nike shoes, or an overnight document delivery service until advertising came along, parading these products and services in an enticing way.

Our view is that a need ought to be defined in terms of the function the product or service serves, rather than in terms of the product or service itself (as in "no one needed a VCR"). When needs are properly defined in terms of the function, it is easy to see that the only products or services that would be successful in the marketplace are those that serve some function. Thus, a VCR serves the function of enabling time-shifted viewing, and the need to be able to watch a program at your convenience was always a need, albeit unrecognized as a problem and, as such, relegated from consciousness simply as a life condition. The invention of the VCR, like all other inventions, helped surface that latent need. Likewise, in the world of business, there is a product to which every executive and every staff member is addicted — Post-it notes. Yet before their invention, no one even sensed the problem now addressed by this innovative product.

Problem Recognition by Each Customer Role

Problem recognition can occur for each customer role and for each of the six values customers seek. The VCR and Post-it examples illustrate the latent needs of the user role. For business consumers, 3M has a Post-it easel pad which can be stuck on the wall like a white board, used, and peeled off without any paint peeling off the walls. This is clearly fulfilling a latent need of the business customer. For the buyer role, the example of problem recognition is the home delivery of pizza, which others convenience value. Similarly online shopping offers the convenience of searching for information and completing the purchase from the confines of one's home. For the payer, the availability of leasing automobiles to individual customers or for a corporate fleet has improved affordability. Also, availability of credit makes many customers realise the need to buy a new car or furniture. A parallel in business markets is vendor financing.

STEP — 2 : INFORMATION SEARCH

Once the need has been recognized, customers search for information about various alternative ways of solving the problem. That search rarely includes every brand in existence. Consider only a select subset of brands/suppliers, organised as follows:

(i) The awareness set consists of brands/suppliers a customer is aware of

(ii) An evoked set consists of the brands/suppliers in a product or service category that the customer remembers at the time of decision making.

(iii) The consideration set consists of the brands/suppliers from the evoked set that a customer will consider buying after the brands/suppliers that are considered unfit have been eliminated.

Initially, customers seek information about the consideration set of brands which is a subset of the evoked set. New information can bring in additional brands/suppliers into the awareness, evoked, and consideration set. It should he the minimum objective of all marketing communications to place the brand in the consideration set (rather than merely in the awareness or evoked set) of its target customers. Consideration sets will include alternatives from different categories when the consumer experiences goal conflict (a single category cannot deliver on all salient and conflicting goals) or goal ambiguity (a lack of salient goals). For example, when the salient goals for a car are maximum fuel efficiency and capability of driving off-road, the consumer may find that one category does not satisfy all salient goals. Subcompacts may offer fuel efficiency but not off-road driving, and four-wheel-drive trucks would do the opposite. Similarly there is goal ambiguity when the consumer has a fuzzy goal like appeasing hunger or a need for personal transportation. Products from several categories could be used to form a consideration set to satisfy these goals. One of the most significant outcomes of the Intemet revolution is the "democratisation of informations across the vast customer population. Information search is one of the first uses of the Internet. A vast number of alternatives are available to the customer, and it is common to find most consumer decisions being researched on the Internet before the products or services are bought offline or online. Thus, the fundamental benefit of "Interactive Home Shopping" (IHS—shopping electronically from home, that is, via the Internet) is the low cost of information search. Yet, researchers Alba, et al. state that the growth of IHS is dependent on several other factors:

(i) *Selection*: Customers should be able to access a large set of items fairly quickly.

(ii) *Screening*: Consumers should be able to screen the available options effectively. If they are not able to do this, then the benefits of a vast selection will be offset by the high costs of search.

(iii) *Reliability*: The customer should he able to comprehend the benefits from products/services reliably in the IHS shopping format. If experiential information available from stores is better than the inflation from IHS, and the consumer is not comfortable enough with the information available through IHS to make a purchase decision, the IHS format will lose the customer to the store.

(iv) *Product comparison*: The IHS format should provide the consumer with superior methods for comparing between alternatives in order to make the purchase decision.

Three elements characterise the information-search phase of the decision process:

(i) sources of information,

(ii) search strategies, and

(iii) amount of search.

STEP—3: ALTERNATIVE EVALUATION

Now that the customer has all the information, how does he or she use that information to arrive at the choice? In this section, we discuss the specific manner in which customer select one of the several alternatives (e.g., brands or suppliers) available to them. These specific processes and steps are referred to by researchers as choice models. There are two broad categories of choice: compensatory and noncompensatory.

The Compensatory Model

In the compensatory model, the customer arrives at a choice by considering all of the attributes and benefits of a product or service and mentally trading off the alternative's perceived weakness on one or more attributes for its perceived strength on other attributes. A customer may go about making this calculation in two ways. One method of arriving at a choice is simply to add the number of positive attributes and subtract the number of negative attributes each alternative has, and then choose the one that has the most positive and fewest negative attributes. However, often, the individual does not consider each plus or a minus equally significant. Some considerations are clearly more important than others, and every minus may or may not cancel a plus on some other feature. A second and more systematic approach is to weigh every attribute for each alternative in terms of its relative importance. To implement this approach, the decision maker also estimates the degree to which the alternative possesses each positive or negative attribute. This can be done either on a numerical scale of, say, 0 to 1 0 where 10 means a perfect performance on that attribute, or in vęrbal rating categories such as poor, average, excellent, and so forth. The latter ratings are then multiplied by the relative weight of the attribute. The sum of these products for each alternative provides a total score for that alternative. The alternative with the highest score is then chosen.

This model is called compensatory because a shortfall on one attribute may be compensated by a good rating on another attribute. Illustratively, a vacation spot that has less learning opportunity but more activities for fun for the whole family might receive the same overall rating as another destination with few family fun activities but more learning opportunities.

Noncompensatory Models

While there are several noncompensatory models identified in the literature, four are most common and useful. These are called conjunctive, disjunctive, lexicographic, and elimination by aspects.

(i) *The conjunctive model:* In the conjunctive model, the customer begins by setting the minimum cutoff is on all salient attributes. Each alternative is then examined on each attribute, and any alternative that meets the minimum cut-off on an attributes can potentially be chosen. If an alternative fails the cut-off, even on one attribute, it is dropped from further consideration. If all alternatives fail to meet the cut-off levels, then the customer may revise his or her minimum cut-off levels or use another decision model. On the other hand, if more than one alternative meets all the minimum cut-off levels, the customer might resort to another decision model to further eliminate alternatives until only one survives the process.

Consider a customer buying a car. He or she might want a car that is priced below $20,000, gets at least 30 miles per gallon, has at least an average reliability and repair record, and has at least a good safety rating (these latter two ratings can be read from *Consumer Reports,* for example). The customer eliminates cars that fall below these cut-off levels. If more than one car satisfies all these cut-off, the customer may next decide on the basis of style, or may simply raise the desired cut-off on one or more attributes. Online resources like MSN's Carpoint (http://www.carpoint.com) and Autotrader (http://www.auto trader.com) allow consumers to specify the minimum features/criteria that they want in an automobile and then provides a list of products that meet these criteria, thus helping the customer with his or her conjunctive model in decision making. The conjunctive model can be used by both household and business customers. Since businesses often buy components and raw materials that have to fit into finished products and production processes, meeting the minimum specifications becomes a necessity. For example, in the chemical industry, required chemicals have to meet certain minimums on such attributes as purity, side-effects, and disposability.

Business-to-Business exchanges like ChemConnect (http://www.chemconnect.com) allow businesses to specify their minimum criteria and generate efficiencies and cost savings through the Intemet. Such indispensable minimums serve as cut-off in the conjunctive model. The conjunctive model is, therefore, especially important in business-to-business markets.

(ii) *The disjunctive model*: The disjunctive model entails *trade-offs between aspects of choice alternatives.* Sometimes the customer is willing to trade off one feature for another. For example, a home buyer might say that the house he or she would be willing to consider buying should have either five bedrooms or, if it has only four bedrooms, it should have a finished basement. A business customer buying a copy machine might be willing to trade off copying speed if the machine has dual-side copying capability because, in a sense, automatic dual copying saves time and inconvenience. Although these trade-offs are made also in the compensatory model, there are important differences. First, the disjunctive model considers the sheer presence or absence of attributes, rather than the degree or amount in which these attributes are present. Thus, the attributes tend to he those that do not vary on a graduated scale. For example, gas mileage rating tends to be used in a compensatory fashion, whereas the presence or absence of a finished basement tends to be traded off in a disjunctive model. This categorical (Is it present or not?) rather than graduated (How much of it is there?) appraisal of an attribute makes the disjunctive model simpler to execute than the other models. Customers could use attributes such as country of origin as a required attribute and drop all alternatives that are foreign made. Similarly, when customers came to know that Nike shoes and the "Kathie Lee" line of clothing were manufactured by underpaid and underage workers, the presence of this information was enough to drop these products from their choice set. Second, in the compensatory model, the attributes traded off need not serve the same purpose while in the disjunctive model they tend to. Thus, in the compensatory model, lower gas mileage of a car can be compensated by superior rating on a totally unrelated attribute, such as safety. In the disjunctive model, on the other hand, gas mileage could be traded off only with other cost-saving features, such as low-maintenance costs. Or for copiers, the high speed and the dual-copying capability address the same time and convenience utility.

(iii) *The lexicographic model:* Another model customers use to make a choice is termed the lexicographic model. In this model, attributes of alternatives are rank-ordered in terms of importance. Customers examine all alternatives on the most important criterion and identify the one with the highest level on that criterion. If more than one alternative remains in the choice set, then they consider the second most important criterion and examine the remaining alternatives with respect to that criterion. The process continues until only one alternative remains.

For an example of business-to-business service, consider a business traveller (a sales- person, say) deciding on a hotel for an out-of-town trip. His most important criterion might be the hotel location within the downtown business district (rather than in the out-lying areas of the city); therefore, he does not even bother looking at the listing of the outlying area hotels (in the AAA guide books, hotels are listed in separate sections for downtown and outlying areas). Since there are several hotels in the business district listing, he next considers the second most important criterion, availability of office and business services (fax, copying, a VCP,-equipped TV monitor in the room, and so on). Suppose only four hotels in the AAA listing meet this criterion. He next considers the third most important criterion, say price. He then chooses the one with the lowest price, and the decision is made. But if two (or more) hotels had the same low price, the customer would have to go through the next round of processing the alternatives on the criterion next in importance, such as the availability of a health spa on the hotel property. The process stops when one alternative is identified.

(iv) *Elimination by aspects:* The elimination by aspects (EBA) model, first proposed by psychologist Amos Tversky, is similar to the lexicographic model but with one important difference. The customer rates the attributes in the order of importance and, in addition, defines cut-offvalues. He or she then examines all alternatives first on the most important attribute, admitting for further consideration only those that satisfy the minimum cut-off level on this most important attribute. If more than one alternative meets this requirement, then the customer goes to the next step, appraising the remaining alternatives on the second attribute, delineating those that meet the minimum cut-off level on this attribute, and so on.

How and When the Models are Used?

Several concepts shed light on how and when various choice models are used. These are processing by brand/supplier or by attribute, comparative features of various choice models, the two-stage choice process, rapid heuristics, and satisficing

(i) *Processing by brand or by attribute:* Customers making choice decisions employ various models according to the choice situation facing them. An important characteristic of these models is the manner in which the evaluation proceeds: one brand/supplier at a time or one attribute at a time. Conjunctive models entail considering one brand at a time with respect to all the attributes. The process of assessing one brand/supplier entirely before moving on to the second brand is called processing by brands. Note that the term *brand* is being used here to connote any alternative from which the choice must be made. Thus, the model is applicable to supplier choice as well as to choice of products and services.

In contrast to conjunctive models, the lexicographic and EBA processes entail processing by attributes (i.e., processing all the brands simultaneously on one attribute at a time). This is simpler to execute than processing by brands. However, processing by brands allows a more thorough evaluation of brands than does processing by attributes. Furthermore, the lexicographic model is simpler to execute than the EBA, but the lexicographic loses the opportunity to purchase a brand that may be superior on the next set of attributes.

In processing by attributes, brands are also subject to a "direction-of-comparison effect." When two brands are compared, one brand becomes the focal subject of comparison, while the other brand is the less focal referent of comparison. This process of comparison naturally leads to an elicitation of more thoughts about the focal brand compared to the referent brand. As a result of this process, the unique attributes of the focal brand gain prominence in the comparison, and if these attributes are positive, they gain more weightage in the evaluation of the two brands. The attributes of the referent brand are compared against these attributes of the focal brand, and given that the referent brand does not have the unique attributes of the focal brand, it is more likely that the focal brand is preferred over the referent brand. In the same way, when the unique attributes of the focal brand are negative, they work against the focal brand's favour, and the referent brand is preferred. The direction-of-comparison effect is marked in judgments made by people who have a high need for cognition because they are more likely to use an attribute-based processing strategy. This effect is least when consumers use an attitude-based processing strategy that involves the use of general attitudes, summary impressions, intuitions, or heuristics to nuke judgment.

(ii) *Comparative features of various choice models:* The conjunctive, disjunctive, lexicographic, and EBA models are all Compensatory models, since the deficiency on one attribute is not allowed to be made up for by excess on another. An alternative may be eliminated in the first step for being only marginally interior to an otherwise substantially better alternative on the second most important attribute; it doesn't matter that the eliminated alternative is much superior on all other attributes. The compensatory model eliminates the possibility of nudding such suboptimal choices. The compensatory model is more burdensome to execute, however, because the customer has to consider several dimensions or attributes at the same time and somehow weigh them in his or her mind. Typically, therefore, the compensatory model is used sparingly and only for important decisions." Most low-ticket items are likely to be chosen with the help of noncompensatory models.

Thus, a customer may buy table salt based simply on a single criterion, such as familiarity with the brand or whether or not it is iodised, or perhaps on price alone. Another customer buying an entree might use fat content as the important criterion and then either choose the one with the lowest fat content (thus employing a lexicographic model) or consider all entrees with fat content not exceeding 15 percent of total calories (thus employing EBA). Calories per serving might then be used as the second criterion, and, if need be, price as the third.

In terms of the three routine/limited/extended problem-solving strategies, the compensatory model is likely to be used generally for extended problem solving. Noncompensatory models are likely used for limited and routine problem-solving situations. Furthermore, noncompensatory models may also he used in the initial stage of an extended problem-solving decision situation, as explained next.

(iii) *Two-stage choice process:* For the more important decisions, a customer might first use a noncompensatory model and then, to further identify the choice, use a compensatory model. Customer researchers Bettman and Park have described customer decision process as a two-stage process, termed phased decision strategy." In the first stage, termed alternative-elimination stage, customers narrow the set of alternatives for closer comparisons. In the second stage, termed alternative-selection stage, the smaller set of alternatives is further examined. The objective of the first stage is to identify the *acceptable* alternatives, whereas the second stage is meant to identify *the best*.

Since noncompensatory models are easier to execute, a large number of alternatives can be examined relatively quickly, particularly if processing is done by attributes rather than by brands. In the second stage, when only three or four alternatives remain, customers can more efficiently employ the compensatory model. Even here, if one or more attributes are matching across the alternatives, one simply ignores this attribute and applies the compensatory model on the smaller set of attributes. In this way customers can take advantage of the compensatory model to make an optimal decision without incurring the information-overload cost that would have accrued if all of the initially available large number of alternatives were to be processed by the compensatory model throughout.

(iv) *Rapid heuristics:* For a common, repeat purchase of low-risk, low-ticket items such as shampoo, snacks, cereals, or office supplies in the business context, customers are unlikely to spend much time or effort. These purchases are perceived to be low-risk, low- involvement decisions. As such, hardly any information is examined, and brand choice is made by using a heuristic (simple rule of thumb). Examples of heuristics used for such repeat purchase items are: "Purchase the known brand only;" "Purchase whichever brand is on sale;" and "I saw my friend using this brand, so I too will purchase this one." A study illustrating this was done by professor Wayne D. Hoyer of the University of Texas at Austin on U.S. customers; the study was later replicated on Chinese customers by the National University of Singapore's professor Siew Meng Leong. In these studies, customers were observed in a supermarket selecting a common, repeat purchase item (namely, detergent and shampoo) and later approached and asked the basis of their decision. In a subsequent experimental study, customers were given a product that could be examined by taste (namely, peanut butter in one study and cheese in another). Of the three brands presented to research customers, one was a well-known brand.

The researchers found that customers in the supermarket study spent very little time (less than 15 seconds) to complete their in-store decision, examined a small number of packages (about 1.5 on an average), made few brand comparisons, and looked at only a few shelf tags. In response to the question as to why they chose the brand they did, an overwhelming majority (approximately 95 percent) mentioned a single reason. This single reason, for the largest majority, was, 'It worked better." In the experimental study where customers were making a choice a new (since none of their usual brands were in the choice set), and where one of the three brands was known but the other two were not, customers overwhelmingly (97 percent) chose the "own brand.

Thus, "purchase the known brand" is a choice heuristic customers use most often, especially in a new choice task of a low-ticket, common, repeat purchase item. Not in vain, then, do advertisers spend considerable monies keeping their brands in the top-of-the-mind awareness of their target customers.

(v) *Satisficing*: No matter what decision model they use, customers as decision makers can never consider and appraise an of the alternatives exhaustively. Indeed, customers *do not* typically make the most optimal choice. As already pointed out, the use of lexicographic or EBA or other noncompensatory model might eliminate a brand from further consideration based on the first attribute even though the brand's other features could have made the brand more attractive overall. Yet customers are perfectly happy making a choice by non-compensatory models. This is a concept that Nobel Prize-winning psychologist Herbert Simon calls satisficing. Satisficing refers to customer's (or decision maker's) acceptance of an alternative that he or she finds satisfying, rather than pursuing the arduous search for the most optimal alternative there might be. Thus, even the ardent comparison shoppers finally give up and buy the product or service they find most acceptable from among those they have considered so far, even though they recognise that there might well be a slightly or even substantially better product or service or deal at the next store. In the business context, cost of searching for information for a myriad of alternatives and then evaluating them is enormous. Hence, satisficing is common even in the business context.

STEP —4: PURCHASE

Once the customer has evaluated the alternatives, he or she makes the purchase. This at first appears a straightforward step, but even here customer behaviour at times becomes intriguing. In fact, this behaviour can be broken down into three substeps. The first substep occurs when the customer identifies the most preferred alternative, based on the alternative evaluation process just described. The next substep is to form a purchase intent — a determination that one will buy that product or service. The final substep is implementing the purchase. This entails arranging the terms of the transaction, seeking and obtaining the transfer of the title or ownership from the seller, paying for the product or service, and receiving possession of the product or the service commitment from the seller. The first substep (choice identification) is the conclusion of a process where the customer's user role and his or her needs and wants as user become most salient. Although the payer's concern (e.g., whether it is affordable) and buyer's concern (e.g., where to get it) may also be taken into account, the emphasis is likely to have refflained on the fit between the product/ service and the performance and social/psychological values the customer seeks in the user role. In the second substep (purchase intent), the payer's concerns become most salient. If the payer is different from the user, a formal budget approval may be needed. The payer may have to assess whether the product or service is overpriced, whether the required cash or credit is available at this time, whether it sits well with established guidelines for allocating the budget over different categories of products or services, or whether it offers equity to other users (e.g., other members of the household or other employees in the organisation) who may have claims on the budget pool.

Finally, the purchase implementation substep activates the buyer role and is influenced most by the concerns of the buyer. The buyer's market values (convenience and service values) become the determining forces. This may influence the store or supplier from whom the preferred item is bought, the day and time it is bought, how soon or late it is bought, and whether it is even bought. For example, a 13-year-old boy we know wanted to attend a space camp run by NASA. He called the camp organisers, got the brochures, identified the specific program he wanted to attend, and got his parents to agree to pay for the trip. The final task of putting together and sending the application was left to the older brother, who procrastinated until the deadline expired. Even when the same person plays the payer, user, and buyer roles, the buyer role may hinder the implementation of the choice identified and approved by the other two roles. Thus, as the above example shows, the customer journey from choice identification to purchase implementation does not always proceed in predictable ways. Sometimes, the purchase intention may not be implemented, as, for example, when a customer almost decides to join a particular weight-reduction program but somehow never gets around to actually doing it. But even if the purchase implementation eventually occurs, the customer journey may take a different route. Two factors can potentially derail the journey: postponement or delay in implementation and deviation from the identified choice.

Delay in Implementation

Causes of delays in implementation occur throughout the customer decision process, from problem recognition through alternative evaluation to purchase. We discuss these here for convenience and because it is the purchase step that they ultimately delay. A recent consumer study by consumer researchers Eric A. Greenleef and Donald R. Lehmann identified the reasons consumers give for delay in their purchase decisions. The study interviewed recent buyers of such products as home appliances, electronics, personal computers, clothing, furniture, sports equipment, and automobiles. The consumers were asked to describe the reasons that caused them to delay the decision in buying these products, and also the reasons or factors that subsequently caused them to close the decision. The top three reasons for delay in buying the products was time pressure, need for more information, and inability to afford the product at the time. Top reasons for closure are deciding on another alternative and finding the time to make the decision. Delays in purchase implementations occur among business customers as well. One reason for such delay is a change in management: the new management may want to review all capital equipment procurement plans and/or redesign the procurement policies. Another possible reason is declining financial performance; if sales and profits fan below projected levels, then some capital equipment purchase plans may be put on hold. Decisions may be delayed because of fourth-quarter syndrome: businesses typically postpone making major purchases until the last quarter of the accounting year; thus, purchase decision making may be delayed until the fourth quarter, either to avoid continuing money early in the year or because time pressure did not permit decision making earlier. Interest rates and the economic situation — domestic or global — may also cause delay in purchase implementations.

An ATKearney report states that four out of five shoppers abandon their shopping carts on the Internet. Customers stated that the top reason for not completing the purchase was that the site required too much personal information before making the purchase. This shows that customers are not very comfortable sharing a large amount of personal information at their first visit to a site. They are willing to part with more information only when they trust the retailer and believe that providing more information will lead to increased benefits. Reluctance to give credit card details, Web site malfunction and an inability to find the desired products are other reasons stated by customers for incompletion of a purchase.

Understanding these reasons is important for marketers because it helps them facilitate the customer journey from problem recognition to purchase. By identifying the particular reason and the step where it has a delaying effect, marketers can work to overcome that baffler. Furthermore, marketers can implement separate actions directed individually toward the three roles of the user, payer, and buyer.

Deviation From the Identified Choice

The second factor that may derail the customer purchase implementation is deviation from the identified choice. Several conditions may account for this. First, the preferred brand may be out of stock, thus forcing the customer to buy a brand different from the one identified, especially if one needs the product immediately. Second, new in-store information may reopen the evaluation process. Third, financing terms may render a purchase infeasible, forcing the customer either to abandon the purchase altogether or to substitute the purchase with a lower-level model or another brand available on preferred terms. In the business context, stock-outs at the regular supplier may force a change to another supplier. Financing of the project, say from World Bank or the Import-Export bank, may change the options considered. These conditions may also shift the relative impact of the customer roles. While the values of the user are most influential in the alternative evaluation phase, the values of the buyer (e.g., convenience of buying) or of the payer (e.g., the financing available) become influential at the purchase stage.

STEP — 5: POSTPURCHASE EXPERIENCE

The customer's decision process does not end with the purchase. Rather, the experience of buying and using the product provides information that the customer will use in future decision making. In some cases, the customer will be pleased with the experience and will buy the same product from the same supplier again. In other cases, the customer will be disappointed and may even return or exchange the product. The consumer may also experience *regret* as a result of comparing one's outcome with a better outcome that would have occurred had a different alternative been selected. Regret has a negative influence on satisfaction with the chosen alternative and on repurchase intentions for the chosen alternative. In general, the post-purchase process includes four steps: decision confirmation, experience evaluation, satisfaction or dissatisfaction, and future response (exit, voice, or loyalty) in that order.

Decision Confirmation

After a customer makes an important choice decision, he or she experiences an intense need to confirm the wisdom of that decision. The flip side is that he or she wants to avoid the disconfirmation. Methods of reducing dissonance and confirming the soundness of one's decision are seeking further positive information about the chosen alternative and avoiding negative information about the chosen alternative. Thus, customers. Reread product literature reviewing the brand's positive features, and avoid competitors' advertisements or negative information from others. They seek out friends to tell them about their purchase, hoping that their friends will validate their decision by praising the selected brand. Marketers can put this principle to use: After the purchase (say, during product or service delivery), sales-people can review with customers all the features of the product or service, and this review during the postpurchase phase is likely to bring to customer attention a few positive features previously ignored, thus improving the perceived attractiveness of the product. In the business context, the company could arrange for a formal celebration with customers or could provide customer testimonials in its advertisements to reassure prospective customers.

Experience Evaluation

Following purchase, the product or service is actually consumed. Marketers need to know whether customers consume it routinely or while consciously evaluating it. This depends on the level of enduring involvement in the product or service and the finality of the preference that caused this purchase. Enduring involvement was defined as the interest customers take in the consumption of the product or service on an *ongoing basis.* We use most products and services routinely and notice them only if something does not work as expected. On the other hand, we are very enthusiastic about some products or services. In consuming these, we are conscious of the consumption experience, appraising and relishing it continually (e.g., wine drinking by wine connoisseurs). These, then, are the products and services that undergo conscious evaluation during use. In the business context, companies would be enduringly involved in a service contract or a single-source supplier, but the appraisal and evaluation would be more formal than in the case of an individual customer's evaluation of a product in which he is enduringly involved.

Secondly, customers buy some products and services on a trial basis, without making their preference final yet. These products, even if not of enduring involvement, are the ones that the customer is likely to use with an eye to appraisal. Free samples received are usually used routinely without conscious appraisal of the performance of the product. Sampling is productive when the product's or service's superiority is substantial and would be conspicuous in consumption, and when the samples are targeted at customers who are not satisfied with the current solutions. Because of their dissatisfaction, they would be actively appraising the sampled product or service. Airbus is using this strategy and offering its, airplanes to several U.S. airlines on a trial basis to break into the market.

Satisfaction/Dissatisfaction

Whether or not they actively evaluate a product or service during product use or consumption, users do experience the usage outcome. This outcome is characterised as satisfaction or dissatisfaction. Measuring overall satisfaction/ dissatisfaction is easy. Customer researchers can simply ask, "How satisfied or dissatisfied are you with-(the product or service name)?" What is more challenging is to understand *why* customers feel the way they do. There are two approaches to this challenge. One is to get the customer to rate a product or service on its various attributes, such as handling, gas mileage, acceleration, and braking for a car, and satisfaction or dissatisfaction with these product attributes can then be used to explain the customer's *overall* satisfaction or dissatisfaction with the product.

But this approach raises another question: What causes satisfaction or dissatisfaction with individual attributes? This question is successfully addressed by a theoretical approach to understanding satisfaction.

Customer behaviour scholars have proposed that satisfaction depends not on the absolute levels of performance on various attributes but rather on how the actual performance compares with the *expected* performance. Thus, if the product or service experience fulfils prepurchase expectations, then satisfaction results, and if doesn't, dissatisfaction results. Therefore, satisfaction or dissatisfaction stems respectively from the confirmation or disconfirmation of our expectations. The theory makes intuitive sense in our everyday experience. For example, we may find a particular level of cleanliness unsatisfactory in a Marriott hotel but quite satisfactory in, say, an economy motel. This is because our expectations about the Marriott are quite high compared to those we hold for the economy motel. A new type of market-based performance measure for firms, industries, economic sectors, and national economics, named the American Customer Satisfaction Index (ACSI), was first introduced in the fall of 1994, with information on 40 industries and seven major sectors of the U.S. economy. The index is produced through a partnership among the University of Michigan Business School, the American Society for Quality, and the CFI Group. It is a national economic indicator of customer satisfaction with the quality of goods and services available to household consumers in the United States. "

An individual firm's ACSI represents its customers' overall evaluation of total purchase and consumption experience, both actual and anticipated." An industry ACSI represents an industry's customers' overall evaluation of its market offering; a sector ACSI is an overall evaluation of that sector, and the national ACSI gauges the nation's total consumption experience. Hence, ACSI represents "a cumulative evaluation of a firm's market offering, rather than a person's evaluation of a specific transaction." The American Customer Satisfaction Index uses a 100-point scale and presently measures satisfaction with 164 companies and 30 government agencies. The score fell from the baseline level of 74.2 in 1994 to a low of 72.6 in the fourth quarter of 2000. The value of the index has increased every year since 1997, but remained flat in 2000. The flat index could be a result of low customer service levels and low productivity improvements in this period. In the online context, a study of "e-satisfaction" customers' satisfaction with e-retailing — by researchers Szymanski and Hise shows that shopping convenience (represented by total shopping time, convenience, ease of browsing), site design (represented by uncluttered screens, easy search paths, and fast presentations) and financial security of ordine transactions are the three most important drivers of e-satisfaction. Surprisingly, product information (quantity and quality of information) had a very small impact on e- satisfaction, and product offerings (number and variety of offerings) had no impact at all." The cost and effort of voicing dissatisfaction online with products and services is also rapidly declining for customers. With services like Planet Feedback (http://www.planetfeedback.com) and the Better Business Bureau (http://www.bbbonline.org), it is much easier for customers to voice their grievances addressed. This puts added pressure on marketers since the impact of dissatisfied customers is also magnified through the medium of the Intemet (higher reach). The theory of satisfaction has important implications for shaping expectations. If marketing communications and other elements of the marketing mix (e.g., advertising, salespersons, price, appearance of the store) promise too much, they may create expectations that the product or service would almost surely fail to fulfil, thus risking customer dissatisfaction. Of course, if the expectations are too low, the sale may not result. The right strategy, therefore, ought to be to create realistic expectations, implying a performance level that the target market finds attractive enough to select the brand.

Future Response: Exit, Voice, or Loyalty

Following the experience of satisfaction or dissatisfaction, customers have three possible responses: exit, voice, or loyalty.

(i) *Exit*: If customers are dissatisfied with their experience with a brand, they may decide never again to buy the brand. This places them back to the start of the decision process the next time the problem recognition arises. They have to go through the arduous process of information search, alternative evaluation, and so on, all over again. This "churn" in customers is very common in credit-card services, and long-distance carriers as customers tend to switch from suppliers when they are dissatisfied.

(ii) Voice. Dissatisfied customers may complain and then decide either to give the brand or marketer another chance or simply to exit. What accounts for customers' tendency to complain or not complain? A customer's likelihood of complaining depends on three factors: dissatisfaction salience, attributions to the marketer, and customers' personality traits.

(a) *Dissatisfaction salience: Not* all dissatisfaction is salient (i.e., bothersome to customers). Generally small gaps between performance and expectations are ignored; moreover, even substantial gaps are not likely to be noticed if the product or service is trivial. Thus, importance of the product or service and the degree of performance — expectations gap determine dissatisfaction salience, which, in turn, determines the likelihood of customer. Malfunction of the vending machine at a supermarket or the nonavailability of the desired product in the vending machine is a matter that causes dissatisfaction, but not enough for it to be salient.

(b) *Attributions to the marketer*: Customers make attributions about who is to blame for poor product or service performance. For example, in the case of airlines, delays are more often than not attributed to the marketer, even though the actual delay may have been caused by weather problems. If customers blame themselves or circumstances, then complaining would not occur; on the other hand, if they attribute failure to the marketer, then they are likely to complain. Furthermore, if customers thought that the failure was not likely to be repeated, they would be less motivated to complain. Finally, customers must also believe that the marketer is likely to take the corrective action; if they think that redress from the marketer is unlikely, they may consider complaining a waste of effort.

(c) *Customers' personality traits*: Customers' personality traits play an important role in complaining. Customers differ in self-confidence and in their degree of aggressiveness/submissiveness. Complaining requires self-confidence, and aggressiveness drives customers to assert themselves. These traits, therefore, lead customers to complain rather than meekly accept poor marketer performance.

Following the complaint, negative word-of-mouth is less likely and repatronage more likely if the complaint is successfully redressed. An important concept here is perceived justice. Perceived justice is customers' perceptions that they were treated with respect during the conflict resolution process, the policy and procedures followed were fair, and the decision outcome itself was fair." When perceived justice seems not to have occurred, then hostility increases.

Research has found that customer complaint is actually good for the marketer. According to one research study, about 19 percent of dissatisfied customers complain; of the complaining customers, a significant majority continue to buy the product or service, compared to those are dissatisfied but do not bother to complain. Thus, complainers care enough to complain. Noncomplainers simply walk out, taking their patronage to a competitor.

(iii) *Loyalty*: The third response is, of course, loyalty. Customer loyalty means the customer buys the same brand repeatedly. The concept of loyalty has been debated in the literature in various definitions of *brand loyalty*. First, brand loyalty can be defined simply as the consistent repurchase of the same brand. This definition has two problems. First, in many product or service categories, customers buy an assortment of brands to satisfy their need for variety in the consumption experience. For example, eating the same cereal every day or eating lunch every day in the office cafeteria would not be satisfying. This problem of variety can be handled by asking customers if the focal brand is consistently at least a part of the assortment the customer buys, if not an exclusive purchase. In the business context, companies are loyal to multiple vendors. The second problem with defining and measuring brand loyalty as a consistent repurchase is that one does not know if the consistent repurchase is merely due to convenience, is a routinisation of the purchase decision, or reflects genuine preference for the brand. To overcome this uncertainty, some researchers have defined brand loyalty in attitudinal terms: the brand attitude underlying the repurchase. Only if a favourable brand attitude underlies repurchase is brand loyalty thought to exist.

At first thought, one would think that if customers are satisfied, they would not switch brands. Thus, a satisfaction rating may be deemed to ensure loyalty. Percent customer research has shown, however, that while customers are less likely to switch when they are satisfied than when they are not, being satisfied does not guarantee loyalty. One study showed that despite satisfaction, as many as 30 percent of customers were likely to switch suppliers." Several potential reasons explain why satisfied customers may still switch. First, customers report being satisfied with a brand, but they may also be satisfied with some other brands. The implication of this is that one should measure customer satisfaction with a brand *relative* to competitors' brands. The second reason is that the marginal utility of a repeated use may decline simply due to familiarity, and need for variety can drive brand switching. Research shows that increasing the variety in the context — that is, providing variety in a different product category — that is purchased simultaneously with the focal category may reduce variety seeking in the focal category. This happens because consumers try to achieve an optimal level of stimulation by balancing the stimulation that comes from variety seeking and the stimulation available from the context." Finally, customers may switch brands because they expect to receive even greater value or satisfaction from some other brand.

CUSTOMER RELATIONSHIP MANAGEMENT AND THE THREE BASIC CUSTOMER ROLES

The central concept of this chapter is setting the relationship between CRM and three basic customers roles. This relationship between the CRM and the three customers roles comprises customer motivations for and outcomes of relationship-based buying. Among the motivations are cost-benefit factors (search costs, risk reduction, switching costs, and value-added benefits) and sociocultural factors (early socialisation, reciprocity, networks, and friendships). Search costs occur in terms of the time and effort of the buyer role. Risk reduction is a benefit to the user in that the current product or service from the current supplier, tried and tested, is devoid of uncertainty as to its performance. Switching costs can relate to each of the three roles. Penalties for breaking the contract, if any, and costs of new investments, such as retooling to become compatible with the new supplier, are costs to the payer. Time and effort expended to learn to do business with the new supplier are costs to the buyer. Learning to use the new supplier's product is a cost to the user. Finally, value-added benefits offer an advantage generally to the user, but if these relate to, say, an improved financing plan or terms of payment, then the payer role is benefited as well. Among the sociocultural factors, early socialisation is the learned behaviour both of using a product or service and of buying from a particular source (i.e., it is a socialisation of both the user and buyer roles). Reciprocity affects at least two of the three roles, the buyer and the payer. The buyer is assured of a source and its commitment since the latter (i.e., the supplier) depends on the buyer for receiving the product or service it (the supplier) in turn needs. The payer is certain to be able to pay since it has the resource the other party values, its own product or service.

Networks affect all three roles. Buyers find it easy to do business with other firms in the network due to a history of interaction. Users gain by being assured of performance, and social values suppliers in the network are accountable to one another for delivering the quality product or service, and they command the social approval as a source. Payers are affected by getting an improved price value over time, by being assured of getting credit terms favourably altered in case of future financial exigencies, and by knowing that film in the network will not abandon the customer in times of financial hardship.

Finally, friendship helps all three roles in the same way as do networks. The user can trust the friend for product or service performance, the buyer gets friendly service, and the payer might get a better price and better credit terms. The process of nurturing suppliers is driven by the buyer search for both user and payer values. We enumerated the benefits of this process as substantially improved quality, substantially improved performance, better delivery schedule, extended service support, and lower costs over the long run.

Of these, the first four are benefits to the user role, and the fifth is a benefit to the payer role. These same benefits occur from supplier partnering. Because suppliers are on board from the design stage, better performance value results from customized design of components and parts or service. Mutual data sharing improves joint production planning for the user role. The payer role benefits from the joint pursuit of long-term total cost reduction goals. And since the users interface closely with suppliers on a continual basis, the buyer role becomes more efficient; ordering and delivery transactions can also become automated.

CASE STUDIES

Introduction

1. Customers are the backbone of business and the purpose of business is to create and retain a satisfied customer. Retention of existing customers tends to be less costly than that of gaining new customers. In essence the customer is the mool mantra for success in any business.
2. With the foregoing as background, the process of customer relationship management from the stage of customer role specification (dividing customer roles as user, payer and buyer), causes of role specification, customer wants and needs, factors of wants and needs, the customer as aperceiver, factors that shape perception, biases that shape perceptual process, managerial uses of perceptual process, customer emotions and customer decision process till purchase of the goods and services has been analysed. Thereafter, future response from the customer in terms of exit, voice or loyalty have been discussed.
3. The central concept of this case is setting the relationship between CRM and three basic customers roles. This relationship between the CRM and the three customers roles comprises customer motivation for and outcome of relationship-based buying. Among the motivations are cost-benefit factors (search costs, risk reduction, switching costs, and value-added benefits) and sociocultural factors (early socialisation, reciprocity, networks, and friendships). Search costs occur in terms of the time and effort of the buyer role. Risk reduction is a benefit to the user in that the current product or service from the current supplier, tried and tested, is devoid of uncertainty as to its performance. Switching costs can relate to each of the three roles. Penalties for breaking the contract, if any, and costs of new investments, such as retooling to become compatible with the new supplier, are costs to the payer. Time and effort expended to learn to do business with the new supplier are costs to the buyer. Learning to use the new supplier's product is a cost to the user. Finally, value-added benefits offer an advantage generally to the user, but if these relate to, say, an improved financing plan or terms of payment, then the payer role is benefited as well. Among the socio-cultural factors, early socialisation is the learned behaviour both of using a product or service and of buying from a particular source (i.e., it is a socialisation of both

the user and buyer roles). Reciprocity affects at least two of the three roles, the buyer and the payer. The buyer is assured of a source and its commitment since the latter (i.e., the supplier) depends on the buyer for receiving the product or service it (the supplier) in turn needs. The payer is certain to be able to pay since it has the resource the other party values, its own product or service.

4. Networks affect all three roles. Buyers find it easy to do business with other firms in the network due to a history of interaction. Users gain by being assured of performance, and social values suppliers in the network are accountable to one another for delivering the quality product or service, and they command the social approval as a source. Payers are affected by getting an improved price value over time, by being assured of getting credit terms favourably altered in case of future financial exigencies, and by knowing that firm in the network will not abandon the customer in times of financial hardship.
5. Finally, friendship helps all three roles in the same way as do networks. The user can trust the friend for product or service performance, the buyer gets friendly service, and the payer might get a better price and better credit terms. The process of nurturing suppliers is driven by the buyer's search for both user and payer values. Benefits of this process have been enumerated as substantially improved quality, substantially improved performance, better delivery schedule, extended service support, and lower costs over the long-run. Of these, the first four are benefits to the user role, and the fifth is a benefit to the payer role. These same benefits occur from supplier partnering. Because suppliers are on board from the design stage, better performance value results from customized design of components and parts or service. Mutual data sharing improves joint production planning for the user role. The payer role benefits from the joint pursuit of long-term total cost reduction goals. And since the users interface closely with suppliers on a continual basis, the buyer role becomes more efficient lending itself to automated transactions.

Case of Diversify Bank of India

6. There is a lot of baggage attached to being a nationalised bank. They are accused of incompetent customer service, low employee motivation and inertia. A turnaround requires vision, dedication and perserverance.This is the case of the Kolkata-based DIVERSIFY BANK OF INDIA which apart from being accused of incompetent customer service, low employee

motivation and inertia was also labeled by the Verma Committee as one of the weakest public sector banks.

7. Thus graded, the Kolkata-based DIVERSIFY BANK OF INDIA decided to focus on its people and achieve a turnaround. The result: over a period of 15 months, it generated one million new accounts.

Background of the Case

8. In 1997, DIVERSIFY BANK's accumulated losses were Rs. 1,434 crore (Rs. 14.34 billion). It got rid of the "weak bank" tag in 2002, after posting profits from 1998 onwards, but this was primarily from the money generated by selling government securities.

9. According to a 1999 report by the Reserve Bank of India, the reasons for DIVERSIFY BANK's poor performance were weaknesses in the areas of operations, HR and management. In 2004, Business Standard Research Bureau's ranking placed DIVERSIFY BANK squarely last in the pack, ranking it 23rd. Then, in March 2006, DIVERSIFY BANK presented a clean balance sheet to a packed press conference in Kolkata. Business had crossed Rs. 45,000 crore {Rs. 450 billion (up from Rs. 37,187 crore (Rs. 371.87 billion) in 2004-05)} and the bank's gross non-performing assets had dropped to 4.66 per cent from 6.14 per cent. The credit-deposit ratio improved from 46.5 per cent to 54.6 per cent. And, for the first time in 14 years, the bank paid a dividend of Rs. 46 crore (Rs. 460 million) to the government.

10. As performance improved, DIVERSIFY BANK climbed the ladder in Business Standard Research Bureau's ranking as well—it was in the 10th place in 2005. In Feb. 2007 announcing the results for April-December 2005-06—business stood at Rs. 54,190 crore (Rs. 541.9 billion). Mr. P.K. Gupta, Chairman and Managing Director, DIVERSIFY BANK OF INDIA, announced that the bank is targeting a business of Rs. 100,000 crore (Rs. 1000 billion) by March 2009.

11. Getting rid of the losses was the easy part. As mentioned above, sales of government securities ensured that the bank registered profits, but the money was being used to balance earlier losses: accumulated losses of Rs. 14,200 crore (Rs. 142 billion) in 1997 came down to Rs. 278 crore (Rs. 2.78 billion) by March 2005.

12. That's when the bank requested the government to set off the losses against its capital. The government agreed—this escape route of nationalized banks has been used in the past by Dena Bank and UCO Bank as well. "One could wish the bank had exercised this option back in 1997 itself," rues Mr P.K. Gupta now.

CRM Aspects Related to Case Study of Diversify Bank of India

13. The real challenge for Diversify Bank, though, was with its people. With over 18,000 employees and 1,310 branches, it is one of the most overstaffed banks in the country. The issue wasn't one of laying them off or even downsizing—not really an option in trade union West Bengal, in any case. Rather, it was to energise them to go seeking fresh business. The track record hadn't been too encouraging, after all: from Rs. 22,300 crore (Rs. 223 billion) in 2000, business had grown just Rs. 5,000 crore (Rs. 50 billion) over the next two years, when the bank mobilised Rs. 27,100 crore (Rs. 271 billion). Compare that with Good Bank of India: deposits grew from Rs 196,821 crore (Rs. 1968.21 billion) to Rs. 270,560 crore (Rs. 2705.6 billion) over the same period. Things clearly needed to change. And fast.
14. "*Diversify Bank* employees needed a change of attitude. From being tight-fisted bankers waiting for customers, they needed to switch to a feet-on-street mindset," says Prof. Prashant Mishra, professor of marketing, Indian Institute of Management, Calcutta, who was involved with training the bank's staff.

Setting of the Target—Mission Million or Mission Impossible?

15. When Gupta took over as CMD of Diversify Bank in May 2005, in his first meeting with regional managers itself, he made it clear that he would be going after growth. "To increase our business, we need more customers," was his emphasis. Diversify Bank isn't—or rather, wasn't—a bank used to competing or setting goals. Known as the "tea bank", it had gotten used to the slow pace of business in East India, as generated by the tea estates and managing agency houses. And then came Mission One Million.
16. In June 2005, Mr. Gupta and his team announced the bank's new goal : one million new savings accounts to be mobilised in the next 12 months. As officers across the bank's 1,300-odd branches threw up their arms in despair, the managing team broke the seemingly-unattainable goal into more manageable targets. In 2005, Diversify Bank had opened 300,000 new accounts—that meant less than one account a day for each branch. A million accounts, then, would translate into just three or four new accounts everyday for each bank (making allowances for holidays and the like). Now, that a target had been set, it seemed more achievable.

Achieving Goals

17. Setting up of the Insurance Marketing Division. Even as Mission One Million kicked off, the bank decided to revitalise its tie-ups with Tata AIG and Bajaj Allianz. Although the associations had been created a

couple of years earlier to distribute the insurance companies' products through the bank, little had really been accomplished. Diversify Bank's board then put forward a proposal to the insurance companies—would they train 1,000 bank employees in the finer details of marketing financial products? Tata AIG and Bajaj Allianz agreed to conduct week-long sessions each, and the bank created a marketing division—a first—under a general manager, to focus on the new products in its portfolio.

18. *Training*: Meanwhile, the bank employees seemed to have reacted favourably to training and it was decided to go ahead with training of managers. This time, the bank turned to professionals. Two hundred high-performing managers were identified from the most efficient branches (the ones generating the most business).They were then sent to the Indian Institute of Management, Calcutta, to brush up on market planning, identifying segments, invigorating sales teams and customer relationship management. "The bank realised that it was time for it to realign practices with current demands," points out Mishra.
19. *Training on Improved Customer Interaction*: Bank employees also needed to go back to school for lessons on customer interaction. This time, DIVERSIFY BANK turned to rather more unconventional sources. It brought in trainers from leading hotel management institutes to educate its frontline staff on the correct way of greeting customers, dealing discreetly with trouble-makers, and being pro-active with addressing complaints. In addition, the Ramakrishna Mission sent over instructors for introductory lessons on yoga and meditation.
20. *A Lesson in Espirit-de-Corps and Motivation*: A survey by the National Institute of Bank Management study had brought out that most employees of Diversify Bank did not have even basic knowledge about the bank, its management or the products it offered. Of course, this isn't an issue confronting only Diversify Bank—"all public sector bank employees need to be reskilled and retrained," points out Ananda Bhoumik, senior director, Fitch Securities. Still, it was a problem that needed to be addressed and solved immediately. The result was a "know your bank" test, which has now become a regular twice-yearly exercise. As a form of recognition—and to drive participation—those who scored more than 60 per cent were given a cash prize of Rs. 2,000, as well as a signed certificate from the CMD. Gupta claims that what started, as competition has now become "a natural exercise in staying abreast of changes in the organisation".
21. *Importance of Communication and Keeping the Employees Informed*: There was another welcome fallout of the NIBM study results: it drove home

to *Diversify Bank* the need for constant communication with its people. The bank, therefore, launched more than five intra-department newsletters, which not only tell the employees what is happening in their department at other branches, but also is a medium of communication for top management. The regular newsletters mark a distinct change in communication style at *Diversify Bank*—earlier, interaction was limited to announcements of changes in management.

Gurumantra—Reaching out to the Customer

22. *Orientation Towards the Customer*: How did all these initiatives help Mission One Million? Gupta and Mishra both point out that Diversify Bank employees now have a distinct bias towards customers—and are more welcoming of new business than before. The results of the training programmes, enhanced communication and empowering initiatives were visible almost immediately. While the Hooghly region organised 100 customer meets and 12 road shows, apart from local advertising, the Ernakulam branch in Kerala celebrated the bank's nationalisation day by organising a Deposit Mobilisation Camp. Door-to-door campaigns and camps during important festivals such as Chhath and Sankranti were held in Bihar, while the Kolkata (north) region invited local footballers such as Biswajit Bhattacharjee and Bikas Panji as guests of honour at deposit camps.
23. *Account Monitoring System*: Next came a new accounts monitoring system for the head office to get daily reports from each branch, something that was not done earlier. The reports were shared among regional heads and monthly "report cards" were printed and distributed to all employees, which showed everything from the number of new accounts, the regions and branches that fared the best, down to star performers of the month. "It was a way of recognising excellence and making the process transparent," says Gupta. Here too, *Diversify Bank* took note of the need for recognition—each month, the five top branches were awarded Rs. 5,000 each, to be spent by consensus (choices varied from music systems to family picnics).
24. *Measures to Enhance Service and Retain Existing Customers*: Customer management experts point out that the biggest danger in acquiring new customers is to forget existing ones. With a nationalised bank, the challenge of retaining customers is even greater. Accordingly, *Diversify Bank* made this a priority area within the Mission One Million goal—it has devised 17 programmes for clerks and six for peons and messengers, all of which focus on customer management. Among the areas covered

were issues like communication, team work and customer service. Six batches of 200 people each have already completed the training and management consultant and trainer S.M. Devdason claims the difference in attitude is already being noticed in several branches.

25. *Dignity of Labour*: A Lesson in Motivation of the Frontline Contact with the Customer: Perhaps the most noteworthy change is in the role of the office boy: new uniforms, new attitude (thanks to the training) and now, new designation. The lowly peon is now a Diversy Mitra (friend). The office "boys" (some of whom have been with the bank for decades) are being educated on the importance of their role: as frontline staff, they are often the first point of contact with the customer and may well help define the customer's entire experience and opinion of the bank and its services. "We are trying to make them look beyond their job profile and realise how important their role is," points out Gupta.
26. *Of course, it's not been too easy*: There has been some resistance from employees and breaking established practices has been tough at times. Devadason points out, for instance, that many managers are still reluctant to conduct feedback meetings with the staff after a training session—although it is mandatory to do so. "Attitudes take time to change," he says.
27. *Mission Accomplished*: Still, the results made the effort worthwhile. In July 2006, DIVERSIFY BANK had a million new savings accounts—it had generated Rs. 500 crore (Rs. 5 billion) worth of low-cost deposits. Of course, it was three months past the deadline, but Gupta isn't complaining. "This was Mission Impossible to begin with. So making it happen in an extra 90 days is good enough."

Areas Meritting Attention

28. *Upgradation of Facilities*: Where financial institutions are into the next phases of IT upgradation, DIVERSIFY BANK lags behind in basic facilities such as tele-banking, ATMs, debit cards and mobile banking. While its branches are computerised, they aren't networked. Now, core-banking solutions are planned, with Ernst & Young being roped in as consultant for the project.
29. *Expansion and Growth*: Also, the bank will have to consider expansion which has so far been neglected. Although Gupta is positive DIVERSIFY BANK will further penetrate parts of India other than the East and the North-East— where it has 75 per cent of its branches—not much is being done.
30. *Advertising*: Although there are ads in newspapers in the Hindi-speaking

belt, the effort is miniscule. Even in East India, the bank has just the odd ad on Bangla TV channels, which fail to grab attention.

Analysis

32. *Diversify Bank of India* has undertaken a concerted drive towards improving CRM. Their focus has been on human resource development by imparting training at various levels and in various spheres. Performance of the bank has been commendable and it has achieved the laid down target. However, there is much to be desired as far as offering of new schemes and upgradation of facilities is concerned. Plans for expansion too haven't taken shape.
33. *The million dollar question remains*—"Will PSUs ever match up to private companies in providing customer satisfaction ?"

STUDY–QUESTIONS

1. Explain the roles of the customer. Discuss the wants and needs of the customer.
2. Explain the factors that shape perception.
3. What do you mean by the emotions? Also explain the various types of emotions in brief.
4. Elaborate the customer decision process in short.

3

THE EVOLUTION OF CRM

INTRODUCTION

As we know that CRM has emerged as one of the latest management terminology. CRM, for some, means 1 to 1 marketing while for some it means a call centre. Others call database marketing as CRM. There are many others who refer to technology solutions as CRM. Popularised by the business press and marketed by the aggressive CRM vendors as a panacea for all the ills facing the firms and managers, it means different things to different people. In our traditional businesses, merchants and traders have been practising customer relationship for centuries. Their business was built on trust. They could customise the products and all aspects of delivery and payment to suit the requirements of their customers. They paid personal attention to their customers, knew details regarding their customers' tastes and preferences, and had a personal rapport with most of them. In many cases, the interactions transcended the commercial transactions and involved social interactions.

Even today, this kind of a relationship exists between customers and retailers, craftsmen, artisans — essentially in markets that are traditional, small and classified as pre-industrial markets. The industrial revolution changed these relationship-oriented practices. Businesses adopted mass production, mass communication and mass distribution to achieve economics of scale. Manufacturers started focusing on manufacturing and efficient operations to cut costs. Intermediaries like distributors, wholesalers and retailers took on the responsibilities of warehousing, transportation, distribution and sale to final customers. This resulted in greater efficiencies and lower costs to the manufacturers but brought in many layers between them and the customers. The resulting gap reduced direct contacts and had a negative impact on their relationships. The post-industrial era (information era) saw the re-emergence of relationship practices. The following factors are identified for this shift in orientation:

(1) Advancement in Technology

The advances in information, communication and production technologies have helped marketers come closer to their customers. Firms operating in diverse sectors ranging from packaged goods to services started using these technologies to know their customers, learn more about them and then build stronger bonds with them through frequent interactions. Marketers could gain knowledge about customers, which helped them respond to their needs through manufacturing, delivery and customer service. Technology also enabled customers undertake some of the responsibilities, normally performed by marketers, like ordering and product—use related services. Though the emergence of CRM in recent times coincided with the information age, we must remember that technology is just an enabler. Technology enabled marketers overcome several long felt shortcomings of mass marketing. Some of these included:

(i) *Lack of fast, effective and interactive modes* of customer contact, feedback and information.

(ii) *Lack of consolidated information* about customer interactions, purchase behaviour and future potential.

(iii) *Inefficiencies of mass marketing*: 1980s and early 1990s witnessed some of the most radical business transformations that resulted in cost reductions in almost all functional departments except marketing. Manufacturing and related operations costs were reduced through business process reengineering, human resource costs were reduced through outsourcing, restructuring and layoffs, financial costs were reduced through financial reengincering but marketing costs kept increasing due to increased competition and product parity in virtually every industry.

(2) Competition in Most Markets

Studies have shown that it costs up to 6-8 times more to attract a new customer than to retain an existing customer (Gruen). Marketers have now started focusing on the lifetime value of customers. They are moving away from just trying to sell their products to understanding customers needs and wants and then satisfying their needs. This has led to a relationship orientation which creates opportunities to cross sell products and services over the lifetime of the customer.

(3) Growing Importance of the Service Sector

In India, the services sector contributes to over 50 per cent of the economy. One of the characteristics of the service industries is the direct interaction between the marketer and the buyer. In services, the provider is usually involved in the production as well as delivery directly. For example, professional service providers like a doctor or a consultant are directly involved in production as well as delivery of their services. Similarly, the customers are directly involved in the purchase and consumption of these services. These direct contacts create opportunities for better understanding, a better appreciation of needs as well as constraints and emotional bonding all of which facilitate relationship building. Therefore, it should come as no surprise when one sees the service firms pioneering many of the customer relationship initiatives. Firms operating in the financial services, hospitality business, telecom, and airlines are the early adopters and extensive users of CRM practices. The service sector contributes to over two-third of the GDP of most advanced economies.

(4) Adoption of Total Quality Management (TQM) Programs

The adoption of total quality management programs have helped companies offer quality products and services to customers at the lowest prices. To enable this value proposition, organisations needed to work closely with their customers, Intermediaries as well as suppliers thus fostering close working relationships with members of the marketing system.

Companies such as Intel, Xerox, and Toyota formed partnering relationships with suppliers and customers to practice TQM. Other developments such as an increase in the number of demanding customers, increased fragmentation of markets, and generally high level of product quality forced businesses to seek sustainable competitive advantages. A competitive advantage is sustainable only when it is not easily replicated. One such sustainable competitive advantage is the relationship that a firm develops with its customers.

GROWTH OF SCHOOLS OF THOUGHT ON CRM

Researchers in different countries observed this shift in marketer's orientation towards customer relationship and started exploring the phenomenon. The initial approaches (early 1990s) to CRM (Coote, 1994) can be very broadly classified as:

1. The Anglo-Australian Approach

The Anglo-Australian approach integrated the contemporary theories of quality management, services marketing and customer relationship economies to explain the emergence of relationship marketing.

2. The Nordic Approach

The Nordic approach views relationship marketing as the confluence of interactive network theory, services marketing and customer relationship economics. The interactive network theory of industrial marketing views marketing as an interactive process in a context where relationship building is an area of primary concern for marketers.

3. The North American Approach

In contrast, the initial focus of the North American scholars was on the relationship between the buyer and seller operating within the context of the organisational environment which facilitated the buyer seller relationship. One of the broader approaches to CRM emerged from the research conducted by academics at the Centre for Relationship Marketing and Service Management at the Cranfield University, UK. The broadened view of relationship marketing addresses a total of six key market domains, not just the traditional customer market. It also advocated for a transition for marketing from a limited functional role to a cross-functional role and a shift towards marketing activities for customer retention in addition to the conventional customer acquisition. The six markets are as follows:

(i) Customer markets—existing and prospective customers as well as intermediaries,

(ii) Referral markets—existing customers who recommend to other prospects, and referral sources or 'multipliers' such as doctors who refer patients to a hospital or a consultant who recommends a specific IT solution,

(iii) Influence markets—government, consumer groups, business press and financial analysts,

(iv) Recruitment markets—for attracting the right employees to the organisation,

(v) Supplier markets—suppliers of raw materials, components, services, etc., and

(vi) Internal markets—the organisation including internal departments and staff.

COMMON MISCONCEPTIONS ABOUT CRM

Common misconceptions about CRM as follows:

(1) "CRM means recognizing a customer wherever he interacts with our company, a 360' view of the customer."

This is a critical first step, but simple recognition isn't enough. We must learn to use the information we've collected in the past to interact effectively in each future interaction. Information about customers is critical to increased understanding and improved service. You also need tools and training so people know what to do with it.

(2) "CRM means scoring and measuring Customer Value."

A very important use of CRM information is to be able to identify who our best customers are. We must have ways to use this knowledge to increase the number of loyal customers and the value of each.

(3) "CRM is sales rep productivity tools."

Some companies still believe that the only way they can build relation- ships is through the sales force, so CRM must be about automating sales. The sales function is only one of those that directly touch customers and make up CRM.

(4) "CRM is the solution that will solve all our customer problems; it's all the software tools that make it easier for a customer to do business with us."

Absolutely not. There is no magic, no sorcerer's stone, and no silver bullet. This effort takes vision, planning, investment, and patience. Software is certainly a necessary enabler, but not the total solution. The trouble with the magic software myth is that it allows business managers to think CRM is just an Information Technology problem. Application software vendors not surprisingly, abet this common misconception. If it were that easy, why wouldn't everybody be doing it already?

(5) "CRM is the internet."

The Internet has greatly increased the opportunity and need for better information, tools, and the processes that can take advantage of them. But relationships are built on understanding and trust. People who understand the customer's perspective must be the ones who design the web experience.

(6) "CRM is just the latest name for Direct Marketing.'

Using information and automation to understand and improve customer relationships has been practised by Direct Marketers for years. CRM is a shift in focus from marketing (communicating "to") to relationship management (communicating "with").

None of these statements is totally wrong, but none tells the complete story. CRM is not just the Internet or just sales rep productivity; it is an entire discipline for interacting with customers that touches all the front office functions.

CASE STUDIES

CRM can be defined as "it is a comprehensive strategy and process of acquiring, retaining and patterning with selective customers to create Superior value for the company and the customer."

A CRM PROCESS FRAMEWORK

The broad framework of CRM process comprises of four sub-processes:

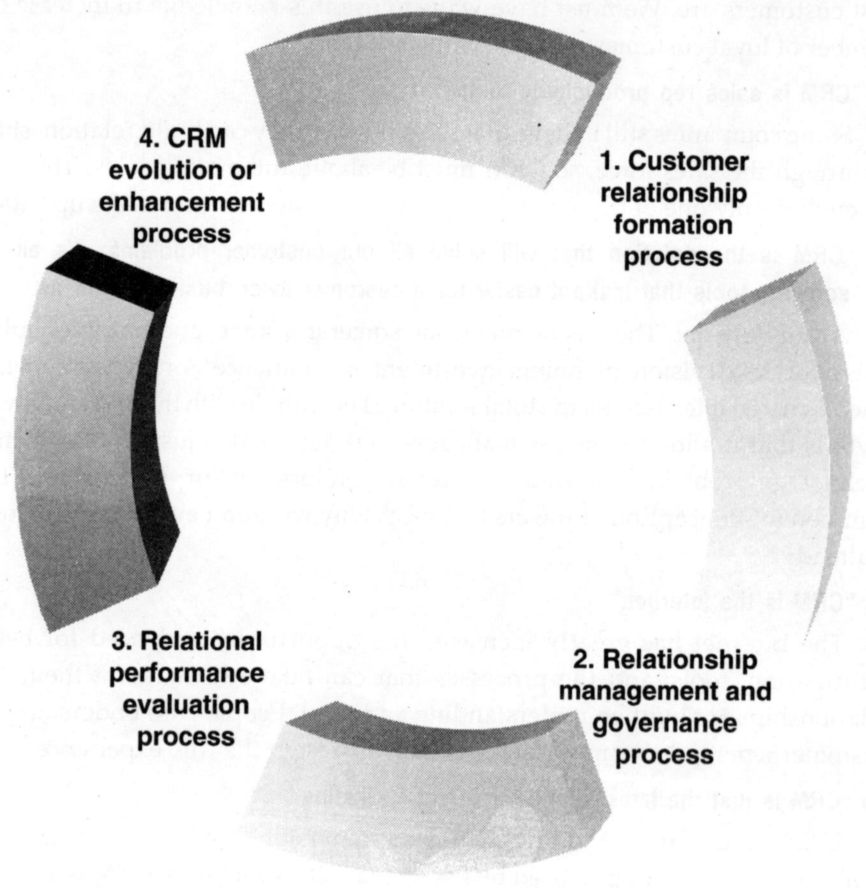

GOALS OF CRM

1. Differentiating Customer

All the customers are not equal, recognize and reward the best customer. For this the CRM needs to understand.

Sensitivity, tastes, preference and personalities.

Life-style and age

Culture background and education

Physical and psychological characteristics.

2. Differentiating Offering

A CRM solution needs to differentiate between low value customer and a high value customer.

High Value customer requiring high value customer offerings.

Low Value customer with potential to become high value in near future.

High Value customer requiring high value service.

3. Keeping Existing Customer

Grading customer from satisfied to very dissatisfy shall help the organization in always improving its customer satisfaction level and scores. As satisfaction level of each improves so shall the customer retention with the organization.

4. Customer Life Time Value

By identifying life stage and life event trigger the points by customer, marketers can maximize share of purchase potential.

THE CRM VALUE CHAIN

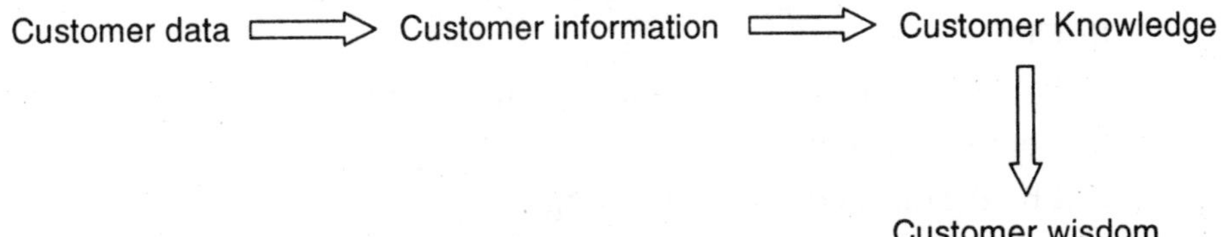

BACKGROUND OF INDUSTRY OR COMPANY

The scenario is of banking industry as a whole but regarding history and code of conduct and ethics we have shared only that of IJIJI bank.

HISTORY OF IJIJI BANK

1994 : IJIJI Bank set-up.

1996 : IJIJI Ltd became the first company in the Indian financial sector to raise GDR.

: SCICI merged with IJIJI Ltd.

: Mr. K.V.Kamath appointed the Managing Director and CEO of IJIJI Ltd.

1997 : IJIJI Ltd was the first intermediary to move away from single prime rate to three-tier prime rates structure and introduced yield-curve based pricing.

: The name The Industrial Credit and Investment Corporation of India Ltd. changed to IJIJI Ltd.

: IJIJI Ltd announced the takeover of ITC Classic Finance.

1998 : Introduced the new logo symbolizing a common corporate identity for the IJIJI Group.

: IJIJI announced takeover of Anagram Finance.

1999 : IJIJI launched retail finance—car loans, house loans and loans for consumer durables.

: IJIJI becomes the first Indian Company to list on the NYSE through an issue of American Depositary Shares.

2000 : IJIJI Bank became the first commercial bank from India to list its stock on NYSE.

: IJIJI Bank announces merger with Bank of Madura.

2001 : The Boards of IJIJI Ltd and IJIJI Bank approved the merger of IJIJI with IJIJI Bank.

2002 : IJIJI Ltd merged with IJIJI Bank Ltd to create India's second largest bank in term's of assets.

: IJIJI assigned higher than sovereign rating by Moody's.

: IJIJI Bank launched India's first CDO (Collateralized Debt Obligation) Fund named Indian Corporate Collateralized Debt Obligation Fund (ICCDO Fund).

: "E Lobby", a self-service banking centre inaugurated in Pune. It was the first of its kind in India.

: IJIJI Bank launched Private Banking.

: 1100-seat Call Centre set-up in Hyderabad

: IJIJI Bank Home Shoppe, the first-ever permanent aggregation and display of housing projects in the county, launched in Pune,

: ATM-on-Wheels, India's first mobile ATM, launched in Mumbai.

2003 : The first Integrated Currency Management Centre launched in Pune.

: IJIJI Bank announced the setting up of its first ever offshore branch in Singapore.

: The first offshore banking unit (OBU) at Seepz Special Economic Zone, Mumbai, launched.

: IJIJI Bank's representative office inaugurated in Dubai.

: Representative office set-up in China. IJIJI Bank's UK subsidiary launched.

: India's first ever "Visa Mini Credit Card", a 43% smaller credit card in dimensions launched.

: IJIJI Bank subsidiary set-up in Canada.

: Temasek Holdings acquired 5.2% stake in IJIJI Bank.

: IJIJI Bank became the market leader in retail credit in India.

2004 : Max Money, a home loan product that offers the dual benefit of higher eligibility and affordability to a customer introduced.

: Mobile banking service in India launched in association with Reliance Infocomm.

: India's first multi-branded credit card with HPCL and Airtel launched.

: Kisan Loan Card and innovative, low-cost ATMs in rural India launched.

: IJIJI Bank and CNBC TV 18 announced India's first ever awards recognizing the achievements of SMEs, a pioneering initiative to encourage the contribution of Small and Medium Enterprises to the growth of Indian economy.

: IJIJI Bank opened its 500th branch in India.

: IJIJI Bank introduced partnership model wherein IJIJI Bank would forge an alliance with existing micro-finance institutions (MFIs). The MFI would undertake the promotional role of identifying, training and promoting the micro-finance clients and IJIJI Bank would finance the clients directly on the recommendation of the MFI.

: IJIJI Bank introduced 8-8 Banking wherein all the branches of the Bank would remain open from 8 a.m. to 8 p.m. from Monday to Saturday.

: IJIJI Bank introduced the concept of floating rate for home loans in India.

2005 : First rural branch and ATM launched in Uttar Pradesh at Delpandarwa, Hardoi.

: "Free for Life" credit cards launched wherein annual fees of all IJIJI Bank Credit Cards were waived off.

: IJIJI Bank and Visa jointly launched m-Chq—a revolutionary credit card on the mobile phone.

: Private Banking Masters 2005, a nationwide Golf tournament for high networth clients of the private banking division launched. This event is the largest domestic invitation amateur golf event conducted in India.

: First Indian company to make a simultaneous equity offering of $1.8 billion in India, the United States and Japan.

: Acquired IvestitsionnoKreditny Bank of Russia.

: IJIJI Bank became the largest bank in India in terms of its market capitalization.

: IJIJI Bank became the first private entity in India to offer a discount to retail investors for its follow-up offer.

2006 : IJIJI Bank became the first Indian bank to issue hybrid Tier-1 perpetual debt in the international markets.

: IJIJI Bank subsidiary set-up in Russia.

: Introduced a new product—'NRI smart save Deposits'—a unique fixed deposit scheme for non-resident Indians.

: Representative offices opened in Thailand, Indonesia and Malaysia.

: IJIJI Bank became the largest retail player in the market to introduce a biometric enabled smart card that allows banking transactions to be conducted on the field. A low-cost solution, this became an effective delivery option for IJIJI Bank's micro-finance institution partners.

: Financial counseling centre Disha launched. Disha provides free credit counseling, financial planning and debt management services.

: Bhoomi puja conducted for a regional hub in Hyderabad, Andhra Pradesh.

2007 : IJIJI Bank's USD 2 billion 3-tranche international bond offering was the largest bond offering by an Indian bank.

: Sangli Bank amalgamated with IJIJI Bank.

: IJIJI Bank raised Rs 20,000 crore (approx. $5 billion) from both domestic and international markets through a follow-on public offer.

: IJIJI Bank's GBP 350 million international bond offering marked the inaugural deal in the sterling market from an Indian issuer and also the largest deal in the sterling market from Asia.

: Launched India's first ever jewellery card in association with jewelry major Gitanjali Group.

: IJIJI Bank became the first bank in India to launch a premium credit card—The Visa Signature Credit Card.

: Foundation stone laid for a regional hub in Gandhinagar, Gujarat.

: Introduced SME Toolkit, an online resource centre, to help small and medium enterprises start, finance and grow their business.

: IJIJI Bank signed a multi-tranche dual currency US$ 1.5 billion syndication loan agreement in Singapore.

: IJIJI Bank became the first private bank in India to offer both floating and fixed rate on car loans, commercial vehicles loans, construction equipment loans and professional equipment loans.

EVOLUTION OF CRM IN BANKING SECTOR

Regulation and technological improvements are responsible for the vast majority of innovations in banking over the past quarter century. The introduction of personal computers and the proliferation of ATMs in the 1970s captured bank management's attention. The regulatory changes in the 1980s fueled much of the industry's growth, then downsizing as:

Bankers focused on amassing market presence which resulted in significant merger activity. Recent technological improvements are at the root of Bankers' focus as well as a target for their significant investment dollars today. In fact, according to recent projections, bankers and their financial service company brethren will spend almost $7 billion this year on CRM and ncrease that by 14 percent each year for then next several years. Looking at this CRM phenomenon in light of the drivers of banking innovation since the 1970s, one might wonder if CRM itself is the innovation, or (conversely) the technology, once again.

Much is being written about CRM. Bankers at all points of the CRM spectrum are looking for a way to quantify their return on investment—Either what it actually is or, if just starting out, what it should be and over what period of time should the value is realized. Ironically, the answer to this question may lie in a simple review of a few known quantities generated from historical innovation. Look, for example, at ATMs. What drove many bankers to invest in ATMs? Was the promise of reduced branch cost, since customers would use them? Instead of a branch to transact business. But what was discovered is that the financial impact of ATMs is a marginal increase in fee income substantially offset by the cost of significant increases in the number of customer transactions. The value proposition, however, was a significant increase in that intangible called customer satisfaction. The increase in customer satisfaction has translated to loyalty that resulted in higher customer retention and growing franchise value. Internet banking, a product of the 1990s, shows similar characteristics. Again, bankers invested believing that the Internet was a lower-cost delivery channel and a way to increase sales. Studies have now shown, however, that the primary value of offering Internet banking services lies in the increased retention of highly valued customer segments. Again, the intangible called customer satisfaction drives the value proposition.

Now we explore CRM. CRM is not another ATM or Internet bank. It is not a checking account, a stock or a mortgage. In fact, CRM is not anything a customer should even know about! You will never sell your customer your CRM, will you? So, one can conclude that CRM is not tangible. If it's Intangible, can it be expected to produce a tangible return? Probably not, or at least not with any direct financial value exclusively linked back to the investment in CRM. CRM is primarily driven by the innovation of technology, but unlike other technological innovations, CRM has power to help bankers quickly and directly improve customer satisfaction. CRM is an added dimension to ensure that what the customer expects is consistent with what the bank is prepared to deliver. One expert in bank CRM initiatives recently said that CRM is an approach that is less focused on providing the right services to the customer than attracting customers who are the right fit for what the bank has to offer. Further, the primary value of CRM is its potential as customer retention tool. People are starting to measure CRM in terms of increased customer satisfaction. Rather than ROI.

WAYS OF CRM IN BANKING SECTOR

Technology Led Delivery of Products

M-Banking	Call centers Banking	Internet	ATMs
Private Banking	Credit/ debit cards	Loans—Home, Car etc.	Deposits

- Young Stars/Student Banking Services
- Investments—Mutual Funds, GoI bonds
- Savings account (Quantum optima)

Extended Reach by Multi-channel Offerings

	Channels
Internet Banking Services	❖ Electronic bill presentment and payment. ❖ Online bill payments for shopping travel and donator transactions. ❖ Funds transfers 24X7 facility. ❖ Money to India for NRI customers. ❖ All routine transactions regarding Banking, Cards, Loans and Investment services.
Automatic Teller Machine	❖ Routine Banking transactions like balance enquiry, cash withdrawal, funds transfer, cheque book requests, etc. ❖ Features like airtime recharge for pre-paid mobile phones, donations to temples/trusts. ❖ ATMs for visually challenged customers.
Mobile Baniking	❖ SMS alerts for salary credit, account getting credited/debited, cheque bounce. ❖ SMS alerts for credit card due date reminders, approaching credit limit reminders.
Call Centre	❖ Customer contact through Voice, IVR, e-mail, correspondence, video conferencing. ❖ Wide range of solution offerings to customer right from balance enquiry to execution of banking transactions like funds transfer, bill payment over phone.

Facts: Regarding M-BANKING, etc.

Which option would you prefer—Mobile or online Banking?

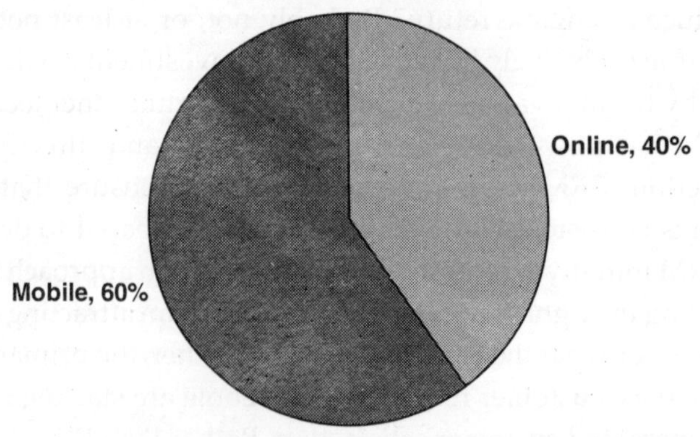

Base : 360

Source: DATAQUEST

WHAT MOBILE BANKING SERVICES

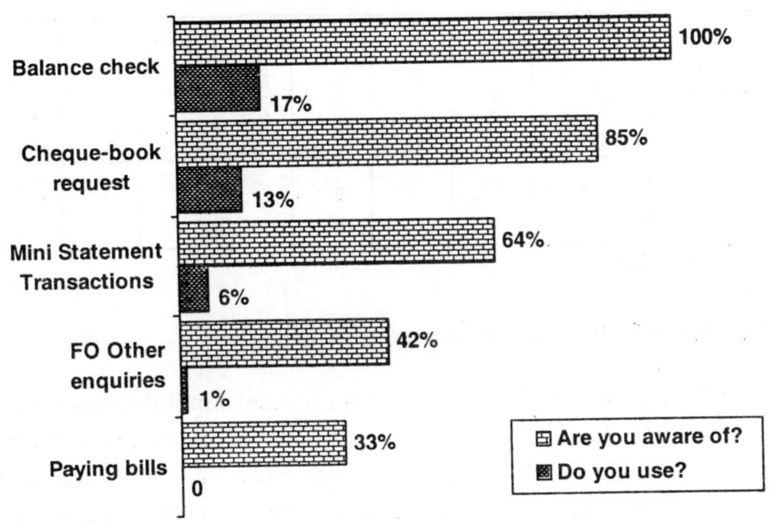

Base : 95 respondents aware of m-banking services.

Clear Mismatch between awareness and usage; On this base of 95 respondents who were aware of m-banking services, only 24% (or 23 respond-nets), were actual users of these services. And given the overall sample size of 360, this usage number amounted to around 6%. Among these users, "checking of account balance" scored high, followed by requests for chequebooks and mini-statements. While the 6% user rate may seem high, the sample selected for the survey was 'A' class—people with a higher awareness of (and access to) services available. If the spread of the survey were to be expanded to smaller towns, the rate would possibly drop to 1-2%. However, banks offering these services say numbers are growing, with the biggest draw being balance enquiries.

M-BANKING: THE SERVICES BOUQUET

	IJIJI Bank	*BDFC Bank*	*ICBI Bank*	*HSBC*	*Bank of America*	*Citibank*	*ABN Ammo*
Balance enquiry	✓	✓	✓	✓	✓	✓	✓
Last few transactions	✓	✓	✓	✓	✓	✓	✓
Cherub payment status			✓	✓	✓	✓	✓
Stop payment of chouse		✓					
Statement request	✓	✓	✓	✓	✓	✓	
Cherub book request	✓		✓				✓

"We have 1.75 lakh registered users for mobile banking services today. And we are already hitting 4,000 transactions per day"

CN Ram, IT chief, BDFC Bank

Are you aware of mobile banking and do you use it?

	All	Delhi	Bangalore	Collate	Mumbai	Chennai	Headband	Trivandrum	Hyderabad	Pune	Chandigarh
Aware?	48	73	45	58	36	65	3	58	11	19	63
Use?	7	12	15	8	3	13	0	4	0	5	1

All figures in percentage
Source : Voice and Data
Sample Size : 754 mobile phone subscribers across 10 cities.

While 47.7% of Indian cell phone users are aware of mobile banking services; only 7.4% of them actually use the facilities. The level of awareness was highest in Delhi (72.8%), followed by 65% in Chennai and 63.4% in Chandigarh. Cell phone users in Headband, Hyderabad and Pune were the least aware, with awareness levels of 3.4%, 11% and 18.5%, respectively. Also, while none of the respondents reported using the facility in Headband and Hyderabad, Pune showed a much higher usage trend—5.3%. Interestingly, despite a #3 position in terms of awareness, Chandigarh was much below in the usage table, with a hit ratio of only 0.6%.

Have you heard about mobile banking?

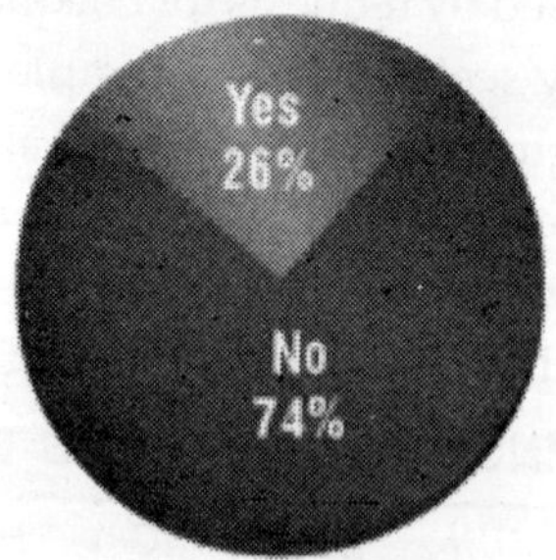

Base: 360 IT industry and corporate users of mobile phones and banks offering M-banking
Source: DATAQUEST

Given the profile of the people surveyed, it's no surprise that over 26% of the sample had heard about mobile banking services. Dataquest did a mix of 60:40 (non-IT: IT people) in the NCR region. As many private/MNC bankers cater to the IT industry, awareness about mobile banking services was higher among 'IT people'. BDFC Bank's CN Ram agreed—"We have 1.75 lakh registered users for mobile banking services. And we are hitting 4,000 transactions per day."

Would you like to use mobile banking services?

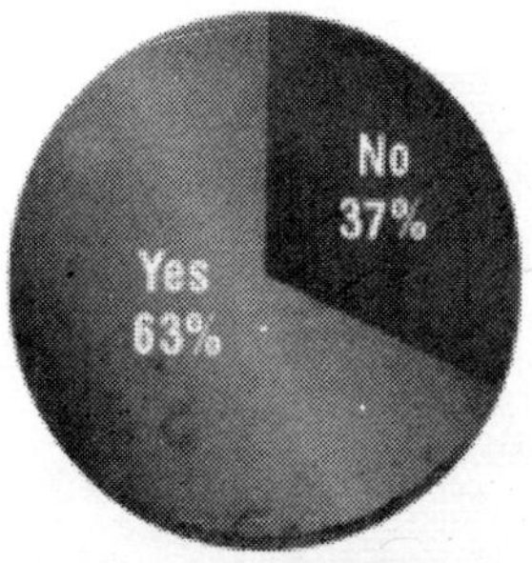

Base : 265 respondents not aware of m-banking services.
Source : Dataquest.

While awareness remains at 26%, people are keen to try out mobile banking. 63% of the respondents evinced interest in the services. Given the convenience factor—the fact that mobile banking can be used from anywhere in the world as long as one can send and receive SMS'—most were interested. Since m-commerce is still about the core virtues of mobile communication, issues like mobility, any-time access and ease of usage emerged as the driving factors in the ongoing year.

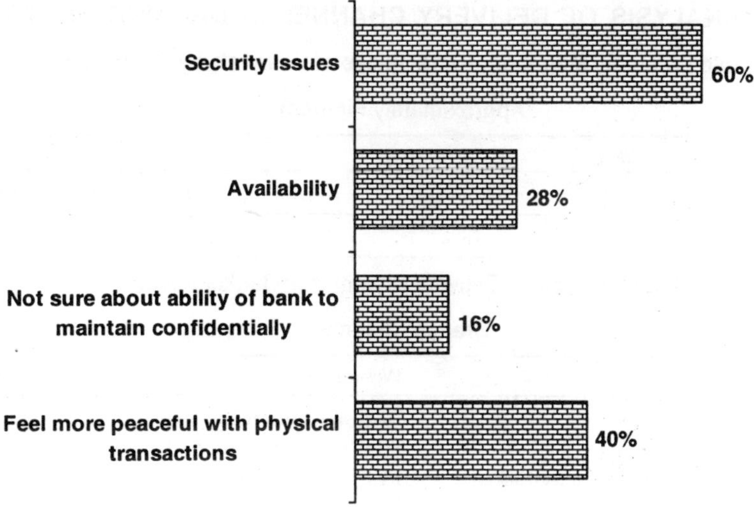

Base : 95 (Those who said there are aware of mobile banking and/or their bank provides the service)
Source: Dataquest.

WHY DO YOU USE M-BANKING SERVICES

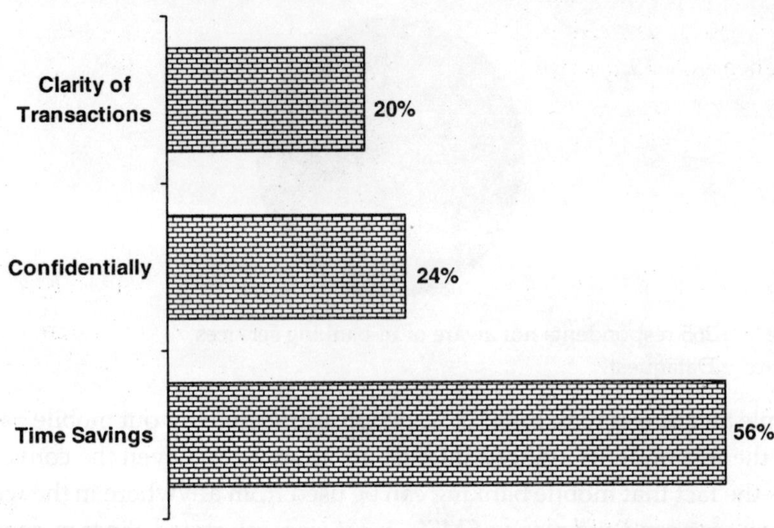

Base : 95 (Those who said there are aware of mobile banking and/or their bank provides the service)
Source : Dataquest.

SWOT ANALYSIS OF DELIVERY CHANNEL IN BANKING SECTOR

Table : Channel Migration—Data on use of Channels by Customers

(Approximately Figures)

2000				*2004*			
ATM	*Call Centre*	*Internet*	*Branch*	*ATM*	*Call Centre*	*Internet*	*Branch*
15%	5%	2%	78%	46%	12%	12%	30%

SWOT Analysis of Delivery Channels in Banking Sector

Branch Channel

Strenghts	*Weaknesses*
Personal touch Personalized information Facilitates complex banking activities Customer retention Deepening of relationships Brand visibility Inculcates customer loyalty Perceived as a trusted advisor	Requires high manpower High infrastructure cost Restricted timings Limited accessibility Time consuming
Opportunities	*Threats*
Financial advisor Facilitates channel migration Effective crioss selling	Increasing cost of transactions in the branch High footfall vis-a-vis employee ratio

ATM Channel

Strengths	*Weaknesses*
Cost effective Better reach Brand visibility Round the clock availability Quicker transactions Networked to centralized database enabling online updating Adds a fillip to Bank's customer base	Cost of set-up Limited cash dispensing ability Lack of human interface Waiting time is not eliminated completely
Opportunities	*Threats*
Flatform for cross selling Value added services like donations mobile phone prepared recharging Shared ATMs to reduce cost and to maximize reach Mobile ATMs to reach remotely located customers	Security concerns Lower brand loyalty

Internet Channel

Strengths	*Weaknesses*
Lowest cost per transaction Reach Minimum physical infrastructure Round the clock availability Convenience banking Account integration for single relationship view Waiting time eliminated Information gateway	All transactions not possible Slow adopters to internet banking lack of human interface Poor penetration of internet in India
Opportunities	*Threats*
Flatform for cros selling Value added services like ticket reservations Virtual banking	Security concerns Lack of strong trust environment Perceived notion that intenet is not a safe place to conduct financial transactions No accessible to masses

Phone Channel

Strengths	*Weaknesses*
Cost effective accessible Most of the banks offer 24"7"365 days service Convenience banking Economies of scale	Cost of set-up Limited transactions Communicaton barrier High AHT (Actual Handling Time)

Single point of contact for multiple products Supports complaint resolution	
Opportunities	*Threats*
Campaign and cross selling opportunities Accessibility across locations	Communication gap Customer perception of incurring cost while transacting
Deepening of relationships Acquisition of new customers	

FOOD FOR THOUGHT

1. Is e-banking and m-banking really a way of customer relationship management?
2. Whether the data about m-banking users encouraging or discouraging?
3. Is CRM really working in India or it is a concept meant for western countries only?

STUDY–QUESTIONS

1. Explain the various schools of thought on CRM.
2. Discuss the various common misconception of CRM in brief.

4

Building Customer Relationships

INTRODUCTION

For several decades marketing theorists have drawn a clear difference between marketing and selling. Selling conjures up for us the image of a door-to-door peddler who tries to sell us something we don't want, and then gets out of town as quickly as possible. The marketing concept, on the other hand, teaches firms to profit by selling what customers really want for a value that competitors can't match. The rationale for this second approach is twofold. First, it assumes that the marketer represents a going concern with every intention of remaining in business in the same market. Second, it supposes a goal of satisfied customers who will be a source of repeat purchases and positive recommendations. In spite of this underlying concept, the focus of marketing education and marketing practice has been on the attraction of new customers through the use of the four P's (product, price, promotion/communication, and place/distribution), rather than on the retention of current customers. Until recently, then, marketing efforts have been focused on "creating exchanges" rather than managing long-term relationships with customers.

Maturing markets, lower population growth, and global competition have forced managers to examine the costs of winning new customers versus retaining their old ones. We now see the focus of marketing shifting to managing relationships with customers. The following definition of marketing captures the new spirit.

Marketing is to establish, maintain, enhance (usually but not necessarily always long-term) relationships with customers and other partners, at a profit, so that the objectives of the parties involved are met. This is achieved by a mutual exchange and fulfilment of promises.

The concept of promises made and kept by both sides is a key to this definition. The promises made by the seller include the obvious ones that are part of any selling contract, such as product quality, delivery and inventory management, attendant services, and others, but for a long-term relationship they must also cover deeper commitments to the buyer's success. The promises made by the buyer also must be beyond those of the contractual terms of payment. One British executive described his understanding of the role of the customer in a strong relationship:

> *I describe 'loyal' customers as those who will call me as a supplier immediately [when] they receive a visit from a competitor with a new product and feel that they have a unique relationship with me and my staff.*

The role of services marketing is critical in relationship building. Consider the following quote from Raymond Langton, the head of SKF North America, a firm in an industry that many would consider to be as far from the "service sector" as any could be (it manufactures bearings for industrial customers), "In today's world, to retain business you cannot look at is as if you were selling a product. You are providing a value-added service." In addition to selling bearings the firm now provides its customers with assistance in the mounting and maintenance of its bearings to reduce downtime in their factories. It is particularly in this critical area of relationship marketing that any organisation begins to realise that it is in the business of marketing services. Relationships, whether with consumers or industrial customers, are built on service.

In fact, in spite of the obvious benefits of relationships to sellers of establishing long-term markets for their products, much of the impetus for closer ties has come from industrial buyers who have found that partnerships with their. suppliers are essential to producing high-quality products while cutting costs. After all, continuous quality improvement is difficult when a firm frequently changes suppliers. On the other hand, long-term, stable relationships are important to building and maintaining quality by allowing both parties to learn each other's businesses and develop cooperative solutions to problems.

Levitt called this form of relationship "reciprocal dependency" and insisted that the seller is responsible for initiating and nurturing it. Research has shown that buyer firms tend to consider the granting of further sales in the future to he a privilege earned through careful attention to the buyer/seller relationships. In fact, buyers in large transactions often see themselves as having granted the sellers special favours, rather than having participated in mutually profitable exchanges. Moreover, having "awarded" these contracts, they expect to be appreciated and further rewarded to even the debt, perhaps by extraordinary service, continued investment in quality improvements, and discounts on further purchases.

Because of the level of commitment required for these relationships, the decision cycle for firms choosing suppliers has become, much longer. For example, banks that used to evaluate and choose providers of stationery supplies in three to six months now take up to 18 Months. This is because the decision to buy is not just for a single transaction, but has become a commitment to enter a long-term relationship, with the attendant risks. In fact, Levitt compared this decision to a romantic encounter. Doing business is no longer a decision to have a "one-night stand," but a commitment to a marriage, which will require cooperation, nurturing, mutual problem solving, and conflict resolution to keep the arrangement productive and mutually beneficial.

Baxter International, the healthcare products and services giant, demonstrates how far relationship building has gone. Its hospital customers have felt tremendous pressure on their earnings due to the growth of alternative healthcare delivery systems, government restrictions, and insurance company pressures. Baxter has negotiated arrangements with some hospitals in which cost targets for supplies are determined and Baxter shares the savings or the costs depending on how well it does in meeting that target. It provides consultants who advise the hospitals on standardising products and streamlining inventory procedures. In fact, Baxter now manages the inventory systems for some of its clients and may deliver supplies to individual floors many times a day. The companies sales through the inventory management program rose by more than a third in 1993, while the supply costs to its hospitals decreased by about $300,000 for one hospital. Baxter and its customers now have a common goal in bringing down costs, because they share the same profit and loss.

Not all relationships are such strong partnerships. In many industries, the burden is on the seller to develop the relationship. For example, firms that originally supplied cheques and stationery items to banks have found other ways to make themselves valuable partners with their clients. Most now offer such additional services as marketing research, sales training, assistance with direct marketing programs, and development of other printed sales materials. Providing such important strategic services helps to develop a close partnership between the two firms, thereby making competitive inroads very difficult.

CONSUMER RELATIONSHIPS

The concept of relationships has become particularly popular in describing these new arrangements between corporations, but, as we will see, it can also be applied to consumer marketing. Relationship building in consumer markets tends to put most of the burden on the seller, since it is generally not as contractually based as business-to-business marketing. But the idea for the seller is the same to develop reasons for the buyer to consider the seller more than the source of single transactions, but rather as a dependable source for solving many needs. For example, banks offer products and services to meet evolving customers' needs over the life cycle, and many assign "personal bankers," individuals who take responsibility for keeping in personal touch with sets of customers, cross-selling new products and handling customer problems. Bank One, headquartered in Columbus, Ohio, uses its extraordinary database of information on its customers to track their financial and life-cycle progress, so that it can offer appropriate services. For example, its systems are programmed to identify customers with large checking account balances as prime candidates for the sale of investment products. This relationship makes it more difficult and undesirable for customers to switch banks. In another category, *Anne Klein*, the designer of women's business clothing offers an "At Your Service" hot- line, that promises to "create a look just for you," with the help of fashion consultants who can assist in shopping at more than 900 stores."

(1) Benefits

Developing a strong relationship marketing orientation is not without costs in money, time, and effort. So, before a firm rushes out to establish stronger relationships with customers, it is good to identify the benefits that it is likely to realise. Advocates list many. One of the most familiar: customer retention. Higher retention means higher market share, which in turn means higher revenues. In addition, sales calls or other contacts are more efficient and productive with familiar customers, than with new ones. New arrangements can require complex, costly negotiations. Long-time customers often purchase greater quantities than new customers, and it is easier (and less costly) to sell new products to them. In high-contact industries, customer service representatives.who are switched from lost accounts may require significant retraining to make them of value to new customers. *Reichheld* proposes that a cycle of success can begin here as the improved economics lead to better profits, allowing higher pay to workers and improved morale. Satisfied employees will deliver better service, which leads to further productivity, and so on.

In addition to the benefits of improved retention, offering customers the advantages of close relationships can have other benefits to the seller. In particular, for products that are sold through distribution channels, providing customers with an incentive to establish a direct relationship with the manufacturer will circumvent the difficulty that many producers have with channel members who refuse to share their customers' names. For sales to industrial buyers, where most negotiations go through a purchasing agent, the establishment of relationships with individual users allows the seller to identify and learn the needs of key influencers in the organisation's buying centre that may otherwise be hard to reach.

(2) Degrees of Relationship Building

However, before getting too swept up in the possibilities, we need to consider the costs of building relationships as well. *Kotler* identified five different levels of relationship marketing at which a firm may choose to operate.

(i) Basic: No lasting relationship is really established. The transaction is made and both parties go their own ways.

(ii) Reactive: The seller offers to respond if the buyer has any problems.

(iii) Accountable: The seller contacts that buyer after the sale to find out how the product has been received and whether it could have been better.

(iv) Proactive: The seller calls the customer from time to time with updates on improvements to the product and other services to make the product's consumption more satisfying.

(v) Partnerships: Both parties work together to find solutions to mutual problems and opportunities for mutual success. This arrangement is generally limited to business-to-business marketing.

The ideal level for a particular firm depends upon several things, particularly on the number of customers and the margins on products. Due to the sheer numbers of customers buying small quantities at low margins, most package goods marketers operate at the basic level. However, Procter & Gamble and some others have operated at the reactive level for many years, by providing 800-number customer complaint and advice lines for each of their products. It has not been feasible for P&G to operate at a higher level, although, as we will discuss later in this chapter, database management and telecommunications technology may allow consumer products firms to improve communication with and learn about their customers.

Knowing that relationship marketing is important is not the same as knowing how to do it well. We will now turn to particular steps firms can take to improve their relationship, marketing.

AIMS OF RELATIONSHIP MARKETING

The primary aim of relationship marketing is to *build and maintain a base of committed customers who are profitable for the organisation*. To achieve this aim, the firm will focus on the *attraction*, *retention*, and *enhancement of customer relationships*. First, the firm will seek to attract customers who are likely to become long-term relationship customers. Through market segmentation, the company can come to understand the best target markets for building lasting customer relationships. As the number of these relationships grows, the loyal customers themselves will frequently help to attract (through word of mouth) new customers with similar relationship potential.

Once they are attracted to begin a relationship with the company, customers will be more likely to stay in the relationship when they are consistently provided with quality products and services and good value over time. They are less likely to be pulled away by competitors if they feel that the company understands their changing needs and seems willing to invest in the relationship by constantly improving and evolving its product and service mix.

Finally, the goal of customer enhancement suggests that loyal customers can be even better customers if they buy more products and services from the company over time. Loyal customers not only provide a solid base for the organisation, they may represent growth potential. This is certainly true for USAA, whose officer members' need for insurance increase over their lifetimes as well as the lifetimes of their children. Other examples abound. A bank checking account customer becomes a better customer when she sets up a savings account, takes out a loan, and/or uses the financial advising services of the bank. And a corporate account becomes a better customer when it chooses to do 75 percent of its business with a particular supplier rather than splitting the business equally among three suppliers. In recent years, in fact, many companies have aspired to be the "exclusive supplier" of a particular product or service for their customers. Over time these enhanced relationships can increase market share and profits for the organisation.

MEANING OF PORTFOLIO

'Portfolio' this term is also used to describe the collection of financial instruments held by an investor or the array of loans advanced by a bank. In financial services, the goal of portfolio analysis is to determine the mix of investments (or loans) that is appropriate to one's needs, resources, and risk preference. In an investment portfolio, the contents should change over time in response to the performance of individual portfolio elements, as well as reflecting changes in the investor's situation or preferences.

We can apply the concept of portfolio to service businesses with an established base of customers. If managers know the annual value of each category of customers (revenues received minus the associated costs of serving them) as well as the proportions represented by each category within the customer base, they can project the ongoing value of all these customers in terms of future revenue streams. Models exist for projecting the future value of the customer portfolio, based upon historical data of customer acquisitions, classes of service purchased, service upgrades and downgrades, and terminations. These historical data can be adapted to reflect pricing and cost changes, as well as the anticipated impact of new marketing efforts. *Weinberg* and *Lovelock* developed such a model for use in cable television systems.

The cable TV industry builds its subscriber base from a variety of segments and is notorious for its "churn", reflecting the continuing need to replace customers who terminate service". Marketing efforts also seek to encourage existing subscribers to trade up from basic levels of service by purchasing the more profitable premium channels. However, the growth of satellite broadcasting and the widespread use of VCRs for playing rental videos present competitive threats to cable TV, with the result that subscribers often choose to downgrade from one or more premium channels to just basic cable service. These are just some of the challenges being faced by marketing managers in this industry as it matures.

Many service firms still focus on the number of customers they serve—an important issue for operations planning—without giving sufficient attention to the *profitability* of each customer. In fact, when service businesses (especially professional firms like accounting or medical practices) are sold, a specific value is often assigned to current clients: The larger the practice and the more profitable each client relationship, the more the business will sell for. A case in point is Comprehensive Accounting Corporation, a franchised bookkeeping service based in Aurora, Illinois. Typically, a privately-owned accounting practice can be sold at a price equivalent to 80% -120% of its current annual billings. However, when a franchisee comes to sell an ongoing comprehensive practice, he or she can expect to get double that amount reflecting the greater profitability resulting from more efficient back office systems.

Another risk is to pay little attention to a particular market segment because individual customers are small and do not generate much revenue. On the other hand, when the segment itself is huge, then the collective value of all the customers may be substantial. British Telecom made the mistake of ignoring the needs of its hundreds of thousands of small business customers, focusing its sales efforts on larger customers. When a new account management program was instituted for the small business market, with contact delivered through inexpensive telephone channels rather than through expensive field visits, satisfied customers responded by sharply increasing their purchases of telecommunications services and equipment.

In talking about customer portfolios, it's important to distinguish between existing relationships —all the customers with whom the firm does business— and the mix of customers being served *at any given point in time*. The former determines valuation, based on current and future earnings potential; the latter is central to decisions on how to optimise use of available capacity over time.

CREATING AND MAINTAINING VALUED RELATIONSHIPS WITH CUSTOMERS

What is valued relationship? It's one in which the customer finds value because the benefits received from service delivery significantly exceed the associated costs obtaining them. For the firm, it's a relationship that id financially profitable over time and in which the benefits of serving a customer may extend beyond revenues to include such intangibles as the learning obtained from working with what customer. Having a good working relationship between two parties implies that they relate positively to one another, as opposed to just conducting a series of almost anonymous transactions. In a healthy and mutually profitable relationship, both parties have an incentive to ensure that it extends for many years. And the seller, in particular, recognises that it pays to take an investment perspective, justifying the upfront costs of acquiring new customers and learning about their needs — which may even make the account unprofitable in its first year — by an expectation of future profits.

Some service businesses conduct a series of discrete transactions with their customers, as in food service, theatre, travel, and freight transport, whereas others enter into a formal agreement to provide continuing service delivery, as in banking, insurance, and telephone service. In theory, it's relatively easy for service firms into the latter category to establish formal relationship with their customers, since each one is identified as a specific account and is billed periodically for the services consumed.

Firms in industries that sell discrete transactions have to work a little harder to establish relationships. In small businesses such as haircutters, frequent customers are (or should be) welcomed as "regulars" whose needs and preferences are remembered. In large firms with substantial customer bases, transactions can still be transformed into relationships by opening accounts, maintaining computerised customer records, and instituting account management programs that may involve a telephone number to call for assistance or even a designated account representative. Long-term contracts between suppliers and their customers take the nature of relationships to a higher level, transforming them into partnerships and strategic alliances. An example of a strategic alliance at a global level is found in the long-term contract between Federal Express's logistics services division and the worldwide operations of the Laura Ashley manufacturing and retail business.

PATHWAYS OF GROWTH

Service businesses can grow in one or more of the following ways:

1. Attract new customers.
2. Encourage existing customers to purchase more units of service.

3. Encourage existing customers to purchase higher value services (for instance, travel first class rather than economy).
4. Reduce the extent of turnover—or "churn"—resulting from desirable customers withdrawing their patronage (a particular problem in easily terminated subscription services such as cable television).
5. Terminate unprofitable, stagnant, or otherwise unsatisfactory relationships and replace them by new customers who better match the firm's profit, growth, and positioning goals.

Traditionally, marketing has overemphasised attraction of new customers. But a well-managed organisation will work hard to retain and grow its existing customers. A widely circulated statement is that on average it costs a firm five to six times as much to attract a new customer as it does to implement retention strategies to hold on to an existing one.

Berry and *Parasuraman* suggest a variety of strategies that service firms can use to maintain and enhance relationships, including such basics as treating customers fairly, offering service augmentations, and treating each customer as though he or she were a segment of one— the essence of mass customisation. *Jackson* argues that service extras often play a key role in building and sustaining relationships between vendors and purchasers of industrial goods. And *Levitt* has this to say about relationship management in professional firms.

It is not surprising that in professional partnership, such as law, medicine, architecture, consulting, investment banking, and advertising, individuals are rated and rewarded by the client relationships they control. These relationships, like other assets, can appreciate or depreciate... Relationship management requires company wide programs for maintenance, investment, improvement, and even for replacement.

The fact is that not all existing customer relationships are worth keeping. Some customers no longer fit the firm's positioning strategy, either because that strategy has changed or because the nature of the customer's behaviour and needs has changed. Careful analysis may show that many relationships are no longer profitable for the firm: they cost more to maintain than the revenues they generate. Just as investors need to dispose of poor investments and banks may have to write off bad loans, so each service firm needs to regularly evaluate its customer portfolio and to consider terminating unsuccessful relationships. Legal and ethical considerations, of course, will determine whether it is proper to take such actions.

CUSTOMER AS ESSENTIAL PART OF THE PRODUCT

Of particular interest for segmentation strategy are those services which are not only delivered to the customer in person but also require each user to share the same facility with many others. Examples of these high-contact, shared services include theatres, restaurants, hotel, airlines, and retail stores. The composition of the customer base has important implications for both the image of the service organisation and the nature of the service "experience". Marketers of may goods and services try to associate their products with particular types of users, often defined in demographic or life style terms. Because this positioning is achieved primarily through advertising, the actual mix of customers is not always clear to each individual user.

In the case of high-contact, shared services, however, the nature of the client base is readily apparent. Any observant customer can quickly determine whether a service such as hotel, theatre, or airline is well or poorly patronised and what sorts of people are using the service — their appearance, age range, apparent income bracket, dress (formal or casual), and whether they appear to have come alone, in couples, or in groups. Also apparent (sometimes obtrusively so!) is how these other customers are behaving: Are they quiet or noisy, slow or active in their movements? Do they appear glum or cheerful, rude or considerate toward others?

Recognising that customers contribute strongly of many high-contact services, marketers need to ensure, first, that they attract customers from the most appropriate dress and behaviour. A restaurant that thrives on business from casually dressed undergraduates would probably not seek middle-aged people in business attire. A hotel that is trying to build up a clientele of business executives may be concerned about how they will react to the presence in the lobby or dinning room dining room of large tour groups on vacation. Similarly, in banking, a high mix of retail business on the floor my discourage business patronage. Audience members at a symphony concert are expected to be quite during the performance so that they do not disturb others' enjoyment of the music. By contrast, active audience participation usually adds to the excitement of attending a rock concert or sports event. There is a fine line, however, between spectator enthusiasm and abusive behaviour by hooligan supporters of rival sports teams.

Many services marketers would probably like to be able to refuse admission to prospective customers who do not fit the market position sought by the organisation. There are ways to discourage unwanted persons from requesting services — for instance, by insisting on certain standards of dress — but outright refusal to admit someone to a service facility may be viewed as illegal or unethical if that person has the ability to pay and is not behaving in a disorderly manner.

One of the marketing's roles is to inform prospective customers in advance about the specific nature of a service, so they know what to expect. This increases the chances of a satisfactory "fit" between different customers — and employment may have to play police officer and either resolve the problem or ask the offending individuals to leave the premises. Failures to do this quickly and efficiently may seriously damage the impression that other customers have of the service, destroying the chances of obtaining repeat business from them.

Homogeneity of the customer base is not always possible or even desirable for many service organisations. Two or more distinct market segments may each contribute importantly to the organisation's success, yet they may not mix well. Ideally, potentially conflicting segments should be separated in their use of the facility; that is they should use the facility sequentially rather jointly, so that they never encounter each other. If this isn't possible, then it may be possible to adopt a strategy of physical separation. Examples include separating airline passengers into first class and economy cabins, placing conventioneers on a different floor of a hotel from other guests, and assigning bank customers with substantial accounts a separate entrance and transaction area from holders of more modest accounts.

POSITIONING PROBLEMS IN CAPACITY-CONSTRAINED ORGANISATIONS

Certain types of service organisations experience significant variations in demand over time. This is particularly true of those involving tangible actions to customers in person or actions to customers in person or actions to their physical possessions. When demand exceeds capacity, then some business will have to be turned away or put on awaiting list. Does it matter whether there are sharp variations in the customer mix between periods of high and low demand? If the off-peak business is financially profitable, can be handled effectively by the service organisation, and is not going to hurt the latter's image, then it is presumably worth taking. Little harm is probably done to an airline's positioning strategy if it uses its uses for charter flights when business demand is low. But if a hotel or restaurant gains a reputation for attracting a totally different type of customer in the off season, there is a risk that this may negate its desired high-season image, particularly if a few high-season customers visit during another season expecting the same types of customers and service levels. One way of resolving this situation is to be quite explicit about the different positioning strategies.

Thus, in the winter months, Boston's Symphony Hall offers classical concerts by the Boston Symphony Orchestra offers classical concerts by the Boston Symphony Orchestra (BSO) with high-priced seats sold to discriminating music lovers. In the spring and early summer, the BSO season is replaced by the Boston Pops. Prices are reduced; tables and chairs replace the orchestra-level seats; and concerts of popular music are played to sociable audiences who talk, drink, and eat as the concert proceeds. The overlap between BSO and Pops audiences is probably quite small, and the distinctions between the two series are generally well known.

FOUNDATIONS FOR RELATIONSHIP STRATEGIES

The preceding discussion should have you convinced that it is good business to focus on current customers, to understand them, and to build strategies around retaining their business, Later in the chapter we describe specific retention strategies that firms use to keep their current customers. But first, in this section, we discuss the foundations needed to begin focusing on retention strategies:

(1) Quality in the Core Service

Retention strategies will have little long-term success unless there is a solid base of service quality and customer satisfaction to build on. This doesn't necessarily mean that firm has to be the very best among its competitor, or "world class" in terms of quality and customer satisfaction. It must be competitive, however, and frequently better than that. All of the retention strategies we describe later are built on the assumption of competitive quality being offered. It does no good to design relationship strategies for inferior services.

(2) Process for Market Segmentation and Targeting in Services

Many aspects of segmentation and targeting for services are the same as those for manufactured goods. The most powerful difference involves between basic marketing principles for segmentation and targeting, the *need for compatibility* in market segments. Because other customers are often present when a service is delivered, service providers must recognise the need to chose compatible segments or to ensure that incompatibles segments are not receiving service at the same time. A second difference between goods and services is that *service providers have a far greater ability* to customise service offerings in real time than manufacturing firms have. The steps and involved in segmenting and targeting services, and a brief discussion of each step follows:

(i) *Identify Bases for Segmentation the Market* : Market segments are formed by grouping customers who share common characteristics that are in some way meaningful to the design, delivery, promotion, or pricing of the service. Common segmentation bases for consumer markets including demographic segmentation, geographic segmentation, psychographic segmentation, and behavioural segmentation. Segments may be identified on the basis of one of these characteristics or a combination. For instance, an urban YMCA may provide services for demographic segments determined by age: preschool and gymnastics for those under 6; basketball for boys and girls ages 5 to 16; and weight training and fitness classes for adults. Within these demographic segments there may be more finely defined services based on lifestyle or usage, for example, fitness classes offered at 5:00 A.M. and 5:30 P.M. for adults who work from 8 A.M. to 5 P.M.

(ii) *Develop Profiles of Resulting Segments*: Once the segments have been identified it is critical to develop profiles of them. In consumer markets these profiles usually involve demographic characterisation or psychographic or usage segments. Of most importance in this stage is clearly understanding how and whether the segments differ from each other in terms of their profiles. If they are not different from each other, the benefits to derived from segmentation, that is, from more precisely identifying sets of customers, will not be realised.

(iii) *Develop Measures of Segment Attractiveness*: The fact that segments of customers exists does not justify a firm's choice of them as targets. The size and purchasing power of the segments must be measurable so that the company can determine if the segments are worth the investment in marketing and relationships costs associated with the group. Later in this chapter, the idea of customer profitability segmentation is presented as an approach for defining and selecting target segments. The chosen segments also must be accessible, meaning that advertising or marketing vehicles must exist to allow the company to reach the customers in the segments.

(iv) *Select the Target Segments*: Based in part on the evaluation criteria just discussed, the services marketer will select the target segment or segments for the service. The firm must decide if the segments is large enough and trending toward growth. Market size will be estimated and demand forecasts completed to determine whether the segment provides strong potential. Competitive analysis, including an evaluation of current and potential competitors, substitute products and services, and relative power of buyers and suppliers, will also help in the final selection of target segments. Finally, the firm must decide whether serving the segment is consistent with company objectives and resources.

(v) *Ensure That the Target Segments are Compatible*: This step, of all the steps in segmentation strategy, is arguably more critical for service companies than for goods companies. Because services are often performed in the presence of the customers are compatible with each other. If during the nonpeak season a hotel chooses to serve two segments that are incompatible with each other — for example, families who are attracted by the discounted prices and college students on their spring break — it may find that the two groups do not merge well. It may be possible to manage the segments in this example so that they do not directly interact with each other, but if not, they may negatively influence each other's experiences, hurting the hotel's future business. In identifying segments it is thus important to think through how they will use the service and whether segments will be compatible.

(vi) *Individualised Service; Segments of One*: When carried to their logical conclusions, both segmentation and customisation lead to "segments of one" or "mass communication," — products and services designed to fit each individual's needs. The inherent characteristics of services lend themselves to customisation and support the possibility of segmenting to the individual level. That is, because services are delivered to people by people, they are difficult to standardise and their outcomes and processes may be inconsistent from provider to provider, from customer to customer, and even from one time period to the next. This inherent heterogeneity is at once a curse and a blessing. On the one hand it means that service delivery is difficult to control and predict, and the resulting inconsistencies may cause customers to questions a firm's reliability. On the other it presents opportunities to customise and tailor the service in ways typically not possible for manufacturers of goods. Because the service itself is frequently delivered in "real time" by "real people" there is an opportunity for one-to-one customisation of the offering. Heterogeneity pursued in a purposeful manner can be turned into an effective customisation strategy.

While segments of one my be practically unrealistic in some cases, the underlying idea of crafting a customised service to fit each individual's needs fits very well with today's consumers, who demand to be treated as individuals and who want their own particular needs satisfied. For service providers who have a limited number of large customers, the segments of one marketing strategy may be obvious. For example, a food management company that provides cafeteria and other types of food services for large manufacturing facilities will customise its services for each large account on the basis of the specific needs of the organisations. Or an advertising agency that specialises in providing communication services for *Fortune* 500 companies will develop individualised plans for each client. In such situations, a relationship manager or an account manager will likely be assigned to a particular customer or client to develop a marketing plan tailored to that client's needs. But even in consumer markets where a company may have hundreds, thousands, or even millions of moments of truth per day, technology combined with employee empowerment is leading the way to mass customisation.

(3) Market Segmentation and Targeting

A second basic foundation of relationship marketing segmentation — learning and defining who the organisation wants to have relationships with. In earlier chapters we discussed consumers of services and described their behaviours, expectations, and perceptions. If we were to aggregate all the behaviour, expectation, and perception information for all the customers in a particular market, we would probably be overwhelmed with the variations across customers. At one extreme, service firms — historically those with a relatively small number of customers, each of whom is vitally important — treat customers as individuals and develop individual marketing plans for each customer. For example, a law firm, an advertising agency, or even a large manufacturer like the *Boeing Airplane Company* will develop service offerings customised specifically and individually for their large corporate clients.

At the other extreme, some service firms offer one service to all potential customers as if their expectations, needs, and preferences were homogeneous. Providers of gas or electricity, for example, often view the needs of customers as varying only in terms of quantity purchased; for this reason their marketing approach is standardised. Between these two extremes are options that most service marketers choose — offering different services to different *groups* of customers. To do this effectively, companies need market segmentation and targeting.

(4) Monitoring Relationships

A thorough means of monitoring and evaluating relationship quality over time is other foundation for relationship marketing. Basic market research in the form of (at a minimum) annual customer relationship surveys can be the foundation for such a monitoring strategy. Current customers should be surveyed to determine their perceptions of value received, quality, satisfaction with services, and satisfaction with the provider relative to competitors. The organisation should also regularly communicate with its best customers in person or over the telephone. In a competitive market it is difficult to retain customers unless they are receiving a base level of quality and value. A well-designed customer database is critical. Knowing who the organisations's current customer are (names, addresses, phone numbers, and so on), what their buying behaviour is, and relevant segmentation information (like demographics, lifestyle, and usage patterns) forms the foundation of a customer database. In cases of customers leaving the organisation, information on termination would also exist in the database. By having such a detailed database on its customers. American express is able to tailor its corporate card member newsletter on the basis of cardholders's spending patterns and preferences. The result of this tailoring is 1,349 versions of the newsletter, targeted at specific customer needs and interests.

These two basics (relationship and customer database) are combined with variety of other types of marketing research as (for example, trailers calls, complaint monitoring, lost customers surveys, and customer visits) to develop a profile of the organisation's customer relationships. With a foundation of customer knowledge combined with quality offerings and value, a firm can engage in retention strategies to hold onto its best customers.

DEVELOPING RELATIONSHIPS

Reichheld maintains that strong relationship marketing depends on the development of four components: products that will build loyalty, employees who are adept at relationships, the appropriate set of customers, and measurement to monitor and improve. We will explore each of these components in turn.

(1) Products

The basis of the new marketing concept is still delivering products that customers want. But sellers no longer think about needs as static; they consider the evolution that needs are likely to follow over time. Because winning new customers is harder than keeping familiar ones, the marketer's best strategy is to develop products and services for the evolving needs of current customers, rather than passing them off to other sellers and trying to find new customers for the same old products. For example, insurance companies provide a range of products that become relevant at different times in a customer's life. They may be able to initially sell a young individual automobile and renter's insurance. As the person matures and his or her needs change, the company should be alert to the opportunities for selling homeowner's insurance' and investments. As the person reaches maturity, services such as health insurance and retirement planning assistance become more important. AT&T's Universal Card is developing its services to meet the changing needs and technological capabilities of its credit card customers. It is currently developing what it calls a "21st Century Personal Servant," an individualised computer account that will extend its current credit service by pulling together all of a consumer's monthly bills into a single statement, allowing the cardholder to pay them electronically, balancing the chequebook, making reservations, and even making recommendations about sales.

This evolution of customer needs over time is typical of most products. Most students today find it hard to imagine that 50 years ago there were retail stores that sold only radios, later adding television sets, because the average customer was intimidated by the technology and wanted a great deal of advice and after-sale service. As the products became commonplace and easier to use, the need for attendant services disappeared and these items could be sold through discount stores with no clerical assistance.

Companies pass through similar life cycles with the products they buy from vendors. A subcomponent may be of keen interest to top management when initially purchased. Its quality, the availability of technical support, and timely delivery schedules will provide the basis for frequent discussions and relationship building between corporate executives at the beginning. However, these concerns will eventually become the routine responsibility of the purchasing agent and the customer firm's own technical staff. If the supplier wishes to remain an important partner in the buyer-seller relationship it must continually enhance the product with value-added enhancements and services. We have-seen how check and stationery suppliers have managed to add services to their product lines that keep their relationships of interest to the top managers of their clients. Similar activity is necessary for any firm that seeks to keep partnerships vibrant and closed to competitive inroads.

In addition to the inevitable evolution of any customer's needs, larger trends are at work as supplier firms throughout the economy have realised the importance of providing products that "entangle" customers in longer-term relationships. *Levitt* anticipated most of these changes a decade ago. As he predicted, sales over time have progressed from selling core products, to augmented products (products with service, installation. guarantees, etc.), integrated systems of products and services that will address many buyer needs. This type of evolution requires expanded commitments by both parties. These relationships are intended to maintain frequent, meaningful contact between partners. The implications for the product offerings necessary to compete in this environment are daunting. No more small ideas or hit-and-run selling. Relationship marketing requires continued attention to the needs of customers, and constant development of new products and services to address their evolving needs.

(2) Employees

Relationship marketing obviously involves the efforts and skills of more individuals than just those in the sales or marketing departments. The need for service and support implies that employees in design, engineering, and manufacturing and/or service delivery must also be intimately acquainted with the needs of the customer and be prepared to deal with individuals from the customer firm. This observation is true for almost any support function in the company. For example, information systems may need to be coordinated to enhance ordering, billing, and other data exchange with customers. Each of the people involved will contribute to the image of the vendor among the buyer's employees. *Gronroos* has spoken of the need to train all employees of service firms to be "part-time marketers," because their interactions with customers are important in maintaining corporate relationships. But it is also true for many employees of manufacturing firms, given that relationships are built upon personal interactions and serving the customers' needs.

What are the implications for human resource policies of this new approach? *Reichheld'* insisted that the key to loyal customers is maintaining loyal employees.

Long-term employees know the organisation's systems better, know how to deal with customers better, and build up personal relationships with customer employees that form the basis of trust so important to the interfirm partnership.

Therefore it is important to design jobs that encourage employees to stay.

Higher compensation can help, of course, but it isn't the only requirement. Career advancement opportunities and empowerment are also important to attracting and keeping top-performing employees. Firms should be aware of the value of personal relationships that employees have with their customers and seek to keep them in contact with the same people. Companies that routinely rotate managers destroy this opportunity for long-term relationships to develop, making it easier for customers to consider defecting. Our research in the banking industry found that many customers become very dissatisfied when personnel are switched from one branch to another.

Reichheld also recommended that firms hire employees on the basis not only of skills and experience, but also of their expected long-term service to the company. For example, he pointed out that the Olive Garden restaurant chain prefers to hire as prospective managers people with strong ties to the communities in which they are expected to develop businesses, and they are kept in those positions to leverage the relationships they develop with the local community. The chain also rewards its staff for loyalty by paying higher wages to those with longer experience with the firm.

Hiring should also consider certain personal characteristics of salespeople and others who will have high interactions with customer personnel. Research has shown that salespeople who are perceived as similar to clients with respect to appearance, lifestyle, and socioeconomic status tend to be more successful, although a rigid policy in this regard could be the basis for discrimination suits. The same research also suggested that potential hirees be screened for social abilities that promote long-term interpersonal relationships.

In general, employees with expected longer tenure with the firm also justify a greater investment in training, which is likely to further increase customer satisfaction. This training must include information and skills necessary to building long-term relationships, lessons that are evidently not part of many current training programs. A recent study of life insurance agents in the United Kingdom found that a large majority of the sample did not feel that suggestions for change and service improvement should come from the needs of the client base. Moreover, most said that they gave a higher priority to attracting new customers than to servicing existing ones. These attitudes against relationship building had not been addressed in their training, which tended to concentrate primarily on the technicalities of insurance. But, such attitudes can be changed.

In the United States, State Farm Insurance has a training program and an incentive system that put equal weight on servicing new and current policies, and the firm is an industry leader in customer loyalty.

A study of the role that sales representatives play as relationship managers between firms found that their training should specifically address several skills. In particular, training in trust-building activities, and skills in questioning and listening to customers are necessary. This includes preparing salespeople to deal with some common ethical dilemmas. In particular, customers occasionally disclose selective information to contact people to test their trustworthiness and honourable intentions, as well as the willingness of the seller firm to reciprocate with equivalent disclosures. To help employees deal with such situations and to maintain cordial relationships with customer firms, training should emphasise rigid corporate standards of integrity regarding the use of such information.

To manage, expand, and grow the relationship, the study's author also recommended that sales reps be trained in a broader set of discipline than those narrowly defined by the current product line. Training in related disciplines such as financing methods or other service management areas that may be of value to customers (again, as in the case of the bank cheque suppliers) can help the sales staff to become truly valuable problem solvers for customers.

Finally, if employees are to be allowed to nurture long-term relationships with customers, the structure of their jobs and organisational responsibilities may need to change. For the past decade major consumer product firms, such as Procter & Gamble and Kraft/General Foods, have experimented with new operating structures that cut across brand lines. The traditional brand management structure doesn't suit itself well to the management of relationships with ever more powerful retail chains and special-needs market segments. In response, manufacturers have experimented with positions such as "segment manager," an individual or team whose job is to coordinate the firm's marketing efforts to address the needs of important customers or segments. Due to the confusion of responsibilities, no single standard has achieved universal acceptance, as the P&G brand management model did for over fifty years. Companies are each seeking their own solutions to the organisational problems of managing products and customers simultaneously. Assigning responsibilities for profit and loss and setting corresponding incentives in these multiply structured environments is likely to remain unsettled for a long time.

Employees must also be trained to calculate the value of customer relationships, so that they can allocate their efforts appropriately. Not every customer is worth the cost of establishing a long-term relationship.

(3) Customers

Not all customers are suitable for long-term relationships. Customers worth pursuing are those that have the greatest lifetime value, and, in particular, those for whom the lifetime value exceeds the cost of acquiring them as customers. We have spoken with bankers who insisted that they lose money on most checking accounts, but then offer large price and merchandise inducements to all customers who open accounts with them. These programs may well attract some customers who will establish long-term relationships with the bank, but in the short-run they will also attract a large number of expensive, nonloyal customers who may put the financial viability of the total program in jeopardy.

Loyalty-based marketing should not be confused with short-term price promotions that seek to generate momentary bursts in sales. They should be carefully focused to identify customers who are likely prospects for long-term relationships. Demographic factors and past purchase histories can be useful in this search. In particular, by identifying segments of similar customers, the firm improves its prospects of tailor-making services that generate high loyalty. For example, older people tend to be more loyal banking customers and also have many similar service needs, whereas younger customers with low balances can be notorious brand switchers. Sometimes a firm may identify a customer segment whose loyalty is counterintuitive and turn its attitudes to its own advantage. For example, USAA, an insurance firm, specialises in policies to military personnel, a community that makes frequent moves and has been notoriously unprofitable to insure. However, USAA created a system that specialises in this group's unique needs, including an immense centralised database that keeps track of clients around the world. This tracking system has provided great convenience to clients who have rewarded the firm with an astonishing 98% retention rate on its automobile insurance policies. Incidentally, the firm's products have also evolved to meet its customers' needs, now including credit cards and investment products.

Based on information obtained from doctors, hospitals, and prenatal training programs, Kimberley Clark, the manufacturer of paper products including Huggies diapers, spent more than $10 million on a database system containing over three-fourths of the names of expectant mothers in the United States. During pregnancy the women receive a series of mailings containing information on maternity and child care, and upon the birth of the baby a coupon for Huggies-which can be tracked to determine whether it is used. How can Kimberly Clark justify this expense? It is the company's feeling that it is building a relationship with the mothers which will result in loyalty to the firm's products. The prize: an average $1400 per year spent on disposable diapers, enough to justify significant expenditures on relationship building.

Identifying and keeping in touch with potentially loyal customers is essential, and computer technology now makes it possible on a scale unimaginable just a few years ago. In fact, an excellent database and the capability to organise, analyse and segment it are absolutely essential to make relationship marketing work. The file must not only contain basic names and addresses but purchase histories and other relevant information that will allow the firm to anticipate a customer's future needs. Vendors are rushing to fill this information need. For example, Equifax Check Services, known to many as a clearinghouse for authorising consumer purchases by cheek at retail stores, actually captures information about each purchase and enters it into the database using the purchaser's driver's license number. The database now contains purchase records on 92 million individuals, including the amount of each purchase, the specific store and the time of day. Equifax can manipulate the database on behalf of its clients to produce lists or even direct mailings.

How can one decide which customers are profitable enough to keep or to pursue? Myer recommended a measure of customer value called Customer Return on Assets (CRA). The basic idea is to measure the profitability of relationships with individual customers, something often overlooked by accounting systems that tend to focus more on product performance. Systems that measure revenue only, combined with a dedication to high service levels at any cost, are likely to lead to terrible misallocations of effort by the sales force and other customer relations personnel. Relationship managers should also he tracking the costs of maintaining relationships. These costs can he traced to individual accounts and include sales, costs, service costs, and other costs related to serving the particular account. The formula for computing CRA was developed primarily for manufacturers selling to wholesale and retail chain customers, but the formulas can be computed for other sellers of products and services as well.

The CRA for this client is 24.6%, slightly lower than the 30% average for many of the actual customers in Myer's study. The first category of costs contains the usual measures of costs of sales, indicating a 48% gross margin on sales. The second category includes the costs of marketing to the particular customer. Specifically, it consists of the costs of selling, promotion, the development of specific products, storage and transportation, and extra service required to keep the account satisfied. Note, for example, that this customer is receiving extra services amounting to 10% of revenues. When these marketing costs are subtracted from the gross margin, the result is the contribution of the customer's sales to corporate overhead. This amount is the return on the manufacturer's investment in the customer.

The manufacturer's investment in the customer is the amount of capital tied up in maintaining the account. In particular, the manufacturer is carrying accounts receivable from the customer, and holds certain finished goods in inventory for later shipment to the customer. For this particular client, average accounts receivable amount to 17% of annual revenues, equal to more than two months of sales, indicating that this customer is slow in paying bills. The average value of equipment and materials held in inventory for this customer represent 2% of sales.

What levels are appropriate for a given seller will depend on the nature of the product and its stage in the life cycle, competition, the state of the economy, and other factors. So each firm must determine what standards are acceptable for its own situation. Even without identifying ideal objective standards for the CRA items, the calculations are useful in comparing the costs to serve different customers. Firms that applied this formula found wide variation in costs of serving customers, particular in promotion expenses because of the fact that some customers bought only on promotions. Other wide variations were discovered in selling costs and in accounts receivable. Interestingly, the analysis also found that the fastest-growing customers were generally the least profitable.

Myer recommended several actions to take to deal with the variability in demands and profitability of different customers, based on the calculation of CRA for each account. Some customers may not be worth the expense of keeping, but others may be attractive long-term partners if the pricing schedules they now pay can be adjusted to reflect more accurately the higher costs of serving them. The challenge is to make those with low CRA more profitable without scaring them away. In particular,

1. The firm should decide what range of CRAs is acceptable. The key is long-term viability more than the current immediate return.
2. A menu of highly flexible options should he drawn up to reflect the range of service options required by different customers, including a greater number of discount schedules, delivery options, promotional packages, and electronic ordering options than the one or two now generally offered.
3. Prices should then be assigned to each service option to reflect the cost of providing it. This will allow customers to specify the services they need and are willing to pay for on an *a la carte* basis. The different prices should be defensible to customers as reflecting the costs of offering the options.
4. Finally, selling the new pricing schedule to customers may be difficult, particularly to those who in the past demanded and received lots of services for no extra cost. Myer recommended a two-pronged strategy to help customers accept the new pricing option: First, rather than positioning additional services as extra charges, present the deletion of services as discounts from the full-service price. Second, these programs must be phased in gradually over time, with a small initial spread that is gradually widened over time.

Although many marketing firms don't do analyses of this type, such calculations are clearly prerequisites to choosing and developing profitable relationships. A CRA analysis may also reveal segmentations based on account service needs that will enable the seller to serve them more profitably than would the usual segmentation based on size or region. Speciality teams can be assigned to deal with customers with similar service needs, a practice that may help reduce the costs of selling to them and managing their accounts. The result can also be improved quality of the relationship.

(4) Measurement

As with any investment, measures of outcome are necessary to control the process, to assess its success, and to provide feedback for assessing the relative effectiveness of various programs. *Reichheld* asserts that most relationship-building programs will not produce measurable bottom-line results for several years. Instead, his recommendation is to track a leading indicator of profits, customer retention, in the discussion of the ROQ model. As we have warned, monitoring satisfaction alone is insufficient, since satisfaction levels are often very high, even though retention is not.

Myer recommended that market share with key accounts be tracked. Because of his recommendation that financial data be kept for each Account, he also suggests that CRA be tracked by account. However, he also recommends keeping some softer measures that directly address relationship marketing. For example, to what extent have we improved the cooperation and participation of key accounts? Have all members of the supply chain benefited, and are customers sufficiently aware of those benefits? These last measures are not easy to define objectively, but they seem well worth following.

Unfortunately, evaluating expenditures in terms of their long-term value to the firm runs counter to standard accounting practice. Currently there are no standardised approaches to measuring the value of a firm's customer relationships. The subjectivity of the judgments necessary to quantify this concept makes it an unlikely prospect for standardised accounting standards in the near future. Therefore marketing must press forward in its effort to find useful measures to track and control this key activity.

(5) Other Implementation Issues

In summary, successful relationship marketing is a three-stage process. *First* of all, the company must have an excellent knowledge of its customers. For consumer marketers and industrial marketers with large numbers of customers, an extensive database containing information on current and potential customers is required. *Secondly*, the company must have the capability of tailoring its marketing programs to individual customers based on customer characteristics and preferences. *Finally*, it must be able to track individual purchase histories to be able to assess the costs of acquiring and servicing each customer compared to the customer's lifetime value.

For many years Sears Roebuck & Company has been at the forefront in tracking sales to individual customers and in running loyalty programs for many of its retail customers. Programs such as its Mature Outlook, New Movers, College Advantage, and its recently launched Sears Best Customer program are all intended to increase customer loyalty to the chain and to add a more personal touch to its customer dealings, in spite of the firm's image as a retail giant. A Sears executive recently outlined three important factors in establishing relationships with individual customers. These are:

1. *Keep it Local:* Because a relationship implies person-to-person contact, all of the Sears programs are the responsibility of individual store managers, rather than of the chain itself.
2. *The Program Must Include Both 'Hard" and "Soft" Benefits:* Hard benefits include discounts, promotions, etc. that are available only to program members that give the program meaning. Soft benefits include giving special priority attention to program members with problems and special requests.
3. *Communication is Essential:* Sears continually reinforces its message to its better customers that they are special, using between six and eight communications per year, including announcements, promotions, and surveys.

Managers insist that the value of these programs are cumulative, and that the impact on loyalty becomes more powerful each year.

STAGES OF RELATIONSHIP STRATEGIES

Leonard Berry and *A. Parasuraman* have developed a framework for understanding types of retention strategies. The framework suggests that relationships marketing can occur at different levels and that each successive level of strategy results in ties that bind the customer a little closer to the firm. At each successive level, the potential for sustained competitive advantage is also increased. Building on the levels of the retention strategy idea. There are four types of retention strategies, which are as follows:

STAGE 1— FINANCIAL BONDS

At Stage 1, the customer is tied to the firm primarily through financial incentives — lower prices for greater volume purchases or lower prices for customers who have been with the firm long time. Examples of level 1 relationship marketing are not hard to find. Think about the airline industry and related travel service industries like hotels and car rental companies. Frequent flyer programs provide financial incentives and car rental companies do the same. Long-distance telephone companies in the United States have engaged in a similar battle, trying to provide volume discounts and other price incentives to retain market share and build a loyal customer base. One reason these financial incentive programs proliferate is that they are not difficult to initiate and frequently result in at least short-term profits/ gains. Unfortunately, financial incentiveness do not generally provide long-term advantages to a firm because, unless combined with another relationship strategy, they don't differentiate the firm from its competitors in the long run. Many travellers belongs to several frequent flyer programs and don't hesitate to trade off among them. And there has been considerable customer switching every month among the major telecommunication suppliers. While price and other financial incentiveness are important to customers, they are generally not difficult for competitors to imitate because the primary customised element of the marketing mix is price.

Other type of retention strategies that depend primarily on financial rewards are focused on bundling and cross-selling of services. Frequent flyer programs again provide a common example. Many airlines link their reward programs with hotel chains, auto rental, and in some cases credit card usage. By linking airline mileage points earned to usage of other firm's services, customers can enjoy even greater financial benefits in exchange for their loyalty.

In other cases, firms aim to retain their customers by simply offerings their most loyal customers the assurance of stable prices, or at least lower prices increases than those paid by new customers. In this way they reward their loyal customers by sharing with them some of the cost savings and increased revenue the firm receives through serving them over time.

While widely and increasingly used as retention tactics, loyalty programs based on financial rewards merit caution. As pointed earlier, these programs are often easily imitated. Thus any increased usage or loyalty from customers may be short-lived. Second, these strategies are not likely to be successful unless they are structured so that they truly lead to repeat or increased usage rather than serving as means to attract new customers and potentially causing endless switching among competitors.

STAGE 2 — SOCIAL BONDS

Stage 2, strategies bind customers to the firm through more than financial incentives. Although price is still assumed to be important, level 2 retention marketers build long-term relationship through social and interpersonal as well financial bonds. Customers are viewed as "clients," not nameless faces, and becomes individuals whose needs and wants the firm seeks to understand.

Social, interpersonal bonds are common among professional service providers (lawyers, accountants, teachers) and their clients as well as among personal care providers (hairdressers, counsellors, health care providers) and their clients. A dentist who takes a few minutes to review her patient's file before coming into the exam room is able to jog her memory on personal facts about the patient (occupation, family details, interests, dental health history. By bringing these personal details into the conversation, the dentist reveals her genuine interest in the patient in the patient as an individual and build social bonds.

Interpersonal bonds are also common in business-to-business relationships where customers develop relationships with salespeople and/or relationship managers working with their firms. Recognising the value of continuous relationships in building loyalty, Caterpillar Corporation credits much of its noted success to its extensive, stable distribution organisation worldwide. Caterpillar is the world's largest manufacture of mining, construction, and agriculture heavy equipment. Although its engineering and product quality are superior, the company attributes much of its success to its strong dealer network and product support services offered throughout the world. CEO David Fites contends that knowledge of the local market and close relationships with customers that Caterpillar's dealers provide is invaluable: "Our dealers tend to be prominent business leaders in their service territories who are deeply involved in community activities and who are committed to living in the area. Their reputations and long-term relationships are important because selling our products is a personal business."

Sometimes relationships are formed with the organisation due to the social bonds that develop *among customers* rather than between customers and the provider of the service. This is frequently the case in health clubs, country clubs, educational settings, and other service environments where customers interact with each other. Over time the social relationships they have with other customers are important factors that keep them from switching to another organisation. One company that has built a significant strategy around customer-to-customer bonds is Harley Davidson with its local Harley Owners Groups, HOGs. HOGs are involved in local rallies, tours, and parties, as well as participating in national HOG events organised by the company.

Social bonds alone may not tie the customer permanently to the firm, but they are much more difficult for competitors to imitate than are price incentives. In the absence of strong reasons to shift to another provider, interpersonal bonds can encourage customers to stay in a relationship. In combination with financial incentives, social bonding strategies may be very effective.

STAGE 3 — CUSTOMISATION BONDS

Stage 3 strategies involve more than social ties and financial incentives, although there are commonly elements of level 1, level 2 strategies encompassed within a customisation strategy, and vice versa. For example, in the Caterpillar dealership strategy just described, dealers are relied on not just to form strong personal commitments to customers. They are also relied on to feed information back into the system to help Caterpillar customise services to fit developing customer needs.

Two commonly used terms fit within the customisation bonds approach: *mass communication* and *customer intimacy*. Both of these strategies suggest that customer loyalty can be encouraged through intimate knowledge of individual customers and through the development of "one-to-one" solutions that fit the individual customers' needs. Mass communication has been defined as "the use of flexible processes and organisational structures to produce varied and often individually customised products and services at the price of standardised, mass-produced alternatives. Mass customisation does not work harder for what they want; rather, it means providing then through little effort on their part tailored services to fit their individual needs.

STAGE 4 — STRUCTURAL BONDS

Stage 4 strategies are the most difficult to imitate and involve structural as well as financial, social, and customisation bonds between the customer and the firm. Structural bonds are created by providing services to the client that are frequently designed right into the service delivery system for that client. Often structural bonds are created by providing customised services to the client that are technology based and make the customer more productive.

An example of structural bonds can be seen in a business-to-business context with Allegiance Healthcare Corporation. By working closely with its hospital supply ordering, delivery, and billing that have greatly enhanced its value as a supplier. For example, Allegiance developed "hospital-specific pallet architecture," which meant all items arriving at a particular hospital were shrink-wrapped with labels visible for easy identification. Separate pallets were assembled to reflect the individual hospital's storage system so that instead of miscellaneous supplies arriving in boxes sorted at the convenience of Allegiance's internal needs, they arrived on "client-friendly" pallets designed to suit the distribution needs of the individual hospital. By linking the hospital through its ValueLink service into a database ordering system, and providing enhanced value in the actual delivery, Allegiance has structurally tied itself to its more than 150 acute care hospitals in the hospitals in the United States. In addition to the enhanced service ValueLink provides, Allegiance estimates that the system saves its customers an average of $5,00,000 more each year.

Another example of level 4 strategy can be seen in the competitive battle between UPS and Federal Express. In the mid 1900s, both firms attempted to tie their clients closer to them with free computers — Federal Express's Powerships and UPS's MaxiShips — that stored addresses and shipping data, printed mailing labels, and helped track packages. By tying into one of the systems a company saved time overall and could better track daily shipping records. As technology has continued to advance, the two companies have tied their customers to them through the Web and now through wireless technology.

But there is also a potential downside to this arrangement from the customer's perspective. Customers may fear that tieing themselves too closely to one provider may not allow then to take advantage of potential price savings from other providers in the future.

IS CUSTOMER ALWAYS RIGHT?

The assumption that all customers are good customers is also very compatible with the belief that "the customer is always right," an almost sacrosanct tenet of business. Yet any service worker can tell you that this statement isn't always true, and in some cases it may be preferable for the firm and the customer to not continue their relationship. This section presents a view of customer relationships suggesting that all relationships may not be beneficial, and that every customer is not right all of the time.

(1) The Wrong Segment

A company cannot target its services to all customers; some segments will be more appropriate than others. It would not be beneficial to either the company or the customer for a company to establish a relationship with a customer whose needs the company cannot meet. For example, a school offering a lock-step, daytime MBA program would not encourage full-time working people to apply for its program, nor would a law firm specialising in government issues establish a relationship with individuals seeking advice on trusts and estates. These examples seem obvious. Yet firms frequently do give in to the temptation to make a sale by agreeing to serve a customer who would be better served by someone else.

Similarly, it would not be wise to forge relationships simultaneously with incompatible market segments. In many service businesses (such as restaurants, hotels, tour package operators, entertainment, and education), customers experience the service together and can influence each other's perceptions about value received. Thus, to maximise service to core segments, an organisation may choose to turn away marginally profitable segments that would be incompatible. For example, a conference hotel may find that mixing executives in town for a serious educational program with students in town for a regional track meet may not be wise. If the executive group is a key long-term customer, the hotel may choose to pass up the sports group in the interest of retaining the executives.

(2) Not Profitable in the Long Term

In the absence of ethical or legal mandates, organisations will prefer not to have long term relationships with unprofitable customers. Some segments of customers will not be profitable for the company even if their needs can be met by the services offered. This may be the case when there are not enough customers in the segment to make it profitable to develop a marketing approach, when the segment cannot afford to pay the cost of the service, or when the projected revenue flows from the segment would not cover the costs incurred to originate and maintain the business. For example, in the banking industry it has been estimated that 40 to 70 percent of customers served in a typical bank are not profitable in the sense that the costs of serving these customers exceed the revenues generated.

At the individual customer level, it may not be profitable for a firm to engage in a relationship with a particular customer who has bad credit or who is a poor risk for some other reason. Retailers, banks, mortgage companies, and credit card companies routinely refuse to do business with individuals, whose credit histories are unreliable. Although the short-term sale may be beneficial, the long-term risk of nonpayment makes the relationship unwise from the company's point of view. Similarly, some car rental companies have begun to check into the driving records of customers and are rejecting bad-risk drivers. This practice, while controversial, is logical from the car rental companies' point of view because they can cut back on insurance costs and accident claims (thus reducing rental costs for good drivers) by not doing business with accident-prone drivers.

Beyond the monetary costs associated with serving the wrong customers, there can be substantial time investments in some customers that, if actually computed, would make them unprofitable for the organisation. Everyone has had the experience of waiting in bank, a retail store, or even in an education setting while a particularly demanding customer seems to use more than his share of the service provider's time. The dollar value of the time spent with a specific customer is typically not computed or calculated into the price of the service.

In a business-to-business relationship, the variability in time commitment to customers is even more apparent. Some customers may use considerable resources of the supplier organisation through inordinate numbers of phone calls, excessive requests for information, and other time-consuming activities. In the legal profession, clients are billed for every hour of the firm's time that they use in this way because time is essentially the only resource the firm has. Yet in other service businesses, all clients essentially pay the same regardless of the time demands they place on the organisation.

It should be noted that the best customers are not just the ones that generate the most profit. Especially in business-to-business settings, those customers that inspire the best ideas and innovations are also good relationship customers even if they don't necessarily generate the highest profits. Customers, who are willing to be involved in new service development or who are on the cutting edges of their own industries can help the organisation develop and maintain quality services for the entire marketplace. These customers benefit the organisation beyond the profits they generate.

(3) Difficult Customers

Managers have repeated the phrase "the customer is always right" so often that it should be accepted by every employee in every service organisation. Why isn't it? Perhaps because it simply isn't true. The customer isn't always right. No matter how frequently it is said, it doesn't become reality, and service employees know it.

Employees recognise that beyond the monetary and time loss that can be traced to some customers, there are customers who are simply difficult to work with for a variety of reasons. Because of the stress they place on the organisation and its employees, some organisations may choose to avoid relationships with these customers.

Although often these difficult customers will be accommodated and employees can be trained to recognise and deal with them appropriately, at times the best choice may be not to maintain the relationship at all—especially at the business-to-business level where long-term costs to the firm can be substantial. Take, for example the view of some of Madison Avenue's major ad agencies. "Some ad agencies say some accounts are so difficult to work with that the simply cannot —or will not— service them. Difficult clients paralyse, the ad agency for a variety of reasons. Some ask that a particular ad campaign work for all of their diverse constituencies at the same time, which in some cases may be next to impossible. Others require so much up— front work and ad testing before selecting the agency that the work is essentially done for free by those agencies not selected. Other clients are stingy; require dozens of storyboards before settling on a concept; or require a lot of direct, frequently disruptive, involvement in the production process. As a result agencies have become more vary of chasing every client that comes along. "As in a marriage, all agencies and all clients don't work well together."

(4) Should Firms "Fire" Their Customers?

A logical conclusion to be drawn from the preceding sections is that firms should somehow get rid of those customers who are not right for the company. More and more companies are making these types of decisions based on the belief that troublesome customers are usually less profitable and less loyal, and that it may be counterproductive to attempt to retain their business. Another reason for firing a customer is the negative effect that these customers can have on employee quality of life and morale.

This is exactly what one company concluded when a client, the CEO of an Internet start-up company, paged one of their employees at her home on the West Coast at 4 A.M. asking her to order a limousine for him in New York City. This was enough to push the employee over the edge and cause her boss to agree that they should "fire" this client. They did so by directly telling him the relationship wasn't working out and to take his business elsewhere.

Another company that took reducing its customer base to the extreme is Nypro — a global, employee-owned company specialising in moulded plastics applications for such as Gillette, Abbott Laboratories, Hewlett-Packard, and other large organisations. In the 1980s Nypro reduced its customers base from 800 to approximately 30 clients on the belief that it could better serve those clients and grow more effectively if it focused on fewer relationships. Nypro adopted a customer intimacy strategy and tied itself closely to this much smaller number of clients. Some of these clients have now been with Nypro for over 40 years. Over time Nypro has selectively added clients to this base, and the company has enjoyed 15 consecutive years of record sales and profit growth with profits up 41 percent in 2000 over the preceding year.

Although it may sound like a good idea, "firing" customers is not that simple and needs to be done in a way that avoids negative publicity or negative word of mouth. Sometimes raising prices or charging for services that previously had been given away for free can move unprofitable customers out of the company. Helping a client find a new supplier who can better meet its needs is another way to gracefully exit a nonproductive relationship. If the customer has become too demanding, negotiating expectations or finding more efficient ways to serve the client can also salvage the relationship. If not, both parties may find an agreeable way to end the relationship.

REALISING THE FULL PROFIT POTENTIAL OF A CUSTOMER RELATIONSHIP

How much is a customer worth in terms of profits? In 1990, Reichheld and Sasser analysed the profit per customer in different service businesses, categorised by the number of years that a customer had been with the firm. The industries studied (with their average profits from a first-year customer shown in parentheses) were : Credit cards ($30), industrial laundry ($144), industrial distribution ($45), and automobile servicing ($25). They found that the longer customers remained with a firm in each of these industries, the more profitable they became to serve. Annual profits per customer, which have been indexed over a 5- year period to easier comparison.

Underlying this profit growth, say the two researchers, are four factors working to the supplier's advantage to create incremental profits. In order of magnitude at the end of seven years, these factors are:

(i) Profit from increased purchases (or in a credit card or banking environment, higher account balances).

(ii) Profit from reduced operating costs.

(iii) Profit from referrals to other customers.

(iv) Profit from price premium.

Reicheld argues that the economic benefits of customer loyalty often explain why one firm is more profitable than a competitor. Loyal customers often become less expensive to serve as they become more efficient in their dealings with the supplier and increase their spending over time (not just in volume but also in terms of willingness to pay a price premium on occasion. Further, the upfront costs of attracting them can be amortised over many years. Finally, because they are satisfied, these customers act as unpaid sales representatives, recommending the supplier and its products to prospective buyers.

For profit-seeking firms, the potential profitability of a customer should be a key driver in marketing strategy. Grant and Schlesinger declare:

" Achieving the full profit of each customer relationship should be the fundamental goal of every business... Even using conservative estimate, the gap between most companies' current and full potential performance is enormous."

They suggest analysis of three gaps between actual and potential performance:

1. What percentage of its target customers does a firm currently have (market share) and what percentage could it potentially obtain?
2. What is the current purchasing behaviour of customers in each target segment? Now, what would be the impact on sales and profits if they exhibited the ideal behaviour profile of (say) buying all services offered by the firm, using these to the exclusion of any purchases from competitors, and paying full service?
3. How long, on average, do customers remain with the firm? What impact would it have if they remained customers for life?

Many elements are involved in gaining market share, cross selling other products and services to existing customers, and creating long-term loyalty. The process starts, as we suggested earlier, by identifying and targeting the right customers, then learning everything possible about their needs, including their preferences for different forms of service delivery. Doing an outstanding job of satisfying these goods lies at the basis of service quality programs. The big challenge for service marketers lies not only in giving prospective customers a reason to do business with their firms, but also in offering them incentives to remain customers and even increase their purchases — but without giving away all the potential profits in the process. To conclude this section, we look at the evolution of programs to reward frequent flyer programs to reward frequent users of a service, focusing on frequent flyer programs in the airline industry. We then examine details of the British Airways' Executive Club for insights into strategies for gaining as high a share as possible of a business passenger's travel expenditures.

Rewarding Frequent Users of a Service

The original "frequent flyer" program was established by American Airlines in 1983. Targeted at business travellers (the individuals who fly the most), this promotion enabled passengers to claim travel awards based on the accumulated distance they had travelled on the airline. "Miles" flown became the scoring system that entitled customers to claim from a menu of free tickets in different classes of service. American was taken by surprise at the enormous popularity of this program. Other major airlines soon felt obliged to follow and implemented similar schemes of their own. Each airline hoped that its own frequent flyer program, branded with a distinctive name such as "Advantage (American)" or "Mileage Plus (United), would induce a traveller to remain brand loyal, even to the extent of some inconvenience in scheduling. However, many business travellers enrolled in several programs, thereby limiting the effectiveness of these promotions for individuals carriers.

To make their programs more appealing, the airlines signed cooperative agreements with regional and international carriers, as well as with "partners" hotels and rental car firms, allowing customers to credited with mileage accrued through a variety of travel-related activities. What had begun as a one-year promotion by American Airlines was soon transformed in to a permanent — and quite expensive — part of the industry's marketing structure.

As time passed, airlines in the US started to use double and triple mileage bonus awards as a tool for demand management, seeking to encourage travel on less popular routes. A common strategy was to award bonus miles for changing flights at an intermediate hub rather than taking a nonstop flight or for flying during the low season when many empty seats were available. To avoid giving away too many free seats at peak time, many airline offered more generous redemption terms during off-peak periods; some even blocked key vacation periods like Christmas and New Year, making them ineligible for free tickets.

Competitive strategies often involved bonus miles, too. Bonus wars broke out on certain routes. At the height of its mid-1980s battle with New York Air on the lucrative 230-mile (370 km) New York-Boston shuttle service, the PanAm Shuttle offered passengers 2000 miles for a one-way trip and 5000 miles for a round trip completed within a single day. Bonus miles also came to awarded for travel in first or business class. And bonuses might also be awarded to encourage passengers to sample new services or to complete market research surveys.

To record the mileage of passengers enrolled in their frequent in their frequent flyer programs, the airlines had to install elaborate tracking systems that captured details of each flight. They also had to create systems for recording and maintaining each member's current account status and to devise procedures for redeeming miles for free travel (some of these activities were often outsourced to independent contractors).

American Airlines was probably the first carrier to realise the value of its frequent flyer database for learning more about the travel behaviour of its best customers, enabling it to create highly-targeted direct mail lists, such as travellers who flew regularly between a certain pair of cities. The airline was also able to examine bookings for individual flights to see what percentage of seats was filled by frequent flyers, most of whom were probably travelling on business and therefore not as price sensitive as people travelling on vacation or pleasure trips. This information proved to have great value when countering competition from low-cost discount airlines, whose primary target segment was price-conscious pleasure travellers. Rather than reducing all fares on all flights between a pair of cities, American realised that it only needed to offer a limited numbers of discount fares, primarily on those flights known to be carrying significant numbers of non-business passengers. Even on such flights, the airline would seek to limit availability of discount fares by such means as requiring an advance purchase or an extended stay in the destination city, so that it would be difficult for business travellers to trade down from full fare to a discount ticket.

A number of other service businesses have sought to copy the airlines with frequent user programs of their own. Hotels, car rental firms, telephone companies, retailers, and even credit card issuers have been among those that seek to identify and reward their best customers. Although some provide their own rewards-such as free merchandise, class of vehicle upgrades, of free hotel rooms in vacation resorts-such as free merchandise, class of vehicle upgrades, or free hotel rooms in vacation resorts-many firms denominate their awards in miles that can be credited to a selected frequent-flyer program. In short, air miles have become a form of promotional currency in service sector.

Rewarding Value of Use, Not just Frequency, at British Airways

Many international carriers initially resisted creating frequent flyer programs of their own. They were concerned not only about the expense, but also that these programs required the airline to give award claimants free seats that could have been sold, during periods of high demand, to paying passengers. However, the competitive threat presented by these programs, especially on routes served by North American carriers, eventually became too strong to resist. Progressive airlines, such as British Airways, also recognized the potential of frequent flyer programs for helping a carrier learn more about its best customers and for building brand loyalty.

British Airways (BA) created its own program, known as Executive Club. In the light of operating experience, modifications to the program were introduced in 1996. Unlike many programs, in which customer usage is measured simply in miles, Executive Club members receive both Miles toward redemption of air travel wards and points towards silver or gold tier status. Travel on BA's partner airlines US Air and Qantas (in each of which it holds a minority share) both qualify for miles: in addition, US Air flights also qualify for point for points.

For example, silver and gold cardholders are entitled to special benefits while they are actually travelling, with particular reference to priority reservations and the quality of on-the ground service. For instance, even if a gold cardholder is only travelling in economy class, he or she will be entitled to first-class standards of treatment at check-in and in the airport lounges. But whereas miles can be accumulated for up to five years (by US-based members), tier status is only valid for fifteen months beyond the calendar year in which it was earned. In short, the right to special privileges must be re-earned every year. The objective of awarding tier status (which is not unique to BA) is to encourage passengers who have a choice of airline to concentrate their travel on British Airways, rather than belonging to several frequent flyer programs and collecting mileage awards from all of them. Few passengers travel with such frequency that they will be able to obtain the benefits of gold tier status (or its equivalent) or more than one airline.

The assignment of points also varies according to class of service: BA seeks to recognise higher ticket expenditures with proportionately higher awards. Longer trips earn more points than shorter ones (a domestic trip in economy class generates 15 points, a transatlantic trip 60 points, and a trip from the UK to Australia or New Zealand, 100 points). To reward higher ticket prices, passengers earn points at double the economy rate if they travel in Club (business class), at triple the rate in first class, and more than four times the economy rate if flying

Concorde supersonic service between London and New York. Likewise, passengers get first class-of-getting mileage bonuses for both Club (+25%) and First (+50%) UK-based passengers get even higher bonuses. In contrast, certain discounted fares do not qualify for either miles or points.

To encourage gold and silver card holders to remain loyal to BA at continuing high levels of expenditures on tickets, BA offers incentives for Executives Club members to retain their current tier status (or to move up from silver to gold card). Silver cardholders receive a 25% bonus on all air miles, regardless of class of service, while gold cardholders receive a 100% bonus; in other words, it doesn't pat to spread the miles among several frequent-flyer programs. The airline also makes it slightly easier to retain existing tier status once this has been achieved. For instance, it takes an annual total of 700 points to qualify for silver status and 1700 points for gold tier status, but once a traveller has reached that level, requalification requires only 500 points for silver or 1200 points for gold. Although the airline makes no promises on complimentary upgrades, members of BA's Executive Club are more likely to receive such an invitation than other passengers, with tier status being an important consideration. For obvious reasons, however, BA does not wish its most frequent travellers to feel that they can plan on buying a less expensive ticket and then receive an upgrade!

Of course, rewards alone will not suffice to retain an airline's most desirable customers. If customers are dissatisfied with the quality of service they receive, they may quickly become disloyal. Neither BA nor any other service business which has instituted an awards program for frequent users can ever afford to lose sight of its broader service quality goals.

THE FUTURE OF RELATIONSHIP MARKETING

Technology holds the key to the future of relationship marketing, particularly with individual consumers. Marketers in many consumer categories now have the technical capability to track purchases of individuals and build databases from these records. The cost of doing so has fallen to a thousandth of what it was in 1970.33 Firms like Lands' End, L. L. Bean, and American Express consider their databases to he among their most valuable assets. Artificial intelligence programs as well as simpler models can be used to infer individual customer needs and preferences from these databases. In this way, customer purchases are the equivalent of a continuous conversation with the seller.

The seller's ability to speak directly back to the buyer is also improving. The databases can be combined with new printing technologies to communicate with consumers on an individual basis. It is now technically possible for a firm like Lands' End to print individual catalogues for each customer on its mailing list, although the cost is probably yet too great to make it practical. Nevertheless, the day is coming. Magazine publishers already print thousands of slightly different editions of their publications targeted to customers with different needs and backgrounds. Coming developments in telecommunications technology, will also give marketers the ability to communicate directly and interactively with customers. The potential for relationship building is enormous. The deciding factor will be how fast costs fall to make these activities feasible.

The future of relationship marketing is hard to predict with certainty because the tools on which it will rely are evolving so rapidly. At the same time, relationship marketing does not have a particularly long history on which to base assessments of its strategic potency or to justify massive expenditures. Nevertheless, the natural next step for marketing to take would seem to be getting back to the one-on-one interactions that marketers thought they had lost when their markets expanded beyond their local communities.

CASE STUDY

Introduction

It's a whole discussion about marketing and selling concept. It describe how the time changed, the way marketing concept changed and in this today's singing and dancing world we have so many marketing and customer relationship theories.

Now-a-days companies focusing on marketing education and marketing practice by using 4 P's, product, price, promotion, and place.

Companies adopting concept of promises made and kept by both sides. Industries providing value-added services, now they bother about customers with assistance in the mounting and maintenance of it's bearing are to reduce downtime in their factories.

Down or reduce price is other factor, which is used for alluring or enticing customers.

Now-a-days the customer relationship become more demanding having benefits too but need money time and effort. The kind of relationship directly effect shares of that particular company.

Relationship marketing depends upon several things particularly on the number of customer and the margins on products.

The main aim of relationship marketing is to build and maintain a base of committed customers who are profitable for the organization and for to achieve this aim they focus attraction, retention and enhancement of customer relationship.

At the same time the valued relationship is in vogue customers are essential part of the product the success and fall today totally depends on customers. Now the main pillars for relationship strategies all quality in the core service, market segmentation, etc.

With the passage of time every industry and company need some supervillaince or want to keep right vigil over their customers, so that they can check out the upcoming problems.

The marketing concept have on more aspect developing relationship where it depends on four components, products, employees, set of customer and monitor and improve.

To achieve this target there are some strategies of relationship (strategies) like-wise financial bonds, social bonds, customization bonds, structural bonds.

Now companies or industries are in tenterhook that every time whatever he feedback given by customers is right or wrong. If companies get wrong perception then it can be detrimental for nuclear disaster for that particular company.

To reduce such kind of problems companies have some particular strategies or some watchdogs who can always keep a tight vigil over customers.

PESTICIDE COCKTAILS IN PEPSI

On Aug. 5, 2003 the center for science and environment, in a startling revelation, said that aerated waters produced by soft drinks manufacturers, including multinational giants, PEPSICO and COCA COLA, contain pesticides and insecticides.

Sunita Narain, director of CSE told that 12 major cold drink brands sold in Delhi and around contain a deadly cocktail of pesticides residues. According to the test conducted by the pollution monetary laboratory of CSE, all samples contained residuals of 4 extremely toxic pesticides and insecticides—linedane, DDT, MALATHION, and CHLORPYRIFOS. The PML team involved in the tests was doctor H.B. Mathur, Dr. Sapna Jonson and Avinash Kumar.

After the tests it was found that these pesticides include potantcarcinogens, which could cause cancer and reduce bone mineral density. The levels of pesticides residues for exceeded the maximum residue limit for pesticides in water used as food, set down by the European economic commission (EC) in all PEPSICO brand, total pesticides and average where 0.0180mg/ltr, 36 times higher than the EEC limit of total pesticides at 0.0005mg/ltr.

In this entire episode, the most shocking part is the double standards of these global players, to talk of corporate responsibility and maintaining global standards. The bottles of COKE and PEPSI that we purchase from stores in the USA for study had no residue, while the residue is 37 times higher in PEPSI in INDIA.

Also to take matter worst, there are no norms for "This food industry".

Due to such a huge amount of pesticides found in Pepsi there was a lot of hue and cry and as a result soft drinks of this company were banned in various states. The southern state of Kerala banned the sale of PEPSI and its product and the decision was extended to its production also. The implications of these tests were far more than expected as a ban was imposed on PEPSI in government and educational institutions by several states in India, including Rajasthan, M.P., Karnataka, Chhattisgarh, Andhra Pradesh, Gujarat and Delhi. Also, the Indian Parliament banned COKE and PEPSI from being sold in its cafeteria.

A great blow came on Pepsi, when a coalition of environmental groups organized under the "Quit India" banner conducted a "human chain" event as well as a series of public awareness campaigns to force Pepsi cola and Coca cola to leave India.

PEPSICO INCORPORATED

PepsiCo Incorporated is a global American beverage and Snake company. The company manufactures, market and sells a variety of carbonated and non-Carbonated beverage, as well as salty, sweet and grain-based snakes, and other foods. Besides the Pepsi-Cola brand (including Mountain dew), the company manufactures Quaker oats, Gatorade, Frito lays, sobe and Tropicana. In many ways PepsiCo differs from its competitors, the Coca Cola Company, having almost three times as many employees and larger revenue. The company formed for distribution and bottling is The Pepsi Bottling Group. PepsiCo is a SIC 2080 (beverage) company.

HISTORY

Headquartered in Purchase, New York. The Pepsi Cola company began in 1898, but it only became known as PepsiCo when it merged with Frito Lay in 1965 until 1997, it also Kentucky Fried Chicken, Pizza hut and Taco Bell, but these fast food restaurants were span off into Tricon global restaurants, now Yum! Brands, inc. PepsiCo purchased Tropicana in 1998 and Quaker Oats in 2001.

PEPSICO BRANDS

PepsiCo owns five different billion-dollar brands. These are Pepsi, Tropicana, Frito Lays, Quaker and Gatorade. The company own many other brands as well.

- Pepsi including Pepsi cola, caffeine free Pepsi, diet Pepsi light, caffeine free diet Pepsi, caffeine-free Pepsi light, wild cherry pepsi, pepsi lime, pepsi max, pepsi twist and pepsi one.
- Other US carbonated soft drinks, including frawg, Mountain Dew, Mug root beer, sierra mist and Tropicana twister soda.
- 7 UP (International Distribution).

- Other US beverage, including Aquafina (flavour splash, alive and twist/ burst, doll, Gatorade, Izze, Mountain Dew, AMP, propel fitness water, SOBE, Quaker Milk chillers, Ben & Jerry's Milk-shake and Tropicana.
- Frito Lays Brands: Baken-ets, Barcel, Bocabits, Cheeso Tris cheetos. Chester's, Craker Jack, Chizitos, Churrumais, Daritos, Fandangos, Fritos, Funyuns, Gamesa, Go snakes, etc.
- Quaker Oats Brands: Aunt Jemima, Cap'n Crunch, Coquireo, Crisp'ums, Cruesli, FresAvena, etc.

SHARE HOLDERS

PepsiCo shares are traded principally in the New York Stock Exchange in the United States. The company is also listed in the Amsterdam, Chicago and Swiss stock Exchanges. PepsiCo has consistently paid cash dividends since the corporation was founded.

CORPORATE OFFICERS

- Indra K. Nooyi
  Chairman of Board & Chief Executive Officer
- Mitch Adamek
  Senior Vice-President and Chief Procurement officer
- Peter A. Bridgman
  Senior Vice-President and Controller
- Richard Goodman
  Chief Financial Officer

PEPSICO IN INDIA

PepsiCo gained entry to India in 1988 by creating a joint venture with Punjab Government owned Punjab Agro Industrial Corporation (PAIC) and Voltas India Ltd. This Joint Venture marketed and sold Lehar Pepsi until 1991, when the use of foreign brand was allowed; PepsiCo bought out its partners and ended the joint venture in 1994.

DISCUSSION

Study by the Center for Science and the Environment has found that the soft drinks contained residues of dangerous pesticides. No law bans the presence of pesticides in drinks in India. Coke and Pepsi opposed the Lab tests, arguing that lab tests aren't reliable enough to detect minute traces of pesticides in complex drinks. India's Supreme Court ruled that both Pepsi and Coca-Cola Company must label all cans and bottles of the respective soft drinks with a consumer warning after tests should unacceptable levels of residual pesticides. First Indian state to oppose the production and sales of Coca Cola and Pepsi was Kerala. Due to this incident, sales of pepsi was affected.

Pepsi, Inc. selects SAP Business suite to support Business Transformation with single platform for operational excellence and growth in June 2004. SAP Business suite provided Pepsi with a common information systems platform to effectively integrate Business processes across its enterprise. So one of the worlds largest convenient food and beverage companies, Pepsi manufacturers, distributes and markets global brands such as Frito-lay snacks, Gatorade Sports drinks, Tropicana juices and Quaker foods with Business suite, Pepsi was able to streamline distribution and delivery, improved planning and forecasting, increased information transparency and linked supply chain and inventory with customer-facing activities in a single, integrated process. SAP established as the industry standard of excellence for consumer products companies, to help Pepsi leverage technology to achieve growth and innovation.

Marketing Management analysts has announced that Pepsi has selected Avista by MMA Decision support services (Avista DSS) to help maximize the return on its marketing investments with Avista DSS, pepsi have the system to integrate advanced analytics into their planning process to improve the bottom line. Its Analytic tools support scenario planning, optimization, forecasting, portfolio allocation, continued tracking and diagnosis of marketing performance to help companies generate the maximum return for their marketing investment. Pepsi have many benefits from Avista DSS. It includes the ability to maximize the return on marketing investment, deliver rightly accurate forecasts, respond quickly to market changes and improve the alignment among marketing, sales and finance.

ISSUES REGARDING PEPSICO

The pesticides, which were found in the soft drinks—Indane, DDT and its metabolites, chloropyrifos and malathion have extremely harmful effects on human health. In their case a Joint Parliamentary Committee (JPC) was constituted on Pesticide Residues in and safety standard for soft drink, fruit juices and other beverages decided to withdraw the writ petition from Delhi High Court. The conclusion recommendation drawn by the JPC on soft drinks and related aspects are significant. Some of that recommendations are as follows:

1. The committee noted with deep concern that the soft drink industry in India with an annual turnover of Rs. 6000 crores is unregulated. It is exempted from Industrial licensing under the industries Act, 1951 and get a one time license to operate from the ministry of food processing industries under fruit products order (FPO), 1995.

2. The standard should be fixed after proper consultation involving experts, scientists, farmer representative, etc. The committee also emphasized the need for taking the opinion of the central committee on food standard which is a statuary body under the PFA Act, 1954.

The committee designed that option should be made available to the consumer to choose between caffeinated and non-caffeinated soft drinks and that there should be no difference in the quality of products being marketed in India as compared to those which are being sold in the USA or other European countries.

The committee also recommended that use of caffeine and its effect on human health. The committee made a further important recommendation that whether PepsiCo and Coca cola are doing manufacturing directly in their own bottling units or through franchisees.

These recommendations speak volumes about total lack of concern on public health by the government and absence of safety standard. This is unfortunate phenomenon, which has been noticed in various other issues related to the protection of human health and environment where there is lacuna, it is exploited for making profit and even where law exits, it is not implemented which creates chaotic situation and corruption flourishes at the cost of permanent damage to the human health and environment. PFA at requires drastic arrangements not only with regard to packaged drinking water and soft drinks but also in several other areas keeping in view the present liberal market situations where all kinds of imported food items are being dumped for human consumption.

CUSTOMER PRIVACY

Pepsi Company takes following steps to protect the privacy of their customers:

Collection

They collect personal information in the course of their business dealing with us usually and as appropriate they will tell us why we are collecting personal information, when they collect it and how they plan to use or these things will be obvious when they collect the information. They usually collect personal information like name e-mail and address and neglecting sensitive information as defined in privacy act.

Use and Disclousure

They use customer information to provide and market their product to us and to fulfil administrative function associated with their business activities. They may share customer information with our members of PepsiCo group of companies, including those which are located in Australia PepsiCo may disclose our information to service providers, contractors and strategic partners from time to time to help customers providing information about their product.

Security

They use a variety of physical and electronic security manicures including retracting physical access to your offices firewall and secure databases to keep personal info secured from misuse loss or unauthorized use or disclosure.

Approach

They are bound by the national privacy principles in the privacy act where appropriate we will handle personal information relying on related bodies corporate exemption and the employ exemption in the privacy act. It is also unworthy that PepsiCo had withdrawn all the elevation of malafied made against the CSE in the writ petition. The petition was taken up by the Delhi High Court and the court directed that the samples of various products of PepsiCo be taken and sent for testing by the government labs. The test conducted therefore belied the contenting made by PepsiCo in their writ petitions that they follow EU standards although PepsiCo claims of following high standards in maintaining quality and safety of its soft drink products, but the expert committee appointed by the (CSE), reports on pesticide residue in soft drinks and sayed it cannot be accepted on its face value. Indian sales of drinks made by pepsi have fallen by ten percent following bans imposed by some states over the report they contain pesticides.

Measures Taken

- PepsiCo is one of the premier consumer products companies in the world and therefore it would do all its level best to maintain good customer relations and upright its image. PepsiCo has all set to go on air with its new television campaign to soften the impact of pesticide controversy.
- Pepsi has decided to take a break from starry ads in the wake of pesticide row senior company's executives said that company may approach scientists instead of film stars to endorse its beverages in order to regain public confidence and help blosters sales.
- Echoing the problem with reaching end consumer directly, a Pepsi India official points out to the recent controversy that broke over Pepsi and Coca-cola being charged in court for damaging the environment, by painting advertisements of their products on rocks in Manali, this shows the extent of brands penetration, with locations being so remote reaching the consumers directly is tough therefore they inculcate regular global practice like setting up national level call centers to address consumer complaints. It trains Consumer Response Co-ordinators (CRCs), who in turn train their sales loans to understand and implement its global systems.
- PEPSICO has selected SAP to provide the primary business platform to unify operations. Standardize process and increase efficiency across its enterprise.
- PEPSICo will be able to streamline distribution and delivery and link supply chain and inventory with customer facing activities in single integrated process.

FOOD FOR THOUGHT

1. By keeping double standard in Indian market does they put their credibility at stove?
2. Does CRM really help these companies in such type of issues?
3. Most of the people know that PepsiCo brands like Pepsi, Mirinda, etc. contains more amounts of pesticides, than people still run after such type of cold drinks?
4. For such a great loss in PepsiCo, which department should be held most responsibility behind all this sapa?

Ponder over it; it's really a burning issue. It may be detrimental l or nuclear disaster for innocent population.

STUDY–QUESTIONS

1. Discuss the relationship marketing or retention marketing is different from the traditional emphasis in marketing. Also describe the goal of relationship marketing.
2. Explain the concept of portfolio. Discuss the pathways to growth for service business.
3. Discuss the various benefits for customers and firms customer relation.
4. "The customer is not always right" describe.
5. What is the meaning of relationship value of customers? Also describe the factors that influence relationship value.
6. Describe the logic behind "customer profitability segmentation" from the company's point of view.

5

The Concept and Components of CRM

INTRODUCTION

The CRM infrastructure is made up of four key components: information, process, technology, and people. Each of these components is critical to delivering a successful CRM program. These four components are:

1. Information

Information is the raw material of CRM. These types of information are useful to CRM:

(i) *Identification data*: Name/address/phone data collected from customers to complete a business transaction.

(ii) *Marketing data*: Descriptors/traits/preferences collected from customers during a transaction (either by asking questions or tracking behaviour).

(iii) *List data*: Names/addresses collected by a third party, which can be bought or leased.

(iv) *Overlay data*: Customer profile data collected by a third party, which can be leased and appended to existing customer records.

2. Process

Customer-centred processes are the "product" of CRM. Some examples are:

(i) All current future processes that directly touch the customer.

(ii) Touch points, or means by which we interact with customers, such as phone, e-mail, etc.

(iii) Identifying and elimination process disconnects and white space.

(iv) Integrating and rationalizing processes from the customer's point of view

3. Technology

Technology is the machinery that enables CRM to work. These are examples of technologies that CRM may find useful:

(i) Software products (process automation tools, analysis tools, website development, and management tools).

(ii) Networking and integrating applications and databases.

(iii) Databases, either purchased solutions or home-grown, central or distributed.

(iv) Security features, such as encryption tools and firewalls.

4. People

People are the power supply of CRM. The energy source must be set to the right voltage for the entire system to work. People are "reset" through various change management tools and support mechanisms, such as:

(i) Training and education.

(ii) New tools.

(iii) Measurements and rewards.

CRM CONCEPTS

There are several important concepts that support the CRM definition. These concepts must also be commonly defined and understood, because they are critical to any successful CRM effort.

1. Customer Life Cycle

The customer life cycle is the total time that the customer is engaged with your company from the customer's experience and viewpoint. The CRM concept includes the definition of the customer life cycle. The customer life cycle is your customer's view of her relationship with your organisation over the long term. The customer life cycle is *not* your company's view. For example, "Product Support" is not part of the customer life cycle. It is certainly a function that your company provides to help customers use your products or service. But from the customer's perspective, the perfect world is where everything always runs perfectly and she never needs any help from you while using your products.

There is a high-level life cycle that is consistent for all customers, no matter the product or service and no matter how much time the customer spends in each stage:

1. *Consider*: Customer becomes aware of a need and investigates alternative solutions.
2. *Purchase*: Customer evaluates and chooses the best alternative and places an order.

3. *Set up*: Customer installs the product and learns how to use it.
4. *Use*. Customer operates and maintains the product and finally makes the decision to retire it or to upgrade, which starts the cycle all over again.

A typical customer life cycle covers these four major stages and includes a layer that you should make specific to your customers and your business. Of course, there is no single life cycle that is identical for all companies and all customers. You'll need to determine the life cycle of your own customers. The basic framework is relatively consistent, but service companies, for example, are not likely to find the concept of "install" relevant to their customers' experience.

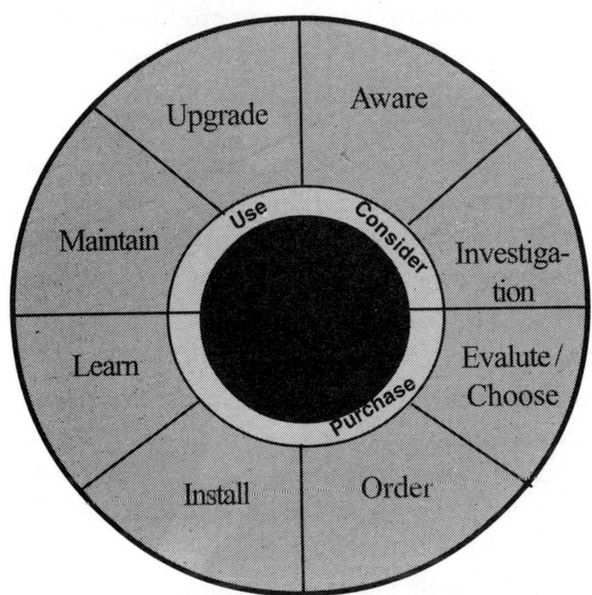

Fig. 1: *The Customer Life Cycle.*

2. Business-to-Business CRM

CRM in the business-to-business (B2B) marketplace is plagued by all the same misconceptions of CRM misconception which are discussed earlier. But B2B CRM suffers from one additional misconception. These are:

B2B customers are companies — Although it is true that company information is an absolutely critical element of any B2B CRM effort, B2B customers are still human beings. We build relationships with the people who work at customer companies. Company information is very important because it helps us describe and understand the people who make up that company, but the company is not a customer. There are some differences between how consumer and B2B CRM programs are implemented (information requirements) and managed (multiple contacts at the same business), but the basic definition of what CRM is remains the same.

3. Customer Asset

The concept of the customer being one of your company's assets is just now beginning to be widely accepted. This concept is a very important one because investing in customer relationships often does not generate short-term gains, and we know that most companies today are focused on the short term.

CRM delivers value because it focuses on lengthening the duration of the relationship (loyalty). CRM makes good business sense because loyal customers buy more product, buy more often, cost less to sell to and support, and often pay a premium. Loyal customers continue to buy our products because they perceive value in the relationship itself. Based on the experiences (with our people, products, processes, etc.) that they have had over time and on the relationship we have been able to establish because of our knowledge of their situation, preferences, and needs, these loyal customers continue to buy from us. Of course, even the most loyal customers must be willing to pay enough that there is some profit on each sale. A company can't stay in business just by having loyal customers if they lose money on every transaction. This was one of the lessons from the dotcom bust.

Customer information

Customer information is a tangible company asset that can (and should be) inventoried and managed. It is a critical component for building loyalty because it's impossible to build strong relationships if you don't know who your customers are and you don't know what their needs and experiences have been. It is an asset that must be protected and maintained.

Asset management requires money and resources because poor data won't support any of the goals of CRM; in fact, it will probably make things worse. Data is the raw material that goes into building relationships and should he valued the same way you value the raw materials that go into building your products. Just like raw material in a manufacturing environment, information has a value. That is becoming clearer as customer databases are beginning to be offered for sale as part of a company's assets. Of course, this has raised all kinds of privacy issues, such as the recent situation where bankrupt retailer Toysmart.com tried to auction off its customer database even though it had promised never to do so. The Federal Trade Commission (July 2001) did rinally approve the sale of this asset, but under very limited conditions. The company acquiring Toysmart's customer information could not change any of the original privacy policies without notifying and asking permission from every customer. How do you put a value on this kind of asset, especially considering the legal limitations? The difficulty with valuing the information asset is that, like all assets, its value is based on what the marketplace is willing to pay for it. We don't have enough experience yet on a standard definition of the precise value of customer information.

There are no Generally Accepted Accounting Practices that cover customer information. We have the feeling that customer data is valuable, but we don't know how valuable. The value of customer information is related to the largely intangible concept of the loyalty the customers themselves. You may be able to sell your customer database, but you don't control and therefore can't sell your customers' loyalty. The most buyer can be assured of is receiving an accurate and up-to-date list of people who have bought your products. Of course, any customer list is made up of both happy and unhappy customers. And the unhappy customers aren't valuable at all.

Customer value

CRM is not about treating all customers the same. Everyone knows that not all customers are alike, so why would we want to treat them all the same? CRM is about identifying and rewarding your most loyal customers so they remain loyal and their value to your company increases. CRM is also about moving the next tier of customers up to loyal (and, therefore, higher value) behaviour. Knowing which customers are the most valuable allows us to follow the important customer-centered concept outlined by Peppers and Rogers (1993) of achieving increased share of *customer* instead of increasing share of *market*. This means that we want our very best customers to buy more of what they need from us. This is much more profitable than the price manipulation and discounting that usually occurs to increase market share. Who cares where the low value customers are shopping?

CRM is about being able to recognize your most valuable customers and doing everything you can to deliver high value experience and to ensure that they remain (or become) more loyal. By the way, value is another place where managing consumer and B2B customers are different. Consumer value is calculated based on the purchases made by an individual. In the B2B marketplace, value is based on the purchases of the entire customer company. Each individual generally has the same "value" as the company account has. In either case, CRM helps you identify your best customers so that you're in a position to treat your *best customers best*.

CRM IN INDIAN PERSPECTIVES

Imagine buying a new car, your first one. And realizing within three months that the tyres need replacing. And the dealer doesn't want to solve your problem either, "Go tell the manufacture about it" he says. Imagine moving to a new city and applying for a phone connection. And having to wait for 2 months before the Telephone Company installs the instrument. Another month before the connection is activated. And then, 2 days later, it goes dead. Imagine losing your travellers cheques during a trip to the US. And the issuer doesn't replace them within 48 hrs as promised in the ads. You finally get the replacement 2 months later when you are back home.

Frightening, isn't it? Yet none of this horror stories are imaginary. If anecdotal evidence is anythin to go by, it leads to just one conclusion: Service stinks! The bad news is that most Indian firms still don't give a damn about the way they treat customers. The good news is that a few smart companies are trying hard to change the state of affairs.

Apart from being more customer- oriented in their attitude, there is one other factor common among the companies mentioned below. They have all adopted technology smartly to create better customer care solution and systems. Some are experiencing with centres, which will help a customer try out a product virtually before buying it. Others are building database to understand individual customers better and tailor products and services to be offered to them. And others are creating information systems that will help a customer locate and buy spare parts much more conveniently. As it is observed that these companies are not making small adjustments here and there in marketing and sales departments. They are pushing through fundamental changes that involve the whole company; the way people are trained, evaluated and compensated. They are adopting a new mantra called *Customer Relationship Management* (CRM).

Customer Care Begins Before the Sale

Lakme Lever unveiled a radically new customer service: interactive kiosks that allow women to choose products that suit them. How do they work? Branded as Lakme Beauty zones, these kiosks first take a picture of the customers face. Then as the customer chooses different shades of eyeshades of lipsticks, these are superimposed on the image in front of a button. That way, she is able to decide whether the colour suits her before she buys the product. What's Lakmes rationale? At Rs 500 crore, the cosmetics category in India has remained relatively small compared to other world..markets. Indian women still lack knowledge about all the permutations and combinations of beauty products. They are not sure which shade suits them best.

There is resistance to some products because facial makeup is concerned cheap in some sections of society. They found that for many products, particularly foundations cram, the number of lapsed users who bought it once and then stop the buying were high. Which means women had bought the product and then found it unsuitable. For long time, Lakme organized Beauty Clubs, where experts offered beauty tips.' But overtime, organizing these gatherings proved to be a logistic nightmare.

Now with these kiosks, Lakme is hoping to reach out to more women right at the point of sale. Currently, given the high cost of the machines, Lakme Lever is concentrating on a few locations, primarily high traffic malls like Crossroads and Shoppers Stop in Mumbai. Godrej-Ge appliances have also found that customer care starts much before the sale takes place. Godrej-Ge doesn't have interactive kiosks like Lakme, but it has found its own innovation solution-Customer Care Call censers manned by executives who have complete description of ;Ill the appliances sold under the Godrej-Ge brand name. Everyday, the call centres across Mumbai, Chennai and Delhi receives close to 3,000 calls, quite a few from people who haven't bought the product. Most of the pre-sale calls pertain to sales. Will a 200-litre fridge fit into my kitchen? Sometimes, customers also ask for other information to help them decide which model will suit them better. The call centres go a long way in helping them make up their mind.

Understanding Buying Patterns

Many Indian companies are facing a big stumbling block in providing better customer service. They are realizing that they simply don't know their customers well enough. In fact most companies, today still practice the art of "reactive CRM"-waiting for their customer to providing feedback rather than proactively asking for it. That's largely because data capture in the Indian environment is still difficult. Food World is trying to put CRM system into place, but unless all products are bar coded, the process will not be up and running. They do the bar coding themselves and that's how they keep a track of the stock keeping. At the moment the parent company RPG is putting together a system to understand purchase patterns better.

Apart from regular customer meets and formal research, it has invested in Data mining software in Chennai that allows it to understand "product adjacencies". What that essentially means is figuring out which products are typically bought together. For example, do people buy cosmetic along with medicines? Or with soaps and detergents? It allows them to understand the combination of products bought against a single billing, at a macro level, it helps RPG formulate its products placements, undertake cross promotions, or develop new pack sizes. Every month, the 41 RPG properties including Food World, Health 'n' glow and Music world-generate close to 8,00,000 bills, which translates into 1.5 million stores visitors. The data captured in these bills are analysed at the Chennai centre.

Understanding the Customer

Almost all firms agree that the starting point is setting up a data warehouse that will hold all the information about each customer. ICICI is doing just that. With 600,000 customers, 2 million bondholders and 25,000 cardholders, the universal- bank-in-the making is sparing no effort to integrate its most privileged asset-customers. They are trying to offer the customer a seamless and consistently good quality experience, regardless of the point of contact, much the same way that the customer know what that expect when they go to a McDonalds outlets or a Marriot hotel.

The CRM team at Acacias their first task was to build a customer information system to help it to understand the multiple relationship a customer has with different parts of the organization. So they started asking customers about the other ICICI products they also had, and asking them for permission to look the accounts. That way, ICICI can fill up a bond folio number. Of course, that's something every neighbourhood grocer has always done perfectly. If you are a regular customer buying Rs 1,000 worth of goods every month, the chances are that the grocer will he ready to deliver even a loaf of bread to your home. That's because in his mind, he has a data warehouse and he knows you are an Rs 1,000 a customer a month.

The issue is how do you replicate this in a large institution that has lakhs, of customers. All the customers' information will be centralized in ICICI's server farm at Mahalaxmi in Mumbai. Apart from the data warehouse there will also be live production warehouse, which will be linked to the various consumer channels and gather information real time. Take the case of loans, which are the most difficult products to price. That's because you need to know the cost of funds, take into account the credit risk and then top it of with the profit margin. Now suppose an ICICI bond holder calls the ICICI call centre for a car loan, there is a 75% chance that he will be offered at least half a percentage point off the loan straightway. Even Direct marketing agents will have access to customer data through a secure Internet connection or a wide area network. Lakme Lever plans similar database for its customers. Not through the interactive kiosks though. The company is beginning the first phase of rolling out 200 franchised beauty parlours. The salons will be set up in cities that have a population of 500,000 or more.

The customers usually shared a rapport with the beautician and so were open to given details when queried on products and services. The franchise will be linked to a central database. When a customer asks for an appointment, the franchise will be expected to take down her name, telephone and the kind of service she needs. Once the customer makes her third visit and it is apparent that she is a regular visitor, the franchise will be asked to get more insightful information on them. They may also give incentives to the customer by offering a 20% discount on her next visit, if she fills out the response coupon. In the next 5 years, Lakme Lever hopes to build a database of at least a million premium customers. Then the company will be in a position to offer them the entire gamut of products from the HLL.

Rewarding Customer Loyalty

CRM's biggest task is to constantly track customers, so that the firm knows it's best customers. That way, it gives the organization a better chance to hold on them, 'But in times of competition, there's no guarantee that they will stay with you. So how do you ensure that they do? Simple, you reward them for loyalty. Airlines, credit card companies do it all the time. Now with its Petro bonus program, even Bharat petroleum joins a part of the loyalty club initiators. For the past few years, the oil companies have been under pressure to differentiate themselves in the customer's eyes.

How could BPCL establish a lock over the customer so that he continued to buy at the petrol pumps owned by BPCL? From March this year, the oil major pushed through a smart card programmed, enlisting select petrol pumps, where the customer is assured of a minimum level of quality service. The pumps had to have the ability to upgrade their facilities, practised good house keeping and customer care and of course, provided the right quality and quantity of product. The Petro card functions as a prepaid card. So every time you use the card, the value of the transaction is debited. You also get points for transactions made on the card-items worth Rs 100 bought at the pumps convenience stores means 100 points, while Rs 100 worth of lubes bought is 250 points. These bonus points are redeemable through gifts. So far, 40000 members have enrolled for the program and by the end of this year, BPCL hopes to net close to half a million members. The program is delivering results.

Making After-sales Service Easier

Technology is also plying a major role in providing customers with the care they want' At Samsung Electronics, that's exactly the game plan. Assume that you are reporting a defect in the hard disk drive that is replaceable during warranty. All you have to do is log on to the companys website and key in the product serial number and your own address.

Out pops the name and the contact number of the nearest Samsung dealer as well as a complaint number. If the dealer does not have the part, then the software deflects the customer to the nearest dealer who has the part. But given the Internet penetration is still low in India, efficiently managed call centres are still the best for handling customers complaints and service requests. The call centres help to reduce loop in the after sales service. There's a common thread running through all these organizations. Talking, listening, understanding what the customer is all about. It is about igniting the employees that caring for the customer is above all else.

CASE STUDY

WHAT IS CRM?

Business approach that understands anticipates and manages the need of current and potential customer of an organization. Integrating People, Processes and Technology of an organization. Effective use of Information about customer to maximize customer satisfaction as well as cost reduction and increased profitability for an organization

FOUR C's {ELEMENTS} OF CRM PROCESS

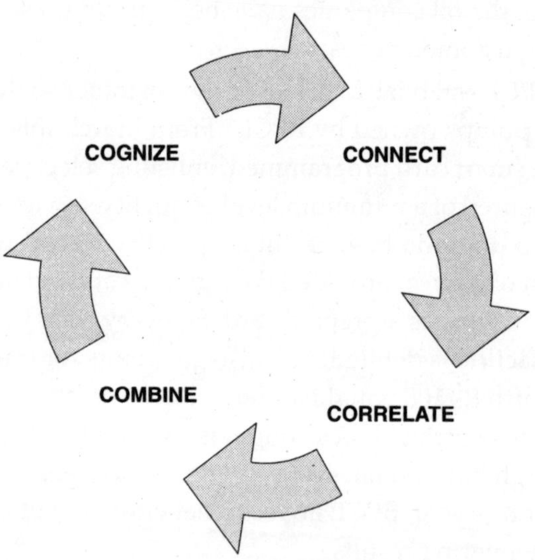

WHY ORGANIZATION LOSE THEIR CUSTOMERS

It is needless to mention the need for retention of customers by an organization for which designing an efficient customer retention plan is very essential. Obviously for preparation of such plan knowledge on the reasons behind losing customers is required. The possible reasons are listed below:

Price-related reasons
Product-related reasons
Service-related reasons
Benefit-related reasons
Competitors-related reasons
Personal reasons

Moved away from the market area where the brand is sold.

Role changes in life cycle, consequently leading to changes in brand preference.

Anger, disgust, distress developed with in the process of product delivery.

Sentimental reasons

Influence of other members of the family or friends.

The organisation must periodically analyze the reasons behind losing customers and accordingly develop a customer retention plan that would serve as the basic tool towards building a strong and long-standing relationship with customers.

Strategies for Building Relationships

An organisation's strategies towards developing and maintaining sustainable relationship differ from one organisation to another depending upon on certain factors, these includes nature of business, its size, its market share, nature of product type, volume of sales, geographical concentrations, social-economic status and rest of paper provides a wide spectrum of strategies that are practiced by customers' driven organisations with national and global perspectives, the reader may concentrate on those strategies or combination of several strategies that suit his business context.

People

People within the organisation have the basic role in developing and maintaining relationship with customers, everyone in the organisation must realise the fact that their work is towards satisfying customers, everyone from the lowest to the highest level is irrespective of their functional specialization and responsibilities must integrate their activities towards one of the main objectives of the organization-customer satisfaction. The marketing department can coordinate integrate activity towards customer satisfaction, obviously, people within the organisation from the basis for customer relationship.

Process

Process involves a logical sequence of activities right from the need identification of potential customers to need fulfillment requires manufacture to products with desired attributes. The process has to be derived from the customers' viewpoint which paves way for total customer satisfaction. The performance of each link must be objectively analysed and concerned in time with the internal and external customers' expectations.

Product

The product offered must constantly provide value addition, the expectations of the customers may always be on the increase due to various reasons. A customer satisfied with a given product may soon become a dissatisfied customer in view of the changes that take place in his expectations, customer's expectations go much beyond physical tangible things. As an anonymous commentator puts in:

Do not offer me things.

Do not offer me clothes, offer me attractive looks.

Do not offer me book, offer me the benefit of knowledge.

Do not offer me things, offer me ideas, emotions, feelings and benefits.

Please do not offer me things.

Organisation

In order to build customer relationship, an organisation should be aware of the technology advancements and provide quality services in tune with the customer's expectations, it should concentrate on total satisfaction and respond to the requirements of the customers faster than its competitors.

Unethical Approach to Build and Maintain Customer Realtionship

Addition : Creating a sense of addition to the brand by adding ingredients that are harmful to body and mind, as in the case of beverages, soft drinks, food items, etc.

Fear: Developing a sense of fear in mind of the customers, that once a brand is continuously used, any brand is continuously used, any brand is continuously used, any brand switchover would cause problems as in the case of cosmetics, food, drinks, medicines, etc.

Initiating : Initiating the attributes of well-accepted brands in an unlawful way.

Promises: Making promises to customers with no intentions to perform.

Commitment: Developing misleading commitments and obligations.

Discriminations: Discriminations on the quality and services among buyers.

Forcing: Making promises to customers with no intentions to perform.

Rewarding: Extending undue benefits in the form of cash or equal means of benefit to the members of purchase team in case of industrial organisational purchase.

Insisting on sentiments: Making use of the faith of sentiments of customers to the best advantage of the organisational purchase.

Communal affiliations: Extending communal affiliations and drawing the attention of customers of selected community.

Negative publicity: Making negative publicity to competitors brand.

Many more unethical ways are also being practiced building relationship. However, a customer can be retained permanently only by mans of quality products and services.

The pressures of competitive and dynamic markets have contributed to the growth of CRM in the Financial Services Sector.

Background

The case is based on the CRM practices being followed in one of the prominent Indian Insurance Sector Companies, IJIJI Prudential Life Insurance Co. Ltd. The company is there into the market since December 2000.

Before discussing the case, lets go through the company's profile.

An Overview

India's leading private life insurer, IJIJI Prudential Life Insurance Company is a joint venture between IJIJI Bank—one of India's foremost financial services companies and Prudential plc—a leading international financial services group headquartered in the United Kingdom. Total capital infusion stands at Rs. 2602 crore, with IJIJI Bank holding a stake of 74% and Prudential plc holding 26%.

They began their operations in December 2000 after receiving approval from Insurance Regulatory Development Authority (IRDA). Today, their nation-wide team comprises of over 680 offices, over 235,000 advisors; and 23 bancassurance partners.

Functions

IJIJI Prudential offers exciting career opportunities for people from a variety of streams. Read on to find out more about how each of the functions contribute to our growing business.

Sales Distribution

Tied Agency

Tied Agency is the largest distribution channel of IJIJI Prudential, comprising a large advisor force that targets various customer segments. The strength of tied agency lies in an aggressive strategy of expanding and procuring quality business. With focus on sales and people development, tied agency has emerged as a robust, predictable and sustainable business model.

Bancassurance and Alliances

IJIJI Prudential was a pioneer in offering life insurance solutions through banks and alliances. Within a short span of two years, and with nearly a large number of partners, B & A has emerged as a vital component of the company's sales and distribution strategy, contributing to approximately one-third of company's total business.

The business philosophy at B&A is to leverage distribution synergies with our partners and add value to its customers as well as the partners. Flexibility, adaptation and experimenting with new ideas are the hallmarks of this channel.

Group

The Group Business of IJIJI Prudential has been in existence for over 2 years. Today, we are the Number 1 player among private life insurance companies in Group Business excluding Mortgage Reducing Term Assurance (MRTA) with a market share of 26% (FY 2004-05). We offer the entire gamut of products including Gratuity, Superannuation Term Insurance, Leave Encashment, Employee Deposit Linked Insurance (EDLI), Mortgage Reducing Term Assurance (MRTA) and Informal Group Term covers.

Customer Service and Operations

The Operations department oils the work processes between the customer and the company to ensure consistent and quality service to the customer. To streamline the operations, the Operations department interfaces between the clients and the agents, the branches and the underwriters, and manages work processes.

The Vision at Customer Service is to deliver 'World Class Service' at every opportunity. Units such as the 9 to 9 contact centre, Outbound Call Centre, Customer Care and Query Resolution Unit are all committed to providing effective solutions to over lakhs of customers across the country.

IT

The Information Technology function at IJIJI Prudential is committed to enable business through the use of technology. It is segmented into 4 groups to enable highest levels of delivery to the customers: Life Asia Solutions Group that provides flexibility in designing better product offerings to end-users, the Solutions Group-Web that provides real-time information to customers and is responsible for customer relationship management. IT Architecture and Corporate Solutions Group is in charge of developing and maintaining a blueprint for the IT architecture for the enterprise as a whole. This team works as an in house R&D Solution Group, exploring new technological initiatives and also caters to information needs of corporate functions in the organization. IT Infrastructure group is responsible for providing hardware, software, network services to the whole organization. This group runs the 'Digital Nervous System' of the Enterprise at the highest levels of efficiency and provide robust, scalable and highly available platform for deployment of business application.

Marketing

The Marketing function at IJIJI Prudential covers an array of activities—brand and media management, channel support, direct marketing and corporate communications. The Brand and Communications team is in charge of advertising, consumer research, media planning and buying and Public Relations; that helps develop and nurture IJIJI Prudential's corporate identity while effectively communicating its varied product offerings to the customer. Channel marketing provides support to the sales force by streamlining the design and development of collaterals and sales tools across distribution channels. The Direct marketing team was set-up to generate high quality leads for profitable business. The team achieves this through target database acquisition and communicating customised product information through e-mailers, telemarketing and innovative direct mailers.

Finance

Finance function in IJIJI Prudential is committed to create an infrastructure that is aligned to shareholder expectations. Finance basically comprises of four functions. Corporate Planning and MIS provide feedback on business strategies. This includes driving the budgeting process, providing strategic inputs for decision-making and management reporting and analysis. The Accounts function includes preparation and maintenance of financial records, funds management, and expense processing and treasury operations. Compliance ensures that every action is within the regulatory framework. This includes reviewing compliance requirements and supporting the ethical framework of IJIJI Prudential life. Internal audit provides assurance to the management over the organizations' control framework and includes process risk management, information security assessment and business continuity assessment.

HR

The people strategy of IJIJI Prudential is "To build a committed team with a culture of innovation, learning and growth. The Human Resource Function at IJIJI Prudential drives the people strategy of the business. With its initial focus on operational excellence to deliver benefits and services to staff members, HR is now committed to building capability through state of the art processes. A robust performance management system, compensation system and a segmented training architecture enable it to deliver value to the organization.

Business

Excellence: The Business Excellence function is committed to building a quality mindset across the organization. IJIJI Prudential is the first organization in the Insurance Industry that has adopted the Six Sigma Methodology for process efficiency and measurement.

THE CASE

It was in August 2006, that a tele caller in IJIJI PRUDENTIAL LIFE INSURANCE CO. LTD., Ms. Anjali Chawdhary, contacted a customer, Mr. Ajay Singh, vice- president, Bedi Group, Delhi for selling insurance plans. The customer as per his requirements agreed to invest with the premium of Rs. 1,80,000 p.a. on the monthly mode. The cheque was of Rs. 30,000 as the first payment is always for two months and the renewals were agreed to be paid on Electronic Clearance System (E.C.S.) mode. The insurance cover applied was Rs. 10 lacs against natural death and of Rs. 10 lacs against accident. The rule is that while applying for insurance if the customer wishes to avail tax benefits U/S 80 (C) and sec. 10 (10) D, he should apply for insurance cover minimum of 5 times of the annual premium paid by him. Mr. Ajay applied with the documents through the advisor Ms. Sunaina Sharma, a gold card member, i.e. a Grand perks card holder of the company. She was the top advisor of her team. Her boss, the Senior Agency Manager, Mr. Sachin Sharma was the top manager in the Delhi branch. Now, the customer was 53 years old. The insurance he applied for was of Rs. 10 lacs and the plan in which he was investing was a ULIP PLAN, i.e. a unit linked insurance plan, LIFETIME SUPER. The case as handled by Sunaina and Sachin with complete forms and documents cross checked was logged in Sunaina's agency code and Sachin's employee code. The underwriting was taken care by Mr. Manu Sharma, the operations head. As the customer was investing premium more than Rs. 50,000 p.a. so he was added among the Priority Circle of the company and was sent a letter for the same.

As per the underwriting rules, the customer had to pass some medical tests which would be borne by the company itself. The company has its licensed doctors in various parts of city. So the underwriting team demanded six different medical reports for the case to proceed.

Sunaina was updated about the status though mail and so was Sachin. In the mean time they both were in regular contact with Ajay and also informed him that he may be required to get some medicals done as he was above 40 years of age and also because he had applied for an insurance cover more than 5 lacs. So Sunaina had also asked him to keep himself free on a day so that when the tests would be demanded he should be ready for it.

The problem occurred when the client was not fixing dates for tests. Sunaina had to send the status for the same to the sales manager Mr. Ajay Kwatra. The first mail sent by her and Sachin, the sales manager, Ajay Kwatra was when the client was outstation as told by the client.

Now as per the underwriting rules if the medicals are not done within one month, the case gets cancelled. It was almost one month and the customer was not fixed with the details. Sunaina was also in contact with the concerned doctor whose clinic was nearest to the customer's residence. It was becoming tougher for her to get the medicals done. Pressure was also there from the seniors. The sales manager, Ajay Kwatra did not want the case to be cancelled or withdrawn as the premium was good enough to add to their target performance.

Sachin came out with solution and asked Sunaina to send the doctor to the customer's residence and get the medicals done. Sunaina coordinated with the doctor and customer and the customer too agreed with it. All the tests were done except T.M.T. test which is also known as Treadmill E.C.G. Now this test could be done only if the customer visits the clinic.

It was then the customer was again followed by the sales team and again the flow of e-mail is began so as to prevent the case from cancellation.

Meanwhile the customer was also asked for changing the insurance cover in the name of his daughter and was advised that he should be the proposed. But Ajay Singh did not agree to this as he wanted this cover on him only. This also increased the suspicion of the underwriting team. Instead, Ajay asked Sunaina to get the fake medical report done and to pass the case just like that. Sunaina did not followed the unethical means and refused him. Ajay then himself asked the doctor directly and offered him bribe for the same. The doctor also refused. Now the customer had no other solution but to go and get the medicals done (TMT) so that the case could proceed further.

The twist came when Ajay asked Sunaina that he would like to with the case draw the case and since as customer has to provide some reason he said it was because of poor customer handling. As per underwriting rules, if a client gets the case withdrawn after the medicals, he/she has to bear the cost of the tests, else it's the company paying for him/her. Here too Ajay could have been asked to pay. But Sunaina prevented that to Happen.

She didn't even followed the unethical means to get the case passed. Sachin and Sunaina are now in dilemma as Ajay Singh had already said that he would get the case cancelled by providing reason of mis-selling. The customer will be out of it safely and the sales team and the sales manager Ajay Kwatra are in a state of what to decide.

FOOD FOR THOUGHT

Question; What do you think should Sunaina and Sachin do ?

Question: Is CRM over practiced here?

Question : How can one be on track of CRM and also identify the customer's true interest to the product and the company?

STUDY–QUESTIONS

1. Explain the various CRM concepts in brief.
2. Discuss the essentiality of CRM in Indian perspective.
3. Elaborate the customer life cycle in short.

❖❖❖

6

A JOURNEY FROM CRM TO E-CRM

INTRODUCTION

CRM in its prehistoric 1990s, was characterised most frequently with technological and functional terms. The mantra, "It isn't a technology, it is a system," actually came into vogue because of reaction to the strong technological wind stirred by CRM and what was at the time the dot.com boom, primarily because of vendor marketing. The standard definition was developed in 2000.

But in early 2002, perception of CRM began to change and with that, a new round of attempts at a definition emerged, as companies contended with a number of new factors that affected institutional CRM. Among them:

(i) The ongoing transition of the business ecology from corporate to customer-centric;

(ii) The transition from a data-driven CRM model to a process- focused CRM;

(iii) The effect of September 11, 2001, on the world economy and the global psyche;

(iv) The rate of and reasons for CRM failures; and

(v) The explosive tangible value of and reasons for recorded CRM successes.

WHOLE-APPROACHED CRM

In whole approaches, the first approach is considered the rational side that governs language, logic, interpretation, and arithmetic. The second approach governs geometry, nonverbal processes, visual pattern recognition, auditory discrimination, and facial skills (the intuitive side). This is the CRM that you know and maybe love, maybe not. It is why the initial CRM was defined as a "system, not a technology", back in the day. The historic CRM was defined in a rather odd fashion. While there has always been talk of improving customer satisfaction, increasing customer loyalty, refining the customer experience, enhancing customer interaction-all subjective factors — CRM has been very much a mathematical/statistical and operational endeavour, with analytic algorithms segmenting data to better understand how to use the data to improve the relationship that you had with the customer.

The proofs of success were the top and bottom lines of corporate revenue. Benchmarks and metrics were created to measure how well it performed against the planned return on investment. CRM was seen as a result, more than as an ongoing process. Nothing was wrong with that — except that how to get the result was actually what CRM is, not the result itself. It has also been tarred as ERP redux. It was a big system that was data-driven and transactional. It cost lots of money to implement, was implemented as a project, and dropped to the end-user without regard to the end-user's thoughts on the matter. After all, ERP captured business actions and automated many, allowed cross-functional interdepartmental data views, and provided a central repository for data that made planning somewhat easier. CRM did the same thing but for customer data, didn't it? Well, if you saw CRM as a technology and a system, yes, that's what it did. Its value seemed to be related to lowering costs or increasing revenue. Not too bad. But it also seemed to fail a lot. The most common reasons for those failures have been the result of ignorance of the second-approach aspects of CRM. At this point, you might be asking yourself, what are 'second-approach aspects, may I ask?" Well, the failure to understand that the corporate culture was going to undergo a dramatic change or the fadure to engage the users, both internal and external, in the planning and execution of the strategy and the implementation. The failure to understand the culture of the chosen vendor. The disregard for the politics of the corporation.

Over-concern for senior management buy-in and stakeholder participation to the exclusion of the users from that stakeholding team. In other words, a fundamental disregard for the human performances in this very human endeavour. By making its definition predominantly first approach, CRM direction was often skewed and distorted, notably when cultural transformation was at stake. That led to problems with how training was handled. The stakeholders were chosen in a one-sided fashion, senior management only passively supported initiatives, IT departments ran the initiatives, and user adoption rates were low. The corrective key? A balanced "whole-approached" approach to CRM which acknowledges that we are dealing with human beings who have interests, concerns, their own agendas, and probably think somewhat differently than we do. We have to map those human performance issues and criteria to a strategic business initiative to make sure that CRM succeeds.

Elements of First-Approach Elements of CRM

(i) Senior management buy-in;
(ii) Total cost of ownership;
(iii) ROI;
(iv) Benchmarks and metrics;
(v) Application selection;
(vi) Implementation planning; and
(vii) End-user training.

Elements of Second-Approach Elements of CRM

(i) CRM and attitude;
(ii) Human performance support;
(iii) User adoption and self-interest; and
(iv) Culture change.

CONCEPT OF E-CRM

The concept of adding 'e' to CRM and make it as 'e-CRM' seems to get attached to everything in CRM space. The 'e' stands for electronic or web-based technology and architecture. The 'e' enables an organisation to extend its infrastructure to customers and partners in ways that offer new opportunities

(i) to reach new customer;
(ii) to do all this in real time;
(iii) to learn customer needs;
(iv) to gain new economics; and
(v) to add value.

e-CRM is a strategy and therefore requires the direction and involvement of top management. To be successful and to gain the advantages one must have a thorough understanding of the capabilities of this electronic technology and to translate it, into specific opportunities that leverage the competitive advantage. e-CRM is a new face in Relationship Management of Customers with which the organisation presents itself to the world. It provides the organisation with the required technology to involve the customer intimately right from the design level, to that of the finished product level.

Use of internet helps in enhancing the relationships. e-CRM gives global real time view to the customer. Organisations can acquire, retain and built loyalty customer groups. There can be two way communication between customers and the organisation from any where, at any time, and by any means. The modes of communication include e-mail, internet (web), chat, Telephone, fax, WAP, interactive voice response (IVR) and other electronic methods that lets a business to, deliver one to one experience to customer, helps to manage a vast customer database and to serve the customers better and faster. e-CRM systems can handle business volumes that are much higher than what could be handled by physical operation and traditional CRM. This directly translates and generates higher revenues for a business.

The virtual channels used by e-CRM systems help to achieve broader reach with no great incremental cost. Once e-CRM system is in place, one can visualise the dropping down of per-transaction costs resulting in a substantial increase in ROI. e-CRM transactions are faster. The e-CRM can lead to the benefits like:

(i) Call centers,

(ii) Customer information systems,

(iii) System integration,

(iv) Automation of customer support process,

(v) Life time value of customer,

(vi) EPOS (electronic point of sale), and

(vii) Customer database.

IMPORTANT STEPS TO IMPLEMENT E-CRM

Among the great lessons learned from the dot com recession are that, unless you're selling porn, the Internet is not a great sales channel, not a great advertising medium, nor even great a direct marketing tool. First we must learn to better use the Internet as a CRM tool. This is a pretty safe bet, because we still have a lot to learn. It is however, a potentially powerful and cost-effective customer intelligence-gathering and relationship-building channel, which few companies have fully exploited. With a better understanding of the new mediums strengths and- weaknesses (e.g., the web is better at selling known products like books, than selling products that require trial or personal examination, like blue jeans), businesses will design on-line customer-facing strategies that are more consistent with on-line human behaviour. Second - We'll get smarter about how to use client data in the 1990's, the push was to get in front of the customer and "own the relationship." Most companies realised, as witnessed by the huge investment in sales force automation and customer relationship management suites over the past decade, he who owns the relationship owns just about everything. We're not just talking about the lion's share profits along the supplier/producer/ wholesaler/retailer "value chain.'

More importantly, were talking about the value of knowledge about customer needs and buying habits. Why has customer data become so important? Because in the new global economy of white-hot competition and frenetic change the only real sustainable competitive advantage in attracting and retaining customers will be to know them individually and better than anyone else does, and to be able to offer them what they want, when they want it. This means providing them financial, emotional and other behavioural incentives to stay, and offering personalised, valued services and add-ons. While most organisations have the ability to collect information, they don't have a coherent and effective strategy to analyse and process this tremendous amount of data into actionable information. The current wisdom in both the on-line and off-line worlds is that, with storage memory-costs continually failing, if you don't know what information to keep, keep it all. Such economies have forced businesses into a data-rich, information-poor scenario'.

Corporations that have undertaken data warehousing projects have learned the hard way just how complicated and difficult it can he to decide what information to look at, how to analyse it, and what to do with the results. Despite accumulating huge amounts of data, most businesses have quickly come to realise (or at least strongly suspect) that a customer data aren't created equal. While the science of data analysis is not new, the art of- discovering what customer information has predictive value is. Most techniques employed today are still based on traditional, sales- respected-oriented metrics, such as recency, frequency and money analysis, which tracks customers by how much, recently and frequently they purchased your products, techniques which have been around for decades. For better and for worse, the Internet has its own set of metries. The good news is that every move a site visitor or on-line customer makes can be automatically captured in a web server log file. 'Because this information is already electronic, it is relatively cheap and easy to analyse and manipulate. The bad news is that many companies get carried away with the beauty of the reporting.

Some companies spend tens of thousands of dollars on detailed reports of on-line visitor behaviour with absolutely no clue how to recover this cost in the form of smarter marketing, more targeted sales, or more informed product development. Many businesses are waking up to the fact that just because it is cheaper to track every move a visitor makes on your site doesn't necessarily mean it's worth doing. While some click stream trends are predictive (for example, increased frequency of a unique visitor to a site indicates likelihood to make and on-line purchase, and collaborative filtering can be an effective sales suggestion engine), on-line behaviour modelling is far from mature.

Is there a common theme in these e-CRM industry trends and predictions? Well, it could go something like this: despite its youth, e-CRM has done a lot of growing up lately. Despite snazzy lingo, fiendishly complex technology, and the continued novelty of the Internet, in many ways, it's back to the future: managing by the numbers. Compared to the gut-wrenching hoopla investors, technologists, sales people and consultants have suffered through, maybe that's not such a bad idea. Tune in two weeks from now for the next three trends in e-CRM: multi-channel integration, impact on the supply chain and implementation.

DISTINCTION BETWEEN CRM AND E-CRM

CRM is philosophy of interaction with the customers and e-CRM is electronic CRM, which is conceptually the same as CRM, but the difference being it is a new term where all integration in the purview takes place with help of web enabled electronic media. e-CRM beverages technology solutions to offer such businesses in sight in a manner that integrates various functions in an organisation like call centre, marketing, sales, support, manufacturing. and billing. The following are some differences between CRM and e-CRM:

(i) In CRM emphasis made on personal selling while in e-CRM there is customer database is readily available at every time.

(ii) In CRM customer contact by mail, telephone, in person while in e-CRM customer information system is readily available.

(iii) In CRM services of After sales; Complaint handling; Account management; Customer care; and Customer Satisfaction is available while in e-CRM services of EPOS sales force; Automation of customers: support processes; Call centers; System integration and Life value of customer.

The e-CRM solution providers are baan, clarify, oracle, pivotal, mySAP, Siebel-2000, vantif, peoplesoft, broad vision, J.D. Edwards. Samsung Electronics India and Tata Telecom Ltd. are successful e-CRM companies. With advent of Internet revolution, successful customer service today means having a successful CRM strategy that integrates web-based self-service with traditional service capabilities.

Web based tools and services are integral part of customer care programs for virtually every business, and their role in customer service will continue to increase successful customer care calls for integration of People, Process, Technology, which is critical. People are crucial for evaluating how well the system meets their needs. Process is important for driving workflow development, which in turn is the result of technology. Technology is the key for developing and modifying the actual applications that customers and customer service agents will be in need and use.

CUSTOMER FOCUS WITH E-CRM

There is a shift from a Uni-dimensional product centric model to 'multi-dimensional' customer as the focus of the organisations' strategic business vision. Customer related information has made it imperative for organisations to go in for e-CRM tools and applications in their marketing mix, so as to strengthen the value chain. e-CRM should not be looked upon a mere concept or a quick fix mantra but as a broader business strategy used to understand, anticipate and manage both current and potential customers, and tailored to unique market segments. The success of e-CRM lies in top-to-bottom re-examination of how companies do business and treat customers. e-CRM applications are designed to optimise customer interaction by collecting relevant data about the customer at progressive stages of interaction. e-CRM tools and its applications uniquely capture a 3-D view of every customer while analysing the synthesised information generated from customer database. The premise here is to get closer to the customer and thereby proactively respond to changes in customer perceptions, needs and wants more quickly and efficiently. It is not that e-CRM is a 'silver bullet' solution or a panacea to address all business related problems that co-operation can turn to during down turns.

e-CRM focus on those customers that are 'business generators' rather than laggards'. This ensures that the companies marketing, advertising and promotional efforts are uniquely directed to that 'critical set' of customers who are most likely to generate business in any given market conditions and for sustained periods of time. From an internal frame of reference, e-CRM applications cut costs and assists in charting out a focused sales plan for the marketing and sales teams thereby cutting overheads and maximizing revenues. As customer acquisition costs continue to inflate in a slow economy, numerous companies are turning to e-CRM tools to help them realise their existing customer value.

EMERGING TRENDS IN E-CRM

e-CRM applications are straddling across business functions to retain, capture and capitalize on customer data, i.e., integrating all aspects of business process and systems by keeping the customers as the core.

According to an IDC'report, e-CRM projects are no longer viewed as stand-alone implementations but are now being increasingly pursued in context of larger business objectives and core strategic agendas. Corporations realize that the true value of their customers in down turn are the ones that will be better equipped, tied over the slump and jump start, consolidate and thrive.

The two emerging trends are —

(i) The measurement of benefits from the e-CRM infrastructure investment,

(ii) Realization that e-CRM is more than a technology solution.

COMPONENTS OF E-CRM

(i) Data synchronisation functionality: mobile synchronisation with multiple field devices, enterprise synchronisation with multiple databases/ application servers.

(ii) EPP integration functionality: legacy systems, the web, third-party external information.

(iii) *Marketing functionality:* campaign management, opportunity management, web-based encyclopedia, configuration, market segmentation, lead generations/enhancement/tracking.

(iv) *Time management functionality:* single user and group calendar/scheduling, e-mail.

(v) *Customer service and support functionality:* incident assignment, escalation, tracking/reporting, problem management/resolution, order management/promising, warranty/contract management.

(vi) *Service support functionality:* work orders, dispatching, real time information transfer to field personnel via mobile technologies.

(vii) *Sales management functionality:* pipeline analysis (forecasting, sales cycle analysis, temporary alignment and assignment, roll-up and drill-down reporting).

(viii) *Executive information functionality:* extensive and easy-to-use reporting.

(ix) *Sales functionality:* contact management profiles and history, account management activities, order entry, proposal generation.

(x) *E-commerce functionality:* manages procurement through EDI link and web-server, and includes B2B and B2C applications.

(xi) *Telemarketing/Telesales functionality:* call list assembly, auto dialing, scripting, order taking.

e-CRM aims to increase the profitability of the customer portfolio, which comprises of many elements. For example, customer acquisition, price, cost to serve, cross sales (further sales to the same customer), up sales (the customer makes greater use of the same product or services), number and size of transactions, expected value of losses and longevity and (or) attrition. The attraction and retention of a firm's most valued customer is the bedrock of any CRM implementation.

It is generally accepted that it costs five times more to acquire a customer than to retain an existing one. In the new web-economy e-mail is the predominant form of return business communication. The new economy business mandate for business success is clear that the companies must exceed their customer's expectations all the time. Companies believe that to achieve this goal is to put all their basic business activities-marketing, sales, financial transactions on the web.

PRINCIPLES OF E-CRM

The following four key principles form the basis upon which the e-business can evaluate the success of e-CRM implementation and its transition to the new economy.

(i) The e-business knowledge is captured and given context during the customer interaction.

(ii) The e-business delivers real value to the customers with every interaction.

(iii) The e-business systems are integrated throughout the value chain, not just at the level of the financial transaction.

(iv) The e-business offers its customers multiple channels for communication.

EXPECTATIONS FROM E-CRM

Examine the relationship between business and customers, as it exist right now. Do not be under the impression that there is a good relationship with customer simply because the customers visit the web site are too many. They may not complain even if they are unhappy. If the business is not getting any information by e-mail, it does not mean that what is being done is right. It may be true that the customers no longer care and are actively looking for another supplier to replace you. Firstly, one must assess the current state of relationship with the customers honestly and sincerely. Next is to map out the journey to e-CRM from the current state. Decide and chart a course that takes the business to the ideal state. It must be remembered that achieving e-CRM is not an end in itself- it is a means to success. The vehicle used for the journey mostly will be the Internet, but every channel of communication available right from the telephone to a brick-and-mortar storefront, is acceptable. All the details and knowledge about the product is poured into these channels. Similarly, the customers will pour all of their information into the channels. Synthesis results in so that a new way of meeting customer's needs will emerge creating opportunity in the new economy.

BENEFITS OF E-CRM

For a business enterprise to achieve ROI from e-CRM, investment in the application domain and technology of e-CRM must contribute to measurable benefits, in addition to intangible benefit (say, customer loyalty). The benefit categories that enterprises should consider are:

(i) *Cost savings:* Cost savings results from the elimination of non-value added activities and can significantly reduce transaction processing cost.

(ii) *Intangible benefits:* Intangible or soft benefits are difficult to quantify.

(iii) *Efficiency:* Efficiency results from performing and operating quickly and accurately in the least wasteful manner.

(iv) *Effectiveness:* Effectiveness results from operating in the most impressive and extraordinary manner.

(v) *Marketing costs:* Reduce marketing costs by developing effective and targeted campaigns.

(vi) *Profitable customers:* Identify the most profitable customers and treat them accordingly. Roughly 20% of the customers generate 80% of the profits.

(vii) *Customer retention:* Increase customer retention by enhancing satisfaction as a result of higher responsiveness.

(viii) *Competitive advantage:* Increase sales and customer loyalty to generate competitive advantage.

(ix) *Customer understanding:* Improve understanding of customer needs by using their preferred channel of communication.

(x) *Prediction of future:* Project after estimating, the future sales, marketing and service activities expected by the customers, based on the analysis of past performance.

CHALLENGES TO E-CRM

The following problems in terms of technical aspects are likely to arise in the way of successful implementation of e-CRM:

(i) Designing an overall architecture that allows rapid integration with legacy systems while creating an open-ended platform positioned for new customer contact channel growth.

(ii) Achieving optimal performance of a system that is hybrid in nature (transactional and data warehousing).

(iii) Managing work flow around extraction, transformation and load process to ensure data quality, buying key components such as data models, middle ware tools and front-end applications.

(iv) Right tools with right strategy and data are key to successful adoption of E-CRM.

FEW EXPERIENCES AND PROJECTIONS

According to NASSCOM, the CRM market in India is currently estimated around $2 million and is slated to grow to $17 million by 2006. By 2004, only 35 per cent of enterprises will adequately define the cost and benefits metrics desired from their e-CRM strategies before implementing tactical projects. These enterprises will be able to quantify the benefits of leveraging technology to enable their e-CRM strategy. By 2004, 55 per cent of CRM and e-CRM initiatives will fail to meet measurable benefit objectives and will fail to positively affect ROI due to lack of business processes for Conducting ongoing measurements. Gurbaxani of 24/7 customer.com opinions that 'Now SCM and CRM are complementary applications and need to work in tandem to get a job done. Knowledge management (KM) is a part of CRM and is used for analysis and to cross-sell and up sell. Thus, CRM along with SCM and KM are going to be important aspects for companies to be successful in the future".

Gartner study says that companies in the future are going to commit 16 per cent of their investments in CRM, 5 per cent in ERP and 13 per cent in SCM.

According to Cartner group, atleast 80% of the enterprises underestimate the time and resources required, with many exceeding their budgets for this effort, by 2 or 3 times. According to a report from IDC the CRM software sales will grow from US $6.2 billion in 2000 to $14 billion in 2005 demonstrating a five year Compounded Annual Growth Rate (CACR) of 25.2%. This growth rate remains well above that of overall IT services market, which shows a CAGR of 12 per cent during 2000-2005. Giga Information Group says that CRM is the least likely category of software that companies will cut. The prediction of Giga indicates a growth rate of 5% or more for CRM. World wide the CRM applications sector clocked over 84% growth in 2000-01 and despite the slow down, the CACR for 2001-02 is expected to be in the 55-60% range.

E-CRM IN DOWN TURNS

Keeping in view of growing demand in CRM, by making use of IT efficiently, organisations achieve lot of benefits even in the down turns. During down turns, the companies often failed to take any initiative or program which is not certain to offer instant success. Many of them are not taking risk, laying off their work force, auctioning their meager physical assets to pay creditors. The willingness to reorganise the significant process from the company is very important. During downtimes the companies must identify the failure parts of their customer service and try to resolve them.

FUTURE OF E-CRM

According to Gartner, with today's dazzling and seductive technology, enterprises must carefully calculate and understand the benefits they will gain and must realise that E-CRM investments may not show quantifiable benefits in the short term. A healthy balance of hard and soft benefits is a sign of a well-thoughtout justification for pursuing e-CRM. However, enterprises at put both justification and measurement processes in place will have the greatest chance to gain a competitive edge.

During the last few years, glabalisation in the field of e-commerce has challenged the companies to make customer communication truly interactive. The e-CRM is drifting away from *one-to-* many mass-communication philosophy to more individualized, *one-to-one* communication. Real-time, automated marketing communication in relation to the effective, personalized sales and services will make the firm's communications to the consumer relevant and timely.

In future, there will be nothing like e-business since all businesses will have an e-layer. In a similar way, the difference between CRM and e-CRM will disappear. As mentioned already, todays market is facing increase in customer expectations and customer relationship complexity, which is caused not only by the new and continuously evolving-technology but also due to greater mobility in the field and faster development of new products. Firms must keep increasing the relationship-complexity function between its customers and themselves. They must shift away from the old paradigm of mass production to the new paradigm of mass customisation to meet the exact and specified demands of the customer.

The rapidly growing Internet based technologies are making a major impact on managing customer's relationships, where companies are establishing one-to-one customer relationships online. The Internet is increasingly serving customers, either directly or in combination with traditional channel-intermediaries.

CASE STUDY

Introduction

CONCEPT OF CRM

CRM, or Customer Relationship Management, is a company-wide business strategy designed to reduce costs and increase profitability by solidifying customer loyalty. True CRM brings together information from all data sources within an organization (and where appropriate, from outside the organization) to give one, holistic view of each customer in real time. This allows customer facing employees in such areas as sales, customer support, and marketing to make quick yet informed decisions on everything from cross-selling and upselling opportunities to target marketing strategies to competitive positioning tactics.

Once thought of as a type of software, CRM has evolved into a customer-centric philosophy that must permeate an entire organization. There are three key elements to a successful CRM initiative: people, process, and technology. The people throughout a company—from the CEO to each and every customer service rep—need to buy into and support CRM. A company's business processes must be reengineered to bolster its CRM initiative, often from the view of, How can this process better serve the customer? Firms must select the right technology to drive these improved processes, provide the best data to the employees, and be easy enough to operate that users won't balk. If one of these three foundations is not sound, the entire CRM structure will crumble.

This sounds like a panacea, but CRM is not without its challenges. For CRM to be truly effective, an organization must convince its staff that change is good and that CRM will benefit them. Then it must analyze its business processes to decide which need to be reengineered and how best to go about it. Next is to decide what kind of customer information is relevant and how it will be used. Finally, a team of carefully selected executives must choose the right technology to automate what it is that needs to be automated. This process, depending upon the size of the company and the breadth of data, can take anywhere from a few weeks to a year or more. And although some firms are using Web-based CRM technologies for only hundreds of dollars per month per user, large companies may spends millions to purchase, install, and customize the technology required to support its CRM initiative.

The initial part of the case study is about the definition of CRM in 1990's and how it changed by 2002 as a result of number of new factors that emerged in the business environment like the companies becoming more customer-oriented in approach and the transition from data driven CRM model to a process focus CRM, etc. Further the case study discusses about the two approaches to CRM by discussing in detail the elements of both the approaches. First approach is governed by language, logic, interpretation and the other one is governed by geometry, non-verbal processes.

CONCEPT OF E-CRM

e-CRM (also occasionally e-CRM) is the electronically delivered or managed subset of CRM. The user of an e-CRM solution uses the resources of the internet or other digital media (for example SMS, mobile data or interactive Television) to deliver elements of a marketing relationship with the customer.

Some web-based CRM tools can help manage the relationships between Central Sales Management, Regional Sales Offices and salespeople by creating rules-based links between different data-sets based on customer purchase cycles, product cycles, sales cycles and other product development, marketing or behavioural patterns. Other e-CRM systems can act as an automated data mining tool, enabling system owners to automate customer communications based on sets of pre-defined rules.

At its most sophisticated, e-CRM can be defined as an enterprise-wide technology-driven approach to the management of all data relating directly or indirectly to customers, in turn helping to define overall product development and marketing strategies.

The term e-CRM is also be used to describe the customer-facing, digitally-delivered portion of CRM. The term usually implies capabilities like self-service knowledge bases; automated, semi-automated or structured e-mail marketing communications (based on preference, behaviour, previous response, etc.); personalisation (either by an individual member of the database or according to rules set by the administrator) of content, etc.

DISTINCTION BETWEEN CRM AND E-CRM

Both the conceptually same, but the way of implementing the process is different in the other words we can say that e-CRM is the automated version of CRM.

Some of the main differences between CRM to e-CRM are:

In CRM emphasis is made on personal selling while in e-CRM there is a customer database, readily available every time

In CRM customer is contacted by male, telephone, in person while in e-CRM customer information system is readily available

In CRM services of after sales; complaint handling; account management; customer care; and customer satisfaction is available while in e-CRM services of EPOS sales force; automation customers: support processes; call centers; system integration and life value of customer

The Indian Hotel Industry

Some facts about Indian Hotel Industry

In 2004-05, Visakhapatnam was the market leader in terms of occupancy, registering occupancy of 80.6 per cent. Bangalore achieved the second-highest occupancy at 79.8 per cent. It also had the highest (ARR), across all categories among the 30 cities, with an ARR of Rs. 6,762. New Delhi was the second highest, registering an ARR of Rs. 5,498. All India average occupancy was 63.6 per cent, an increase of 3.9 per cent occupancy points above the previous year's level, or 6.5 per cent in real terms. All India ARR increased by 26.9 per cent over the previous year.

Star category-wise occupancies ranged between 46.3 per cent to 72.1 per cent. Average rates showed a much greater spread, from Rs. 5,499 for five-star deluxe hotels to Rs. 643 for one-star hotels, an increase of Rs. 1,052 and Rs. 140, respectively, from the previous year.

The All India average revenue per available room (RevPAR) increased substantially, from Rs. 1,605 in 2003-04 to Rs. 2,170 in 2004-05, reflecting an increase of 35.2 per cent. In the eight years of the survey, this has been the second-highest RevPAR growth (the highest was 46.2 per cent in 2003-04).

Rooms revenue, generally considered being the most important source of a hotel's overall profitability, was 57.7 per cent of total revenue for five-star deluxe hotels, 60.1 per cent of total revenue for five-star hotels and 56.6 per cent for four-star hotels. Overall (across all hotels) it represented 57.3 per cent of total revenue (an increase of 5.7 per cent from 2003-04).

Food amp; Beverage revenue represented 28.3 per cent of total revenue across all hotels, a decrease of 4.6 per cent from last year. (This reflects the increased share of rooms revenue in the total of 100). The all India average of Rooms department expense as a percentage of Rooms revenue declined further from 17.8 per cent in 2003-04 to 14.7 per cent in 2004-05.

Similarly, the all India average Food amp; Beverage department expense as a percentage of Food amp; Beverage revenue declined from 55.9 per cent in 2003-

04 to 53.9 per cent in 2004-05. Minor Operated department expense as a percentage of Minor Operated department revenue registered an increase from 53.7 per cent in 2003-04 to 58.8 per cent in 2004-05.

Telephone and other department expense, at 64.3 per cent of total revenue, was the highest departmental expense. Total departmental expense as a percentage of total departmental revenue reflected a further decline, from 37.4 per cent in 2002-03 and 33.7 per cent in 2003-04 to 30.9 per cent in 2004-05. This is partly owing to higher ARRs.

Percentage of foreign guests increased to 28.3 per cent in 2004-05, compared to 25.0 per cent in 2003-04, primarily as the percentage of foreign business travellers grew. Of the foreign guests, the UK provided the largest demand, at 16.2 per cent, followed by USA, at 12.8 per cent, and France at 7.2 per cent. Domestic guests continue to be the most important segment for the Indian hotel industry, accounting for 71.7 per cent of all guests in 2004-05, though this has decreased marginally from 75 per cent in 2003-04 and 76.9 per cent in 2002-03.

All India average stay of a business traveller has increased from two days to 2.4 days. There is an increase in foreign business travellers utilising five-star deluxe, five-star, four-star hotels and heritage hotels from 27 per cent, 18.6 per cent, 11.4 per cent and 11.7 per cent, respectively, in 2003-04 to 28.1 per cent, 21.4 per cent,13.7 per cent and 14.1 per cent, respectively, in 2004-05.

Owing to all India increased occupancy, property operations and maintenance expenses per available room (PAR) has increased from Rs. 69,735 in 2003-04 to Rs. 91,981 in 2004-05.

Average monthly occupancy was highest in December (at 71.7 per cent), followed by November (at 67.8 per cent) and January, February (at 65.8 per cent).

Direct enquiry and advance reservations by travel agents and tour operators cumulatively comprise 75.9 per cent of reservation source for the Indian hotel industry. Five-star deluxe hotels are making the best use of GDS as 8.1 per cent of the total reservations for five-star deluxe hotels come from GDS, against the all India average of 1.7 per cent. GDS reservations generally provide higher room rates compared to the other channels.

Print advertising is the most popular medium used by the Indian hotel industry with the all India average at 92.2 per cent of hotels using it, followed by 82.5 per cent using direct mails.

Radio advertising features as the least utilised marketing media at 8.4 per cent, followed by merchandising at 24.5 per cent, by the Indian hotel industry in 2004-05. All five-star deluxe hotels (sample size 32) used the hotel website at 100 per cent as a marketing medium in 2004-05.

Credit cards as a mode of transaction increased from 27.7 per cent and 30.4 per cent in 2002-03 and 2003-04, respectively to 32.5 per cent in 2004-05. Credit cards remained the most popular method of payment at five-star deluxe hotels at 47.4 per cent. Visa (41.8 per cent) was the most widely used credit card by hotel guests in 2004-05, followed by Mastercard (37 per cent). American Express charged the highest credit card commission at 2.9 per cent against 1.7 per cent by Visa and Mastercard.

Comparison with the results of the survey in 2004-05 with the previous year, shows that nearly all categories (except one-star hotels) saw an increase in occupancy and a significant increase in average rate (except heritage hotels). This resulted in a major increase in RevPAR across all categories with the highest RevPAR growth in four-star hotels at 41.9 per cent and an all India RevPAR growth at 35.2 per cent. The demand for rooms has been positive and owing to lack of adequate new supply, hotels in nearly all categories have managed to simultaneously increase the occupancy and average rates.

Among environmental issues, electricity consumption is the most monitored attribute, followed by water consumption. Five-star deluxe and five-star hotels continue to monitor environmental issues most closely. Energy expenses accounted for 8.9 per cent of total revenue in 2004-05 against 10.5 per cent of total revenue in 2003-04 and 12.3 per cent in 2002-03. This may be partly attributed to rising revenues and partly to the increase in efforts made to conserve energy by the industry.

AVERAGE OCCUPANCIES AMP; RATES FOR CITIES IN INDIA

	Average Occupancy					*Average Rate*				
City	*2000-2001*	*2001-2002*	*2002-2003*	*2003-2004*	*2004-2005*	*2000-2001*	*2001-2002*	*2002-2003*	*2003-2004*	*2004-2005*
(1)	*(2)*	*(3)*	*(4)*	*(5)*	*(6)*	*(7)*	*(8)*	*(9)*	*(10)*	*(11)*
All India	55.60%	53.20%	54.80%	59.70%	63.60%	Rs. 2,046	Rs. 2,058	Rs. 2,004	Rs. 2,689	Rs. 3,413
Agra	55.40%	42.90%	42.20%	51.00%	62.70%	Rs. 1,615	Rs. 1,269	Rs. 1,232	Rs. 2,201	Rs. 1,895
Aurangabad	44.80%	ID	34.10%	63.00%	61.10%	Rs. 1,378	ID	Rs. 1,733	Rs. 2,998	Rs. 1,784
Bangalore	72.10%	62.80%	72.40%	78.90%	79.80%	Rs. 2,570	Rs. 1,921	Rs. 2,149	Rs. 4,109	Rs. 6,762
Bhopal	53.90%	ID	62.30%	59.60%	71.20%	Rs. 1,288	ID	Rs. 1,145	Rs. 1,677	Rs. 1,785
Chennai	75.10%	65.00%	63.90%	61.60%	73.30%	Rs. 2,118	Rs. 1,936	Rs. 2,048	Rs. 2,061	Rs. 2,384
Cochin	68.20%	58.70%	57.60%	69.00%	64.80%	Rs. 816	Rs. 1,306	Rs. 1,089	Rs. 1,368	Rs. 1,062
Coimbatore	56.40%	ID	ID	64.50%	67.50%	Rs. 1,366	ID	ID	Rs. 1,407	Rs. 1,401
Darjeeling	26.30%	28.20%	ID	62.60%	66.30%	Rs. 671	Rs. 1,630	Rs. ID	Rs. 1,902	Rs. 1,570
Goa	57.10%	56.10%	60.20%	65.30%	60.10%	Rs. 2,174	Rs. 1,756	Rs. 1,982	Rs. 2,147	Rs. 2,704
Hyderabad	71.40%	67.20%	71.00%	72.80%	75.20%	Rs. 1,842	Rs. 1,131	Rs. 2,049	Rs. 2,406	Rs. 2,729
Indore	65.10%	77.50%	64.70%	61.40%	60.00%	Rs. 874	Rs. 850	Rs. 782	Rs. 521	Rs. 661
Jaipur	52.30%	56.20%	56.90%	62.60%	71.50%	Rs. 2,051	Rs. 1,543	Rs. 1,289	Rs. 1,628	Rs. 1,791

(*Contd.*)

Table Contd.

(1)	(2)	(3)	(4)	(5)	(6)	(7)	(8)	(9)	(10)	(11)
Jodhpur	34.70%	32.50%	37.40%	45.90%	56.20%	Rs. 2,117	Rs. 1,290	Rs. 1,561	Rs. 1,226	Rs. 3,346
Kolkata	66.70%	61.70%	63.60%	64.60%	67.10%	Rs. 2,465	Rs. 1,417	Rs. 1,342	Rs. 2,520	Rs. 2,210
Kullu-Manali	44.40%	39.80%	ID	34.50%	47.00%	Rs. 760	Rs. 1,498	ID	Rs. 1,964	Rs. 2,668
Lucknow	53.30%	56.50%	56.60%	66.30%	66.70%	Rs. 2,019	Rs. 1,166	Rs. 1,129	Rs. 1,642	Rs. 1,867
Mount Abu	ID	42.10%	38.10%	51.80%	47.10%	ID	Rs. 980	Rs. 922	Rs. 1,084	Rs. 1,255
Mumbai	66.10%	63.80%	62.60%	66.30%	74.90%	Rs. 3,591	Rs. 2,075	Rs. 1,822	Rs. 3,063	Rs. 4,307
Mussoorie	52.90%	ID	ID	70.00%	61.00%	Rs. 1,766	ID	ID	Rs. 2,685	Rs. 2,997
Mysore	52.50%	ID	51.10%	34.80%	ID	Rs. 660	ID	Rs. 1,120	Rs. 878	Rs. ID
Nagpur	55.00%	60.00%	57.20%	51.30%	46.10%	Rs. 643	Rs. 1,113	Rs. 1,032	Rs. 985	Rs. 931
New Delhi	59.30%	55.90%	58.30%	69.10%	76.60%	Rs. 3,911	Rs. 3,434	Rs. 2,918	Rs. 4,247	Rs. 5,498
Pune	58.10%	58.00%	59.90%	62.10%	77.20%	Rs. 2,036	Rs. 1,044	Rs. 1,141	Rs. 1,820	Rs. 1,295
Shimla	48.10%	43.60%	46.70%	45.00%	53.80%	Rs. 1,062	Rs. 1,578	Rs. 1,022	Rs. 2,080	Rs. 1,679
Thiruvananthapuram	57.00%	55.40%	60.30%	51.10%	47.50%	Rs. 1,153	Rs. 966	Rs. 983	Rs. 1,302	Rs. 1,805
Udagamandalam (Ooty)	ID	38.00%	ID	48.80%	44.40%	Rs. ID	Rs. 947	Rs. ID	Rs. 1,609	Rs. 1,861
Udaipur	44.00%	44.30%	46.60%	45.70%	54.50%	Rs. 3,402	Rs. 1,924	Rs. 1,644	Rs. 2,473	Rs. 3,800
Vadodara	58.00%	43.50%	46.40%	62.50%	62.60%	Rs. 1,116	Rs. 1,039	Rs. 1,110	Rs. 458	Rs. 467
Visakhapatnam	65.60%	56.60%	ID	70.10%	80.60%	Rs. 877	Rs. 1,184	ID	Rs. 1,293	Rs. 1,531

ID - Insufficient Data.

Other Significant Trends

All India average revenue per hotel has grown significantly, from Rs. 9.15 crore during 2003-04 to Rs. 11.49 crore during 2004-05, and is expected to see further improvement in the next few years owing to an increase in occupancy and average rate.

House Profit (Gross Operating Profit after deducting franchise and management fees) as a percentage of revenue increased from 34.8 per cent in 2003-04 to 40.7 per cent in 2004-05. The all India average net income (income before depreciation, interest payments and taxes) per hotel also increased, from Rs. 2.80 crore (34.8 per cent) in 2003-04 to Rs. 4.08 crore (40.7 per cent) in 2004-05, reflecting the overall health of the industry.

July has the lowest monthly occupancy in the year. However, occupancy for all months was higher in 2004-05 compared to the last five years.

RELEVANCE OF INDUSTRY TO TOPIC

The topic is "journey of CRM to e-CRM"

The Indian hotel industry is relevant to the topic in a way that it was just a few years back that the concept of e-CRM has been employed in Indian hotel industry. Before that the traditional methods of CRM were being used. So in a way Indian hotel industry had its journey from CRM to e-CRM. e.g earlier customer contact was being made through mail or telephone but now its done via e-mail. Customer can enjoy the benefits of online booking, online payment and can also get the readily available information via hotel's website. Earlier customer feedback was obtained through long questionnaires but now the entire process has been automated.

E-CRM STRATEGY IN HOSPITALITY

The Internet has transformed Customer Relationship Management (CRM) in hospitality. A large majority of your customers are planning and booking their hotel stay online. How do you nurture, grow and retain your customer base when the competition is just a click away? How do you prepare for the future in this very dynamic and transparent online environment? How do you beat the competition for the most lucrative customer segments? By building a comprehensive e-CRM strategy and creating interactive mutually beneficial relationships with your customer, any hotel company can ensure its survival in this new environment.

On average approximately 2% of hotel website visitors will make a booking while the other 98% will read, scan, and then leave your site. Without a comprehensive CRM strategy in place hoteliers will never know much about their website visitors, bookers or lookers. Even if Internet users book on the hotel website and hoteliers draw some information out of them, the blending of business and leisure customers makes it hard for hotels to differentiate who they are and follow up with appropriate marketing messages. Many hoteliers know next to nothing about their customers and their travel planning and purchasing behavior.

A Customer Relationship Management strategy and the rise of low cost e-CRM tools to help support this strategy have helped many hoteliers address the question "Know your customer." Many of these low cost tools can interface with the PMS, and when done right they allow for high quality data gathering either online or at check in. Do not underestimate the value that a CRM strategy can provide. Have your strategy in place and then find a technology that will fit this strategy.

Rewarding loyalty is one way to know your customer. A loyalty program need not be complicated, expensive, or labor intensive. A few small brands and ownership groups have introduced such programs in the past few years and most are used to combat the use of third-party intermediaries. The loyalty movement in hospitality continues and when performed effectively can produce meaningful results for your hotel, the brand, and most importantly your customer.

BACKGROUND

The traditional CRM focus in hospitality has always been Customer Satisfaction.

The presumption is very simple: customers will appreciate good service so much that they would not go to your competitor. In other words: customer satisfaction + quality of services = customer loyalty.

The truth is that customer satisfaction does not always equal customer loyalty:

A new study published in August 2004 by Cornell University also calls into question the widely held belief that guest satisfaction means repeat business. The results of its recent study challenged the theory that satisfied guests generate repeat business in the lodging industry. Analysis showed only a weak connection between satisfaction and loyalty, which is a precursor to repeat business.

Dr. Kano, a prominent Japanese quality expert, believes that customers experience value at 3 dimensions: the Basic, the Expected, and the Unanticipated Value. The Kano Model stipulates that only when companies provide well above and beyond what the customer expects they operate in the Unanticipated Value dimension. Only when companies operate in the Unanticipated Value environment they can build strong customer loyalty.

E-CRM IN HOTELS TODAY

Electronic customer relationship management (e-CRM), in the context of the exploding Internet distribution and marketing in hospitality, is a business strategy supported by Web technologies, allowing hoteliers to engage customers in strong, personalized and mutually beneficial interactive relationships, increase conversions and sell more efficiently.

e-CRM cannot exist in isolation. Today's multi-channel marketing model requires a single brand image to be communicated across all channels. In the same time it requires interactive customer relationships to be established and maintained across all channels.

Anytime an Internet user lands on a hotel website, a branding interaction occurs. This branding interaction can be positive (brand-building) or negative (brand-eroding). Unfortunately for some hoteliers on many occasions a visit to the hotel website turns out to be the last point of contact with this particular customer.

Two key questions are facing hoteliers today:

Who owns the customer in this new online environment? The online intermediary, which made the booking, or the hotel where the guest stayed?

How can hoteliers establish mutually beneficial interactive relationships with the customers in order to increase repeat business, boost revenues, and retain loyalty?

Here are the main aspects in e-CRM in hospitality:

Know Your Customer

Customer Service

Personalization

More Efficient Marketing

Building Customer Loyalty

The main aspects of e-CRM in hospitality:

Know Your Customer

Knowing your website visitors is an extremely important consideration when conceptualizing and designing your hotel website and your e-CRM strategy. After all, addressing your key audiences and providing them with relevant information is one of the key aspects of any hospitality site.

Different customer segments should easily identify areas on the site that speak to them. Internet users visit a hotel website not as John Smith or Jane Smith, but as a Business Traveler, Meeting Planner, Special Event Planner, Family Traveler, Spa Services Seeker, Golf Outing Seeker, Vacation Planner, Convention Attendee, Wedding Planner, etc. If you do not speak to each of these audiences, you will lose most of them to your competition.

It is a matter of perspective on what is truly important to the customer. Different characteristics of the property can appeal to different customer segments. For example, to the business traveler, choosing a hotel may be influenced by the availability of a function room, high-speed Internet access or proximity to an area corporation, while a leisure traveler may find the same hotel a great location for local area attractions; same hotel, same destination, different purpose.

Personalization

Personalization is more than providing the right information to the right person at the right time. Personalizing the customer experience on the hotel website is a powerful conversion and retention tool. Customizing your interaction with your most valuable customers (those 20% that generate 80% of your business) will provide significant long-term rewards.

Personalization on the property level should start by identifying all electronic touch points with your customers (hotel guests, meeting planners, travel professionals, etc.) and creating an action plan. Personalize all electronic communications with your customers. Adopt a policy on how to address your guests via e-mail (first name only, Mr./Mrs. + Last Name, etc). Addressing the customer segmentation issues on the property website is a logical next step. Creating a targeted e-mail marketing campaign is another good step.

For the major hotel brands, the personalization efforts are much more complex and expensive. Customization tools used by some major brands and airlines allow website users to actively personalize their website experiences using over 250 criteria. Here are some of the efforts by the major travel and hospitality companies to make the user experience more personable.

Personalization agents using a variety of customization applications, capable of creating Behavioral Profiles and a Real-time profile for each customer.

Collaborative filtering: Using preference matrix and artificial intelligence to capture and predict customer interests.

Decision-support applications utilizing various applications for Behavioral Profiling, Predictive Modeling, Collaborative Filtering and Click-Stream Analysis, capable to sense the purchasing behavior and patterns of the user. By providing a customized booking experience these applications can boost the conversion rates.

Customer Support

It is important to understand that customer service is only one aspect of e-CRM and is primarily a reactive function aiming to improve performance and efficiency, while e-CRM as a whole is a proactive long-term strategy.

We believe that on the Internet the customer support aspect of e-CRM is an extremely important trust building and customer retention tool. A well positioned Contact Us or Help button or Push-to-talk feature speaks volumes about the hotel brand ("They care about us") and builds trust. 57% of online shoppers actively seek sites with good customer service.

Only 50% of those searching travel online actually make their bookings online. The other 50% look online, but book offline, due to privacy issues, security concerns, purchasing habits, or need to speak with a live agent to finalize the travel booking, etc. Therefore, a hotel website should take extra steps to accommodate these 50% of the potential bookers by providing online help desks, live agents, push-to-talk features, very visible 1-800 numbers, TTY phone numbers, etc.

Customer support in the Internet age relies on a wide range of tools and techniques:

Web Self-Service Tools: Intelligent service channel management and natural language search engines, directing customer requests to most appropriate support information and services; FAQs; Ask the experts self-service chat rooms, interactive maps and directions and business locators, etc.

Live Service Tools: Push-to-talk functionality and real-time interaction with live agent; instant messaging and chat-room type of assistance; Voice-over-

Internet Protocols (VOIP) applications; automation to pre-screen live support (selective approach).

E-Mail Service Tools: Inbound e-mail management; automated e-mail response systems, capable of automating 80%-90% of e-mail volume with 98% accuracy, and dramatically improving service and reducing support staff by up to 40%.

More Efficient Marketing

e-Marketing plays a crucial role in establishing interactive relationships with your customers. E-Marketing is a marketing strategy that uses the Internet as its medium. This includes display ads (e.g. traditional banners), keyword search, classifieds, e-mail marketing, referrals and sponsorships, etc.

The main issues facing e-Marketers in hospitality today are:

Guest profiling and one-to-one marketing.

Accurate segmentation: focused segmentation equals higher response rates.

Create narrow-focused marketing campaigns.

Utilizing lifestyle data and personal preferences in the marketing.

Building opt-in e-mail lists and precision e-mail marketing (fivefold higher response rates).

Internal benchmark of customer lifetime value.

Cross-selling opportunities.

Campaign tracking and ROI analysis.

Developing a robust and effective e-Marketing strategy requires not only an extensive knowledge of your customers and precise customer segmentation, shifting marketing finds from offline to online channels, but deciding what your marketing objectives are. E-Marketing can be successfully used as a direct response vehicle (short-term, results-oriented) or as a branding tool (long-term and strategic goals).

Customer Loyalty

True loyalty on the Internet is difficult to achieve your competition is just a click away. Loyalty Programs of the major hotel brands provide a crucial competitive advantage over online discounters and intermediaries who do not have such programs.

Loyalty programs are very popular with online travelers, and especially with people who book online. Forrester reports than in 2002 over 80% of Online Bookers belong to some kind of a travel loyalty program, and more than 60% to a supplier-sponsored one. Here are the most obvious benefits of a well-functioning loyalty program in hospitality:

Identify your most loyal customers

Market to your most loyal customers

Accumulate guest-centric customer intelligence

Optimize Lifetime Guest Value

Yet hoteliers do not need just any customer loyalty. A low-attachment loyalty (e.g. inertia loyalty, price loyalty) can bring only limited results. Hoteliers should strive to achieve a true Premium Loyalty (i.e. emotional or brand loyalty), which is characterized by high level of attachment and repeat purchases. This is the ultimate loyalty valued most by companies.

CONCLUSION

e-CRM is an integral part of online distribution and marketing in hospitality. The Internet provides the best direct means to reach existing and potential customers. Establishing interactive relationships with your customers, which is the essence of e-CRM, will help you retain your customers, increase revenues, and build brand loyalty.

BENEFITS OF E-CRM

BENEFITS TO CUSTOMERS

Online bookings can be made by the customers, online payments can be made by the customers, any information regarding the check-in and checkout time can be posted on website, queries can be posted in hotel's website, to be answered by the concerned person, various details regarding the hotel are readily available to customer, the customer could get all the information about the hotel without making much efforts, customer may also have the advantage of site-seeing via hotel's website, it's a cost effective way to surf information for the customers, and the customer can easily compare the various hotels on various parameters by visiting web-sites of different hotels.

The following benefits can be made available to customers through various methods:

Site Customisation

When the company operates a web site (which are very useful e-CRM tools), it has the opportunity to make a lot of information available to the customers. Giving the right information at the right time to the customers is part of good CRM practices. However, a piece of information that is appropriate for one customer may not be appropriate for another customer and this is when companies are falling in the trap of the information overload. This is why site customisation features are so important, it will allow the customer to personalize her access to the site by choosing during her first visit to the site her preferences. A password protected entry and/or a cookie that will be left in her computer will allow the company server to recognize her during her next visits and will display only the information she desires. The example of AnyYahoo.com is the most famous example of this customisable web site.

Alternative Channels

The information and communication technologies will offer a variety of new ways for the company to get in touch with its customers. Examples are electronic mails, Short Message Service (SMS), voice over IP, which can be added to the list of older channels such as fax and phones.

Local Search Engine

This kind of function is very important to the customers since it allows searching the site on keywords in order to locate quickly specific information they are looking for.

Membership

As specified before, the company can ask the customers to request a password in order to navigate on password-protected parts of the web site. One advantage of such a feature is that it makes the customer feels special since she has access to a load of information, which is not available to everybody. But the most interesting advantage in term of CRM is the fact that the company will be able to gain valuable information from the customer when she registers to get the password.

Mailing List

In that case, the company will use different opportunities (the customer is browsing on the site, phone call, etc.) to have the customer register on the mailing lists which means that the company will be able to send newsletters or any customised information to the customer, by e-mail and on a regular basis.

Site Tour

The customer can follow a tour through the web site, which gives her an idea of the organization. Then, she will be able to easily find her way to appropriate pieces of information during her next access to the site.

Site Map

A map of the site is proposed to the customer in order for her to find her way easily through the different layers of pages contained in the site. It is a hierarchical diagram that can also be called site overview or site index.

Introduction for first-time users

This feature is very close from the "site tour" feature. In this case, the first-time visitors of the web site to access an introduction page that contains information about how to use the site the most efficiently.

Chat

This feature exploits the tremendous advantage of the internet which is the interactivity it provides. Indeed, the interaction between different customers and some company's representative can, in a number of cases, generate information for the company and content for the site which are both very interesting elements.

Electronic Bulletin Board

Also called forums, this feature has the same advantages as the chat with the exception that the interaction won't be instantaneous. A customer can use the bulletin board to post a message in order to ask a question or give her opinion about a product or a service. Then the message will remain on the forum and other customers of specific company's employees will be able to react to this message. Again, this can produce interesting content for the site and the company can get interesting information about its customer.

Thus, Customer Relationship Management (CRM) is about finding, getting, and retaining customers. It is in fact a combination of business processes and technology that seeks to understand a company's customers from a multi-faceted perspective: who they are, what they do, and what they like. Application of the above stated e-tools will give a tremendous boost to the Hospitality industry.

BENIFITS FOR THE HOTEL

The emergence of remote data access led to sales force automation aimed at reducing the cost and increasing the effectiveness of sales.

The growth of call centres added the customer service component providing the opportunity to service clients needs at reduced cost, further freeing the expensive sales force to perform higher value tasks.

The development of sophisticated data mining systems enabled management to devise highly focused marketing campaigns aimed at up-selling and cross selling products and services.

e-CRM technology means that the traditional internal boundaries of a company are starting to blur. Very soon, the principles of e-CRM start to merge into e-Procurement, e-Fulfilment, and eventually the total supply chain. Technologies are starting to be assessed in terms of the potential impact on the holistic customer experience of a company.

Adopting an e-CRM strategy means businesses can arm themselves with an understanding of what their customers want, and how and when they want it—driving business strategy, building brand awareness and attracting and retaining their most profitable customers

Issues in Applying e-CRM to Hospitality Industry

Negative Perception: Negative perceptions about CRM have discouraged many companies from going ahead with CRM. But many such decisions are based on the bad experiences of other companies.

Expensive: e-CRM is an expensive activity, most of the hotels in India are not having large capital base, so its become difficult to implement E-CRM, moreover Indian Hotels are considered to be expensive than the counterparts in world over, under such circumstances most of them will try to reduce cost burden and e-CRM looks to be a distant dream.

Standardisation : CRM/e-CRM is based on the customer, but in hotel industry it is very difficult to perceive what value addition customer do perceive, when he stay at a hotel, moreover, there are various types of customer having different needs, so it is very difficult to have a standardized pattern of CRM/e-CRM.

Specialisation: Application of e-CRM requires special knowledge and techniques, which require different set of skill possessed by professionals. In India e do not have these agencies which provide specialized e-CRM solutions for hospitality industry.

Customer Behaviour

Though Internet has forced Indian Hotel industry to think toward e CRM, but e-Commerce in India has not been able to establish itself very well, Indian customer still go by the travel agent then using internet for their vacation, or business planning, this case is also true with world population also, most of the visitor rely on middlemen, than Internet for booking their room or planning their vacation or business.

Staff Resistance: Human resources in any organization, industry are reluctant to change, so it would not be wrong to have same with Indian Hospitality Industry, with the induction of e-CRM the role and responsibility of each and every personnel will increase manifolds, and at current scenario Indian Human Resources are not equipped with that kind of training needed for implementation of e-CRM

Current Scenario of Indian Hotel Industry

The Indian hospitality sector is all set to witness a flood of the world's leading hotel brands. New brands such as Amanda, Satinwoods, Banana Tree, Hampton Inns, Scandium By Hilt and Mandarin Oriental are planning to enter the Indian hospitality industry in joint venture with various domestic hotel majors.

Hotel developers like ITC, EIH, Bharat Hotels, Viceroy, DLF, Unitech and Royal Palms are currently in negotiations with various hotel brands. ITC wants to extend its existing tie-up with the US-based Starwood Hotels beyond the latter's Sheraton brand and may bring other Starwood brands like W Hotels, Westin, Four Points and Aloft to India in ITC's new projects.

Unitech which is setting up two hotels in Delhi, has already formed a joint venture with Marriot International to run its three new hotels in India, which are expected to start operations by '08. "The three new hotels will be located in Kolkata, Gurgaon and Noida. We are investing around Rs. 700 crore to set-up these hotels," Unitech managing director, Sanjay Chandra said.

Mumbai-based Royal Palms is in talks with Anando, Starwoods, and Singapore based Banyan Tree for its three new hotel projects coming up in various parts of India. The firm has already tied-up with the US-based Carlson Hospitality and bought the Park Plaza brand to India recently.

"For the next decade or so, existing hotels will continue to flourish. We are planning to expand our hospitality business to other places like Chennai, Hyderabad and Kolkata in the next few years and we are in talks with leading hotel chains," Dilawar Nensey, joint managing director, Royal Palms said.

Currently, over 142 luxury hotel projects are coming up in India with an investment of Rs. 7,300 crore. The country is witnessing a spurt in hotels as India is facing a severe shortage of quality hotel rooms because of increased business activity and a spurt in leisure travel by the country's burgeoning middle class, as well as international tourists.

"These factors have generated a great interest in the American and European markets and many hotel brands have been keen to enter the Indian hospitality sector," industry analyst said. International tourist arrivals rose 13.2% in '05 to 3.9m, the highest ever, and the government expects arrivals in '06 to grow by 15%.

DLF sources said that Hilton International will be a minority stake holder in its hotel development company. The properties under DLF-Hilton joint venture would be managed and marketed by Hilton International.

DLF has chalked out plans to set up over 100 business and four-star hotels in 50 cities over the next seven to 10 years. Hilton may bring its other brands like Travel Lodge, Howard Johnson, Galileo GDS and Gulliver Travels to India.

Dubai-based Kingdom Hotel Investments is looking at an investment $1 bn and is currently in talks with leading hotel companies in India and is looking out for land and hotel projects in the country.

Inter-Globe Hotels has tied up with European player According to set-up 12 hotels under the Ibis brand. UK-based hospitality chain Thistle and Guoman Hotels has tied up with Nijhawan Group as its sales and marketing representative in the country.

Here is how hoteliers replied to question regarding their e-CRM programs:

HeBS Poll Results: Do you have an e-CRM Program in place at the hotel?

56% - Yes

22% - No

0% - Planning to implement in 2007

22% - Planning to implement in 2008

OPINION

The Indian hotel industry has witnessed a tremendous and a robust growth during the year 2003. It was first time since the attack at world trade centre that Indian tourism and hotel industry has witnessed such a growth, but in these years there has been an innovation in the Indian hotel industry. Each and every process in the industry has been automated the adoption of the world wide web not as merely a tool for providing information related to the hotels, but also to improve the quality and effectiveness of customer relationship management the process of CRM has begun to be addressed as CRM where CRM process is implemented with the help of electronic data bases and other electronic information.

In India we have not witnessed the boom in e-commerce to the extent it has witnessed in the other parts of World. It is evident to know that one of the biggest hotels chain in India the Taj group of hotel has not been able to implement e-CRM properly and has yet not been able to realize its full potential. Further, It is not been able to implement e-CRM at a scale and a level to which it have been implemented by the other reputed international hotel chains like Hilton which is leading in the process of e-CRM.

Research shows there has been an increase in the hotel occupancy rate via utilization of e-CRM. People across the World first prefer to get the entire information about the hotel; they are likely to book for their stay and moreover there has been increase in online booking in hotel industry.

FOOD FOR THOUGHT

Now million $ question arises

Will Indian Hotel industry be able to adapt self to the change pattern?

Moreover as we know the Indian hotels are expensive then their international counterparts so will they use e-CRM to increase their cost in short-run?

And should they employ e-CRM to incur the long-run benefits and will there be any benefit as regards the Indian Hotel Industry?

STUDY–QUESTIONS

1. Discuss the concept of CRM and e-CRM in brief. Also explain the steps of e-CRM.
2. Explain the various distinction between CRM amd e-CRM.
3. Write down the various benefits of e-CRM.
4. Write a detail note on the emerging trends of CRM.

7

CRM in Business to Business

INTRODUCTION

Companies that are actually communicating with online markets have flung the doors wide open. They're constantly searching for solid information they can share with customers and prospects via Web and FTP sites, e-mail lists, phone calls, whatever it takes. They're not half as concerned with protecting their data as with how much information they can give away. That's how they stay in touch, stay competitive, keep market attention from drifting to competitors. Such companies are creating a new kind of corporate identity, based not on the repetitive advertising needed to create "brand awareness,' but on substantive, personalized communications.' There's no question that the Internet has streamlined business processes, providing efficiencies unmatched by traditional ways of doing business. The Web makes things happen faster. But is speed enough?

In the early days of e-business, companies built their Web sites implementing so-called storefront software that enabled them to accept a customer's credit card information and automatically check inventory. They then ensured that their systems were robust enough to allow customers 24-by-7 access. Dot-com companies had to build organisations to support inventory tracking, delivery, and returns processing, and traditional companies had to quickly incorporate the Web channel into existing business practices. The ability to exploit multiple channels introduces a series of headaches for the IT executive charged with integrating legacy applications such as fulfilment and purchase-order systems with the Web. The better the organisation's current computing power, the more effective will be integration of the new Web channel into existing operations.

Don't get me wrong. The Web shouldn't simply be shoehorned into a company's existing business unless processes are already robust. Simply put, mere automation of business processes isn't enough. Companies will be expected to provide their customers and suppliers with even more information than ever before. To do that, they need the best databases, with the highest-quality data, and the applications and processes necessary to deliver that data, not to mention a cultural willingness to share data with suppliers and customers. Whether the company was a pure-play dot-com e-tailer or a traditional brick-and-mortar general merchandiser, key processes such as ordering, fulfilment, inventory management, and distribution all had to run at Web speed. The challenge of streamlining the supply chain to keep pace loomed ever more large. As companies adopt the mantra of "differentiate or die," they realize that manufacturing, like customer service, is an area of opportunity.

FEATURES OF BUSINESS MARKETS

Buying and selling of goods and services not only takes place between a consumer and a firm but also between two firms or businesses. A firm may buy raw material from the other firm or business to process it further or it may buy finished goods or even services to sell them to the consumers under its brand name. For example, Britannia Industries Limited buys flour from many flour mills to make biscuits, which are finally sold in the consumer as well as institutional markets. The business market comprises of all the organisations that buy goods and services for use in the production of other products and services that are sold, rented or supplied to others. It also includes retailing and other wholesale firms that acquire cnd goods for the purpose of rescuing or renting them to others at a profit. In the business buying process, business buyers determine which products and services their organisations need to purchase and thenfind, evaluate and choose among alternative suppliers and brands . The business market is many times bigger in size than the consumer market.

Each consumer item is a culmination of many operations executed on different raw material. For example, to produce a car, the car manufacturer has to buy tyres, paint, battery, upholstery and other items from different suppliers or firms. Therefore, many sees of business purchases are made for just one set of consumer purchase. Although fundamentally business markets also involve the same factors as consumer markets do, there are some characteristics that make them unique. These include:

(i) Market Structure and Demand

In a consumer market, there are usually many buyers., i.e. individuals or households. However, these buyers buy in less quantity. On the other hand, a business market contains a few but large buyers who buy in bulk. This increases the influence of these buyers, on the market. For instance, business markets are more geographically concentrated depending on where the big buyers lie. To cite an example, chemical manufacturers are more concentrated in the western part of India. Most demands in a business market are 'derived demands', being derived from quantity the firm hopes to sell to its customers. For instance, Maruti Udyog's demand for tyres, paint, etc., ultimately depends on how much it hopes to sell to consumers in India and abroad.

Many business markets have inelastic demands, i.e. the total demand for many business products is not much affected by price changes in the short run unless that is linked to the consumer demand. Finally, business markets have more fluctuating demands because a small change in consumer's demand can cause a large change in business demand. Thus the demand for many business goods and services tends to change much more quickly than the demand for consumer goods or services.

(ii) Nature of the Buying Unit

A business purchase usually involves more buyers involved in the decision-making process and a more professional purchasing effort. There are many purchasing agents whose entire professional life is dedicated towards buying in the business context. As the quantity of purchase and its value increases, the number of people involved in the purchase also tends to increase dramatically. The key players involved include technical experts, management and business markets experts and finally well-trained sales persons.

(iii) Types of Decisions and the Decision Process

Business buyers have to make more complex decisions than consumer buyers. This is because the volume and the value of the purchases are quite high and they have to make complex economic and technical considerations. In the buyer's organisation, interactions continuously take place among many people across different levels with respect to the purchase decisions. The business buying process is more formalised than the consumer buying process because of the complexity involved. Decisions may be made after due considerations of all the factors and this may involve considerable time for deliberation. Finally, in the business buying process, the buyer and the seller are much more dependent on each other.

Therefore, many a time, the business sellers directly work with their counterparts in the buying organisations. They help them make decisions by identifying and defining the problem, providing more information on the related products and informing them about the customisation that could be made. In the long run, it becomes very essential for the industrial marketer to build long-term close relationships with their customers. From the point of view of stimuli for the business buying situations, the major factors that influence the buying process include the four marketing Ps, i.e. product, price, place and promotion, combined with other forces in the environment that consists of economic, technological, political, cultural and competitive forces.

(iv) Types of Buying Situations in B2B Contexts

There are many types of buying situations in business-to-business context. They differ from each other with respect to the kind of complexity associated with the decision-making process. The amount of work that the buyer needs to put in before considering these purchases also varies. At one end of the spectrum is what is called the *straight re-buy*. This involves the buyer reordering something from its past supplier without any modifications. The purchase department, based on the list of past suppliers and their performance, routinely places these orders. An organisation may have an automated reordering system triggered off by a drop in the inventory levels. This saves ordering time and ensures timely supply of parts for the buying organisation.

In the *modified re-buy,* the buyer wants to modify the product specifications, prices, terms or suppliers. This process involves more decision-making efforts on the part of the buyer. Suppliers might feel slightly pressurised and might offer better terms to the buying firm. When a firm buys a service or a product for the first time, then it is referred to as *a new task situation*. In this case, if the cost or risk associated with the concerned purchase is more than the usual, the number of participants in the purchase process correspondingly increases. Initially, a lot of information about the purchase, the market, suppliers, etc., is collected. The suppliers may also send their prospects to the buyer in order to inform the buyers about their products and services and in the hope of getting their contract. The buyer has to decide on many specifications, suppliers, price limits, payment terms, order quantities, delivery terms, etc. The importance attached to each of these terms (factors) varies and influences the outcome from various parties across the organisation.

In many situations, buyers prefer to buy a packaged solution from a single supplier instead of buying the component from various suppliers and then integrating them. This is known as *systems buying*. Systems buying helps the organisation to avoid the tedious process of making multiple decisions involved in a complex buying situation. Systems selling is a key business marketing strategy for winning and holding accounts. The contract often goes to the firm, which provides the best system meeting the customer's needs. For example, many firms such as SAP sell complete ERP solutions to their customers. These packages not only offer a software solution but also help the organisation prepare for the change, train the end users and boost the implementation of various processes.

(v) Participants in the Business-buying Process

In business organisations, major buying decisions are made by its 'buying centre' that consists of individuals and units from across the organisation – each having an interest in the buying decision being made. Each of these units has a different influence on the buying process and members of the units play different roles. The buying centre includes all members of the organisation who play any of the following *five* roles in the purchase decision process:

(i) *Users:* They are members of the organisation who ultimately use the product or service. They initiate the buying process and help in defining the product specifications according to their requirements.

(ii) *Influencers:* They consist of all those members who have the technical capability to help define specifications and provide information for evaluating alternatives.

(iii) *Buyers:* They are the people who have the formal authority to select the suppliers and arrange terms of purchase. Their major role is in the selection of vendors and negotiating with them.

(iv) *Deciders:* They have the formal or informal power to select or approve the final suppliers. Sometimes buyers may play this role in routine purchases.

(v) *Gatekeepers:* They control the flow of information about the products/ services being purchased for use by others within the organisation. This often has an impact on the decision-making process.

The buying centre may not be a formally identified unit and it is usually a set of roles assumed by different people for different purchases. Sometimes one person may assume all the roles and may be the only person involved in the buying situation. The marketer in the selling organisation must know about the participants involvement in the decision-making, each participant's relative influence and the evaluation criteria each participant uses.

Sometimes, informal participants may actually make or strongly affect the buying decisions. Business buyers are highly influenced by environmental, organisational, interpersonal and individual factors as well as economic factors and accountability. More accountability for the purchase means greater attention being paid to details. Finally, it can be said that buying decisions result from the complex interactions of ever changing buyer-centre participants.

(vi) The Business Buying Process

The business buying process is much more complex than the consumer buying process. It usually consists of eight stages and may take quite a bit of time before a decision is finally made. Formally, the different stages are as follows:

1. *Problem recognition:* Here, a person in the firm recognises the problem or

the need that can be met by acquiring certain goods or services. Depending on that person's influence, the proposal may be carried further.

2. *General need description:* In this stage, the firm describes the general characteristics and quantity of the required item.
3. *Product specification:* The buying organisation decides on and specifies the best technical product characteristics for the required !tern in this stage.
4. *Supplier search:* This is the stage where the buyer tries to find the best vendors.
5. *Proposal solicitation:* In this stage, the buyer invites qualified suppliers to submit proposals.
6. *Supplier selection:* The buyer reviews the proposals and selects a supplier or suppliers in this stage.
7. *Order-routine specification:* The buyer decides and specifies the details of the order. The details include, technical specifications, quantity required, expected time of delivery, return policies, warranties, etc.
8. *Performance review:* This is the final stage where the buyer rates his/her satisfaction with suppliers and decides whether to continue, modify or drop them.

Advances in technology have had a dramatic effect on the B2B marketing process. Increasingly, business buyers are purchasing products and services through Electronic Data interchange links or on auction sites over the internet. Such purchasing gives buyers access to new suppliers, lowers purchasing costs and hastens order processing and delivery. Business marketers, in turn, are in touch with customers online and share marketing information, sell products and services, provide customer support services and maintain ongoing customer relationships with the customers.

SIGNIFICANCE OF CRM IN BUSINESS TO BUSINESS MARKETS

These involve close interaction with the customers, long selling cycles, different sets of decision-makers and influencers. Today, business customers demand greater responsiveness, reliability and quality consciousness from their vendors. The business-to-business landscape has changed dramatically due to the ever-evolving customer needs and also due to factors like the internet. The rapid rise of e-commerce and electronic market places has resulted in many innovations taking place in the B2B scenario.

Business marketers often have to face complex decision-making processes in order to satisfy their customers. Firms are able to get instant information on demand and supply situations from the website. Many suppliers place their product information and documentation on the web to enable buyers get an idea of their products so that more pertinent and relevant questions could be asked. Second, the proliferation of web-based industrial service providers has bought services like vendor comparison on various parameters readily accessible to buyers. These service providers also act as intermediaries. Auction sites have been established on the internet, wherein a buyer can quote his requirements while the sellers compete to outbid each other. Companies, can even resort to day-to-day trading to reduce their inventory and get competitive prices for their purchases. All these innovations have given rise to a situation wherein it becomes very easy for the customer to switch from one supplier to another.

In today's business market scenario, industrial customers adopt differential buying approaches. They may go in for an open market purchase for commodity items that are of low value individually and there is not much difference in the quality of the offerings of different vendors in the market place. (In this case the vendors try to outbid each other in the selling process and try to offer better services in terms of delivery time, etc.) For high value items that are very critical, industrial customers may go in for a long-term close collaboration with their vendors. Vendors are selected more carefully in such situations.

Therefore, customers now use various vendor management strategies to cut costs, enhance product quality and responsiveness from their vendors. In addition, they also demand greater value addition, tighter integration with their processes and systems so as to lower the total cost of ownership, higher service levels and more cost-effective solutions.

Thus, fierce competition for the top customers, rising customer acquisition costs, maturing markets, commoditisation of many products and services through e-commerce and lower vendor switching costs have forced vendors to focus on building loyalty with the customers. They seek to develop and nurture long-term and mutually beneficial relationships with their customers. Today, it is not uncommon to see vendors and their customers go in for contracts for products and services that last as long as ten to twenty years. Vendors also agree to integrate their systems with the customers in order to reduce the lead-time required for making purchases. In many industries, the best-in-class companies have taken the lead and implemented CRM concepts. This has resulted in a clear competitive advantage for them. Some of the strategies that the companies in the B2B market landscape have used to generate market leadership includes:

(i) Focusing on key customers and building strong relationships with them.

(ii) Proactively generate high levels of customer satisfaction with every interaction with the customer.

(iii) Anticipate customer's need by careful study of the environment, customer processes and their behaviour The firm then responds to these needs even before the competition becomes aware of it.

(iv) Building closer ties with the customer, sometimes by integrating their systems.

(v) Finally, creating a value perception for the customer. The customer must see the relationship with the vendor as something that brings value and adds to their competitive advantage. Otherwise the customer will take the business elsewhere.

Customers and Technology

(a) Customers

Typically, a small proportion of the customer base (20 per cent or less) accounts for more than 70-80 per cent of a firm's revenue and profits. Therefore, it is essential for a firm to identify these key customers. Identification of key customers is based on two factors mentioned below:

1. *Lifetime value:* It is important to judge what the customer contributes to the vendor over his/her lifetime. Factors that need to be taken into account for such calculations include the estimated annual revenues generated each year, cost of acquisition retention and estimates of the future value of the customer on the basis of the expected business. This exercise is often very difficult in business markets but proves to be of utmost importance to the firm.
2. *Strategic importance of the customer:* A firm should know how much the customer contributes to maintain the competitive edge of the firm. Some of the customers may be important simply because they are major players in the market. The vendor develops prestige-value by servicing these customers and hence cannot afford to lose them. These customers also play a key role in helping the firm achieve its business mission. However, a strategically important customer might have a comparatively low lifetime value.

(b) Technology

In the present industrial scenario, technology is playing an important role in building relationships by facilitating the flow of information across the value chain. Business customers are increasingly investing in technology to collaborate more closely with their vendors. Technology enables the demand of the customers to become much more visible across the extended supply chain. This, in turn, enables the vendors to become more responsive to their customers needs and helps vendors shed excessive inventory and minimise stock obsolescence. The better inflow of customer data also helps vendors analyse purchase behaviour of the customers more closely and take proactive measures to build brand equity with them. At an advanced stage of the relationship, firms provide their data to vendors so as to enable them to carry out their own analysis and predict the customer demands. Thus technology is changing the way relationships are made and managed.

ENTERPRISE RESOURCE PLANNING

ERP was the methodological point for the product-driven corporate ecosystem. It took the MRP systems and expanded them to include other critical business departments such as human resources (labour) and finance (capital). ERP added procurement planning and budgeting to its vast libraries of business processes that impacted the overall production process. It took advantage of technologies like relational databases (such as Oracle or IBM's DB2) and graphical user interfaces (GUIs) to make the systems more accessible and acceptable. It was able to adapt to the new paradigm of distributed computing through the use of client/server technologies. What this allowed the enterprises to do is to plan, report, and analyse the processes and methods that were aimed at continually tweaking manufacturing and related practices. But it was still based in the world that was driven by product creation and consumer demand, though a computerised, much more flexible version of that world.

SUPPLY CHAIN MANAGEMENT

Supply chain management (SCM) is the process of planning, implementing, and controlling the operations of the supply chain as efficiently as possible. Supply Chain Management spans all movement and storage of raw materials, work-in-process inventory, and finished goods from point-of-origin to point-of-consumption. The term supply chain management was coined by consultant Keith Oliver, of strategy consulting firm Booz Allen Hamilton in 1982.

The definition one America professional association put forward is that Supply Chain Management encompasses the planning and management of all activities involved in sourcing, procurement, conversion, and logistics management activities. Importantly, it also includes coordination and collaboration with channel partners, which can be suppliers, intermediaries, third-party service providers, and customers. In essence, Supply Chain Management integrates supply and demand management within and across companies.

Some experts distinguish Supply Chain Management and logistics, while others consider the terms to be interchangeable. Supply Chain Management is also a category of software products. Supply chain event management (abbreviated as SCEM) is a consideration of all possible occurring events and factors that can cause a disruption in a supply chain. With SCEM possible scenarios can be created and solutions can be planned.

Organizations increasingly find that they must rely on effective supply chains, or networks, to successfully compete in the global market and networked economy. In Peter Drucker's (1998) management's new paradigms, this concept of business relationships extends beyond traditional enterprise boundaries and seeks to organize entire business processes throughout a value chain of multiple companies. During the past decades, globalisation, outsourcing and information technology have enabled many organisations such as Dell and Hewlett Packard, to successfully operate solid collaborative supply networks in which each specialized business partner focuses on only a few key strategic activities (Scott, 1993). This inter-organizational supply network can be acknowledged as a new form of organization. However, with the complicated interactions among the players, the network structure fits neither "market" nor "hierarchy" categories (Powell, 1990). It is not clear what kind of performance impacts different supply network structures could have on firms, and little is known about the coordination conditions and trade-offs that may exist among the players. From a system's point of view, a complex network structure can be decomposed into individual component firms (Zhang and Dilts, 2004). Traditionally, companies in a supply network concentrate on the inputs and outputs of the processes, with little concern for the internal management working of other individual players. Therefore, the choice of internal management control structure is known to impact local firm performance (Mintzberg, 1979).

In the 21st century, there have been a few changes in business environment that have contributed to the development of supply chain networks. First, as an outcome of globalisation and proliferation of multinational companies, joint ventures, strategic alliances and business partnerships were found to be significant success factors, following the earlier "Just-In-Time", "Lean Management" and "Agile Manufacturing" practices. Second, technological changes, particularly the dramatic fall in information communication costs, a paramount component of transaction costs, has led to changes in coordination among the members of the supply chain network (Coase, 1998). Many researchers have recognized these kinds of supply network structure as a new organization form, using terms such as "Keiretsu", "Extended Enterprise", "Virtual Corporation", Global Production Network", and "Next Generation Manufacturing System". In general, such a structure can be defined as "a group of semi-independent organizations, each with their capabilities, which collaborate in ever-changing constellations to serve one or more markets in order to achieve some business goal specific to that collaboration" (Akkermans, 2001).

Successful SCM requires a change from managing individual functions to integrating activities into key supply chain processes. An example scenario: the purchasing department places orders as requirements become appropriate. Marketing, responding to customer demand, communicates with several distributors and retailers, and attempts to satisfy this demand. Shared information between supply chain partners can only be fully leveraged through process integration.

Supply chain business process integration involves collaborative work between buyers and suppliers, joint product development, common systems and shared information. According to Lambert and Cooper (2000) operating an integrated supply chain requires continuous information flows, which in turn assist to achieve the best product flows. However, in many companies, management has reached the conclusion that optimizing the product flows cannot be accomplished without implementing a process approach to the business. The key supply chain processes stated by Lambert (2004) are:

(i) Customer relationship management
(ii) Customer service management
(iii) Demand management
(iv) Order fulfilment
(v) Manufacturing flow management
(vi) Supplier relationship management
(vii) Product development and commercialization
(viii) Returns management

Supply Chain Management is so well defined, its components are almost a chant: plan, source, make, deliver, return. Repeat forty times and fall into a stupor. Despite its soporific powers, these five components are a mantra to any company that delivers product to customers. They have the power to make or break your relationships with these customers. These five components are as clearly marked and well known as they are due to the SCOR model developed by the Supply Chain Council.

SCOR — the Supply Chain Operations Reference model — as of this writing is at version 6.0 and is a highly refined, well-optimised standard that combines supply chain-only business processes with key metrics and benchmarks, and comes up with a set of best practices that have been put to practical use by the Supply Chain Council's members. The procedure the Supply Chain Council uses to create the model is interesting on the face of it, and worth understanding as one that is useful in developing any standard. The steps:

1. Identify the "as is" state of a supply chain related business process;
2. Identify the "to be" state of the same process; and
3. Quantify that against the operational practices of existing similar companies (usually members)
4. Extract a series of world class processes, a.k.a. best practices; and

5. Characterise these management procedures and the associated software solutions that result in the best practices.

(1) Plan

Planning is exactly what it sounds like. Make determinations how to build, extend, define, or determine the supply chain and all its components.

(i) Balance resources with requirements and establish/communicate plans for the whole supply chain, including return and the execution processes of source, make, and deliver.

(ii) Management of business rules, supply chain performance, data collection, inventory, capital assets, transportation, planning configuration, and regulatory requirements and compliance.

(iii) Align the supply chain unit plan with the financial plan.

(2) Source

This is all the pieces needed to find the optimal suppliers that will provide you with the appropriate goods and services.

(i) Schedule deliveries; receive, verify, and transfer product; and authorize supplier payments.

(ii) Identify and select supply sources when not predetermined, as for engineer-to-order product.

(iii) Manage business rules, assess supplier performance, and maintain data.

(iv) Manage inventory, capital assets, incoming product, supplier network, import/export requirements, and supplier agreements.

(3) Make

Again, straightforward (if only the entire IT world were as clear and simple as the supply chain definitions). How to produce the goods that you need to get to the customer.

(i) Schedule production activities, issue product, produce and test, package, stage product, product to deliver.

(ii) Finalise engineering for engineer-to-order product.

(iii) Manage rules, performance, data, in-process products (WIP), equipment and facilities, transportation, production network, and regulatory compliance for production.

(4) Deliver

We all know this one. What does it take to get the planned, sourced, made goods to the customer?

(i) All order management steps from processing customer inquiries and quotes to routing shipments and selecting carriers.

(ii) Warehouse management from receiving and picking product to loading and shipping product.

(iii) Receive and verify product at customer site and install, if necessary.

(iv) Invoice customer.

(v) Manage deliver business rules, performance, information, finished product inventories, capital assets, transportation, product lifecycle, and import/ export requirements.

(5) Return

We all know this one too. What does it take to get the planned, sourced, made, delivered goods back to the producer or supplier?

(i) All return defective product steps from authorising return; scheduling product return; receiving, verifying, and disposition of defective product; and return replacement or credit.

(ii) Return MRO product steps from authorising and scheduling return, determining product condition, transferring product, verifying product condition, disposition, and request return authorisation.

(iii) Return excess product steps including identifying excess inventory, scheduling shipment, receiving returns, approving request authorisation, receiving excess product return in source, verifying excess, and recover and disposition of excess product.

(iv) Manage return business rules, performance, data collection, return inventory, capital assets, transportation, network configuration, and regulatory requirements and compliance.

I don't want to call the above a process map, but it is a clear definition of what concerns supply chain and how the supply chain works. What is interesting, though. unspoken, is that this is a highly customer-sensitive set of actions. Think about it. Plan (by employees), source (suppliers), make (employees, suppliers), deliver (to paying customers, partners), return (from paying customers, partners, suppliers). No matter how much you automate a so-called back-office set of processes, the ultimate target is the 21st century customer. SCM is a customer issue, not just an anonymous back-office process, there for the stream-lining. There are live people involved in the creation and movement of inanimate products.

SUPPLY CHAIN MANAGEMENT PROBLEMS

Supply chain management must address the following problems:

(i) *Distribution network configuration*: Number and location of suppliers, production facilities, distribution centres, warehouses and customers.

(ii) *Distribution strategy*: Centralized versus decentralized, direct shipment, Cross docking, pull or push strategies, third party logistics.

(iii) *Information*: Integrate systems and processes through the supply chain to share valuable information, including demand signals, forecasts, inventory and transportation etc.

(iv) *Inventory management*: Quantity and location of inventory including raw materials, work-in-process and finished goods.

(v) Supply chain execution is managing and coordinating the movement of materials, information and funds across the supply chain. The flow is bi-directional.

SUPPLIER RELATIONSHIP MANAGEMENT

If you subscribe to the premise that an enterprise value chain is the real deal, you probably realise that the end client is not the only customer that exists. The suppliers are customers as much as the employees and the business partners in your channel. All of them collaborate to make your end client cry tears of joy while they do business with you. As this has evolved over the past two years to the au courant model we are engaged with now, we've also seen the interest in and growth of both ERM and SRM — employee relationship management and supplier relationship management. The former is a construct from Siebel that Siebel swears will be a $20 billion market. I have seen no evidence of that whatever. Do I write it off entirely? No. But I'm not taking a $20 billion write-off either. To me, ERM is making sure that your employees are fairly compensated for providing quality work. Treat them with respect and make them accountable, reward them for success. Remember that they're human. That should do it for ERM. Granted, I'm being glib, but I also don't see the need for it when you already have human resources strategies, applications, and compensation strategies and the applications support it. SRM is another story altogether. This is an important component of the customer-centric universe.

Comparing SCM and SRM? C vs. R?

SCM is the actual processes and practices that govern production and its delivery. SRM governs the relationships between suppliers and the producing company. It resembles CRM strategically, and certainly resembles partner relationship management or channel management down to its practical level. In fact, it is so close in nature to PRM there is no reason not to include SRM as part of the CRM subset universe. If I describe something as "the software and business processes that create collaborative communications and align an enterprise with its ---," what would you think it is? Put "partner" in the blank space and it's PRM. Put "customers" in and it's CRM. Put "suppliers or vendors" in and it's SRM.

There is a difference between SCM and SRM besides the middle letter. While SCM supports internal processes to external customers of any variety, SRM supports collaborative networks that are integrating their mutual supply chains. The components are very different. SRM deals with the human interactions between the suppliers and the company or companies that use them. It uses automation to make the relationships more effective, rather than making the processes more efficient per se. The most advanced SRM solutions, such as PeopleSoft's SRM, are 100 percent Internet applications that use portals for supplier (and other) access.

So if you were to dissect the SRM machinery, you'd probably come up with a map that includes sourcing, contract management, procurement, presentment and payment, and perhaps spend analysis. Solutions that are more sophisticated throw in catalogue management, trading partner management, order management, product configurators, ports, and a host of analytics beyond spend analysis that can track supplier performance.

GOING DEEPER

It pays to look briefly at the more common components of an SRM solution. Like any other solution of its ilk, it always should involve planning a strategy for how to execute an SRM initiative (if you are doing it separately). The only notable thought beyond the strategic planning norms outlined in this book is that SRM strategies require thinking about the vendors and suppliers as both customers and partners involved in making the ultimate revenue-producing customer happy. That means they are part of the collaborative chain and have to be happy themselves so the chain that leads to revenue creation doesn't break.

Here are the major components:

(i) *Procurement:* SRM solutions can lead to a number of important benefits in the procurement process. By bringing the processes under control, out-of-control spending is reduced. How often is it that you find some departmental budget monkey going wild and spending on the basis of departmental and not enterprise need, no matter what the damage? This can bring the spending under control and reduce the procurement cycle, increase contract compliance, and reduce the per transaction cost of procurement. In the more advanced places, catalogue management is improved because of the improvement in the overall procurement processes. Solid workflow routing is introduced so that the orders can be more effectively managed and approvals assigned more quickly. Shipment notices can be issued automatically. Imagine your weary desire to do some requisitions at 3:00 A.M. because you can't sleep due to your inability to adjust to the time difference in Nepal. You go online, access a catalogue and the supplier sites that are tied to the items in the catalogue. Built-in business rules govern how the procurement requisition is created. You do all this-in Nepal-at 3:00 A.M. The requisition is created and entered into the system for action. It is secure. You can sleep now. The world is as one.

(ii) *Sourcing:* While choosing the right suppliers for a quote or proposal seems to be a matter of both knowledge and the heart, SRM can make this process so much more satisfying and effective. This is not easy. You'll see that when you see what SRM sourcing modules contain. For example, attribute weighing is a way of defining the important criteria that you set for seeing the value of a prospective bidder or an active one based on algorithms that I can't begin to comprehend. Another feature is event scoring and award. These are comparisons of multiple vendors and their responses to a proposal so you can evaluate and choose the winning bidder. Supplier performance is a set of provided or customised metrics that can measure how well a supplier is doing against plan. This can have a real effect on whether you award him a certain piece of business at a certain time. Some of the most commonly used metrics are quality, cost, responsiveness, and delivery speed. Finally, collaborative negotiations have a direct impact on the deals that are going on with spot buys, reverse auctions, or just plain auctions. Negotiations are real time and have to be done that way. The rapid dissemination of the negotiations information has to be handled through multiple organisational levels for both bidder and buyer SRM sourcing provides the real-time workflow and knowledge management tools to do this.

(iii) *Payment:* Who doesn't know how touchy payment processes are? They are the most sensitive of subjects, the foundation for lawsuits. Those processes when flawed create bad communications and/or late payments and that leads to those lawsuits and highly irrational behaviours between the persons owed and the scofflaw company. All make this a thin-skinned and critical function within SRM. Paying the suppliers isn't just the use of your financial applications purchased from an ERP vendor We are talking about managing relationships. If you pay in a timely fashion through an ordinary and comfortably repeatable routine, you don't have a lot of relationship worries. But what if there are conflicts? How does the settlement process, that which comes between procurement and check to your supplier, get handled? Never fear, SRM is here. SRM uses workflow to enable alerts that are triggered when payment disputes are initiated. Perhaps it's a mistake in invoicing or a payment discrepancy. It doesn't matter If you are using SRM's best practices, all the invoicing, dispute resolution, and payment issuance are done online via secure portals with unique IDs and passwords for each supplier.

(iv) *Analytics:* Commonly, the most important analytics for SRM are analytics that help you control costs. For example, there may be a price increase in goods that you regularly order that is not apparent because the ordering process is automatic or automated. You don't want to see this for the first time after it hits the books. By doing what is often called spend analytics, you can carve the procurement process into tiny or big or diagonal pieces and see what's going on with the costs of each part of the procurement. But SRM-related analytics don't stop there. You can monitor employee spending patterns or analyse purchase data.

CASE STUDY

I

INTRODUCTION

Customer relationship marketing or model is basically the strategy implemented by a company to deal with customers which are points that a company management keeps in mind while dealing a customer. CRM in business to business means that how a company deals with other companies from where it imports raw material or exports other things. For e.g. if there is a manufacturing company, it has to import raw material from the suppliers. After manufacturing it sends finished goods to retailer or wholeseller. Then in all these processes company must follow some strategies or policies so that supply chain from both ends can be maintained.

This topic deals with business to business environment. This topic deals with decision-making of management while maintaining smooth flow supply chain two or more companies.

— Marketing strategies followed by different business houses while dealing with their competitors and suppliers or importers.

— Role of internet in maintaining business environment.

— Change of technology on a particular industry and its effects on its associates and subsidiaries.

— Role of management (different levels) while taking a decision.

— What is nature of unit from which a company is buying or selling goods or raw material?

— Different types of situations through which a company passes while dealing with other business houses.

— Who are participants in business-buying process,. i.e. while buying raw-material from other companies which members play roles.

— While business buying process,. i.e. the complexity while purchasing or selling goods to other business houses.
— Different types of methods or procedures followed by industrial customers.
— Supply chain management, i.e. how the planning, implementing, controlling effect the supply chain in business environment.
— Effect of globalization on business environment.
— Effect of different types of government policies on business environment.
— Optimum utilization of resources so that efficiency and effectiveness can be increased.
— Different types of networks used in business environment.
— Problems faced in supply chain management.
— Problems faced in decision-making.
— Mode of payments.
— Analysis of business environment.

So, CRM in business to business environment is model which gives ideas about business dealings and different types of strategies followed by companies while dealing with each other for wealth maximization.

INTRODUCTION OF COMPANY

Historical Background of Bhushan Industries:

1970—Started with very small initial outlay for manufacturing Door Hinges and later on, Rail Track Fasteners.

1973—Manufacturing facilities set-up for Tor Steel and Wire Rod in Chandigarh.

1981—Rolling Mill Project commissioned at Chandigarh for Round and Narrow Strips.

1985—Backward Integration Project for Steel Melting facilities.

1986—Upgrading of Mini Steel Plant with continuous casting and ladle furnace facilities.

1997—Commissioning of Narrow Width Cold Rolling Project at Chandigarh with a project cost of Rs. 65 crores.

1998—Commissioning of Precision Pipe Project at Chandigarh with a project cost of Rs. 57 crores.

2001—Commissioning of Kolkata Project with a project cost of Rs. 290 crores.

2002—Addition of narrow width Cold Rolling facilities.

2003—Expansion of wide width Cold rolling facilities, ERW Water Pipes & Tubes down stream facilities at Kolkata with a capital outlay of Rs. 88 crores.

2004—Further expansion of Cold Rolling facilities at Kolkata with a capital outlay of Rs. 61 crores.

2005—Commissioning of Orissa phase-I project consisting of 4 DRI Kilns, Steel Making Facilities, Coal Washery and 100 MW Power Plant with a capital outlay of Rs. 829 crores.

2006—Orissa Phase-II project consisting of Hot Metal (Pig Iron) 0.70 mtpa, Coke Oven Plant 0.45 mtpa, Sinter Plant 1.00 mpta, Oxygen Plant 1x400 TPD, Lime & Dolomite 2x300 TPD, Steel Making Facilities 0.90 mpta, HR Coil (CSP Plant) 0.90 mtpa with a capital outlay of Rs. 2900 crores is under implementation.

2007—Oxygen Plant and one Electric Arc Furnace (EAF) commissioned under Orissa Phase-II project.

Bhushan powers and steel industry manufacturers precision tubes both in square and round form. Precision pipes are used mainly in automobile and cycle industry. The raw material is imported from SAIL, TATA, Bokaro, and TISCO. But generally raw material is imported from SAIL.

Raw-material comes in two forms.

— HRC (hot rolled) this raw material comes directly from furnace and is of dull color.

— CR (cold rolled): This type of raw material is put again in furnace to bring shine.

The raw material comes in the form of rolls. These are three mills inside this

In first large Precision Tubes are manufactured, the size of which varies from 22.3 mm to 66.5 mm (outer diameter). The length of the Precision Tubes depends upon the order of customer.

In second unit, small Precision Pipes are manufactured, the outer diameter of which varies from 0.8 mm to 3.5 mm.

Steps of Production

(1) *Uncoiler*: This is the first step of manufacturing. As described above, the raw material comes in the form of coils, so that straight strips can be used in pipe-making.

(2) *Welding*: since the coils are of limited length, so to maintain the continuity of the process, coils are welded one after another. In this process Tungsten Inert Gas (TIG) is used form welding purpose. The main advantage of TIG welding is that no material is used for welding.

(3) *Accumulator*: the welded strips are then accumulated in a large accumulator. This accumulator acts the feed backer, i.e. it can accumulate large no strips to continue the production process.

(4) Next process is divided into three parts:
Forming section
Fin section
Welding section

Forming section: as strips are straight and rectangular, so to make Precision Pipes, these strips undergo a deforming process so that the strips can be deformed into Precision Pipes.

Fin Pass: In this process rounding of pipes starts, i.e. edges are molded in such a way to get Precision Pipes.

Welding section: Here process of induction welding is used. In this process high frequency welder of 450-500Hz is used

To melt the edges in such away that the edges get join together.

(5) Cooling zone: after passing through welding process the pipes get very hot. So to cool them a water soluble coolant is used.

(6) Cut of Carriage (CoC): The next process is cutting of pipes according the order of the customers. Standard sizes are maintained in this process.

(7) Conveyer: From CoC, pipes are put on conveyers from where they are 25 or 30 pipes in a single bundle. For large pipes 4 or 5 pipes comprises a bundle.

(8) Use of rust preventing oil: to prevent the pipes from rusting, Bundles are put in rust preventing oil.

(9) Quality checks: There are different of quality checks such dimensions of pipes, welding and dent, etc.

CRM MODEL IN BHUSHAN INDUSTRY

This industry is basically customer-oriented industry. So first preference is given to customer. But there are many steps or strategies which industry follows while dealing with other business houses.

(1) *Supply Chain*: This industry gets its supply of raw material from TATA, Tisco, SAIL, and Bokaro, etc. But a main supplier is SAIL. So we can say that supply chain is based on single supplier. The import of raw material depends upon the order of customer, i.e. the business houses which want to import pipes, mainly Precision Pipe importers are Hero Honda, Hero Cycles, and Automobile Sector, etc. If sometimes there is hindrance or disturbance in supply chain, the management tries to sort it out. But even if then problem exist, then Vice-Chairman takes the final decision.

(2) *Decision-making in Buying Situations*: Whenever company imports raw material from any other business house, the upper level of management takes the decision.

(3) *Market Strategy in Business to Business* : Since the firm is consumer-oriented so market strategies are mainly according to the consumer satisfaction, i.e. the company pays more attention to consumers in Business to Business environment, this takes the help of websites, has agents in many states, uses direct contact policy in foreign investment and export. The Precision Pipes are exported to USA, Sri Lanka and many African countries from Bhushan Industries.

(4) *Role of Government Policies in Business to Business Environment*: According to the market head of the company, the company mainly concentrates on the quality of products. So if due to some government policies the cost of production increases or decreases, the company does not take this into much consideration, as according to marketing strategy of company if some want to survive in this completion, the brand name is must. The brand name can only be created by producing quality products.

(5) *Role of Global Environment in Business to Business*: Global environment also plays an important role in Business to Business dealing. For example, according to the marketing head of the company, the USA was not much interested in their industry earlier. But after Kyoto Protocol in Global Warming, it was decided that USA can manufacture steel products up to a limit. Then USA started paying attention to India and many other developing countries to meet its demand of steel products. So Global Warming also plays an important role in Business to Business environment.

(6) *Effect of Technology*: According to the production manager of Bhushan Industries, it is very necessary to maintain up to date technology to survive in the market. But the change in technology does not affect prices much as quality is the most important thing.

(7) *Enterprise Resource Planning*: The Bhushan industry has a planning unit, which decides on many manufacturing decisions according to supervisor of Bhushan econoany, sometime presence of orders; the management hires unskilled and skilled labor on contract bases

(8) *Relationship with Suppliers*: As described above this industry got supply from many companies but the main supplier is SAIL. The company follows a market policy while importing the raw material. In this market policy, the transportation costs, custom duties are decided while importing raw material. in this market policy, the transportation costs, custom duties are decided while importing raw material from different places.

The total raw material used in the Bhushan industry is of the range between 5000-6000 tons. Total turnover of the company is about 300 crore. The company mainly concentrates on quality maintaining than the pricing policy while dealing with other business houses

COMPARISON OF ORIGINAL MODEL OF CRM AND THE COMPANY FOLLOWED CRM

(1) *Supply Chain*: In the supply chain management given in the topic, the supply chain given is very concrete based on many models and processes such as planning, implementing and controlling. These are different types of models and situations explained in topic. While in real situation like that of Bhushan Company planning is there, implementation is there but no specific model or strategy is followed.

(2) *Market Strategies*: This company is mainly customer -oriented. It has good market policies regarding customer dealing. But while dealing with other business houses has direct contacts with them. If the marketing structure is not widely spread, as explained in CRM topic.

(3) *Government Policy* : According to marketing manager of the Bhushan industries government policies do not have much effect on the cost or price fluctuation though sometimes price may be affected but the fluctuations are very less. On the other hand in CRM topic of B2B government policies may play an important role in price of cost function.

(4) *Resource Planning*: These companies follow resource planning at small scale. All the resource planning is done by the management but it does not include low level management in resource planning such as supervisor level.

(5) *Decision-making*: Decisions are taken by high level management. While making decisions company takes into consideration the customer satisfaction as first choice while in CRM B2B topic all users, influencers, buyers, deciders and gatekeepers play an important role in decision-making.

BENEFITS AND DRAWBACKS IN PRODUCTION FUNCTION

Benefits

Use of TIG (Tungsten Inert Gas): This company uses Tungsten which improves the quality of welding.

The size of pipes is according to standard size which is checked randomly which saves the time of checking.

Skilled labor: Majority of the labor here is skilled which gives the edge over the other companies in production function.

Final checks: Final checks are made after production regarding dimension, length which gives an extra edge to manufacturing unit.

Hub area: This industry is in Chandigarh which is hub of three states, so it gets an extra benefit of location.

Drawbacks

Rejection rate: The rejection rate is quite high, i.e. 2-3%. This is due to welding process in which the welded pipes are rejected.

Role of management only: Only higher management takes decisions. It does not include lower management in decision-making.

Only customer-oriented: This company is only customer-oriented, i.e. the marketing is towards customers only. It does not have a specific marketing strategy towards B2B environment.

No specific supply chain: The supply chain is not specific. Though the supplier is same most of the time (SAIL). But the supply chain as explained in the CRM B2B topic is not there.

Business to Business Buying: No Business to business buying process is followed as explained by CRM Business to Business Model. As the top management only takes decisions.

FOOD FOR THOUGHT

In the light of the above case analyze the difference between real and model of CRM proposed.

II

The Indian State Electricity Board (ISEB) is a statutory body formed on 1-2-1959 under the Electricity Supply Act. Subsequently with the re-organization of the erstwhile State of Indian under the Indian Re-organization Act, 1966 the present form came into existence w.e.f. 1st May,1967.

Starting with the modest installed capacity of 62 MW, the ISEB has grown up by leaps and bounds with generating capacity 6201 MW as on 31-3-2007. The Board's gross generation during the year 2006-07 was 36412.055 MUs.

ISEB operates its own Generation Power Plants and also gets power as its share from BBMB. It also gets power as per allocation from the Central Sector Power Projects. The ISEB also constructs and maintains its Transmission and Distribution system for providing efficient services to the various categories of electricity consumers in the state.

Though the welnit network of Transmission and Distribution System, ISEB is proud of serving more than 62.31 lakh consumers comprising of approximate 51.49 lakh General, 1.09 lakhs Industrial, 9.7 lakhs agriculture connections.

All the power Stations operated at their best ever plant load factor since their installation.

I SEB ORGANISATIONAL SETUP

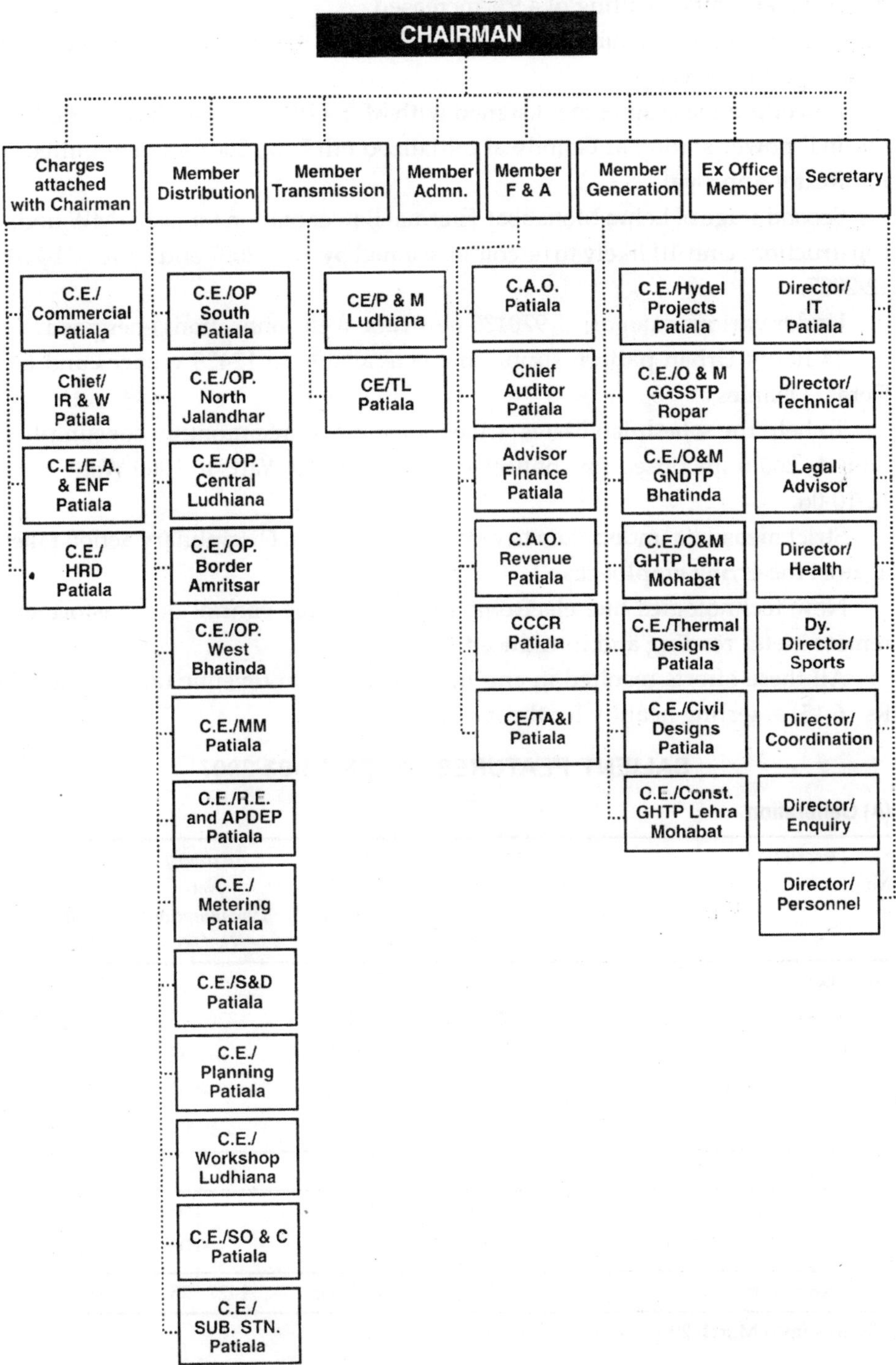

Total Power generated is 34984 lakh units which is more than previous year by 1636 lakh units resulting of 4.9% increased.

The prestigious Ranjit Sagar Dam Project (4x150 MW) commissioned and dedicated to the Nation.

Power purchase agreement signed with M/S GVK for installing 2x250 MW thermal power station at Goindwal initialized 6th Feb., 2007 and submitted to PSERC for approval.

Second stage of Lehra Mohabbat Thermal Power Station for 2x250 MW under construction. Unit-III likely to be commissioned by 30-9-2007 and Unit-IV by 31-12-2007.

Under various categories, 970139 new tube well connections energized.

24 hours Urban pattern supply made available to 12428 villages and 695 Deras/Dhanies.

To help the scheduled castes/tribes consumers, free monthly consumption limit A, 200 units raised for connected load from 500 Watts to 1000 Watts w.e.f. 12-10-06.

Strict measures undertaken to reduce power theft. Disciplinary action taken against the erring employees.

New technologies like electronic meters, remote control of transformers, remote meter reading and introduced.

All these efforts resulted in and increase of 3% in revenue (approximately Rs. 6.15) asserting healthy for the further.

SALIENT FEATURES AS ON 31-03-2007

(A) Generation

Sl. No.	*Description*	*Installed Capacity (MW)*	*Total Generation* (MUs)*	*Auxiliary Net Consumption (MUs)*	*Generation (MUs) Up to 31-03-2007*
(a)	Own				
	Thermal	2120	15434.639	1376.345	14058.294
	Hydro	995	4396.574	51.580	4344.994
	Share from BBMB	1257	3978.260	0.00	3978.260
	Micro Hydel	4	7.959	0.000	7.959
	Total	4376	23817.432	1427.925	22389.507
(b)	Share from Central Sector	1764	12361.601	0.00	12361.601
(c)	PEDA/Captive Plants	61	233.022	0.00	233.022
	Grand Total	6201	36412.055	1427.925	34984.130

*Figures upto March 2007 are final as per REA.

(B) MAXIMUM DEMAND : 6558 MW AT 13.15 HRS ON15.08.2006

(C) TRANSMISSION & DISTRIBUTION SYSTEM :

Sl. No.	Description	No. of (Ckt. Kms.)	Capacity (MVA)	Lines (Ckt. Kms.)
(a)	220 KV	47	10038.700	4325.024
(b)	132 KV	76	4851.600	3035.52
(c)	66 KV	430	9674.250	5666.402
(d)	33 KV	93	1113.000	1574.366
	Total (a to d)	646	25677.550	14601.312
(e)	11 KV	252165	16212	123332
(f)	L.T			173854.000

(D) RURAL ELECTRIFICATION

1	Villages Electrified	13123(100%)
2	Villages provided 24 hours supply on Urban Pattern	13123
3	Agriculture pump sets energized	970139

(E) COMMERCIAL

(a)	Total No. of Consumers	6231240
(b)	Total Connected Load(MWs)	21078.65
(c)	Energy Available for State (MUs)	34984.13
(d)	Transmission Distribution Losses (MUs)	8367.09
(e)	Energy Consumed in State (MUs)	26617.04
(f)	Export to other States(MU) Upto 31-3-2007	977.11
(g)	Revenue from Sale of Power (Crores)	7028.4

(F) PER CAPITA CONSUMPTION

(G) FINANCE AND ACCOUNTS

(Capital Plan Outlay (2003-04) (006-07) 2363

Capital Plan Expenditure (2003-04) up to 30.9.303 2006-07 1721.77

(H) MAN POWER

(a)	Class-I & II	NA
(b)	Class-III	NA
(c)	Class-IV	NA
	Total	72154

(I) COST PER UNIT 374.98

Points to be discussed

Outsourcing/Throw rate: Throw rate is the type of outsourcing in which whole of the work is carried out totally from outside. It means the material and the labour both are provided by the contractors.

Labour rate: In this case the material for the construction is given by the department, whereas the labour is hired from the contractors.

Planning committee: The planning committee consists of the higher authorities, which performs the function of planning, i.e. to whom and how much powers are to be provided.

Store purchase committee: The store purchase committee purchases the stock for future requirements.

D.G.S.D.: The Director General of Stores and Disposal standardizes the firms for purchases. Only, from these firms the material can be purchased. The standardization is done according to rates and quality

Delegation powers: There are different powers assigned to different officers, like: Ex En, S.D.O., J.E. etc. These powers are regarding immediate purchases. The powers are of centralized type.

Works Regulation: The works regulations are the written norms according to which the works are carried out. These include hiring of labour and immediate purchase etc.

Purchase regulation: The purchase regulations are the rules regarding purchases. According to these the powers of purchases lies mostly in the delegation. The powers are highly centralized. The emphasis is on the bulk purchase, rather than according to need. The purchases are made by floating the tender notices in the newspapers and on the Internet as well. The tender notices are floated twice. Second time these are floated fifteen days after their approval. This makes the procedure lengthy

Individual authorities for purchases: The individual authorities for the purchase are very less, since the powers are of centralized type.

QUESTIONS TO BE RAISED: IN LIGHT OF CRM

Is outsourcing creating monopoly?

Are the authorities given sufficient powers?

Is the purchasing procedure of the Board lengthy and expensive?

Is there a chance of increase of prices due to the drawbacks of the system?

STUDY– QUESTIONS

1. Explain the meaning of business to business market. Also describe the features of business to business markets.
2. Discuss the significance of CRM in Business to Business Markets in brief.
3. What do you mean by the supplier relationship management. Also discuss the various problems of supply chain management in brief.

❖❖❖

8

CRM IN BUSINESS TO CONSUMER MARKETS

INTRODUCTION

As the world moves toward a global economy, the service sector has become a very significant contributor. Any major economy that isn't competitive in the services sector isn't competitive internationally. In particulars, services are intangible, inseparable, variable, and perishable. To successfully address the marketing complexities posed by these characteristics, the service marketing mix must go beyond the usual four P's to include three additional mix elements: *people, physical evidence*, and the *service process*. The marketing concept is equally applicable to organisations in the service sector and to manufacturers of physical goods. Understanding and identifying the needs and wants of the market underlies successful marketing for service organisations and other types. In addition, the management of service quality through the monitoring of customer satisfaction is perhaps more critical to the success of service marketing than to the marketing of goods. In fact, we have argued that the distinction between services and goods producing sectors of the economy is an additional is an artificial one in that every firm sells services to its customers. That service consists of four components: *the physical product, the service product, the service environment, and service delivery.*

DEFINITIONS

As we know that *services are deeds, processes, and performances.* According to this definition, the services offered by any organisation are not tangible things that can be seen, touched and felt, but rather are intangible deeds and performances.

For example, IBM, an international software and hardware making company, offers repairs and maintenance service for its equipment, consulting services for information technology and e-commerce applications, training services, web design and hosting, and other services. These services may include a final tangible report, a website, or, in the case of training, tangible instructional materials. But for the most part, the entire service is represented to the client, follow-up calls, and reporting — a series of deeds, processes and performances. Similarly, the core offerings of hospitals, hotels, banks, and utilities comprise primarily deeds and actions performed for customers.

As per this definition of services, you should be aware that overtime *services* and the *service sector of the economy* have been defined in subtly different ways. The variety of definitions can often explain the confusion or disagreements people have when discussing services and when describing industries that comprise the service sector of the economy. Compatible with our simple, broad definition is one that defines services to "include all economic activities whose output is not a physical product or construction, is generally consumed at the time it is produced, and provides added value in forms (such as *convenience, amusement, timeliness, comfort,* or *health*) that are essentially intangible concerns of its first purchaser.

CHARACTERISTIC ELEMENTS OF SERVICES

There are four commonly cited characteristics of services that make them different to market from goods: *intangibility, inseparability, variability,* and *perishability*.

(1) Intangibility

Services are said to be intangible — they cannot be seen or tasted, for example. This can cause lack of confidence on the part of the consumer. As was apparent earlier, in considering pricing and services marketing, it is often difficult for the consumer to measure service value and quality. To overcome this, consumers tend to look for evidence of quality and other attributes, for example in the decor and surroundings of the beauty salon, or from the qualifications and professional standing of the consultant.

(2) Inseparability

Services are produced and consumed at the same time, unlike goods which may be manufactured, then stored for later distribution. This means that the service provider becomes an integral part of the service itself. The waitress in the restaurant, or the cashier in the bank, is an inseparable part of the service offering. The client also participates to some extent in the service, and can affect the outcome of the service. People can be part of the service itself, and this can be an advantage for services marketers.

(3) Heterogeneity/Variability

The fact, that service quality is difficult to control compounds the marketer's task. Intangibility alone would not be such a problem if customers could be sure that the services they were to receive would be just like the successful experiences their neighbours were so pleased with. But in fact, customers know that services can vary greatly. Different front-line personnel have different abilities. Even the same service provider has good days and bad days, or may be less focused at different times of day. Services are performances, often involving the cooperation and skill of several individuals, and are, therefore unlikely to be the same every time. This potential variability of service quality greatly raises the risk faced by the consumer. The service provider must find ways to reduce the perceived risk due to variability. One method is to design services to be as uniform as possible — by training personnel to follow closely defined procedures, or by automating as many aspects of the service as possible. This isn't always a good strategy, however. The appeal of some service personnel — particularly, those involved in such expensive personal services as *beauty parlour treatments* or *home decorating* lies in their spontaneity and flexibility to address individual customer needs. The danger with too much standardisation is that these attributes may be designed right out of the services, therefore, reducing much of their appeal. A second way to deal with perceived risk from variability is to provide satisfaction guarantees or other assurances that the customer will not be stuck with a bad result.

(4) Perishability

The fourth characteristic of services is perishability. Perishability of a service means the service cannot be inventoried or stored. If a pair of jeans does not sell today, a retailer can store it and sell it at a later time. This feature allows firms to mass produce goods and store them in warehouses until consumers are ready to purchase. For services, this is not possible. A US Air flight that sells only 75 of the 200 seats will lose the revenue of the 125 empty seats if the plane takes off with those seats empty. That revenue is lost forever.

Concerts and sporting events are live events in which consumers pay to see the performance. Consumers have no choice as to when or where they can watch the events unless there are multiple performances. If they want to watch, they must go to where the performance is staged, at the time it is occurring. Again, empty seats are lost revenue since they cannot be inventoried and sold at a later time. To maximise revenue, airlines want to fill every seat in an airplane. The same is true for sporting events and concerts. Perishability can cause the reverse to occur. Demand can be greater than supply.

In this situation, the airliner does not have enough seats for everyone. Customers are left at the gate. In sporting events such as football's Superbowl, baseball's World Series, and hockeys Stanley Cup, demand outstrips supply. Potential revenue is lost because of fixed seating capacities.

To reduce the negative impact of perishability, services must develop strategies to cope with fluctuating demand. This goal can be accomplished by making simultaneous adjustments in demand, supply, and capacity. The goal of these strategies is to achieve parity among the three. At the optimum, demand will equal supply, which in turn will equal capacity.

For a service such as Nuuuli Place Cinema on Tutuila Island in American Samoa, demand often exceeds capacity during evening showings of popular new releases while during daytime showings the theatre usually has empty seats. To manage this situation, Nuuuli Place Cinema must make simultaneous adjustments in demand, supply, and capacity.

One method of adjusting demand is to move some of the demand from the high-peak evening showings to nonpeak afternoons. Reducing the price for the afternoon showings is one way of doing this. Supply can be adjusted by having multiple showings of the most popular movies during the evening. Nu'uuli Place Cinema could show the same movie at 7:30, 9:30, and midnight. To increase capacity, Nuuuli Place Cinema could show a popular movie in two or three of the mini theatres at the same time.

CLASSIFICATION OF SERVICES

There are a number of ways of classifying service activity, and there is inevitably some degree of overlap between the methods available. This section outlines some of the methods of classification commonly used, which are as follows:

(i) End-user: Services can be classified into the following categories:

(a) *Consumer:* leisure, hairdressing, personal finance, package holidays.

(b) *Business to business:* advertising agencies, printing, accountancy, consultancy.

(c) *Industrial:* plant maintenance and repair, workwear and hygiene, installation, project management.

(ii) Service Tangibility: The degree of tangibility of a service can be used to classify services:

(a) Highly tangible: car rental, vending machines, telecommunications.

(b) *Service linked to, tangible goods:* domestic appliance repair, car service.

(c) *Highly intangible:* psychotherapy, consultancy, legal services.

(iii) People-based Services: Services can be broker. down into labour-intensive

(people-based) and equipment-based services. This can also be represented by the degree of contact:

(a) *People-based services - high contact:* education, dental care, restaurants, medical services.

(b) *Equipment-based-low contact* automatic car wash, launderette, vending machine, cinema.

(iv) Expertise: The expertise and skills of the service provider can be broken down into the following categories:

(a) Professional: medical services, legal services, accountancy, tutoring.

(b) Non-professional: babysitting, caretaking, casual labour.

(v) Profit Orientation: The overall business orientation is a recognised means of classification:

(a) Not-for-profit: The Scouts Association, charities, public sector leisure facilities.

(b) Commercial: banks, airlines, tour operators, hotel and catering services.

VALUE OF CUSTOMERS OVER TIME

The value of a customer to a firm will increase over time. For example, the profit earned per credit card customer increases by 83% over the first five years that customers are with a company. For industrial laundry services, profits increase 79% from $144 to $258 per customer over the first five years. For auto servicing, profits increase 252%, going from $25 per customer for the first year to $88 for year four and after. This increase in the profitability of a customer is due to the following four reasons:

1. Customers tend to use a service more over time.
2. Service firms become more efficient over time.
3. Customers refer others to the firm.
4. Firms can increase their prices because of quality, dependable service.

Individuals may try a new auto service facility for a small repair. If they are satisfied, they will try them again when other work has to be done. If the satisfaction continues, they will probably switch all of their patronage to the new facility. The same pattern holds for credit card users. They may use the card a few times the first year. If service is satisfactory, they may increase their usage the second year. This pattern should continue year after year. For industrial distributors, the peak usually does not occur until the twentieth year. However, for auto repair services the peak normally occurs after only four years.

Services become more efficient as employees get to know the customers. They learn what customers expect. They learn how best to meet customer needs. Less time is spent on performing the service since the workers know what is expected and how the customer wants the service performed. Also, customers learn the capabilities of the service firm. They know what they can and cannot do. Customers may even contribute to the increased efficiency over time by preparing in advance for the service. For example, after dealing with the same accountant for a long period of time, customers know what receipts and paperwork are needed. Customers learn the best way of preparing the data. These steps taken prior to the service encounter by the customer will allow the accountant to perform the service in less time.

Profits increase because satisfied customers will tell others about the service. When looking for a new service vendor, consumers rely more on word-of-mouth communications than any other source of information. The strength of positive word-of-mouth communications is based on the customer's level of satisfaction. Customers who are at the "OK" state of satisfaction will tell few others about the service and their impact will be minimal. As the level of satisfaction increases to the "pleased" and "excited" states, more individuals are told and others are more willing to give the firm a try. Once a service has built a high-quality reputation, prices can be increased. Most customers are willing to pay more for a service that is dependable and of high quality. Often the cost of gaining a new customer exceeds the profits earned during the first year that the customer is with the company. For example, if a credit card customer left after only one year, the firm would experience a $21 loss. The longer customers are retained, the more profits will grow. Reducing defections by only 5% can increase profits by as much as 85%. For example, in the auto service industry a 5% reduction in defections increases profits by 30%. In the credit card industry profits increase 75% while in the banldng industry the gain is 85%. The gain for insurance brokerage is 50% and for office building management it is 40%.',' Considering that it costs approximately six times as much to gain a new customer as it does to keep current customers, service firms should actively work to reduce defections.

One morning in 1982, Charles Gawley, president of the Delaware-based credit card company MBNA America, assembled all 300 employees of the firm. Frustrated by the constant stream of letters from unhappy customers, President Cawley announced his determination that the company would strive to satisfy and keep every customer. MBNA America started gathering feedback from disgruntled customers about their service. Using this information, changes were made. Eight years later, MBNA America's defection rate of 5% was one of the lowest in the credit-card industry. MBNA America had moved from thirty-eighth in the industry to fourth and its profits had increased sixteenfold.

THE COST OF LOSING A CUSTOMER

Firms underestimate or even worse, ignore the cost of losing a customer. They assume that a lost customer can be replaced and one should not worry as long as the revenues are coming in. However, this is an imperfect thinking. It does not look at the quality aspect and the implicit costs of losing customers (Reichheld et al. 1990). When managers do not measure the actual cost of losing a customer, they will not be able to focus on reducing defections as they will not know the worth of a customer. Defecting customers are clear indicators of a drop in profits in the future..There are many ways in which loss customer cost the firm.

1. A lost customer reduces cash flows for the firm in the future. Served correctly, customers generate increasingly more profits each year they stay with a firm. This is because of the increasing familiarity with the service, that the firm provides to the customers. Familiarity with the service further increases the volume of the business that the customers do with the firm. For example, as a customer grows more comfortable with using a credit card, he/she will use it for more purchases over a period of time.
2. Second, if a firm wants to maintain the same volume of business, it has to attract new customers. Replacing an existing customer with a new customer costs up to five times more in advertising and other costs. Also in the first year the new customer would spend less than an old customer would have done.
3. Servicing customers over a period of time becomes more cost-effective for service firms as they discover new traits of the customer and his likes and dislikes. Therefore, a firm can serve old customers more efficiently than it can serve new customers.
4. Firms with long-term customers, in whom they have developed a higher level of loyalty, can charge more for their products and services. A customer will often willingly pay more to stay at a hotel they know or consult a doctor they are used to rather than take chances with some unknown hotel or less expensive doctor.
5. Finally, highly satisfied long-term customers are likely to refer new customers to the firm. This means that the firm has to spend less on advertising and other expenses for, attracting new customers.

When a firm considers all the costs that result due to the loss of a customer, the managers of the firm become conscious of the actual situation. They realise that the continuous improvement in the quality of the service is not a cost but an investment in form of a customer who generates more profit than the margin on a one-time sale. Estimation of the costs of losing customers makes it easier for managers to justify the cost of continuously improving service quality versus things like cost reduction that have more tangible measures.

DEFECTIONS MANAGEMENT

The process of identifying and reducing defections within an organisation is called defections management. To be successful, the plan must be proactive and be supported by every person in the organisation. There are three principles governing defections managements:

1. Don't try to eliminate all defections.
2. Watch for customers who have defected, are ready to defect, or who have reduced purchases.
3. Develop a service recovery program.

The first principle of defections management is the development of a coordinated plan to reduce defections. Although zero defections should be the goal of all organisations, in reality it probably will not be achieved. At some point, the cost of eliminating defections will be greater than the cost of gaining new customers. It must also he recognised there will always he a certain level of customer attrition. A few customers will defect no matter what you do.

Firms must identify customers who have defected or who are ready to defect. For some services, this is an easy task while for other services it is more challenging. Commercial services such as janitorial or pest control operate under contractual agreements, so identifying defectors is easy. In fact, many times contractual customers will go through a period of complaining prior to canceling a contract or letting a contract expire. They may also mention that a competitor has offered them a better value package. Both are cues that something is wrong and the customer is close to switching.

Identifying defectors in consumer services is difficult, especially for services where there is no identification of the customer. Services such as restaurants, hotels, theme parks, and sports teams fit into this category. The only way most of these services know that the customer is ready to defect or has defected is when he or she complains to management. But for each person that complains, there are 25 dissatisfied customers who do not complain. They just take their business elsewhere. So relying on the number of complaints will allow a firm to identify less than 4% of the defectors. This method will also not identify defectors who leave for other reasons such as a lower price or better service.

A key to identifying defectors is the development of a customer database. The database must contain names, purchase amounts, and purchase frequencies. Personal information about each customer is helpful, but not essential. A credit card company can spot a potential defector when the frequency and amount of their charges starts to decline. A hotel chain can spot when frequent travellers start reducing their stays. The same procedure can be used by other services where customers must make reservations or appointments. It can be more challenging for restaurants, theme parks, and sporting events to identify defectors. Some names and data can be collected if tickets are purchased in advance by phone or through the mail. Restaurants that take reservations are able to capture a few names. These types of services must find ways to develop a customer database if they are serious about defections management.

One way of developing a database is through the use of a frequency purchase program. For example, customers who make a certain number of purchases could receive some type of free gift or financial reward. Monitoring this type of program would require that customers possess a card or ticket which can be punched. Although this is not a perfect method because customers can defect and give their ticket to others, it does identify many defectors. Another method of reducing defections which will be discussed further in the next section is the development of a zero-defections culture in the organisation. Employees need to be trained to watch for defectors. If they can be identified before they leave the facility, chances of retaining them are much greater. Defections management requires the development of a service recovery program. However, it is important to realise companies should not assume that defectors are lost for good. The sooner a defector is contacted, the greater the probability he or she can be won back.

Southland Cleaning Services, a janitorial service in the Midwest, decided to adopt a defections management program when their defection rate rose to 15%. Receiving a cancellation notice from one of their oldest customers, the president of Southland made a visit to the customer. After listening to the complaints, the president of the janitorial service acknowledged the customer had a right to he unhappy. Southland had faded to bye up to their contract. Going one step further, Southland's president asked for another chance to take care of the problems. The customer replied it was too late. However, six months later, the customer called and wanted Southland back. Their new janitorial service had not done a good job and the customer had been so impressed with the attempt to win them back that they were willing to give Southland another chance.

Using this method of trying to win defectors back, the president of Southland Cleaning Service was able to get about 20% of the potential defectors to change their minds and not cancel their contracts. Of the 80% who did cancel, approximately half returned within two years of defecting. Sometimes customers have unrealistic expectations. These unrealistic expectations may have been gained through advertising or a salesperson. It may be the result of miscommunication between service personnel and salespeople or it may be that the wrong marketing message is being delivered. The message conveyed to customers through marketing must he understood by personnel performing the service.

When the defections hit 15%, the president of Southland Cleaning Services started looking for explanations. In visiting with defectors, he found that they were told by the salesperson that they would never have to worry about the building being clean. They were also told that they would never have any problems with Southland Cleaning Service. However, the building was not always clean and problems occasionally arose.

Realising expectations were unrealistic, the president of Southland developed a new sales approach. The Southland representative acknowledged that the firm was not perfect. Problems will occasionally arise. When problems occur, it is the responsibility of the customer to let Southland know. If notified of a problem, Southland promised to respond as quickly as possible. Using this new sales approach, the defection rate of new customers dropped to less than 10%.

CREATING A ZERO-DEFECTIONS CULTURE

To create a zero-defections culture, everyone in the organisation must understand that zero defections is the goal of the corporation. Employees must understand the lifetime value of a customer. Most employees never think about or realise how much revenue one customer brings in during his or her lifetime. Most employees do not realise that losing a customer means losing all of the revenue that customer would have contributed to the organisation during his or her lifetime. The sooner potential defectors are identified, the easier it will be to win them back. Employees should he taught to watch for declining sales and signs of dissatisfaction. Of course, the best method of preventing defections is by keeping current customers happy. Employees must realise the importance of satisfying each customer every time. They must also understand that customers need to feel they are receiving a good value from the service.

A-1 Heating and Air Conditioning redesigned its employee training to emphasize the importance of keeping its business customers rather than emphasizing sales. Customers had complained they did not like being pressured into repairs they had not planned on and did not feel were necessary. Realising their error, A-1 now trains its employees to identify and solve customers' problems rather than maximise sales. Their goal is to prevent defections and spot unhappy customers before they depart. Unless employees receive some type of reward or incentive, they are not likely to pay much attention to defections. One method of tying incentives into defection rates is for a firm to pay a bonus to employees based on rate of defections. This method works well for firms where employees are assigned specific accounts. For example, account representatives for a trucking company could be paid an incentive bonus each Year based on the rate of defections. The fewer the defections, the greater the bonus. If multiple personnel handle accounts, then a group bonus can be used. If the amount of effort put forth by various employees can be determined, the bonus can be prorated based on effort expended. Concerned about the quality of work being performed by its support personnel, management of Southland Cleaning Services developed an incentive for each employee. Believing defections were the outgrowth of complaints and dissatisfaction with work performed, Southland developed a bonus system based on the number of customer complaints. Employees were given a 5% bonus on their paycheck if no complaints were received during the pay period. If one complaint was received, the bonus was reduced to 3%. No bonus was given if two or more complaints were lodged by the customer.

The incentive reduced complaints, which in turn reduced defections. The monies paid out came from a reduction of supervision costs. Because support personnel made a stronger effort to do quality work, less supervision was needed. A zero-defections culture will occur if management has created a customer service atmosphere within the organisation. Management must demonstrate by their example that customers come first. Part of creating a customer service atmosphere is management's commitment to providing employees with the resources necessary to serve customers. When management provides strong support for service personnel, service personnel will in turn provide good service to customers.

THE UNCONDITIONAL GUARANTEE

The possibility of obtaining zero defections is enhanced by unconditional guarantees. An unconditional guarantee is one that customers can invoke for any reason. Unconditional means that the firm does not attach conditions that must be met before the customer can invoke the guarantee. Bugs Burger Bug Killers (BBBK) is a Miami-based pest extermination company owned by S.C. johnston & Son. BBBK specialises in pest control for hotels and restaurants. While competitors promised to reduce pests to an acceptable level, BBBK promised to eliminate them completely. BBBK charges up to ten times as much as competitors. Despite the high price, BBBK has captured large market shares in most areas where they operate. Total sales has topped $30 million. Although BBBK has the most extensive guarantee in the industry, it has never paid out more than $120,000 a year in guarantee claims.

A good guarantee should pass the following five tests. First, it should be unconditional. Customers can invoke the guarantee for any reason. Second, the guarantee should be easy to understand and easy to communicate. Third, the guarantee should be easy to invoke. Customers should not have to 90 through a lengthy process to invoke the guarantee. Fourth, customers should find it easy and quick to collect payments. Fifth, the compensation given to customers should be meaningful to them.

Good unconditional guarantees provide firms with marketing muscle. BBBK's guarantee allowed them to gain substantial market share in cities where they operated. It also allowed them to charge more for their services. An unconditional guarantee forces a firm to focus on customers. Since customers can invoke the guarantee for any reason, firms must make sure customer expectations are met. When they are not and the guarantee is invoked, feedback is obtained. This feedback will identify weak spots in the service process. Correcting these problems will reduce the number of guarantees invoked in the future.

SERVICE FAILURE AND RECOVERY

Service failures are instances where a service is either not performed or is performed poorly. In terms of satisfaction states, service failures are the instances when customers leave a service angry or dissatisfied. In both situations, the service performance is below the adequate expectation level of the customer. Because of the dissatisfaction, customers will be less inclined to purchase from the firm again. In many cases, they will tell others about their bad experience, which compounds the negative impact on the service firm. An unhappy customer will tell 10 or 11 others about his or her experience. The impact of dissatisfaction is quite staggering.

Service Failures

Service failures do not automatically result in firm-switching behaviour and negative word-of-mouth communications. Customers can be recovered. The manner in which postservice failures are handled will have a greater impact on future purchase behaviour than the level of dissatisfaction of the original service experience. Firms have a second chance for making things right with the customer. However, if a firm fails the second time around, the backlash is even stronger since the firm, in essence, has failed twice. It failed during the regular service, then it failed again in the service recovery process. A strong service recovery process can produce positive results and overcome most service failures. Successful recovery will diminish the negative impact of the original poor or failed service for three reasons. First, through postservice communications with the firm, customers come to believe that the service provider is fair because they admitted maldug a mistake or they offered the customer some type of restitution. Second, a good service recovery process takes away all of the negative consequences of a service failure such as loss of time or money. Third, the service recovery process will normally cause consumers to alter their attributions as to the cause of the service failure. The impact of good service recovery can be illustrated by the experience' of a tourist group going from New York to Club Med in Cancun. The flight from New York to Cancun was delayed ten hours, arriving in Cancun at 2:00 a.m. Both food and beverages ran out long before the end of the flight. The landing in Cancun was so hard that the oxygen maslcs were dislodged and luggage fell from compartments above the passengers. Dissatisfaction was beyond the irritated stage. It had reached the angry stage. A lawyer on board was already discussing with the passengers a possible class-action lawsuit. Hearing about the bad experience of the passengers, Club Med Chef Sylvio de Bartok went to work. He took half of the staff to the airport to greet the guests when they got off the plane. They helped them with the luggage and listened to their accounts of horror.

At Club Med, the other half of the staff prepared a lavish banquet that included champagne and a live band. Realising the importance of compatibility management and the role other customers could play in the service recovery process, the staff of Club Med were able to convince most of the other guests to stay up and wait for those arriving late. Instead of being angry, the late-arriving guests were commenting it was the most fun they had experienced since college. Instead of dissatisfaction and a lawsuit, the guests returned to New York with stories about what a great experience they had and what a great place Club Med was to visit. Service recovery requires four steps. First, firms need to develop a service recovery program in their company. Companies such as Enterprise Rent-a-Car have companies on call to handle emergencies for them. If a customer has a flat tyre on a rental car, Enterprise has service companies on call with trucks that can he dispatched immediately. Within minutes, a service technician will arrive to take care of the problem and get the customer back on the road.

Second, firms should encourage customers to complain so that resolution of even irritated customers can be achieved. Third, data from causes of service recovery should be used to correct problems that lead to service failures. Fourth, firms need to allocate sufficient resources to service recovery so that it becomes a company strength. A service recovery program begins with commitment by management. They set the tone and direction for the employees. If management is committed to service recovery, employees will buy into the program. In addition, management must provide employee training in how to handle complaints and how to recover dissatisfied customers. Service recovery can occur at two different stages of the purchase process. The first stage is during the service encounter. At this stage, employees have to be trained in how to spot dissatisfaction and then how to deal with it. For example, a restaurant patron who is not eating his meal may be dissatisfied with it. The waitperson can inquire to see if this is the case. If it is, then an opportunity exists to correct the problem immediately. They said ... A well-informed employee is the best salesperson a company. Sometimes the dissatisfaction occurs after the customer leaves the service. For example, a customer picks up an automobile that has been repaired. It runs fine when she picks it up and even does well for a couple of days. Then the problem reoccurs, and she is dissatisfied and feels the repair service did not fix it properly. At this point, she will probably deal with a complaint department. The same situation may happen with a cable TV service or a pest control service. The service may do well for a period of time, then something goes wrong and the customer is dissatisfied.

The more quickly a complaint is handled, the more likely the customer can be recovered and will purchase from the firm again. If the service problem can be corrected at the time of the service encounter, the negative impact of the experience is almost always diminished. The longer it takes to correct the problem, the less likely it can he resolved satisfactorily and the less likely the customer will buy again. If a business customer calls an advertising agency with a complaint about their service, the more quickly the complaint is handled, the more likely they will keep the client. The worst scenario is for customers to be passed from one employee to another only to have the last one say that they will get back to them later. Passing complaints to someone else forces customers to retell the story. The more they retell it, the angrier they will become and the more difficult it will be to resolve. Customers will feel they are getting the run around and that the firm is just stalling. They may even feel the firm does not really want to correct the problem. Firms that are serious about service recovery will give the first employee contacted by the customer the authority to handle the complaint. If it cannot be done immediately over the phone, the person who made the initial contact should do whatever is necessary to see that the problem is resolved. Once the employee knows it will be corrected, he or she needs to convey the message back to the customer. It should be the responsibility of the first contact person to keep the customer informed of what is happening. Customers who are not kept informed tend to get angrier as time passes.

Employees should be trained to defuse the customer's anger as quickly and tactfully as possible. Normoly all this requires is attentive listening, admitting the firm made a mistake, and acknowledging the customer has a right to feel annoyed. Listening will allow customers to vent their anger and explain why they are unhappy. Admitting the firm made a mistake will offset the attribution. It is harder to be made at someone who admits he or she made a mistake. By agreeing that the customer had a right to be upset and dissatisfied, employees demonstrate sympathy and understanding. With this groundwork, the recovery process is ready to move into the resolution stage.

Many companies begin the resolution stage by asking the customer what the firm can do to correct the problem. Firms that have used this strategy are astounded at the reasonableness of customers and the solutions recommended. Customers seldom recommend drastic solutions. Often they may suggest a partial refund or a coupon for a discount on another purchase. They may just want the service firm to correct the problem. Few customers will suggest solutions that are unreasonable.

Once the customer has made a suggestion, the service employee is then ready to negotiate a viable solution to the problem. The goal of the resolution is twofold. First, the firm wants to eradicate the negative experience and change the dissatisfaction into some type of satisfaction. Second, the firm wants that customer to return and purchase again. With these goals in mind, the employee should negotiate a solution that satisfies the customer and is feasible for the firm. If the problem cannot be corrected at the time it is discovered, then customers need to be kept informed. The customer needs to be kept up to date on the progress that is made. If the same employee can deal with the customer through the whole service recovery process, it will increase the chances of a positive outcome. In the business-to-business area, keeping customers informed through one contact person is very important. Too often, either the problem is passed around or it is assumed the customer knows what is happening.

Reducing Service Failures

Reducing service failures requires that firms keep an accurate record of customer complaints and that they encourage customers to complain. By keeping a record of customer complaints, weak areas in the service process can be spotted. If a number of customers complain about the same thing, then the firm knows it is a problem. Steps can then be taken to correct thc problem. It is important to encourage customers to complain. Those who are angry will normally complain, but those at the dissatisfied or irritated stage will usually not say anything. Encouraging these customers to complain will allow a firm to see any weaknesses in processes or materials used in their service. Strengthening these weak links will allow the service to improve quality.

Encouraging customers to complain will also convey a message that the firm cares about its customers. It promotes a long-term relationship. Displaying and promoting toll-free telephone numbers and Internet addresses is a good way to encourage customers to complain. If these methods are used, the employees handling the problems need to be trained in service recovery and then have the power to resolve the situations. Customers like it when the problem can be corrected with one phone call and, if possible, while they are still on the phone. Using toll-free numbers and Internet technology and then passing the customer on to a complaint department to answer at a later time does not encourage customers to voice complaints. Another method of encouraging complaints is a proactive customer contact program. This method has company personnel call customers after a service has been performed to see if they are satisfied. If they are not, the employee is in a position to immediately correct the problem or start the process of service recovery. Companies should not be content to call only once. Calling two or three times will solidify the relationship with the customer and give them ample opportunity to complain. If no complaints arise, the contacts will strengthen the relationship and encourage brand loyalty and repeat purchases.

RELATIONSHIP MARKETING

Relationship marketing is a hybrid version of database marketing. The purpose of relationship marketing is to build long-term connections between the company and its customers and to develop brand and firm loyalty. Relationship marketing works well for services where transactions tend to be continuous and switching costs for customers are high. Firms operating in the customisation and functional service quality sector do with relationship marketing programs. The long-term goal of relationship marketing is to build brand loyalty. Personal interaction with service personnel is critical in the development of the long-term relationship. Medical, legal, accounting, and janitorial services fit into this category. William Bernbach (1911-1982) said . . . Nothing is so powerful as an insight into human nature . . . what compulsions drive a man, what instincts dominate his action . . . if you. know these things about a man, you can touch him at the core of his being.

Developing a Relationship Marketing Program

The first step in relationship marketing is locating prospects. Prospects are individuals who are likely to purchase the service. Using personal contacts and direct communication from the company, the prospect is encouraged to try the service. When the service is purchased, the prospect becomes a customer. The next step is to turn customers into clients. Most customers will initially make purchases from several firms. A customer becomes a client when most or all of his or her purchases are made at one company. The last stage in this process is turning the client into an advocate for the firm. Advocates are brand and firm loyal. They communicate positive word-of-mouth communications about the firm to encourage others to use the company. Suppose Schneider National trueldng company builds a database of potential customers. Through analysing each company, Schneider can narrow the list down to potential customers who would be likely to use them for their shipping needs. At this point they are prospects. Through personal contact with a salesperson from Schneider, some of the prospects will decide to give Schncider a try. They may have Schneider ship several loads for them. Using the concepts of relationship marketing, Schneider will cultivate the relationships with these customers. Eventually, they will start shipping most or all of their loads with Schncider. Now they are clients. The next step for Schncider National is to convert clients into advocates.

FUNCTIONS OF A RELATIONSHIP MARKETING PROGRAM

A relationship marketing program should be designed to accomplish one or more of six functions. Each of these functions should add value to the service for the customer. The first function is to provide social reinforcement. Social reinforcement refers to a customer's esteem and affiliation needs. Sending a customer a birthday card provides social reinforcement. The second value-added activity is reassurance. Reassurance involves the concepts of trustworthiness, reliability, commitment, and concern. Staying in touch with a customer can provide reassurance. When a State Farm insurance agent calls her customers after a tornado to check that they are safe, she is providing reassurance. When a hair stylist calls his customers to see if they are satisfied with their hair, he is showing concern. A plumbing firm demonstrates reassurance when it calls to make sure a water leak was fixed.

A third function relationship marketing can provide is benefit reinforcement. Benefit reinforcement involves telling a customer why a service is beneficial. Benefit reinforcement will help reduce any cognitive dissonance a customer may be experiencing. An auto mechanic explaining to a customer why a new part was put on rather than repairing the old one is using benefit reinforcement. The same is true when a physician reminds a patient of the benefit of the surgery he received. The fourth value-added function of relationship marketing should be to solve customer problems. Database marketing is primarily concerned with selling a good or a service to a consumer while the concern of relationship marketing is to help solve problems. Making a sale is secondary. A janitorial service may be called in to help solve some particular problem a firm is having cleaning a food manufacturing line. If the janitorial service has developed a relationship with the customer, the best solution may be to call in another firm with greater expertise. The goal is to solve the customer's problem, not just to increase revenue for the janitorial firm. A plumber may see a particular customer need and recommend another person who is better qualified to do the work. The fifth function of relationship marketing should be to provide some customisation of the service. Customers must feel that the firm is moulding the service to meet their particular needs. For firms operating in the customisation operational sector, this would be a natural part of their service philosophy. Firms operating in the functional service quality sector will need to do some customisation of the service. Because of the need to provide some customisation, firms using the cost efficiency and technical service quality operational approaches have difficulty establishing strong relationship marketing programs. The last value-added function of relationship marketing involves service enhancements. Customers are given "extras" to reward them for their loyalty or they are treated in a special way. For their best customers, an auto service centre may deliver vehicles they have repaired. Some services offer VIP cards to certain customers which entitles them to additional services. The goal of the service enhancement is to strengthen the bond between the company and the customer.

STUDY–QUESTIONS

1. What do you mean by the services? Also describe the various features of services.
2. What do you mean by the defections.
3. Describe the various functions of relationship marketing.

9

TECHNOLOGICAL TOOLS FOR CRM

INTRODUCTION TO VARIOUS ASPECTS OF CRM

There are three aspects of CRM which can each be implemented in isolation from each other:

(1) Operational CRM—automation or support of customer processes that include a company's sales or service representative.

(2) Collaborative CRM—direct communication with customers that does not include a company's sales or service representative ("self service").

(3) Analytical CRM—analysis of customer data for a broad range of purposes.

META Group (acquired by Gartner in April 2005) developed this conceptual architecture in the late 1990s, and dubbed it the "CRM Ecosystem".

(1) OPERATIONAL CRM

Operational CRM provides support to "front office" business processes, including sales, marketing and service. Each interaction with a customer is generally added to a customer's contact history, and staff can retrieve information on customers from the database as necessary. One of the main benefits of this contact history is that customers can interact with different people or different contact "channels" in a company over time without having to repeat the history of their interaction each time. Consequently, many call centres use some kind of CRM software to support their call centre agents.

(2) COLLABORATIVE CRM

Collaborative CRM covers the direct interaction with customers, for a variety of different purposes, including feedback and issue-reporting. Interaction can be through a variety of channels, such as web pages, email, automated phone

(Automated Voice Response AVR) or SMS. The objectives of Collaborative CRM can be broad, including cost reduction and service improvements.

(3) ANALYTICAL CRM

Analytical CRM analyses customer data for a variety of purposes including:

(i) design and execution of targeted marketing campaigns to optimise marketing effectiveness.

(ii) design and execution of specific customer campaigns, including customer acquisition, cross-selling, up-selling, retention analysis of customer behaviour to aid product and service decision making (e.g. pricing, new product development etc.) management decisions, e.g. financial forecasting and customer profitability analysis prediction of the probability of customer defection (churn).

(iii) Analytical CRM generally makes heavy use of predictive analytics.

DATA

Don't confuse data with information. Don't confuse data with knowledge or understanding. Don't make data anything useful until it is put in context. It isn't. Data is a fact or multiple facts or a set of values that is raw material stored in a structured manner. Out of context, without interpretation and human intelligence applied, it means nothing other than it is a nugget. With interpretation and human intelligence applied, it becomes (possibly) useful information and thus, valuable to your business. But collecting data and storing it somewhere is not particularly beneficial unless it is part of a strategic plan. For example, if you have a customer record that has a complete history of the purchases of the customer and the complaints of the customer and the other interactions of the customer through various channels, what does it mean unto itself Nothing. It is a listing of events. But what happens when you begin to interpret details? You determine that certain customer purchases were followed by a complaint and a return of that item. You also see that some of the customer's interactions indicated that there was an interest in purchasing items that were entirely unrelated to the class of items that were returned. That suggested that you gear your marketing material to this new set of potential purchases. Perhaps you took it a bit further. You mapped the customer's age and geography to buying patterns of the same age and geography. That suggested some purchasing possibilities that were not obvious until you did this analysis.

Note something very important here. When human brainpower is applied by studying the details, interpreting them, and identifying patterns that are determined to be useful, then data becomes valuable information. Until then it is a structured fact but out of context.

WHAT'S A DATABASE?

A database is a set or collection of these structured facts stored in physical files and managed by a database management system (DBMS). It is a collection of facts potentially valuable to a business when organised and interpreted. The DBMS is the system that handles the data so that you have access to it in a variety of ways. For example, using a relational database such as Oracle allows you to query the data to find out patterns that the data suggests dependent on the components of your query. There is a query language called SQL that is used by most databases for these requests.

So far, it seems easy to understand, doesn't it? Well, easy is over. We're not quite at the head-scratching stage, but we're going to be getting there fast. Now that we've identified what data is and its potential value, we can look at the micro and see how data is structured in the information technology universe that you inhabit at least in an avatarish kind of way.

DATA STRUCTURE

How data is structured is not something you have to remember as a business person, but it does pay to know at least the basics. The structure becomes important when you begin the difficult but potentially rewarding process of deciding what is important to you in that data nugget. For example, when you are collecting data from online registrations you usually see the same-old-same-old to start the process. Last Name, First Name, Address, City, State, Country, Phone, Fax, E- mail. But after that, the questions tend to vary widely. In CRM, they usually take the form of "When are you planning on buying CRM software?" or "Do you want a representative to contact you?" Sometimes they are survey-type questions asking about you; interests and hobbies, occupation, or other personal identifiers. At this initial stage, the data collected is captured and stored but not much is done with it. How data is structured has some importance in the capture and storage, so we'll take a brief look at it.

Entities and Attributes: The Linear

Entities are data defined by a common group of characteristics that are of interest to the business. It could be person, place, thing, concept, event, or any other number of general classes of objects. So "customer" could be an entity. Attributes are the descriptors of particular characteristics describing the entity. So, for example, an attribute attached to the customer entity would be "number of years that the customer was associated with the store." So it would read something like "years- as customer" if placed in a CRM data model. Entity = general data object; Attribute = descriptors attached to entities.

Data Quality

Now that you have structure and definition, you have to begin to concern yourself with the value of the specific data that you have. That means "good" data rather than "bad" data. Good data means accurate and not redundant. Inaccurate and repetitious data (bad data) can clog up your system, waste your precious work time, and slow down the physical IT infrastructure. While desire for good data is obvious, how to get it isn't so clear. Even though deleting the redundancies seems easy enough-after all, we have the delete key-it isn't so simple, especially when you have hundreds of gigabytes or even terabytes of customer data. Think about the following scenario: Are William Smith, Bill Smith, and Will Smith all married to Jada Pinkett? What if Will Smith has a Pasadena address, Bill Smith doesn't, but his address is two years old, and William Smith is listed as a "rapper and movie star" as occupation, but not living in Pasadena. What if they are all listed at 33 years old? How many real Smiths are there? One, two, or three distinct entities-all or none of whom might be the star of Men in Black? Is this serious? Absolutely. In a 2001 survey conducted by Pricewaterhousecoopers, 75 percent of 600 companies reported significant problems because of defective data. Over 33 percent of those surveyed indicated that because of these data problems they had faded to send a bill or collect an invoice, thus losing direct revenue. Even more staggering, the Data Warehousing Institute (TDWI) did a study in 2003 that estimated that defective data (including incorrectly spelled names like "Arun Chudhury" -a regular event for me) costs U.S. industry a mind-blowing $611 billion in overhead for mailing costs and wasted labour time that could otherwise be saved with high rates of data quality. High rates of data quality are equal to about 98 percent accuracy levels.

DWI identifies seven areas that characterize data quality. They are:

(i) Timeliness is the data available when needed? Real-time datawarehouses are a contemporary answer to this question, though not the traditional one.

(ii) Accessibility is the data easily accessible, understandable, and usable? This is defined by the intelligence of the team in charge of the data and data quality. If they understand the user is most likely a nontechnical business unit representative and not one of their own, then the data will be usable and accessible. If they don't, heaven help you all.

(iii) Consistency are data elements consistently defined and understood? Is a "customer" for sales defined the same way as a "customer" for marketing when it comes to data? Imagine the problem when a new field is entered into one system that is connected through several others and the database administrator forgets to let everyone know there is a new field. Or, if "net sales" in department 1 is calculated differently than "net sales" in department 2, there is a difference in definition as a result.

(iv) Completeness is all the necessary data present? For example, the Centre for Data Quality does audits on data quality. In one case, it found an insurance company that was missing the required Social Security number for claims in 82 percent of the audited records. A securities firm had 300,000 records that had at least one blank (but required) field. That was 30 percent of their total records.

(v) Validity do data values fall within acceptable ranges defined by the business? For example, a phone number of 95000-125-3256 is not valid and falls outside the range of acceptable phone numbers. Lack of validation routines is one of the most common mistakes in the land of data cleanliness.

(vi) Accuracy does the data accurately represent reality or a verifiable source? For example, is the name spelled right? This is one of the prime "what can go wrong" areas, because simple incorrect data entry is one of the major problems with data quality. Data defects are common when data migration occurs from one system to another or an ETL (extract, transform, load) tool is used to grab data from one system to bring it to another. Conversion does- not always work so smoothly when the data is migrated but not the business processes that the data is mapped to.

(vii) Integrity is the structure of the data and relationships among entities and attributes maintained consistently? This means is "Last-Name" the structure used across the departments at the company or is "Last Name" used and "last name" used and ... you get the picture. When integration between disparate data systems is attempted, mismatched syntax and formats is often a real problem.

Differences in corporate culture and approaches in defining data can create a huge problem with the integrity and validity of data as each merger occurs. Your customer might not be my customer-at least as far as our converging databases are concerned. But data quality is a science now, so never fear. There are methods of vastly improving data quality that are long established and effective. Many of them mimic any CRM project that you might be aware of. Some are software-driven. All involve judicious human behaviour, a task unto itself.

The Data Quality Program

Good data quality programs resemble tactical versions of good CRM programs. There are executive sponsors and program managers involved. Project planning is part and parcel of the effort. Education, metrics, ongoing communications, process and data element assessment, establishment of change management policy and operations, and the development of ongoing internal processes are all critical to the effort. Where it differs is in the level of scrutiny given the actual data and its structure and storage. For example, a typically important part of the effort is a data audit. A data audit is sometimes internal, if the skills are there, or sometimes done by an external firm such as the Centre for Data Quality. It is a systematic review of the data for the identification of common defects. Once they are identified, metrics to detect the defects as they enter the datawarehouse or the other data stores are created as are rules for fixing the defects. If the work is systematic, then defects ranging from missing data or incorrect data to duplicate records or business rule violations should be discovered. What kinds of defects are found? The British Columbia Ministry of Advanced Education found defects that led to students who were over 2,000 years old (Mel Brooks, 1 wonder?) or not yet born, among other things.

Another aspect of the program that is unique is data cleansing. This is usually a rules-based software solution to providing good data that is bereft of duplicates, missing information, and invalid ranges. There are four methods used for cleaning the data:

(i) Correction: This is the fixing of defective data elements and records. It could involve modifying an incorrect value to conform to the company standard or filling in a missing piece of information. It could involve merging duplicate records-often called by consumers "deduping.' I use reduplication software for ACT! that merges duplicate records for me. It's modestly efficient but it depends on the fields that ACT! defines as duplicable-up to three of them. I change that so I can merge more duplicates. It is not complex, though. It won't find that Will Smith and Bill Smith might be the same person. It is looking more for identical, rather than similar, records to merge. Correction in the world of data cleansing is far more complex and more painstaking a process. Typically, the data analysts fixing Oracle or DB2 are using a data quality tool such as those provided by Trillium Software to correct the defects.

(ii) Filter: This data cleansing method involves deleting duplicate, missing, or spurious data elements that might occur as the result of some bad software process occurring.

(iii) Detect and report: This is for data that has little business value. It is simply what it says. Find the problem and let someone know, but don't fix it.

(iv) Prevent: This is, of course, devoutly to be wished, but not always the case. This means that data entry people are trained in proper data entry given the company's business processes. It also means that codes are up to-date and stay that way, that when it calls for changing business processes or data models, the changes are made.

Benefits of Good Data

Customer satisfaction is perhaps the most important one for purposes of this book. This seems like pretty time-consuming stuff, doesn't it? So why do it? What are a few million data errors? Well, bud, the ROI is so clear and the benefits so material, not doing it seems to be a serious *faux pas*. There are tangible benefits to your bottom line, and top line for that matter. In a TDWI study, 19 percent of the companies queried said the most significant benefit was improved customer satisfaction. Nine percent saw increased revenues, twelve percent saw reduced costs. Having "a single version of the truth" was the result for 19 percent, tying customer satisfaction improvements as the number one reason for doing this.

DATA MODELS

There are several stages to get through to complete the design of a valid data model. There are several that you can glance at and keep upstairs as a reference, but we wouldn't get into this too much.

(i) *Conceptual data model:* This model is essentially the first thinking about the data in the early phases of system development. Data requirements are scoped from a business standpoint here, not from a pure data architecture. Technical details are not part of this design at all. This is the stage where the CRUD matrix is developed.

(ii) *Logical data model*: This follows the conceptual data model. The technical theories of data architecture are used here. Normalisation is an example- this is the process of constraining the definitions of data to prevent redundant data definitions. The relationships established at the conceptual level get absorbed as attributes called pointers or keys within the entities that the logical data model identifies. However, there are no constraints or restrictions that imposed by the database management system at this level, so no database can be created yet.

(iii) *Physical data model:* Once the logical data model is completed, the next step is the mapping of database design data groupings into physical database areas, files, records, elements, fields, and keys while adhering to the physical constraints of the hardware, DBMS software, and communications network. This is the physical data model and is the immediate predecessor to the database itself. The database follows.

But what happens once you have the data structures, and the database and the data itself Datawarehouse.

THE DATAWAREHOUSE

The term "datawarehouse" was coined by Bill Inmon in 1990. Over the years, it has come to mean an enterprise-wide data collection that is organised around subjects, collected from multiple sources and centrally merged into a coherent body over time. If the data store is a single specialised subject, it is a data mart. Piping data from several data marts to a consolidated store can be a datawarehouse. Because data is now so voluminous, usually a datawarchouse has a time period associated with it. For example, if the time period is five years, then data that is one minute old is rolled into the warehouse, but data that is five years and one minute old is rolled out of the warehouse. To function, datawarehouses have several technologies that are actively involved. Data is extracted from operational databases. It is processed and cleaned up to eliminate incorrect and redundant data or add missing data. It is then loaded into a relational database such as Oracle 9i or IBM's DB2 database. Once in the database, analytical operations are run on the data using analytic tools (such as those provided by SAS), online transaction processing (OLAP) tools (such as PeopleSoft's PeopleTools), or data mining tools to provide some historic patterns and interesting results.

A financial services company, can use the nice, clean, accurate data to find the most profitable and most committed customers. The value of the datawarehouse is incalculable. But there are obstacles and dangers along the way to dropping the ring in the volcano.

On the other hand, the analyses could be as simple as a report on 18-49 year olds' viewing habits in prime time: network versus cable. That takes tools like Business Objects' Crystal Reports Enterprise. If you are looking across dimensions and analysing a matrix such as zip codes and the relationship to return rates on direct mall campaigns, then OLAP is for you. The most complex reports come from the data mining tools that can also identify individual historic interaction patterns and their relationship to demographically valid data. Datawarehouses are a necessity for CRM. Think of it in the simplest terms. If you get five letters about the same thing or get "personal" letters that misspell your name constantly, what kind of trust are you going to have in the company committing the snafus? If you are a retailer, a datawarehouse provides you with the data to discover customer demographics, specific shopping patterns, successes and failures in marketing campaign results, and so on.

Possible Problems

Architectural and human issues can turn a datawarchouse into a place ready for repossession and dismantling. Given that this is the repository for what is likely to be all the customer data that is needed for that gorgeous, 360-degree perfect circle of a view of the customer, failure is not an option, but it is a possibility. A very expensive possibility. Here are some of the known problems with datawarehousing:

(i) Conflicting business rules among users-same calculation performed differently;

(ii) Data homogenisation;

(iii) Heavy overhead;

(iv) High maintenance system;

(v) Lack of knowledge of customer management against over concern with resource optimisation (effectiveness, efficiency);

(vi) Query and reporting tools that are so easy to use everyone actually uses them and creates "report request overload";

(vii) Security not assignable without process-driven approach;

(viii) Eighty percent of time is spent on extracting, cleaning, loading—no time for applications; and

(ix) Incompatibilities in the systems that are feeding the datawarehouses. Data not being captured turns out to be important.

Currently, the dominant method of replenishing datawarehouses and data marts is to use extract, transform, and load (ETL) tools that pull data from source systems periodically at the end of a day, week, or month-and provide a snapshot of your business data at a given moment in time. That batch data is then loaded into a datawarchouse table. During each cycle, the warehouse table is completely refreshed and the process is repeated no matter whether the data has changed or not. Using the ETL tools can create data discrepancies, particularly if the data is being refreshed and hasn't changed.

Reasons for Failure

Datawarehouse failures are not unknown. In fact, the Cutter Consortium issued an early 2003 report that stated that 41 percent of all datawarehousing and business intelligence projects fail outright or at least don't meet the business objectives of the company that is implementing it. This is a dangerous place to be. Fully 25 percent of all the companies implementing datawarehouses don't trust the concept, which is a nightmare in the making.

Some of the reasons for failure:

(i) *Technical:* Ignoring the obvious issues related to query volume and network traffic; installing the wrong components; not paying attention to issues like scalability (using terabytes of data is possible—how can the system handle that much?).

(ii) *Design*: A bad architecture; a data-driven methodology rather than a business-driven plan; no definition of metadata, creating confusing data definitions; ignoring configuration by the user or providing too much capability to configure.

(iii) *Sociological*: The politics of datawarehouses are intense since he (or she) who controls the data controls the world (or at least the company); failure to investigate vendor product claims or vendor culture.

(iv) *Procedural*: Always a thorny issue for customers and vendors; poor scope management leading to scope creep (e.g. increasing the feature set — constantly); using a methodology that doesn't involve prototypes or proof of concept; ignoring an iterative approach and isolating the users from the design process; operational and management procedures at data center not measured against the warehouse environment; poor training.

All of these can be reasons for failure, as can others. In order to provide a likely success, it is important to approach a datawarehouse implementation as you would a CRM project.

Real-Time Datawarehouses

Customers run their own universe. This isn't a case of the inmates running the asylum, but of empowerment. As I've established, that means customer volatility is on the increase. That also means that the customer information that a company has needs to be as current as possible to allow that company to make the appropriate and timely decisions regarding that customer as close to real time as possible. Imagine this: you are a pharmaceutical company and you didwt have knowledge that the customer who is buying your medicine recently developed an allergy to something that is in the medicine. The results could be devastating to the customer and to you as a pharmaceutical company.

Most cases of the "need to know real time" are less dramatic than this, but the contemporary nature of the information is often the difference between retention and loss. Datawarehouses are storing customer information. This is good. But when the datawarchouse is replenished in real time, it empowers users by providing them with the most up-to-date information possible.

Imagine the ability to have the data available in the datawarehouse as soon as the data is written and captured. Wow. If done well, real-time datawarehousing provides the data record image prior to and after the new information is gathered. Analysis becomes interesting and very valuable. Think about that pharmaceutical example. Knowing what changed and when becomes important to the health and well being of the customer and the company. In the Internet era, more people are beginning to realize the limitations that snapshot copy replenishment presents and demand better alternatives.

Snapshots do not involve entire database movement but simple captures of parts of database tables-for example, specified columns. In addition, not each individual change is made to a record between copy processes. In this light, the snapshot process can be likened to looking at last week's newspaper or using last week's stock market results to trade stock today.

Data is a perishable commodity: the older it is, the less relevant. Businesses need tools that can provide real-time business intelligence and an absolutely current and comprehensive picture of their organization and their customers-not last week or last month, but right now. Stopping at the datawarehouse is the equivalent of buying everything you purchase at Wal-Mart. Other (data) stores provide other value that might rival datawarehouses, but just might be a complement to the datawarehouse, too.

One of the most popular and often mentioned is the data mart. Where the datawarehouse provides you with all your enterprise data consolidated, the data mart is focused around a single subset of the enterprise data. For example, it may be the repository for all the data related to product sales for the company, while you might have another data mart with all the customer data. You can use the data singularly via the data mart or consolidate the data from both data marts to do analysis that might be valuable to you. It could cover a specific area such as products or be organised around a line of business such as sales or marketing. Data marts are smaller and use software to summarise, store, and analyse data that might be useful to you someday. The architecture still has to be characteristically the enterprise architecture so that the designations for entities, attributes, fields, and so on are consistent with those of other data marts and the rest of the company.

Operational Data Store (ODS)

Operational data stores have been made analogous to "short-term memory" in more than one instance. They are an interim area that is used to store continuously updated recent data gathered through the course of a business day. They are designed to hold small amounts of current data that has simple queries performed on it. For example, when you give Federal Express or UPS your tracking number and then see where your package is, that could well be data from an ODS. A few days after your package is delivered, that short-term memory is wiped out. There are several classes of ODS. Each of them can handle more and more complex transactions in a closer to real-time manner. CRM- related ODS systems are Class 1 systems that provide synchronous or near-synchronous updates for customers receiving validated information. When the legacy system is updated, so is the ODS. There is either no lag or only a few seconds lag. So if I enter an order online and it is captured, its data appears in the ODS about the time I finish and submit the entry. Class II and III use a store and forward approach. That means every few hours (in a Class II system) or every day (in a Class III system), a new file with the new information is captured at the legacy system. Then once an hour or once a day, the file is dumped to the ODS and refreshes the data. Not nearly as effective as the Class I ODS that is most frequently used for CRM.

CORPORATE INFORMATION FACTORY (CIF)

The corporate information factory (CIF) is a logical architecture, developed by CRM and data management guru Claudia Inmhoff and datawarehouse god Bill Inmon. Its advantage is that it concerns itself with the business processes of a company and drives its results (business intelligence) using data provided from business operations. It could equally as well be called a customer information factory because it combines the producers of data and consumers of information into a single architecture. It is a primo example of a decision support system for any CRM or enterprise strategic data architecture. The CIF uses datawarehouses or ODS as the assembly point for data captured from the operational systems and business processes of the subject company. At the datawarehouse or ODS, the information is assembled and presented in a useable format for the ultimate-user of the data. The users then acquire the newly formatted data so that they can slice and dice it and then assemble the new reports into useful information that is available in their own environment-using their interfaces. According to Dr. Imhoff, four operations and administration functions must be implemented to maintain a CIF effectively:

(i) *Service management*: These processes register, prioritize, assign, and track the disposition of all requests for service coming from the business community.

(ii) *Change management*: This is classic change management. When the environment changes, so does the culture. These processes make sure that the culture change is managed effectively with minimal disruption and maximum adoption.

(iii) *Systems management:* These processes manage the changes to new versions of databases, upgrades to software, and installation of new hardware components.

(iv) *Data acquisition management*: These processes monitor and maintain the programs that capture, integrate, cleanse, transform, and load or update data in the datawarehouse or operational data store. They are typical data acquisition processes.

All of the above are typical operations in an enterprise environment. What makes the CIF important to the new generation of CRM is the information workshop. The data and processes integrate here for the business community. Data is mapped to the appropriate process and presented in a way that the business users find easy to understand. Peoplesoft's analytic capabilities use this "workbench" idea with their Enterprise Performance Management (EPM) engines. Workbenches, rather than provide you with a hammer and saw, provide you with visual information tools that help you conceptualise your planning or understand the results of your search for some kind of knowledge.

So if you are looking for patterns related to employee activity and customer satisfaction, you can not only derive them but see them as relationships using a workbench. When it gets down to basics, though, the CIF is only as good as the datawarehouse at its heart. If the datawarehouse design is flexible and can adapt to the changes in business process and in the overall business ecosystem, it can work. If it can remain stable and use the data structures it contains already, regardless of the change, it can work. Finally, if it can handle the different forms of analytic processes that exist from straightforward simple SQL-based queries to complex data mining, it can work.

DATA MINING AND CRM

Recent advances in data gathering and data storage technologies, along with the steep fall in prices has made it possible for companies to gather and store large amounts of data. Large companies generate gigabytes of data daily through their daily transactions. Analysing such large quantities of data requires approaches that are very different from the traditional data analysis approaches adopted in disciplines such as statistics, Artificial Intelligence (AI), machine learning and others. This has given birth to the field of Knowledge Discovery in Databases (KDD) more popularly called as Data Mining. 'Knowledge Discovery in Databases (KDD) is the non-trivial process of identifying valid, novel, potentially useful and ultimately understandable patterns in data. Others look at data mining in terms of a set of tools and techniques that operate on and extract implicit patterns from data.

CHARACTERISTICS OF DATA MINING

Data Mining has many characteristics that are very different from traditional data analysis disciplines. Given below are a few of the more important ones.

(i) Data mining techniques give the search methods some degree of search autonomy resulting in automated or semi-automated nature of the discovery.

(ii) Data mining tools and techniques operate on large and very large databases. Therefore, many techniques that were available to researchers earlier cannot be used without modification to suit large datasets.

(iii) Data mining is usually done on data that has been collected while undertaking the day-to-day transactions of a company. Such data usually has less bias than data that has been specifically collected for the purpose of analysis. However, many a time, attributes might be insufficient to carry out some desired analysis.

(iv) Data mining aims to facilitate the involvement of the end user (e.g. manager, etc.) in the discovery process without need for trained experts either for running the various techniques or for interpreting the results.

(v) Last, data mining is an interdisciplinary field taking its inputs from diverse but related disciplines such as statistics, artificial intelligence, machine learning and large databases, among others.

Data mining tools and techniques operate on large databases and extract patterns that are implicit in them. The knowledge that is extracted from the databases by the data mining algorithms is primarily of two types: predictive and descriptive. Prediction involves finding out the future state of a variable using its past values and the values of other related variables. For example, a manager of a bank might want to find out whether his customer (say A) will default on a loan repayment or not.

The chances of the customer's defaulting can be found out using a classification algorithm, which would assign the customer to either the defaulting set or the non-defaulting set. Description involves finding out the properties that describe the data under consideration. For example, a manager of a retail store might want to know how the profiles of his/her customers change with either age or their income.

Data Mining Tasks

Data mining tasks are operations that extract predictive or descriptive knowledge from the large datasets. The main tasks are as follows.

(i) Segmentation: Segmentation aims to identify a finite set of naturally occurring clusters or categories to describe data. Segmentation is done in such a way that cases belonging to a segment or cluster are more similar with respect to the clustering criterion while they differ significantly from the cases belonging to other segments. The knowledge about market segments is very important to a marketing manager for carrying out his/her day-to-day activities. Based upon this knowledge marketing campaigns are run, advertisement budgets are allocated, store locations are decided, offers made and a host of other activities are carried out. But, before doing any of this, segments are to be identified and their characteristics determined. This is done using clustering algorithms that segment the database based on the required criterion.

(ii) *Deviation detection*: Deviation detection (DD) focuses on discovering the most significant changes in the data from previously measured, expected or normative values. Many of the CRM and other packages routinely keep on checking critical parameters as they change with the market scenario.

In case, the parameters change above a value as defined by the user, then it is reported to the user/manager for appropriate action.

(iii) *Regression*: Regression is the operation of learning a function that predicts the value of a real valued dependant variable based on values of other independent variables. Suppose the effectiveness of an advertisement campaign is measured in terms of brand recall. If a marketing manager has a prior feeling that the ad effectiveness is dependent on the total advertisement budget and the media used, then he/she can estimate the effectiveness of the advertisement campaign in terms of the advertisement budget and other related variables that might be important. If a new campaign is proposed to be launched, the manager can estimate its effectiveness based on the above regression equation that he/she has estimated. The campaign budget and other parameters can then be fine tuned to achieve the required degree of effectiveness.

(iv) *Classification*: Classification is a process that maps a given data item into one of the several predefined classes. In CRM, classification is used for a variety of purposes like behaviour prediction, product and customer categorisation. Classification is used in campaign management to identify prospective customers for a new product from a database of old customers.

(v) *Link analysis*: Link analysis seeks to establish relationship between items or variables in a database record to expose patterns and trends. Link analysis can also trace connections between items of records over time. The most important link analysis application in CRM, called market basket analysis, is an operation that seeks relationships between product items characterising product affinities or buyer preferences. For example: A manager in a retail store will be very concerned about the display of goods. He/she will like to display only those products that are likely to be purchased. Optimising the shelf space with the products that are most likely to be sold would help the manager in improving the revenue from the store. If the marketing manager mines for association rules, rules that details of items that sell together, then using these rules the display space can be redesigned and better utilised. The display can thus be made to accommodate principally those items that sell together. By reconfiguring the display space, the store manager increases the amount of sales.

Most of the data mining tasks are exploratory in nature. They give a pointer to the fact that possible relationships might exist between variables, but might not, in most cases, ascertain the reason for the occurrence of the detected pattern. But their usefulness comes from the fact that they are able to point to the possibility of obscure and hidden relationships existing between variables. The use of data mining tasks must be guided by the questions that need to be asked. Two or more data mining tasks used in proper conjunction on a large database would give a manager rich preliminary insights into the phenomenon taking place and probably ferret out hidden relationships otherwise impossible to recover.

Data Mining Tools and Techniques

Data mining tools and techniques are algorithms and methods used to carry out the above data mining tasks. They differ from each other in type of data handled, assumptions about the data, scope and interpretations of the output. It should be noted that a single tool (say neural networks) could be used to carry out many tasks (e.g. segmentation, classification, etc.).

Similarly, a data-mining task could be performed using two or many tools (e.g. classification can be performed by decision trees, neural networks or rule induction.) We give below a brief introduction about some of the more important data mining tools, which are a part of many of the currently available data mining packages.

(i) *Case-based reasoning*: Case based reasoning (CBR) methods try to simulate the thinking process of human being. Typically, when an example is presented to a CBR solution, it tries to match the current example with other examples that it has in its repository and retrieves the case that is most similar to the current case. Decision is then taken based on extrapolation, i.e. fitting the decision taken by the most appropriate case. The power of case based reasoning packages depends largely on the indexing method used to store cases and the matching method used to retrieve relevant cases.

(ii) *Visualisation techniques*: Visualisation techniques allow the user to view data from various angles using graphic display techniques like charts, diagrams, displays for multi-dimensional data, etc. Used in conjunction with other data mining techniques, visualisation techniques are ideal when users do not know what and where to look for in the data and to discover new knowledge. Managers without any technical knowledge can easily understand properties of a data set, if it is presented in a visual form. Most of the data mining packages include at least one visualisation tool.

(iii) *Clustering algorithms*: Clustering algorithms divide the database into different groups called clusters such that intra-cluster similarity is the maximum and the inter-cluster similarity is the minimum. Research in clustering has occurred simultaneously in many fields, resulting in diverse approaches each having its own advantages and disadvantages. Recent studies have looked at clustering very large data sets. Market segmentation using a clustering algorithm is almost the first thing that every manager does to gain more knowledge about his market and its constituents.

(iv) *Decision trees*: Decision trees are classification tools that classify examples into finite number of classes considering one variable at a time and dividing the entire data set based on it. Decision trees can be used for inducing rules for classification and segmentation.

(v) *Rule induction*: Rule induction is the process of inducing general rules that apply to many cases from a database of specific examples. These rules may be of the classification type, predictive type or may be rules that perform link analysis.

(vi) *Nearest neighbour techniques*: Nearest neighbour techniques use a set of examples to approximate a classification model. Suppose a case has to be classified into a predefined class. These techniques try to find the neighbours of this case. The 'neighbour' is another case that has almost similar properties as the specific case under consideration. A similarity measure is used for this purpose to find the 'closest' example in terms of certain parameters and then it assigns this new case to the class that has the maximum representation amongst its neighbours.

Usually analytics packages obtained from vendors come with many different kinds of tools. These might be used for varying tasks as discussed above. But it must be kept in mind that the choice of the algorithm to be run on the data depends not only on the data that you have but also answers to the questions that you ask. If you want to know whether a customer will repay back a loan or not, then it is more appropriate to run a classification algorithm. On the other hand, if you want to know which items sell together in a retail outlet, it may be more appropriate to run an association rule finding algorithm.

As transactions take place, new data constantly comes into the data warehouse sometimes adding to the new data while at other times updating the old data. Data mining solution for a particular CRM application must be capable of. catering to such kind of dynamism. Running the same algorithm over the entire database repeatedly is an expensive proposition in terms of both time and resources. Tools with incremental knowledge updating capabilities can help in dealing with such situations.

Finally, tight integration between the front end CRM solution like a campaign management solution and the backend data mining solution helps to ensure consistency and timely information dissemination throughout the company. This could be leveraged to make more informed and better decisions.

ROLE OF INTERACTIVE TECHNOLOGIES

Information technology has revolutionised the way we see and do our work bringing in better and more efficient methods of conducting our businesses. With the advent of the Internet, distances and time differences no longer matter. People are able to have instant and reliable access to important and critical information while knowledge can be disseminated efficiently and instantly.

The development of software, hardware and networking technologies have led to the development of new and better technologies not only to be in use our day-to-day lives, but also for conducting business operations. Companies have used such technologies in their operations for cutting costs, improving processes, delivering better services and last but not the least getting close to their customers. The development and deployment of interactive technologies and the proliferation of the Internet as a medium of communication have made it possible for companies to interact more closely with their customers and at the same time get to know them better.

INTERACTIVE TECHNOLOGIES

These are two-way interaction between the communicating parties. They permit a dialogue between the parties concerned. In particular, they permit more than one sense, viz. sight, sound, etc., to be used for communication. Such technologies are easy to use deeply involving and permitting more information to be communicated. For example, consider a web page of a company selling automobiles, especially cars. One way to communicate the offerings is to have a web page in HTML format with just a few pictures about the cars on offer and their specifications. While conveying to the users the essential information such sites are not interactive. Communication is just one-way, the user is not able to respond to this information, the company, therefore, loses out on critical feedback from the user as far as his/her opinions about the product is concerned. A better way of communicating the same offering is to use more interactive web technologies. Significant advances have made it possible for the company to develop its web site in such a way that the user is able to get a three-dimensional view of the selected car, look at it from various angles, change the colour and other accessories and even take a virtual test drive in a simulated environment.

Such interactivity conveys the features of the car better than any words or pictures can express. At the end of the experience, the user can be asked to fill in a small questionnaire and get his/her feedback. Thus the main idea here is better communications with the customer, generating a positive impact in his/her minds about the product. Interactive technologies have become an integral part of all the CRM solutions offered today by vendors. They consist of interactive web sites, kiosks, customer interaction centres and others. Interactive technologies offer many advantages to companies. They include:

(i) Interactive technologies offer customers a chance to voice their opinions to the firm on the products and services on offer in a more proactive fashion. Getting such feedback is the first important step in process, service and product improvement ultimately affecting customer satisfaction. ID The company is able to empower the customers with sufficient knowledge about products and their care. This enables customers solve minor problems they face regarding purchases themselves without involving the company's service engineers directly. Thus, a company affects considerable savings in services and is able to concentrate its resources in solving more critical issues. For example, a company can guide a user step-by-step in the process of preliminary fault diagnosis. The customer solves minor complaints following instructions from the web site or recorded voice, while the service engineer is better equipped with preliminary knowledge to solve a more complicated problem. It has been seen that using an interactive web page to provide such services is five times cheaper than giving instructions through telephone.

(ii) Better communications: This provides detailed features of the product to the customers and enables the customers to get a good idea on what the product has to offer, and thereby offer informed decisions. The company is also benefited, as an informed customer will be able to appreciate the product better, before making a decision. The customer expectations will be grounded in reality.

(iii) Since, the company is able to affect better communications, the call duration and transaction times are reduced significantly thereby allowing the operators to handle more calls. Thus, the company realises significant savings and improves call centre productivity.

EVOLUTION OF INTERACTIVITY IN WEB TECHNOLOGY

Here we will be primarily looking at the evolution of user interface technologies. The first generation of modern interfaces was based on proprietary programming that ran natively in the operating system on the client, thereby reducing the need for network bandwidth. Although they were interactive, the need for a significant amount of software to be installed on the clients, led to high costs for installation, maintenance and upgrades.

Second, they could be used only within the company or a few selected customer interaction points, because of their proprietary nature. Customers could not access such interactive user interfaces from the Internet, thus blocking the major customer segment. In the next stage, standard HTML clients accessed applications functionality that resided on the server. The server generated the user interface for the application functionality as a static HTML based document that could be downloaded from the Web. But since standard web browsers are sessionless and have no application functionality (in other words a dumb client), interactivity was limited.

Each interaction by the user needed the client to send the entire document back to the server and refresh it again, causing inefficient network usage a jamming user experience and deterring user adoption. The present generation is currently seeing the advent of thin client solutions using standard open technologies like ActiveX and Java for implementing lightweight clients that constitute just the presentation layer of the applications. These technologies provide a high level of client interactivity but require only a small amount of software to be installed on the clients. Many of the web browsers now support ActiveX, Java and other interactive interface technologies, thus improving interactivity with the customers.

Client and Server Side Interactions

Majority of the applications today run on client-server kind of architecture. Here, the interaction can be of two kinds, viz.

(i) Client side interaction

(ii) Server side interaction

Server side interaction has both advantages and disadvantages. Some of the advantages are:

(a) The server controls the environment

(b) Code is not downloaded into the client

(c) Less client dependent.

However, there are also significant disadvantages that include:

(a) Heavy computer load (on the server)

(b) Hard to simulate Real-time interaction

(c) Limited access to client resources. The client capabilities are effectively wasted.

On the other hand, client side interaction comes with its own set of advantages and disadvantages. The advantages include:

(a) Distributed computer processing power-running on many clients

(b) Real time interaction

(c) Access to client resources

Disadvantages include:

(a) Takes time to download code

(b) Unknown environment (Internet), so possible security concerns

(c) Client most likely not as powerful as the server

Choosing the right application with the correct type of interaction could he a tricky task. Some of the factors that need to be considered are: where the program runs, the download speed that can be expected and the run time for the application and finally, the platforms the programme is expected to run. CRM applications can he used both within the company and also by customers.

Their set of requirements and content to be delivered are significantly different. Applications that are accessed by the customers using their own infrastructure need to be interactive, but at the same time must be built using open technologies (like Java, CGI, etc.), so that they can be accessed easily. Download times for applets (small Java programmes running on clients) need to he kept as low as possible. However, these applets significantly increase interactivity. A compromise is to download the applets from the server as and when needed. In case, the applications are used by the organisations themselves, then proprietary software can he used. Client side interaction is mostly preferred as it enables the operators to access information quickly as server load is reduced. On the other hand, it requires a significant amount of software to be resident on the clients, making initial start up periods quite long as software has to he loaded on each client throughout the organisation. A compromise is to use a thin client version that uses the web to interface with the server.

(i) ActiveX, CGI, Java and Netscape Plug-ins are some of the interactive web technologies used in CRM solutions.

(ii) *ActiveX*: It is a set of technologies developed by Microsoft that integrates software components in a networked environment using any language. The set of technologies include ActiveX scripting, controls, documents and server framework. ActiveX control is essentially a Windows program that can be distributed from a web page. These controls can do literally anything a Windows program can do and therefore interactivity can be increased by appropriate programming.

(iii) *CGI (Common Gateway Interface)*: CGI is a standard for interfacing external applications with information servers. Basically CGI is the equivalent of letting the world run a program on your system. Therefore, the client is the one that is taking up most of the load, while the server is free to perform transaction processing and other critical operations.

(iv) *Java*: It is a set of three key technologies (Java programming language, Java byte code and the Java Virtual machine) that allow an application to he complied once and run on may platforms. It is basically platform independent and the programs can he downloaded to a client machine and run there.

(v) *Netscape, plug-ins*: These are software programs that mend the capabilities of Netscape Navigator in a specific way - for example, the ability to play audio samples or view movies from within the navigator. In all the above technologies, the fundamental idea is the same - i.e. run a program on the client and make it as interactive as possible. It will use the client to run and therefore, there will not be any delay associated with processing. Once the part of the processing associated with the program is over, then it can be sent over the web to the server.

STRATEGY

Several commercial CRM software packages are available which vary in their approach to CRM. However, CRM is not just a technology, but rather a holistic approach to an organisation's philosophy in dealing with its customers. This includes policies and processes, front-of-house customer service, employee training, marketing, systems and information management.

Hence, it is important that any CRM implementation considers not only technology, but furthermore the broader organisational requirements. The objectives of a CRM strategy must consider a company's specific situation and its customers needs and expectations.

TECHNOLOGY CONSIDERATIONS

The technology requirements of a CRM strategy can be complex and far reaching. The basic building blocks include:

(i) A database to store customer information. This can be a CRM specific database or an Enterprise Data warehouse.

(ii) Operational CRM requires customer agent support software.

(iii) Collaborative CRM requires customer interaction systems, eg an interactive website, automated phone systems etc.

(iv) Analytical CRM requires statistical analysis software as well as software that manages any specific marketing campaigns.

(v) Each of these can be implemented in a basic manner or in a high end complex installation.

KEY FUNCTIONALITIES

A typical CRM system is subdivided into three basic sub modules:

(1) Marketing

(2) Sales

(3) Service

(1) Marketing

Marketing sub module primarily deals with providing functionalities of long-term planning and short-term execution of marketing related activities within an organisation.

(a) Marketing Planning

Long-term Market Plans can be made and Quantitative as well as Qualitative measures (targets) can be set for a defined period and for different product groups, geographies etc. These are then monitored based on the actual performance throughout the defined period. Marketing campaigns with the specific objective of generating leads (Prospective customers who may be interested in a product).

(b) Campaign Management

Short-term execution includes running marketing campaigns via different communication channels targeting a pre-defined group of potential buyers with a specific message referring to a product or a group of products.

(c) Lead Management

One key objective of the marketing function is to generate sales related leads, which finally get converted into sales revenues for the company. Lead management deals with processing these leads, carrying out a sanity check, evaluating the genuineness of the information (Since, there is a lot of information that is gathered during marketing campaigns it becomes necessary to screen these leads), and finally converting them to hot leads or cold leads.

(2) Sales

Sales functionalities are focused on helping the Sales team to execute and manage the presales process better and in an organized manner. Sales team is responsible for regularly capturing key customer interactions, any leads or opportunities they are working on etc, in CRM system. The system helps by processing this data, monitoring against the targets and proactively alerting the sales person with recommended further actions based on company's sales policy.

(3) Opportunity Management

Opportunities help the Sales team by organizing all the relevant data regarding a prospective deal into one place. It is characterized by the details such as Prospective customer, expected budget, total spending, products interested in, expected closing date, Key players in the deal and their key characteristics, important dates and milestones etc.

The Opportunity has several phases, e.g. initiation, identification, qualification, RFP received, quotation sent, final stage, won or lost. Of course these phases can be defined based on individual company needs. A CRM system helps in each phase by "Guiding" the Sales representative to carry out certain suggested activities as defined by the company's sales policy. It creates reminders and planned activities within the system. e.g. if the Opportunity has reached "RFP received" stage, and the deal size is more than (say) 50,000 USD, the system can prompt the representative to hold a review discussion with a senior manager. This is often referred as "Guided Sales Methodology". Opportunities can be directly converted into Quotations or Sales Orders.

(4) Quotation and Sales Order Management

Opportunities if reaches a Quotation phase can be converted to a quotation, and, if won gets converted to a Sales order. Standard features of creating a "linked" Quotation or Sales Order from opportunities are provided. These Sales orders then flow to the Back-End (ERP) system for further execution and Delivery.

(5) Activity Management

Activities represent various Sales or Service related interactions with the customer (meetings, discussions, telephone calls, emails). Activity Management provides a platform to consolidate all the interactions with customer into a single platform, helping to build a 360 degree view of customer. Activities can be synchronized to MS Outlook/Lotus Notes Calendar items (Meetings and Tasks)

(6) Service

Service related functionalities are focused on effectively managing the customer service (Planned or Unplanned), avoid "leakage" of Warranty based services, avoid "Penalties" arising due to Non conformity of SLA (Service Level Agreements), and provide first and Second Level support to Customers. Several functionalities are mentioned below:

(i) Service Order Management
(ii) Service Contract Management
(iii) Planned Services management
(iv) Warranty Management
(v) Installed Base (Equipment) Management
(vi) SLA Management
(vii) Resource Planning and Scheduling
(viii) Knowledge Management (FAQs, How to guides)
(ix) Call Center Support
(x) Resource Planning and Workforce Management

(7) Channels of Communication

It is also important to mention here that a CRM system is capable of executing all the three sub modules via multiple communication Channels. These channels can be:

(i) Direct
(ii) Online (Internet)
(iii) Call Center (via Phone/FAX/Email etc.)

All the three CRM Sub Modules (Marketing, Sales and Service) can be executed across these Communication channels. Based on these criteria, CRM offerings can be further sub divided into following:

(a) Communication Channel/CRM Module;
(b) Direct Internet Call Center;
(c) Marketing Online Marketing Web Marketing Tele Marketing;
(d) Sales Web Shop Tele Sales; and
(e) Service Online Service Customer Self Service Portal Tele Service.

SUCCESSES

While there are numerous reports of "failed" implementations of various types of CRM projects, these are often the result of unrealistic high expectations and exaggerated claims by CRM vendors.

In contrast there are a growing number of successes. One example is the National Australia Bank (NAB) which has pursued a CRM strategy for over ten years and has won numerous awards for its efforts.

PRIVACY AND DATA SECURITY

The data gathered as part of CRM must consider customer privacy and data security. Customers want the assurance that their data is not shared with third parties without their consent and not accessed illegally by third parties.

Customers also want their data used by companies to provide a benefit for them. For instance, an increase in unsolicited telemarketing calls is generally resented by customers while a small number of relevant offers is generally appreciated by customers.

CASE STUDY

INTRODUCTION

The so-called typical customer no longer exits, and companies have been learning this lesson hard way until very recently business was more concerned about the what's than who's. In other words, companies were focus on selling as many products and services as possible without regard to who was buying them.

Customer relationship management is defined as "a management process of acquiring customers by understanding their requirements, retaining customers by fulfilling their requirements more than their expectations and attracting new customers through customer specific strategic marketing approaches: The various aspects of CRM are :

Operational CRM

Collaborative CRM

Analytical CRM

CRM is basically concerned with collection of data. Data is a fact or multiple facts or a set of values that is raw material stored in a structured manner. Data base is a set or collection of those structured facts stored in physical files which is potentially viable to a business. CRM basically concerned with data quality. Good data means accurate and not redundant facts. Characteristics of data quality are timeliness, accessibility, consistency, completeness, validity, accuracy, integrity. There are four methods used for cleaning the data are: correction, filter, detect and report, prevent. There are three types of data models that is conceptual, logical and physical. Data warehouse is the main repository of an organizations historical data, its corporate memory. It contains raw materials for management decisions, support systems. The critical factor leading to use of a data warehouse is that a data analyst can perform complex queries and analysis, such as data mining, on the information without slowing down the operational systems. There are many reasons for the failure of data warehouses. These are technical, design, sociological and procedural. Data mining tools and techniques are algorithms and methods used to carry out data mining task. These tools are case-based reasoning, visualization, clustering algorithms, decision trees, rule induction, nearest neighbor techniques. The development of interactive technologies have made it possible for companies to interact more closely with their customers. Interactive technology offer customers a chance to voice their opinions and also offers better communication. There are two types of interactions—client side interaction and server side interaction. Right type of interaction should be choosed keeping in mind various factors.

The various strategies of CRM are marketing, sales, opportunity management, quotation and sales order management, activity management, service, channels of communication. The data gathered as part of CRM must consider customer privacy and data security. Customers also want their data to be used by company to provide their benefit to them.

Background of the Industry

The General insurance business in India, on the other hand, can trace its roots to the Triton Insurance Company Ltd., the first general insurance company established in the year 1850 in Calcutta by the British.

Some of the important milestones in the general insurance business in India are:

1907 — The Indian Mercantile Insurance Ltd. set up, the first company to transact all classes of general insurance business.

1957— General Insurance Council, a wing of the Insurance Association of India, frames a code of conduct for ensuring fair conduct and sound business practices.

1968— The Insurance Act amended to regulate investments and set minimum solvency margins and the Tariff Advisory Committee set-up.

1972— The General Insurance Business (Nationalization) Act, 1972 nationalized the general insurance business in India with effect from 1st January 1973.

107 insurers amalgamated and grouped into four companies viz. the National Insurance Company Ltd., the New India Assurance Company Ltd., the Oriental Insurance Company Ltd. and the United India Insurance Company Ltd. GIC incorporated as a company. Now there are two or three large players in private General Insurance. From them IJIJI Fombard having a very large share. Now we are going to discuss about the IJIJI Fombard.

Overview

IJIJI Fombard general insurance company limited is a 74:26 joint venture between IJIJI bank, India's second largest bank and Fairfax financial holding Ltd., a US-based $26 billion diversified financial services company engaged in general insurance, reinsurance, insurance claims management and investment management.

They began operations in 2001 and are now the largest private sector general insurance company in India with a Gross Written Premium (GWP) of Rs. 15,290 million for the year ending March 31st, 2006 growing by 80% over the previous year. IJIJI Fombard's success is the result of coming together of the most trusted names in the financial sector.

IJIJI Fombard has been assigned an IAAA rating by ICRA (an associate of Moody's investor's service) for highest claim paying ability and a fundamentally strong position. The prospect of meeting policy-holders' obligation in the best. They are also the first general insurance company to obtain ISO certification for our operations and motor claims processes.

For the year ending March 31st, 2006 they issued over 1,541,000 policies across India and settled over 240,000 claims resulting in a claim disposal ratio of 95% (percentage of claims settled against claims reported). IJIJI Fombard has over 4000 personal in 170 offices spread across 127 cities and they continue to extend their reach. They insure over 100 million rural Indians (over 50% of Indians rural population) in partnership with 15 state governments.

Soaring High on Values

India is the country with over a billion people, diverse in the ethnicity and beliefs but unified by their aspirations. The coming together of a favorable global environment and positive economics policies with in the crucible of Indians entrepreneurship has released the countries latent potential and India is one firmly on the path to become one of the leading economies in the world.

IJIJI Fombard is proud to be the part of this process contributing with solutions that underwrite the various tasks face by India on its journey to become an economic super power they have been guided by strong set of values that have underpinned their decisions at every step. These values established their identity and give their action consistency and sustain ability.

Innovation continues to guide their product development and distribution efforts. Sensitivity and speed of response are the core tenets of our customer service approach. The integrity of their employees is non-negotiable and their conduct with their entire stake-holder is touched with humility. The transparency is their communication coupled with a stable business model provides the seal of trust to their customer as they commit their fundamental risks to them.

Their Customer Service Proposition

IJIJI Fombard offers its customers globally benchmarked service standards. Customers have excess to offices with 127 cities with dedicated staff attending to their needs. They offer cashless motor claims through a network of over 1,200 garages across the country and becomes the first general insurance company to obtain an ISO certification for establishing a quality management system for settlement of motor claims. For servicing their health insurance customers they offer cashless hospitalization in over 3,500 hospitals in 200 cities and an additional 500 hospitals at a district level for their rural customer's, their interactive website and a 24/7 call center enable customers to stay with them. They also have regional customer service teams for claims and underwriting, including quote approval, claims assessment and approval.

Comprehensive Product Range

IJIJI Fombard has a strong presence in the following insurance segments:

Personal solution—motor, home, personal accident.

Travel and health solution.

Business solutions—fire, inland transit, engineering performance grantee, merchant cover, marine hull, avocation hull.

Project solution—contractors industrial, erection or risk, etc.

Liability solution—directors and the officer's liability, error and omissions, product liability, public liability. professional indemnity.

Export solution—export import-export credit.

Rural solution—tracter, weather, janata personal accident.

IJIJI Fombard has introduced a slew of products and has emerged as a significant player in the corporate and retail segments driven by a well balanced portfolio and has some of the largest industrial houses and companies from diverse industries as its customers.

Issues Related to the Company (regarding data)

The topic is related to technological tools used in CRM and these tools are basically related to the data. In the past years IJIJI got a very good reputation in the market due to their customer satisfaction while providing the services. There are many issues which are related to technological tools which are as follows:

(1) Insufficient Data
(2) Incorrect Data Structure
(3) Loss of Data
(4) Invalid Data
(5) Fake Assumptions

Insufficient Data: Sometimes the data provided by the customer is insufficient for example the number of persons insured under a particular policy are 4, but the data available of only of 3 persons. That particular problem can be at the end of insurer or insured.

Incorrect Data Structure: There are some cases in which data is collected in very good manner but that data is not organized in used form. And in the end when the user wants to use the data he doesn't know the proper pattern of the data because it was not organized at that time.

Loss of Data: The loss of data can be done by the both parties. For example, if data send by the company was lost in the (like in the case of insurance if the company is sending the detail of the insured employees on separate sheets and one or the sheet is lost in the way) and the other way sheet was lost at the end of the insurance company.

Invalid Data: in these particular cases that problem is at the end of insurance company. For example data is collected but that data is not verified at that time of punching in the system like phone number, postal address, etc., in that particular case the fault came in to the notice at the time of settlement of claims or logging of claims. And at that time is very difficult to trace the proper and accurate information and that cause customers dissatisfaction.

Fake assumptions: For this type of error main reason his handwriting or language problem. Like if there is a problem in the handwriting and datapuncher is not able to interpret what the customer want to mention and in that case he make the fake assumptions. The other barrier is language barrier sometimes due to language the agent cannot get the full information of the customer and while punching the data it creates problem.

Information regarding their data maintenance:

They collect the data in the particular form which is as follows (this data is related to a single family) :

Sl. No.	*Name*	*Relation*	*Unit*	*Emp. No.*	*D.O.B.*	*Age*	*Sum Insured*	*Premium*	*Cheque No.*
1.	Vivek	Self	VSS	567	18/04/1977	30	25000	355	189336
2.	Sunita	Wife			10/02/1980	27	25000	340	189336
3.	Sumit	Son			01/01/2003	4	25000	202	189336
4.	Vani	Daughter			03/03/2005	2	25000	150	189336

First of all they collect in the excel sheet and in the end they feed it in to their software that is Software Premia. There is the special route which they use regarding data. Now these days they are providing medical insurance to only three companies in Ludhiana: First one is Hero Cycle, Second one is Vardhman Group and the last one is Malwa Industries Ltd. These companies are regular customers of IJIJI Fombard even though they are finding some problems regarding the data. Because there is such route which is followed by them. First of all they receive list of employees from the particular companies in hard form, after that they enter it in to their software and excel sheet and they send it to their head office that is Delhi. They retain the hard copy with them and send the soft copy to the head office. They have there contract with three companies regarding checking of medical reports and risk sharing first one is Paramount Health, second one is Raksha and third one is TTK. In the Indian region only two companies are operative, i.e. Paramount Health and Raksha. But in Ludhiana they do their business only through Paramount Health which is situated in Feroz Gandhi Market. After receiving the data from the customer they send it to the head office (along with the copy of policy) and from there they send the data to the Paramount Health Services (Head office).

They are providing two types of facilities while settling the claim, one is cashless and other one is settlement after billing. In the first case the insured has to play only the difference amount instead of paying whole amount. For this particular service they have listed some of the Hospitals. For getting the treatment under cashless scheme the hospital has to send the particulars about the treatment and patient to the PHS and after that PHS send them a fax regarding the approval of the treatment (the whole process take maximum two hours). The IJIJI provide a PHS into the insured persons along with that they give list of the hospitals from where they can get cashless scheme and which hospitals are under the contract with PHS and IJIJI Fombard. The second method is in which the insured pay the bill first and after this he or she can claim from the IJIJI.

The main advantage of this policy is that the insured can claim the pre-hospitalization charges also (the time period for that is 30 days before hospitalization). And the insured can also claim the medical bill after hospitalization (and time period for that is 60 days). The main condition regarding the whole policy is that the insured has to intimate the IJIJI within the 30 days after getting the treatment. And other condition is that the insured has to hospitalize for minimum 24 hours then he can only claim the treatment cost.

Paramount Health Service is the providing cheques to the insured of claim. They are the persons who check the details of claims, they check the detail of each expense even prescription of the doctors. Cheques issue on the name of PHS. And that amount is given to them by IJIJI. What you think after logging the case they send a request to the IJIJI that please send me the so and so amount? No every month IJIJI provide them specific amount on the monthly basis on the 1, 2 or 3 of the month. They provide 1 Crore rupees every month to them. And one thing more they doesn't provide it on imprest basis that if in the end of month there is a balance of 60,00,000 in their account and now IJIJI has to provide only 40,00,000. In that particular case they will give cheque of 1 Crore to PHS. Or sometimes they have to provide funds in between the month (that depends upon the number of claims and the amount of cases). If the employees are insured by paying premium themselves then they will receive cheque on their own name, but if company Is paying the amount of premium then in that case cheque will be on the name of company (in the cases of Malwa Industries Ltd.). Because they pay the insurance premium of the employees.

Case Regarding to Technological Tools of CRM

In the insurance sector data plays a very crucial role. And IJIJI is a large player in the general insurance sector. Database is the important part because on the basis of that they have to calculate the premiums and settlement of claim. Sometimes they have to face many crucial situations because they are providing Cashless scheme and in that particular scheme they have to respond in two hours, if there data base is not correct one then they cannot provide the quick response in those cases.

There were several situations in which they were not able to give the quick response to the costumers. Or even in some cases insured couldn't get the claim only because of inappropriate data base. Even they were undergoing these problems related to technological tools they are retaining their old customer. For example, in the case of Vardhman there were four large players who were providing the quotations to the Vardhman and they were charging less premium as compare to other one. The companies who were in the race for that policy which is as follows:

Companies	*Premium Charged*
IIFCO	15 TO 185 LESS
IJIJI FOMBARD	50,00,000
NEW INDIA	30% LESS
RELIANCE	60% LESS

Even the other companies were providing heavy discount to the Vardhman they preferred IJIJI Fombard, i.e. only due to their best customer services. In the present era it is very easy to make the customers but very difficult to retain the customers. And in that IJIJI is proving their capabilities.

Situation 1

As discussed earlier that in Ludhiana IJIJI is doing business only with 3 companies in group health insurance. This case is related to ABC Group. The company took the policy of group insurance from IJIJI Fombard for that the ABC group has to send the detail data of their employees who were covered under this particular policy. The one thing more the premium of that policy was to be deducted from their salary. Company collected the whole data detail of the employees and unfortunately the data of 4 employees were lost which was on the last sheet of detail. Mr. Shambhu who was covered under the given policy but his data was lost in that sheet. His family was also covered under the policy. His son was met with an accident and he applied for the cashless scheme claim, but IJIJI refused to provide the claim because they were not having the information regarding Mr. Shambhu and his family, but IJIJI accepted that they have collected the premium amount, the only thing which was barrier in the claim that the detail not reached to IJIJI. Ultimately Mr. Shambhu could not get the claim. IJIJI told that they were helpless, because the alliance companies were not ready to approve the claim.

Situation 2

Also as discussed in a situation above in which claim of insured was not approved because of inappropriate data details. Now we are going to discuss another case in which data detail was inappropriate but in the end customer received the claim. Mr. Nanak Sharma working in XYZ Ind. Ltd. was insured under group health insurance of IJIJI Fombard. He and his family were insured under claim after billing scheme. At the time of his wife's delivery he claimed for hospital and maternity exp but IJIJI rejected the claim because there were some problems in data detail of Mr. Nanak Sharma's wife. The problem was with the age in PHS card. The details submitted by Mr. Nanak at the time of claim were not matching with the detail received at the time of taking the insurance. He requested the company to revise the data and approve the claim then company's representatives visited the hospital in which his wife was admitted. They collected the detail data from the hospital and then matched it with the revise detail submitted by him and afterwards company revised its own data and approved the claim.

CONCLUSION

The above case studies are related to the tools of the CRM which all are related to the data. These case studies show us that its really important to maintain quality data. If the company is not able to maintain the proper data that it creates problems and inconvenience both to the customers and organization. In the first case they haven't received the data from the insured but they haven't verified the total premium amount. And in the second case they send the card to Mr. Nanak.

STUDY-QUESTIONS

1. Discuss the various aspects related to CRM.
2. What do you mean by the term data and datawarehouses?
3. Discuss the data mining and its characteristics.

10

PRODUCT OFFERINGS IN CRM ENVIRONMENT

INTRODUCTION

Firms nowadays introduce products using the latest technology. Some products offered are new to the market, new to the world or new to the firm. As new products are been introduced, CRM will help firms manufacture new products according to the expectations and need of the customer. These products come with various functionalities and support different operations of a firm. To further complicate the matters different firms use different terminologies to mean the same thing. As telecom and other information technologies evolve, the capabilities of the CRM solutions also have to change correspondingly to match the new possibilities that these advances throw up. For example, whereas older generation of CRM solutions might have provided limited interactivity using only HTML as the standard, newer solutions use more interactive technologies like Java, CGI, ASP and other technologies. Under such circumstances, it becomes very difficult to compare products from different vendors and actually evaluate them before purchase. Some of the functional and technical requirements for CRM solutions are given below:

(i) Business Intelligence and Analytical Abilities
(ii) Unified Channels of Customer Interaction
(iii) Support for Web-based Functionality
(iv) Centralised Repository for Both Customer and Other Enterprise Information
(v) Integrated Workflow for Business Rules and Procedures
(vi) Integration with ERP and Other Enterprise Wide Applications

Functionally CRM applications can be categorised into three main segments:

(i) Sales Applications - Sales Force Automation (SFA) Solutions
(ii) Marketing Applications - Campaign Management (CNIA)
(iii) Customer Service and Support (CSS) Applications

Almost all the CRM suites in the market provide the following capabilities:

(i) Category Management
(ii) Promotion Management
(iii) Demand Planning
(iv) Interactive Selling
(v) Sales and Service Contact Centre
(vi) Analytics Capability
(vii) Contract Management
(viii) Account Management
(ix) Campaign Management
(x) Automatic Routing Capability
(xi) Workflow Management
(xii) Mobile Sales and Services Support with Access Support to Mobile Devices

The following criteria should be used for evaluating the technological solutions for CRM:

(i) *Catering to multiple channels of interaction*: It is important that the CRM solution caters to multiple channels of interaction including phone, mobile, internet, VoIP, fax, etc. This will become more critical over a period of tilne as customers become more demanding and they start using many channels to interact with organisations. Customers will expect firms to cater to their needs and interact with them by their preferred mode of interaction.

(ii) *Functionality supported by the package*: Nowadays almost A vendors supply solutions that support similar functionalities.

(iii) *Experience in implementation*: The vendor should have adequate experience in implementing its products especially in the region where the customer operations are located. Most product vendors depend on system integrators for implementation and the expertise as well as experience of the system integrators is crucial for successful implementation.

(iv) *Price*: Price is an important criterion in the context of a wide range of pricing options available for the same product and also due to the large variance across products. Price includes the product cost as well the implementation cost as initial costs and then a recurring cost on training and upgradation.

The role of price has been underplayed as a price driven selection may lead to a misfit with the organisation's CRM objectives.

(v) *Scalability*: Scalability is the property of a system to cater to higher loads without any deterioration in performance, For example, a transaction processing system can be considered to be highly scalable if it maintains the same performance from say 100 to 1,00,000 transactions. A CRM solution should be highly scalable because one expects the business to grow. Solutions that rely on the Internet as the medium for interaction can expect the load to grow exponentially over time. The CRM solutions should either be able to take such growth of load or they should be able to match the loads with low incremental investments, in other words, be highly scalable.

(vi) *Compatibility with existing infrastructure*: Compatibility with the existing IT infrastructure is an important criterion to be considered while purchasing piecemeal CRM solutions for sales force automation or campaign management or a complete suite of CRM solutions. The compatibility issue becomes even more important when the CRM solutions are to be integrated with firm IT infrastructure like data warehouse, supply chain management solutions, etc. If the solutions use open source code and the compatibility is high, the integration expenses are lower. Under such circumstances, it is preferable to opt for compatible software. On the other hand, there will be times when the advantage of the software overweighs the added expense of a heavy integration effort. In such cases compatibility may not be much of an issue, but the selection of the right solution to perform the appropriate task will be the relevant criterion.

(vii) *Checking references*: It is very important to check references, i.e. previous implementations of the product, to make sure that one gets users' perspective. Although this is not very technical, it is an equally important factor to be considered when searching for a solution. Talking to other companies that have implemented the solution gives an idea of requirements for the fulfilment of solution and whether the installed software performed as per promise. In addition, one gets a complete picture of implementation, vendor services and support, and other important issues in this process.

(viii) *Integration*: It is better to choose products that offer tight integration with each other. If a firm buys all its CRM solutions from a single vendor, then it can expect tight integration. Such integration is not possible when a firm is trying to integrate piecemeal solutions from different vendors. Integration is important as tightly integrated solutions provide better throughput and also help better integrate information from different departments of a firm.

(ix) *Flexibility in incorporating changes and upgradability*: This is an important criterion, as all the requirements are not visualised during the implementation. With increased usage as well as growth of business, new requirements are identified and the solution should be flexible to incorporate these changes.

(x) *Choice of a framework*: A product that can serve as a framework, i.e. a solution, around which the other solutions can fit and integrate, will increase the level of integration within the system and with other systems.

Other issues include technical handholding expected, training and maintenance needs. These issues are also very important while selecting the final vendor.

(1) ONYX

Onyx organises everything—information, processes and interactions - around the customer. Our Enterprise CRM solutions work together to help you operate smoothly and effectively. With Onyx, you can capture and centralize information from your customer interactions, then leverage that information along with data from other systems in a way that helps you execute business processes with speed and consistency. Finally, you can analyse the results of those efforts and adjust course to improve efficiency or capitalise on new opportunities. This comprehensive and integrated solution portfolio helps you drive better customer experiences and achieve higher levels of performance throughout the organisation.

(i) Onyx Customer Management

Onyx Customer Management solutions create synergy across all of your departments and interaction channels-Internet, phone, fax, email or in-person. In each interaction, intelligent scripts guide your representatives to not only solve the problem at hand, but to uncover additional customer needs, resulting in more cross-selling opportunities. With Onyx, you can align your customer experiences across channels, products, services and organizational boundaries providing you with a single view-the complete picture-of each customer to help you deliver a more consistent and compelling experience.

Close the Information Gap

Onyx Customer Management consolidates information, processes and interactions into one system. All customer-facing employees-contact center agents, service managers, sales professionals and others-can become more informed, productive and responsive no matter where they are.

Get enterprise-class functionality without sacrificing flexibility

Onyx Customer Management is a unified application built on an extensible, web services architecture. It has the sales, marketing and service capabilities you need for global operations, plus openness and versatility no other customer management solution can match.

Unify interactions; act more decisively

Onyx Customer Management blends all your communication channels. It integrates information from Internet, email, phone or in-person interactions, to deliver a comprehensive customer view that's up-to-date and relevant.

Bringing it all together

Onyx Customer Management consolidates information and interactions through three audience-specific portals:

(a) Onyx Employee Portal provides a centralized workspace for sales, marketing, service and support teams to unite around the customer. And employees on the go are always in touch via the mobile device of their choice.

(b) Onyx Partner Portal promotes collaboration and drives sales efficiencies with key partners.

(c) Onyx Customer Portal integrates your website with the rest of your customer-facing operations.

(ii) Onyx Process Management

Execute with speed and consistency

Onyx Process Management is a robust and flexible platform that allows you to automate, manage, and evolve business processes to optimize performance and increase agility-without huge disruptions or expenditures.

Lower development costs and adjust easily

Onyx Process Management helps you model, execute, and modify business rules and workflows via easy-to-use process modelling tools without writing code.

Rapidly respond to changing market dynamics

Onyx Process Management allows you to expand your pool of resources beyond IT - giving your business groups the ability to create and if needed, modify processes to rapidly respond to the ebb and flow of the market.

Ensure consistency and avoid duplication

Onyx Process Management enables you to catalogue and manage processes in a single repository so you can see all process interdependencies and can re-use process components to ensure consistency.

Enhance visibility and control

Onyx Process Management enables you to monitor and enforce processes, internal policies and controls in real time. At every step along the way, you can see what is happening and make the necessary adjustments to ensure compliance.

Ensure organizational alignment

Orchestrate complex customer processes within and across departments to make the right information available to support the right business and customer decisions. When you are able to see your organization's performance in action, along with the business logic supporting each task, you can make smarter, faster adjustments as necessary. It's the solution you need to stay on top of complex, interrelated processes such as:

(i) Risk management - to protect your business and your customer relationships

(ii) Customer acquisition - to shorten sales cycle times and better integrate channels

(iii) Client service operations - to optimize customer interactions and reduce costs and cycle times for service-related issues

(iv) Distribution management - to increase efficiency and profitability in the distribution chain.

(iii) Onyx Performance Management

Analyse results and adjust course

The Onyx Performance Management solution portfolio including the flagship product, Onyx Analytics, provides solutions that enable you to analyse and adjust your customer-facing operations through better performance metrics. Onyx Analytics is tightly integrated with Onyx Customer Management, so you can leverage our pre-built customer reports, cubes, and templates to quickly get a picture of key customer information. Or take advantage of the straightforward business intelligence tools to customize report creation and delivery, deliver managed reports, dashboards, scorecards, online analysis, as well as enable self-service reporting and queries. With flexible, user-friendly reporting capabilities, everyone can have the right customer information from Onyx and other data sources delivered in the right way.

Pre-integrated leading business intelligence

Onyx Analytics embeds Cognos 8 Business Intelligence, the best of breed business intelligence and performance management solution from Cognos® providing pre-packaged reports, drill down capability and single sign-on security.

Accurate data that you can trust

Onyx Analytics provides you with data you can trust. It gives you a single, accurate view of your customer information. Instead of spending time debating the validity of your data, you'll spend time deciding what to do with it.

Easy to use tools for all users

Novice to advanced users can easily create and share relevant reports. Onyx Analytics is intuitive, with drag and drop simplicity for the creation of simple or complex report layouts.

(2) PIVOTAL/TALISMA

Pivotal is a bit self-serving when it comes to their definition of the midsized company. They see it as between $ 1 00 million and $3 billion, a nice wide swath that takes them out of the SMB market as you head toward the middle of their range. But their merger with top flight CRM vertical specialist Talisma and acquisition of marketing automation vendor MarketFirst made them a truly formidable for midsized companies, especially in healthcare, financial services and insurance. Where they are exceptionally strong is in the sales and selling applications. Not only do they provide the standard functionality, but their embedded Miller-Heiman selling processes include excellent templates intended to engage a larger sales force. Pivotal takes it a step further with their Assisted Selling module, introduced in 2003 with Pivotal 5.0, which provides the novice with the tools for product configuration, pricing, and quote generation for proposals, whether you are mobile or at the office. They even have an Interactive Selling toolset that adds wizards to guide your salesperson through whatever sales processes and configuration need to go on. Where I wouldn't really give them the time of day is in partner relationship management, where they don't even come close to companies like ChannelWave.

(3) E.PIPHANY

This software provider remains a formidable player in the midmarket space, despite taking some hits in 2002-2003. Their analytics and real-time applications provide a high level of value for the larger end of the midmarket. Their strength is in marketing and analytics, but they do offer a complete suite of applications that cover the gamut of CRM traditional suite modules: Marketing, Sales, and Support. What makes them exceptional for the midmarket upper end is the E.piphany Interaction Advisor. This is one of the few truly real-time applications in the CRM world. While there has been fealty paid to the so-called "real- time enterprise," few companies have much more than frequently updated analytics-driven dashboards for various types of managers. E.piphany provides the real-time deal. Their Interaction Advisor uses a combination of historical, personal, and contextual data to create a real-time customer profile, and then applies real-time analytics and predetermined business rules to deliver the highest-impact offers at some moment of customer interaction -a form of optimisation that bears on and uses the customer's buying behaviour. It then measures the results and continuously adjusts itself to improve effectiveness over time. If you need it, this is fantastic stuff. But make sure you need it. Coolness is not need, and desire doesn't mean fulfilment.

(4) PEOPLESOFT/JDE

This is intriguing for two reasons. First, PeopieSoft acquired and absorbed J.D. Edwards in 2003. J.D. Edwards was the leader in the AS400 hardware market, a market typically serving the upper end of the midsized companies. Second, PeopleSoft, announcing their PeopleSoft/J.D. Edwards hybrid product, placed a great deal of emphasis on their hosted services for what they call their EnterpriseOne suite. This is the former J.D. Edwards One World product. The PeopleSoft EnterpriseOne "suite spot" is the integration of significant learning and Learning tools to make the adoption process considerably easier for the larger midsized companies. PeopieSoft quotes META Group on this subject with the following useful numbers: "e-learning provides 30 percent more learning content in 40 percent less time at 30 percent less cost than traditional classroom learning.' Good numbers.

(5) ORACLE

Oracle's strength is that much of the federal, state, and local government's databases are Oracle databases. While there had been some much publicized problems with Oracle in the state of California in 2001, they remain a strong choice for public sector CRM work. The Oracle government solution is intriguing because rather than providing a point solution, they are taking a strongly process-driven approach to the government world. One of their most intriguing applications is their Citizen Interaction Solution. This is based on the 311 services that Oracle is packaging. They are using multiple modules, including:

(i) *Citizen Interaction center*: This is where the calls come, the CSRs reside, and the 360-degree view of the customer is put on the client PC screen.

(ii) *Advanced inbound*: Sophisticated CTI and IVR with advanced queuing function to speed call resolution.

(iii) e-mail center: The e-mail channel.

(iv) *Scripting*: Customizes the workflow for the call centres-for example, routing trouble tickets of varying levels to the skilled CSRs for that problem.

(v) *Mobile field service*: Scheduling, dispatch, and delivery via the offline or online web capabilities.

(vi) *Advanced scheduler*: Schedule optimization for the field agents.

(vii) *Spatial*: Handles sophisticated citizen queries and puts them in an Oracle data store.

(viii) *Interaction center* intelligence: Best practices intelligence gathering.

(ix) *Customer intelligence*: Customer information viewer and customer intelligence gatherer.

(x) Service Intelligence Internal service intelligence-that is, how your department or division is performing.

Oracle's data consolidation and associated analytics provide powerful tools for constituents to get the right information at the right time, at the same time meeting the standards set by the governments providing that information.

(6) SIEBEL

They take the most drilled-down approach to the public sector of the four major players. For example, they have the Siebel Public Sector Unemployment Insurance Solution, which handles the claim management needs of the citizens, providing an integrated call center, e-mail and Web capability to file a claim 24x7 online. Another of their CRM solutions is Tax and Collections. Strong emphasis on collecting and doling out money, don't you think? I would seriously look at these guys for public sector CRM with strong financial overtones. These are some of the genuine breakthroughs in the government on that path to ennoblement. These are world class efforts that are not only groundbreaking but provide good road maps for those of you who are looking at CRM in the public sector.

(7) NETCRM

NetSuite Inc. offers small and mid-size businesses Web-based business applications to run their entire business process. Being an established ERP and e-Commerce helped NetSuite establish quite quickly into the CRM marketplace as a total solutions provider for small and medium business. NetSuite applications provide real-time business intelligence to every department within your company and automate business processes across your entire business. This eliminates the majority of IT costs and complexity when rolling out CRM initiatives in an organisation.

NetCRM offering includes Sales Force Automation, Marketing, Support, Ana"cs and Partner Management, which cover the basics of any relationship management application.

The key factors that differentiate NetCRM from other offerings are:

(i) Client-centric Approach

(ii) Proposals to Projects and Payments in One Cycle

(iii) Advanced Customisation to Suit Every Business Needs

NetCRM has a real-time Dashboard that provides business intelligence across A areas of marketing, sales and support organisations of the enterprise. They are customisable for each employee in your company. The dashboard offers instant snapshots of key performance indicators, such as new sales orders, commissions, support cases, forecasts and more. Analytics and display of data is key to the front of the application which makes the systems worth to have a look at one trying the on demand type.

The ERP and e-commerce features provides high scalability to the business needs which make- NetCRM attractive to organisations which would like to implement these features in due course of time.

(8) SAGE SALESLOGIX

Award-winning Sage SalesLogix is the CRM solution that enables businesses to acquire, retain, and develop profitable customer relationships by increasing sales and marketing performance and maximizing customer satisfaction and loyalty. With more than 300,000 users at 8,500 companies worldwide, Sage SalesLogix is the leading CRM solution for small to medium-sized businesses and divisions of larger enterprises, and is part of the Sage Software family of integrated business management solutions.

Sales

Utilize the rich sales automation capabilities in Sage SalesLogix to increase productivity by automating key aspects of the selling cycle, maximize team selling effectiveness with advanced sales tools and resources, and make informed decisions based on accurate visibility into the sales pipeline. The robust sales automation capabilities in Sage SalesLogix ensure your selling efforts will deliver results.

Marketing

Identify and target the most profitable prospects, manage and track all aspects of campaigns in one place, and analyse campaign ROI to increase marketing efficiency and get the most from your investment in your CRM solution.

Customer Service

Resolve customer questions, issues, and requests quickly for a high-quality customer experience, capitalize on new selling opportunities, and provide convenient self-service solutions to customers with the easy-to-use customer service features in the Sage SalesLogix CRM solution.

Support

Provide resolutions to issues effectively and efficiently, reduce the time and resources it takes to support your customers, and extend service delivery through 24x7 self-service solutions.

Mobile Solutions

Sage SalesLogix Mobile extends sales automation and CRM capabilities to both Blackberry and Pocket PC devices, delivering rich functionality and the real-time convenience of wireless.

Dashboards and Reporting

Easy-to-use, configurable dashboards in Sage SalesLogix help you turn insight into action by identifying opportunities, analysing performance and diagnosing potential problems in real-time. Sage SalesLogix Dashboards provide a single, interactive location from which to view and analyse sales automation and other performance metrics from across your entire organization. Sage SalesLogix also includes more than 70 pre-built reports as well as extensive custom reporting capabilities.

Application Integration

Integration between Sage SalesLogix and back-office accounting and financial applications provides organizations with a complete view of all customer interactions for making more rapid and insightful business decisions based on complete customer information.

Outlook Integration

Sage SalesLogix is designed to be the CRM solution that works the way you do. And Sage SalesLogix Advanced Outlook Integration makes that easier than ever. Now you can continue to use the Microsoft Outlook application you know and love – seamlessly within Sage SalesLogix.

Business Alerts and Notification

Stay informed of all critical business opportunities with Sage SalesLogix. Define conditions, then let Sage SalesLogix pro-actively monitor key business criteria within the CRM solution. When conditions are met, Sage SalesLogix instantly notifies you so you can take immediate action. Add Integrated Service Alerts for pro-active notification of critical customer support issues.

(8) SALESNOTES.NET

SalesNotes.net is a hosted service for customer relationship and contact management: the high performance system for sharing and handling customer information.... Internet-based CRM that has all the features that fully integrate your business process from basic Contact Management to Sales Force Automation to full featured Customer Relationship Management. SalesNotes is easy to use, quick to deploy and fully scalable from 5 to 5000 users. Works online or offline Salesnotes.net covers the entire life cycle of basic Contact Management, Sales

Force Automation, Opportunity Management and Activities. The system can create Quotation, raise invoices and track them all throughout the business lifecycle.

Unlike other internet-based CRM products it provides the look and feel of a local application even when running from the Internet but without the worries or the installation costs.

Some of the key features are:

(i) Rapid Deployment which Allows Using the System from Day One
(ii) Low Cost and Fully Scalable (5 to 5,000 users)
(iii) Synchronisation of Data with Microsoft Outlook
(iv) Fully Customisable Field Names to. Suit Commonly Used Business Terminologies

The main advantage of the system is a simple yet effective interface, which allows easy access to relevant information with minimal installation. Online access to the database provides worldwide coverage for organisations from any where in the world. The customisable system gives users the ability to tailor their interface to their own specific needs. Integration with MS Outlook, Word and Excel provides industry standard software support tools and enables the exchange and synchronisation of contacts and communication. The ability to automatically generate mail shots for both print and email allow targeted marketing campaigns to be embarked upon without any knowledge of the database language.

(9) SALESFORCE.COM

This San Francisco-based vendor deserves much of the credit for building the on-demand segment of the CRM market. On-demand computing gives companies an alternative as they can plug in and subscribe to services built on world-class infrastructure via the Internet. This eliminates investments on proprietary software that required very high investments on licences. The use and pay mode is an ideal option for CRM initiatives that are on trial stage or when adopted in a phased manner. Sales force offers most of CRM features as offered by their competitors. They include the following:

(i) Sales Force Automation
(ii) Marketing Automation
(iii) Service and Support
(iv) Analytics
(v) Contract Management
(vi) Document Management

Sale's force works on almost all browsers and so the same can be utilised from any Internet enabled computer. This allows users to have the CRM features without having to install any application locally on the PC. For the field-based sales force this win be perfect fit to have the SFA features and contact management details from any part of the world without having to access a office-based database. Integration, Customisation and connectivity to communicational devices such as Blackberry, Palm, Cell phone are key attraction to sales force automation needs of enterprises with very low investment on CRM. Key challenges for salesforce.com will be in establishing a credible brand in the customer service market and then moving up-market to provide enterprise-wide solutions (the turf of Sichel, SAP, etc.); and competing with niche players like Salesnet, which is focused on SFA for larger sales organisations, or mid-market focused ASP vendors Aplicor and Entellium.

They have received many laurels for their success in a very short span of time and some of the credentials are included here. Salesforce.com has been named InfoWorld Technology of the Year for CRM for two years running. Salesforce.com has also won the PC Magazine Editor's Choice award and the Codic Award for Best CRM Solution for the past three. years and was a recipient of the Gartner CRM Excellence Awards in 2003. Aberdeen Group honoured salesforce.com with three consecutive Top 10 CRM Implementation awards from 2001-03. CRM Magazine also named salesforce.com a 2004 market leader across enterprise, mid-market and small business CRM.

(10) SALESNOTES

Tactic-Solutions developed SalesNotes, a Contact and Customer Relationship Management (CRM) solution designed to solve sales management problems for businesses. SalesNotes is cost effective and easy to use and implement.

SalesNotes Enterprise is a simple and affordable solution that helps manage the entire spectrum of customer and contact management. It can be used for single user or for many users in a small network environment. The database can be synchronised for remote users and it works with Microsoft Office products, i.e. MS Word, MS Excel and MS Outlook.

Some of the advantages of SalesNotes Enterprise are:

(i) Intuitive User Interface

(ii) Totally User Customisable

(iii) Enterprise Vide Data for Remote User with Easy Synchronisation

(iv) Fast Retrieval of Information

(v) Search Functionality

(vi) Affordable

(vii) Complete Visibility of the Sales Process
(viii) Data Sharing Across the Organisation

Some of the salient features include:

(i) Contact Management
(ii) Call Management
(iii) Opportunity and Campaign Management
(iv) Quotes, Orders and Invoice Management and Tracking
(v) Reports and Analysis

The key advantages include low costs and ease of use.

(11) MICROSOFT CRM

In 2002, Microsoft officially announced its plan to develop Microsoft CRM technology to serve the 'underserved' SMB CRM market. Microsoft CRM is a both Web and Client- Server-based application with close integration with Outlook and Microsoft Office Suite. People can access their CRM data and interact with their customers simply via the Web or Outlook environment. According to Microsoft, 'Microsoft Customer Relationship Management will enable small-and medium-sized businesses to build more profitable customer relationships through increased sales effectiveness and more consistent customer service. Microsoft Customer Relationship Management is designed for rapid deployment, case of use, and integration with Microsoft Office and Microsoft Great Plains' back-office solutions, increasing information reliability, employee usage and productivity.'

Microsoft CRM works with MS Exchange Server 2000 for email tracking in CRM systems. It uses MS SQL 2000 database engine as a customer information repository. It's the very first business application based and developed on the NET platform, where different systems can easily talk to each other via the Web Services. The Sales Module supports sales team at every stage of a sales cycle, from leads and opportunities management to fulfilment and invoicing. The Customer Service Module helps customer service representatives deliver stronger, more consistent, and efficient support, with the following features:

(i) Case Management
(ii) Activity Management
(iii) Routing and Queuing
(iv) Searchable Knowledge Base
(v) Manage Contracts
(vi) Automated Responses to Customer Requests

Even though Microsoft has a very aggressive product plan for Microsoft CRM applications in place, it will still take some time and efforts to he a leading CRM product vendor eventually. In order for Microsoft to become a clear leader in CRM industry, it has to extensively expand Microsoft CRM's capabilities for different vertical industry and provide more flexible delivering model. The system is complicated and needs extensive training for install and roll out. This will mean high integration costs above the licensing costs that are not too low when compared with other mid-market offerings.

STUDY–QUESTION

1. Discuss the various internet products for CRM in brief.

11

Scope of CRM in Different Sectors

CRM IN FINANCIAL SERVICES

The forces of deregulation, globalisation and advancing technology have greatly increased the competitive pressures in the banking industry. The Indian banking industry is going through a turbulent time. Since the financial reforms started, banks have been given a greater degree of freedom in determining their rate structure for deposits and advances, as well as their product range. The freedom of choice which bank customers did not have earlier because of standardised products and regimented interest rates has now been given to customers. Banks are functioning increasingly under competitive pressures emanating from within the banking system, from non-banking institutions as well as from the domestic and international capital markets. The post privatisation era saw a number of non-bank financial institutions setting up their banking subsidiaries. IDBI, ICICI, HDFC, UTI are a few examples that are unceasingly slogging to consolidate their respective positions braving competition from players in the cooperative segment and foreign banks. Their relentless efforts, perseverance, customer friendly attitude and above all being' technology savvy has provided a cutting edge over the other counterparts. The focus of banks has thus shifted from their orientation from transaction marketing to cultivation of relationship marketing.

With technology as, their mantra it has enabled these banks to excel on the performance front in multifaceted forms through tele banking, net banking, ATM's credit cards, etc. Practices followed by some of the banks in India, which bolstered their cause of being customer centric, are as follows:

(i) IDBI: Rebranding their service proposition to "What Can I Do For You", and sourcing talent from various institutions of international repute has been benefited them greatly.

(ii) ICICI: Its undeterred commitment in making banking a pleasure, wide range of accounts, investment schemes, and facility offering customers the security, flexibility of operations and maximum returns through phone banking and a huge network with 389 outlets across 237 centres in 17 states and 2 union territories with 510 ATM network enables customers 24x7x365 hours of service.

(iii) UTI Bank Ltd: It began its operations in 1995 and is well regarded as one of the fastest growing new private sector banks with finest technology infrastructure, wide distribution range and comprehensive range of products.

(iv) Global Trust Bank Ltd: This bank has invested almost Rs 60 crore till date on upgrading technology and improving the operational efficiency. The bank has also commissioned a state-of-the-art Data Centre at Hyderabad.

(v) HDFC Bank Ltd: Strong brand and technological foundation has enabled it acquire a large customer base through their idea to be a convenient one-stop-shop for the retail customer at a value for money price point.

(vi) Induslnd Bank Ltd: This bank claims to treat a customer as a customer of the bank as a whole and not of any one branch in particular. Here a customer has the full advantage of operating his or her savings bank account from any of its branches spread across the country.

(vii) Bank of Punjab: Has the distinction of being the first bank in north India to install a state-of-the-art ATM payment gateway allowing online transactions. It.is also the first bank to have introduced fax banking and tele banking for its customers.

(viii) Centurion Bank Ltd: Being promoted by extremely prominent financial entities (International Finance Corporation - Washington and Asian Development Bank - Manila) it has constantly endeavoured to offer customized services that are driven by customer requirements.

'Net Banking - A Paradigm Shift": 12 Net Banking with its wide variety of services may intensify the existing competition in the banking sector and threatens to move the customers to those banks who will he the first to get on the Net and the competition will he defined by declining prices and rising level of customer satisfaction in a transparent environment, where the customer is bound to dictate terms to the banks. The current picture of Net banking in India is a bit grey due to the following reasons:

(i) The infrastructure costs of providing such services are quite high.

(ii) Reserve Bank of India does not allow interbank funds transfer through the Net since Cyber laws are not in place.

(iii) The verification of digital signature is another major constraint.

(iv) Security aspect continues to he the major hurdle.

(v) Low PC penetration and low access to Internet is another major constraint in India unlike in the West.

At the moment e-Banking has turned out to be just another channel adding considerable costs in the short-run and it is believed that the Bricks (old-economy) has silenced the over optimistic clicks (new-economy) as electronic banking has failed to transform economies of banking'.

Caution is the need of the hour, in the wake of the lessons learnt from the dotcom crash:

(i) The dotcom era is over but the Internet era is beginning.

(ii) The Internet is not a new business; it is a new way of doing business.

(iii) A business is viable online if it is viable offline.

(iv) The number of website hits is meaningless. What matters is the number of paying customers.

(v) Services on Internet won't be free forever but they'll be cheaper than offline services.

CRM IN THE PETROLEUM SECTOR

The petroleum sector has been the longest surviving profit making industry in the world, right from the turn of the 19th century and right into the first years of the 21th century. Exxon-Mobil and Shell continue to post the highest turnover and profits in the world year after year. So do the three major oil companies in India. It is therefore obvious that the oil companies have a little secret up their sleeve that helps keep customers and earn substantial profits in spite of the high dosages of taxation, which Governments all over the world like to levy on oil products.

What type of customers do oil companies have? A wide variety I should say. The retail trade that dispenses petrol and diesel to motorists is the biggest segment. The customer is the retail outlet dealer and the end consumer is the motorist, which is you and me. Oil companies have a close relationship with the dealer community. They recruit them, train them and their employees, keep track of their profitability, punish them if they do not perform as desired and reward them when they deliver the objectives. Oil companies have been using computers ever since IBM started mass-producing the 1401's and historical records of dealers are available for the last 50 years. Dealers consult the Regional Managers before they get their daughters married or their son(s) sets up a new business. I would say that this is one fine example of CRM.

What about the end consumer in the retail trade? One would agree that it is too cumbersome to keep track of 10 million motorists. But, each retail outlet would keep track of the regular customers that come to his outlet. He does that by offering him credit for his purchases. A typical corporate customer for cars would sign a slip and pay at the end of the month. The trucker fills his tank 'with diesel at the beginning of his journey and pays when he returns from his designation after collecting the freight charges. But then the dealer operates this type of transaction and the company has no liability. All the same it keeps the customer loyal to the dealer and the company' profits by it. A primitive form of CRM, one would say.

A more sophisticated version, which has been introduced in the last few years, is the prepaid, card. Most oil companies in India have launched such cards in selected markets. A limitation of service providers to administer the scheme across the country is the constraint that prohibits a national launch. These cards come with bonus points, gifts and prizes for regular customers and more for high value customers. Essentially it ties in the customer to the company's outlets as these cards can be used at most outlets. This is an improvement on the credit offered by the dealer and brings in extra flexibility to the customer who has an option to fill at any convenient outlet of the company.

Management consultants conclude from their research that credit would play a very important part in retaining customers. And therefore it may not be adequate to let credit management be left to the dealers who have severe limitations in this record. Hence, oil companies are getting into arrangements with banks that can offer credit through the dealers and the company and the dealer also profit from this arrangement. The movement of the truck is also tracked efficiently through satellite based communication systems, which also keeps the fleet owner satisfied. Thus came the concept of the fleet card, which is fast gaining popularity amongst fleet owners, as they now do not have to dole out cash to the drivers. The fleet card is typically a prepaid card and is also used for tracking the movement of the truck whenever the driver uses the card.

The second major category of customers for the oil industry is the highly price sensitive LPT consumer. It is normally the lady of the house who interacts with the distributor for her requirements. The dealer and company typically have her name, address, telephone number and few other details in their computer records. The oil industry would have the details of nearly 50% of the town or citys households by location. This database is yet to be exploited for any cross selling of goods and services. The existing data needs to be augmented with income, family size, education, etc., so as to use it for other than accounting purposes. The day is not too far away when such data would be centrally available for consumer marketers to target their products. However, the focus today for CRM is primarily on industrial customers. A small number of customers in the industrial sector purchase large quantities of high value fuels, lubricants and speciality products. These products can be sold on credit at special discounted prices from different locations to multi-unit customers. Customers like their accounts consolidated at the unit level as well as at the centralized level. Details of product despatch become a key factor in maintaining low inventories and also to avoid stock ours. How do oil companies go about it?

RETAIL: THE WORLD'S LARGEST INDUSTRY

In the retail industry over 50 of the Fortune 500 companies, and around 25 of the Asian top 200 companies are retailers. The industry accounts for over 8 per cent of GDP in western economies. The level of consolidation within each country has increased significantly over the last few decades. This trend has led to organised networks capturing upto 80 per cent of the grocery market in the developed economies, and upwards of 20 per cent in developing economies. Further, global markets will progressively get easier to tap as product market barriers are relaxed and tastes converge. Profits in retail have steadily been rising and have generated 18 per cent shareholder returns between 1994 and 1999. When compared banks 9%, insurance 15.2%, consumer goods 11.2%.

Significantly, retail is also one of the world's largest employers, accounting for 16% of the US workforce and 12% of Poland. Wal-mart, Carrrefour, Tesco, Hemp Depot and Kingfisher are benchmark retailers in these fields. Factors such as scale in sourcing, merchandising, operational effectiveness and ambience have driven the spread of organised retail. Grocery, electronics and DIY are examples of categories that compete on the strength of better pricing, which in turn is driven by superior sourcing and merchandising, and cost-efficient operations. The recent evolution of the Internet has helped further broaden the scope of operations of large retailers as a number of large retailers are pursuing innovative demand aggregation and supply chain streamlining initiatives using B2B technology (e.g., Global Net X change, RetailExchange.com).

RETAILING IN INDIA: THE EMERGING REVOLUTION

In its nature, the Indian retail market is in sharp contrast to the global situation. Like the rest of the world, it is large, with sales amounting to $ 180 billion and accounting for 10-11% of the GDP. However it is also exceptionally fragmented and unorganised. With close to 12 million outlets today, India has the largest retail outlet density in the world.

However most of these outlets are basic mom-and-pop stores with very basic offerings, fixed prices, zero usage of technology and little or no ambience. These are highly competitive outlets, drawing on free land (unregistered kiosks or traditional property), unpaid cheap labour and zero taxes in retailing.

There are multiple causes for this low level of modernisation in Indian retail. Primary among them are the stifling restrictions on consumer goods and consumerism that existed till the 1990s. The consumer industry was suffocated by controls; production was paralysed by a license system and companies were either forbidden entry or denied manufacturing scale. Marketer's inability to create economies of scale in sourcing, the high fragmentation in suppliers and the supply chain restrictions on interstate movement and on stocking prevented development of scale.

Further the limited set of organised options prevented retailers from negotiating better terms with their suppliers, the lack of a consumer culture, along with low incomes, prevented the development of retail formats such as department stores that work on superior ambience and design to capture consumers. Limited products put, consumers perpetually on the back foot. The last nail in the coffin was probably the lack of regard for retail as an industry, leading to there being virtually no access to capital, land or people available to aspirant retailers. The lack of retail-oriented education courses made it difficult to get trained people. Constraints on foreign direct investment prevented the entry of most of the world's leading' retailers, organised retailers were cost disadvantaged against their non-organised competitors by the high tax evasion by the unorganised sector, prevented from creating a national sourcing scale due to the inter-state tax complexities, and were additionally bound by complex and often inconsistent legislations. All of this resulted in India having the most basic form of retailing.

We see the opportunities in the Indian retail market as failing into three categories, requiring different approaches to ensure success. These categories are defined by the level of sophistication of the supply chain, and the degree to which change is required in consumer shopping behaviours. "Ready-to-go" sectors are those where the supply chain is reasonably sophisticated and there is little change required in consumer shopping behaviour. These sectors are primarily dry grocery, electronics, apparel and malls. Within the Indian regulatory and infrastructure situation this itself is a significant challenge and only a few will succeed.

"Shape-and adapt" sectors are those where at least one of these two parameters requires to be and can be restructured. These include women's apparel, DIY, fresh grocery and fast food. The challenges in these markets are very different by category. In womens apparel, the prize will go to the retailers who can develop scale in sourcing while ensuring a high level of customisation of ethnic wear. In DIY management of a complex sourcing system will need to he complemented by a marketing effort to change the consumer's mindset towards purchase of such products. In fresh grocery, the winners will be those. Who can make the requisite investments in the sourcing chain to reduce wastage and ensure that high quality fresh products are available at competitive prices.

Finally the "wait and watch' sectors are those that are constrained by market intrinsic or regular barriers and include liquor, pharmacies and fuel. In these cases, the retailers ability to influg and manage regulation is the key to entry. In determining how to capture these opportunities important not to lose sight of the past, it would he' too conservative to infer that these failure proof of the Indian penchant for traditional stores over modern formats. However, the failures should serve as a warning that the Indian consumer like his brethren elsewhere is a savaltie-for-money shopper, and retailers who plan to pursue this opportunity need to be sure they can deliver value. As a result of this concurrent evolution in consumers, suppliers competitors, there has been a noticeable shift in the importance of the organised retail sector a clear base established for future growth.

(i) *Hubs of retail activity have emerged*: Chennai, Bangalore and Hyderabad have been major retail hubs. In Chennai about 17% of food sales flow through supermarkets and 30% of durables sale come from speciality chains such as viveks and vasanth.

(ii) *Scale of operations changing*: Subiksha has over 50 stores in Chennai. Food has 41, spread over Chennai, Bangalore and Hyderabad. This growing scale enabling these supermarkets to eliminate links in the purchasing chain and to deals with food processors directly. In fact, the scale of purchases has made India's largest consumer goods company, HLL dedicates a special team to deal with these emerging retailers.

(iii) *Purchasing habits in metros shifting towards supermarkets*: The increase in variety, quality and availability of products as well as an increase in spending power has resulted in consumption increasingly using supermarkets for their personal shopping.

(iv) *More competitors are eyeing the sector*: Large conglomerates like Tata, ITC and the Rajan Raheja group have initiated investment; the Birlas have acquired the Madura garments apparel business, while Reliance has publicly committed to developing a retail business along with the development of its fuel-retailing network.

(v) *Foreign retailers looking for entry options*: The increasing attractiveness of the sector raising the interest of a number of global retailers.

(vi) *Retailers need to manage the environment*: The retail industry will need to ensure management of these constituencies in order to flourish, all branded goods companies therefore were more than willing to forge strategic relationships with the large retailers the nature of the alliance being determined by the relative bargaining power of stakeholders.

(vii) *Relax the supply chain regulations*: To resolve issuers with the upstream, policy makers need to do away with the constraints on processing, manufacturing and distribution.

(viii) *Relax SSI regulation*: The reservation of large sub-segments for the small scale render processing sector, particularly in food and apparel, inciticient. The reservation shout lifted at least partially to let larger and more efficient players enter these sectors.

(ix) *Remove distributions constraints*: Allow marketers to buy directly from farmers and lift restrictions on food grain movements across states. Further investment in distribution infrastructure should be encouraged through fiscal incentives.

To Develop These Integrated Businesses, Retailers Need to:

(i) *Leverage the net*: Ensure that the power of the Internet leveraged, along with the strengths of the offline business.

(ii) *Concentrate on economics*: Focus and keep strong track of the core economic drivers of the business, namely customer acquisition costs and transaction fulfilment cost.

(iii) *Carve out and integrate*: Ensure integration where required, but do not stifle the creativity and innovation required to manage an Internet business. Retailers entering the Indian market need to determine how best to integrate an online offering with a bricks and mortar presence. At the outset, this is likely to be an issue mainly for booksellers and travel agencies. But almost all types of retailers can proceed with their c-tail plans without the fear of cannibalization, the restructuring of logistics networks, or attacker's. In India, they are the attackers.

WHAT COULD RETAIL LOOK LIKE IN 2010?

If retail continues along its current growth path in India, sales are likely to touch $300 billion by 2010, with 6-7% of this flowing through modern channels. Given the moderate-income growth and the slightly easier operating environment, modern retailers would tread cautiously and certain businesse's and formats might fail. If the leaders, who would also be expanding conservatively, were able to capture a share of 5% of the organised sector in grocery and apparel, India would have companies ranging from $450 million in size in grocery and 90 million in appare (up from $40-45 million currently)

Now imagine this. It's 2010, the second phase of India's economic reforms are successful and per captia incomes are growing by 9-10%, leading to similar growth in spending levels. Retailing is now a recognised industry. In addition, the sector has been unshackled - supply chain constraints have been eased, global retailers are permitted to compete in India, real estate markets made more organised and finally the tax structure rationalised. In this future, retailing in India could be a large as $450-500 billion and organised formats could account for a 20-25% (around $100- 124 billion). This would be similar to where retail in Indonesia is today and would imply a slightly slower pace of change than was witnessed in Thailand. This share of modern formats would imply that 40-45% of purchases in urban centers would switch to organised channels and that these channels would be able to capture a substantial part of demand from the middle income categories. In this aggressive scenario, the leaders in the grocery and apparel markets with market shares of 5% would be 2 billion and in apparel $350-400 million in sales.

What is realistic lies somewhere in between these two scenarios. Incomes and consumer demand are likely to grow at a faster pace as the economy performs well, lifestyles continue to change and better product and shopping options become available.

On the regulations front as well, it is likely that several important changes will take place, e.g., foreign investment will be per limited into the sector constraints impacting the sector will be relaxed, etc. This transition will however, be gradual. In this scenario, the industry is likely to grow to around $350 billion and with organised retailers accounting for 10-15% of the value ($35-50 billion).

This is similar to where China is today - in terms of standards of living, spending and modern retailing. In its tier on e cities, China already has nearly 40-hyperrnarkets, over 4100 supermarkets/convenience stores and 220 department stores, and this figure is expected to increase rapidly. Visualising a similar scenario for India would suggest that India would probably have an average of 2-3 hypermarkets in each of its top 15 cities, each with 2-3 supermarket/ convenience/drugstore chains. China has achieved this position with a more complicated supply chain and strong operational constraints, though with a higher income level and the advantage of global expertise.

Even in Poland organised retailers have grown from a negligible figure to 10% in less than ten years. In this scenario, then the leaders in the grocery and apparel markets with market shares of 5% would be around $1-1.5 billion and in apparel $200-250 millions in sales. Electronics would also boast of at least one or two large retailers with sales of $100-200 million each. It is going to be very difficult to predict if any of these scenarios come true. What is certain is that the opportunity is large and that retailers who wish to capture it need to begin working towards it immediately. And, even though there may be easy pickings, the large opportunities will require significant effort, bold investments and government support.

CRM IN HOSPITALITY SECTOR

An organisation rarely finds its most valuable asset in the balance sheet. Yet this asset - customer satisfaction - has more impact on long-term performance than any other variable in the business today. The customer is back again in the core of the business strategies. We are now driving towards establishing a dialogue with our customer, to understand and anticipate their evolving, individual needs and maximize the lifetime value of these relations. The idea behind developing a relationship with the customers is not new. Customer relationship management in a sense is the way the corner grocer used to treat his customers. What is new now is that the concept is to be applied on an "industrialised" basis for tens of thousands even millions of customers that is what is entirely new.

It is called customer management, customer information systems, customer value management, customer care and sometimes customer centred. But clearly now the term 'Customer Relationship Management' (CRM) has overtaken the market. We have gone back to the old way of doing business, a customer at a time, but millions of customers. That is CRM today. CRM is a business strategy to select and manage the most valuable customers. CRM is customer centric business philosophy and culture that supports effective marketing, sales and service process. CRM applications are effective provided that the enterprise has the right culture, strategy and leadership.

Hospitality product is largely people-based, consumer and experienced in close encounter with the service provider, lasting more than one interaction. This is punctuated by moments of truth leading to dissatisfaction.

Hence people, physical environment (ambience) and process have a significant role to play. The intangibles (service, ambience) along with tangibles (food, lodging) are equally important. Getting the right blend makes the hospitality service fairly complex and challenging. While hotels serve to provide a 'home away from home', restaurants Offer an ambience expected to be different from the home. The interaction with the customers in the hotels is often of a longer duration where the conception of EAI (Extended Affective Interaction) holds. This in turn raises certain expectations, namely responsiveness, empathy and assurance, essential components of total offer.

(i) *The Hospitality Industry*: Traditionally, the hospitality (and service) industry has been perceived to be different from other industries for the reasons of its perishability (a hotel room, if not sold today, cannot be carried as inventory, intangibility (a hotel stay is an experience) inseparability (simultaneous production and consumption of all hotel services) variability (of service delivery). Moreover, the service delivery process becomes part of the marketing process for a hotel.

Simply put, the marketing department communicates a promise to the customers: this creates awareness, expectations, and influences the ultimate purchase decision. However, in order to deliver this promise, it is essential for the organisation to build an internal process and systems that encourage employees to give their best in terms of service to customers. The delivery of the promise is affected by the operational employees who become an integral part of the marketing process, through their interaction with the customer while delivering the promise. The process as described above thus has a fundamental impact on the moment of truth, which is basically every moment when the customer interacts with the employee of the hotel during the process. In the hospitality industry, expectations are created by the promise. Expectations may also be influenced by prior experiences, opinions of friends and associates or on the image of the hotel. Every guest walks into the hotel with an expectation. So it is really the moment of truth that defines value for a guest. For a hotel, therefore, service quality is of utmost importance, especially in view of the fact that a lot of employee-guest interactions are carried out in the absence of direct supervision. Weinstein and johnson (1999) have defined three levels of the service offering such as core benefits, hygiene factors and satisfiers. Applying this to the hospitality where services, the Core benefit: the basic need satisfied by the hotel in response to what the customer is actually seeking. This reflects the basic product the guest wants to purchase (e.g., a room, a meal, status, etc.) Hygiene factors. this is the minimum acceptable level of service attributes that customers would expect in a hotel (e.g., direct dial telephone services, wake up calls, laundry services, air conditioning, restaurants, in-room television, etc). If these services are, not delivered or delivered poorly, customers experience dissatisfaction. However, simply offering 'them or performing them adequately does not lead to customer delight, since customers take them for granted as part of the service package. Satisfiers are those attributes, which differentiate the hotel from its competitors, while simultaneously exceeding customer expectations. They have the potential to create high customer satisfaction levels. 'These are value-added services that go beyond what the customer expects and these create value.

(ii) *Customer relationship*: In the marketing literature the terms customer relationship management and relationship marketing are used interchangeably. As Nevin (1995) points out these terms have been used to reflect a variety of themes and perspectives. Some of these themes offer a narrow functional marketing perspective while others offer perspectives. While others offer a perspective that is broad and somewhat pragmatic in approach an orientation. A narrow perspective of customer relationship management is database marketing emphasizing the promotional aspects of marketing linked in database efforts. (Bickert 1992). Another narrow yet relevant viewpoint is to consider CRM only as customer retention in which a variety of after marketing tactics are uses for customer binding or staying in touch after the sate is made. A more popular approach with the recent application of information technology is to focus on individual or one-to-one relationship with customers that integrate database knowledge with long-term customer retention and growth strategy (Peppers & Rogers 1993)", Thus, Shani and Chalasani (1992) define relationship marketing as an integrated effort to iaentify, maintain and build up a network with individual customers and to continuously strengthen the network for the mutual benefit of both sides through interactive individualised and value added contracts over a long period of time". Gronroos (1990) states: "marketing is to establish, maintain and enhance relationships with customers and other partners, at a profit, so that the objectives of the parties involved are met. This is achieved by mutual exchange and fulfilment of promises. The implication of Gronroos definition is that is the 'raison de etre' of the firm and marketing should he devoted to building and enhancing relationships".

(iii) *The hospitality industry and CRM*: CRM process in hotels is governed by the basic principle that good service does not guarantee customer satisfaction. And satisfaction does not guarantee loyalty. There is therefore, need for strong customer relationships to build loyalty. For the hospitality product, the customer relationship is governed by the moment of truth. This fundamental truth, combined with the unique characteristics of the service industry has traditionally focused the complete attention of the service provider on the customer. Even a market share-oriented approach would necessarily need to take care of the customer. The unique characteristics of the hospitality industry have deep implications on building customer relationships. Perishability is where the hospitality product cannot be stored. While pricing and promotions are normally utilized as strategies to manage demand variation, which may not be sufficient to ensure efficient management of demand.

However, combined with loyalty built through relationships these strategies can result in better demand management, thus minimizing variation and optimizing occupancy and yield. Intangibility while the physical structure and certain components of the hospitality products are tangible, a hotel stay is primarily an experience and is consummated by the service elements of the product. Since the management of the moments of truth essentially depends on intangible factors, these are critical for building successful customer relationships. Inseparability- consumption of a hospitality product is inseparable from its production; that means, unlike manufactured goods, there is no scope for quality checks prior to consumption. Any change in delivery methods can affect the quality and value of the service. Since inseparability defines the moment of truth, it is, critical to manage the moments of truth in order to provide value and build successful customer relationships. Due to the high involvement of customers in the service delivery process in hotels, variability in production standards is a major concern. This is especially true of the many hotel services where employees and customers interact in the absence of supervision.

Extensive and intensive training of employees is required, in order to ensure successful service delivery, and constant attention to motivation and morale is needed in order to ensure successful management of the interaction and therefore customer relationship. Where the service can be deliberately varied to meet the specific needs of individual customers, an opportunity arises for the hotel to utilize the variation to build customer relationships based on the unique preferences and requirements of individual customers. This may take the form of mass customisation for key segments or individual for key guests. The key to CRM in the hospitality industry is the presence of satisfiers. The tangible elements of the hospitality product are manifested in the core benefits and hygiene factors, which are necessary conditions in order to eliminate customer dissatisfaction.

But it is really the satisfiers that create value for the customer. Satisfiers are often intangible in nature and can be critical in building relationships and loyalty. The tangible elements can often be duplicated by competition, and do not sustain competitive advantage other than hotel brands.. But satisfiers, if focused on and developed, have the potential to become unique to a hotel and can help in building and managing the relationships with the customers. Hence, customer relationship management in hospitality is the continuous process of managing the moments of truth and a search for opportunities to create value for the customer with the ultimate objective of generating customer loyalty based on the constant interaction of the customer with the product and employees of the hotel.

(iv) *Objectives*: There are many ways for maintaining customer relationship. The main variables are customer satisfaction, service quality, customer retention strategies, training and retaining the internal customer, developing customer loyalty, complaint management, data management, and effective communication. Where most of these are intangible in nature the study was focused on these areas. Both management of hotels as well as the customers were interviewed with the help of structured questions:

   (a) To study the managerial practices followed by hotel industry in the study areas in building customer relationships through proper segmentation, quality, complaint management practices, customer data collection process, employee retention and training practices, communication process followed.

   (b) An attempt was also made to know the customer opinion on the areas of satisfaction they received and their opinion of quality of services, complaints made and the responsiveness of service providers.

   (c) To find the gaps in building CRM.

(v) *Methodology*: Visakhapatnam the City of destiny - consists of more than 15 lakhs population and is industrial based city with a heavy floating population has been selected for the study.

Basically, Visakhapatnam is a commercial city consisting of two Five Star Hotels and four Three Star Hotels. All six hotels put together have around 600 rooms of different types, to serve to the customers where most of them are regular visitors to the city. For out of six of these hotels and 20 customers (both regular and occasional) have been contacted for gathering the data. By keeping the objectives in mind, care was taken in selecting the respondents from management, customer, as well as in selecting the hotel. The executives and guests of the hotels were interviewed with the help of structured questions. The collected data is presented in the following lesson with through analysis takes analysis is mainly focused on what is required for CRM, the practices observed in the industry and the opinion of the customers. Finally, the important gaps between customer expectations and perceptions have been discussed and suggested suitably.

(vi) *Analysis of findings*: Sometimes companies fail to understand customers accurately because they fail to focus on customer relationships. By adopting a relationship philosophy, on the other hand, companies begin to understand customers over time and in greater depth, and are better able to meet their changing needs and expectations.

Basing on the data collected through structured interviews with the management of hotels as well as with the guests of the hotels on the variables influence, the CRM such as segmentation, quality, employee retention and training, complaints, communication process, customer data collection and customer satisfaction levels. A thorough analysis was organised and mentioned below are the findings.

(i) *Methodology*: The foundation of an effective customer relationship strategy is market segmentation-learning and defining who are the customers organisations one wants to have relationships with. Segmentation helps in understanding the guests likes and dislikes and facilitates in providing customized services—helps in offering different services to different customers. It is observed from the hotels that the basic segmentation variables are price and services (benefits) offered. Mainly concerned on corporate groups, foreign travellers, conferences, group incentives travellers and weekenders. Efforts were on to target the young generation. The consumers expressed their satisfaction on the differentiation showed and facilities provided.

(ii) *Quality*: In service, quality is the delivery of excellent or superior service relative to customer expectations. In hospitality services, it is the consumer who defines quality. Therefore, the human side of service is the key to deliver quality. No doubt many of the determinants for quality of products can be applied to the service, but the human side of service is missing to a considerable extent in case of services. In assessing the hotel quality, customers perceive multiple factors. Such as reliability, responsiveness, assurance, tangibles and empathy. It is observed that initial research is apparently not present from management side to close the expectations perceptions gap. Standard rules were provided to staff to carry out various operations and were mentioned. Around 50% of service employee turnover is observed, except in one case, which resulted in making services more reliable. No in-depth training programs has seen to build responsiveness and assurance with the service provider which is required to improve the willingness and knowledge of service provides. A monotonous room decor is seen depending upon the type and not much efforts have been made to change the decor in the same type. Consumers study confirms that finding new faces of service providers in each of their visit leads to less reliability and assurance. Unfamiliarity also leads to less empathy and responsiveness of service providers and expresses the expectation of different decor at each of their visit.

(iii) *Empowerment*: In the hospitality industry the importance of front line employees in delivering the services is significant. This has given raise to the need for empowerment. The interest shown by the management in empowering their employees is worth examining to understand the customisation of services. When asked, whether their employees are empowered to make decisions in favour of the customers, most of them expressed that their employees have been empowered to take independent decisions within the guidelines nothing but limited empowerment. Customer respondents also expressed that the concerned employees are not fully empowered resulting in normal to abnormal delays in serving and in solving the problems.

(iv) *Complaints*: Hotel industry is largely people based. More and prolonged encounters punctuated by moments of truth leads to problems. Despite the best efforts, there are always going to be situations in which a customer becomes unhappy. The effective complaint management will lead to customer loyalty and results in customer retention. It is observed that on an average the rate of complaints is 10% through unsolicited sources and 30% through solicited sources. Standard feedback forms are also collected. However, it is noticed that in many of the cases it is a reactive approach from the management rather than proactive. It is also observed that not much effort has been taken to prevent the problems. Many disagreed to disclose data on complaints recorded and necessary measures taken. Customers expressed that the small problems are attended immediately which are within the limits of the service provider. But in many cases communication gaps and delay in solving the problems are expressed.

(v) *Customer database*: A well-designed customer database is essential in hotel industry for implementing customer retention strategies. Knowing the current customers, their preferences on room decor, food, usage patterns, likes and dislikes forms the foundation of customer databases. With a foundation of customer knowledge combined with quality offerings and value, a hotel can engage in retention strategies to hold on to its customers.

It is noticed that all hotels are maintaining guest profiles or histories of all guests visiting their hotels but on limited information about contact details, organisation, designation, preferences of food, room type, etc. Effective use of this information is not seen. Customer contact employees are not trained to note the customer tastes, preferences on various encounters to build strong customer data.

(vi) *Communication*: Direct interaction with the guests through executive visits to customers, executive listening helps in having first hand information about customer expectations. In the same way, responding to customer complaints and visits through proper communication channels even on the departure of the customers will help in building relationships. Management responses revealed that they continuously keep on communicating with their regular customers especially on the complaints made. In most of these cases the medium used is telephone. But not much paper communication has seen about the changes taking place in the hotel and benefits offered except in the cast of corporate customers. Rate of executives visits to customers is high. A mix of opinion is expressed by consumers about the communication they receive from the hotels where they stay on various activities of new products, special benefits and on complaints made.

(vii) *Customer satisfaction*: The success of any hotel depends on the satisfaction derived by their customers. Satisfied customer will not only retain with the organisation and also acts as a word of mouth to the service. Customer satisfaction survey can be used to determine the extent to which customers are satisfied and delighted, and they extent to which this influences customer retention. All hotels are using the feedback forms at various service encounters in gathering the customers satisfaction levels. However, not much action is seen on the information gathered. Many times it is a reactive approach.

All hotels are using the feedback forms at various service encounters in gathering the customers satisfaction levels. However, not much action is seen on the information gathered. Many times it is a reactive approach.

Customer perception reveals that collecting feedback is a routine and except on few areas, not much change has taken place.

(i) *Discussion and conclusion*: Effective CRM goes beyond service. It involves implementing systems and processes to ensure that the management process promises, builds an environment for effective delivery, and delivers the promise in a manner that exceeds the customer's expectation, thus adding value and building the relationship.

(ii) Many hotels have built complaint systems around expressed, or registered, complaints. Registered complaints represent only the tip of the iceberg of A customers' complaints. Latent complaints can be generated through all customer contacts. Complaints requiring the most attention are those having the greatest potential impact on customer loyalty. Effective attention to complaints need a database of complaints. Communicating the changes made on customer complaints can be extended to more number of customers. So that the present repeat customer rate of 50% in the occupancy can be increased.

(iii) Selection of service employees is vital because the hotel industry is a people intensive industry. Employee turnover rate reflects on costs as well as on the quality of the services.

Customer contact employees training programs should focus more on retention and in explaining the benefits of their retention. It is also important to define the 'exact role and responsibility the employee plays in interacting with and building guest satisfaction. Customer contact employees need to be more empowered to perform their functions efficiently and to accept the responsibility and to avoid the delays under proper supervision. Communication is restricted to a limited number of customers on complaints made, on the feed back forms of the consumer and about new introductions and benefits. It would be better for the organisations if they extend the list of customers to communicate on these areas. It will result in customer loyalty as well as retention.

Finally, consumer profile organisation process of collecting data and using customer profile effectively is vital in the hotel industry. Hotels should raise to the level of developing customer data on all, aspects through their internal customers. The internal customers should be trained enough in developing the customer profiles and preparing the profiles, which in return, may help to be proactive. The key to successful CRM is to identify key customers based on the profiles developed and ensure that there is a continuous search for opportunities to add value for them. No relationship em be successfully initiated and managed without satisfied, motivated and empowered employees. To the extent possible hotels should customise their services and should continuously monitor the relationships.

(6) HOSPITAL AND NURSING SERVICES AND CRM

The current state of CRM programs and implementation in the service sector in India is very rudimentary. In fact "customer-focus" is very limited. With respect to Hospital service providers, CRM seldom goes beyond a one-sheet patient feedback form. (Set Appendix 1 for samples of patient feedback questionnaires). It is again doubtful whether any of the feedback will be incorporated for rectifying current practices, thereby enhancing patient loyalty. Usually, such hospitals have a marketing wing, which is responsible for closely monitoring the feedback. However, the analysis subsequently carried out by them and the remedial measures implemented are not a streamlined effort or worst still are non-existent. They are also in the nature of 'hospital acceptable" measures of patient satisfaction and not 'Patient driven," measures of satisfaction. The remedial measures are more in the nature of "damage control". They neither seek to delve into reasons for dissatisfaction nor origins of dissatisfaction.

(Usually in the nature of rectifying deviations from "hospital acceptable" levels of satisfaction and not from 'customer-centric satisfaction')

There is a need to focus on additional ways of maximising patient satisfaction with the care received. Staff training, on how to maintain good customer relations; changes in organisation and scheduling to minimise patient discomfort and waiting times; adoption of architectural and design styles that provide warm and appealing as well as functional environments; market research and so on. There is a need to further appreciate that the above activities represent only one side of the coin. The providers need to go outside their walls to cultivate those who act as the distributors of health care.

In health-care provision, someone other than the end user (patient or client) typically decides which provider will supply needed health care services. A large percentage -of hospital volume is tied to physicians and corporate employers. Under such circumstances, there are special requirements for successfully developing enduring relationships with those who distribute health care services - the physicians and employers.

Learning what may create - or promote - customer loyalty is one step of the process that contributes to enduring ties, ensuring that the services offered meet the needs of customers and that changes are made as needed is also an essential step. Tactics that will open lines of communication invite serious interest in what an organisation has to offer, and give confidence that it is responsive to customer needs have to be formulated and implemented effectively. Health care organisations, in other words, need to be customer-driven in the fullest sense of the term.

In todays environment customers cannot be taken for granted. There is an increasing trend towards corporatisation and privatisation of hospital services. Gone are the days when the loss of a patient can be shrugged of. More and more people have incomes and the desire for quality services. The smartest of hospital service providers need to spend time and resources looking closely at the reasons for patient loss and take steps to eliminate them. They must make sure that they may take their business elsewhere. This could be due to quite a few reason such as:

(i) Lack of proper procedures;

(ii) Unsatisfactory service;

(iii) Uncompetitive price charged for the service.

The best way of retaining customers is to deliver a level of high customer (patient). Satisfaction through price, people, processes, physical evidence, place and promotion (product, yet another 'P' of the marketing mix is not mentioned because, in a service sector like a hospital, product is a constituent of all the other P's). This will result in strong loyalty and ultimately will show up on the bottom line as positive customer feedback and increased revenue; and the starting point is the development and implementation of an efficient CRM program, which is inclusive of a SRM program and PRM program.

Current CRM efforts in a hospital are transactional in nature. If the hospital is to move from transactional selling to relationship marketing, the hospital needs a suitable structure. Effective relationship with the patient requires the active cooperation of all departments within the hospital. It also requires the managers to recognise that serving the patient requires more than just good doctors and an infrastructure. It needs to he a coordinated activity across the entire service providers if they are to create a value-laden relationship. Relationship marketing is based on the theory that in order to feel valued by their provider customers' need focussed tailored and continuous attention.

CUSTOMER EXPECTATIONS FROM HOSPITAL SERVICES

In order to better understand how building relationships with suppliers and operations personnel within the hospital services would result in better CRM, it would be useful to list some of the expectations that the customers (patients) have from hospital service providers and also to list, the suppliers, who ultimately are responsible for fulfilling these expectations.

When customers enter into a relationship for buying a service, they have expectations of the service that they should be given. These expectations are shaped by their previous dealings with other service providers in the same category. Their expectations are also shaped by the type of products they have purchased, the price they have paid, is well as such factors as the service providers (hospital's) brand and advertising messages. If the hospital is to successfully build on the relationship it has with the customer it needs to understand the patient's expectations in order that it can meet them, or indeed surpass them if at all possible. While individual patients have different expectations of the service, the company should expect that it probably would not be able to meet absolutely all of them.

There will be, however, many that are common to most patients and these must be met if the hospital is to retain these people and enjoy repeat business from them. Patients will have expectations that relate to the hospitals they visit, the personnel that deal with them, and of the service transaction as a whole. Listed below are some of the typical expectations that patients would have:

(i) Patient (customer) expectations from a hospital:

(ii) Proximity, central location

(iii) Clean environment

(iv) Adequate space to move about

(v) Comfortable lobby seating

(vi) Adequate space in patients rooms

(vii) Attached toilets in, the patient rooms with a geyser facility

(viii) Pure filtered water availability

(ix) Timings to suit their requirements

(x) Diagnostic services, pharmacy and dietary services within the compound of the hospital

(xi) Lift services

(xii) Laundry services

Patient Expectations from Hospital Personnel

Some of the more visible hospital personnel include doctors, nurses, attendants, reception personnel, billing personnel, ambulance personnel, and diagnostic report division personnel. These are the people with whom the customer has an immediate bearing.

From Doctors

(i) To be an expert in the field

(ii) To be gentle, a querier, a confidence booster and wordy

(iii) To be one who can explain the problem in common terminology and put the patient at ease

(iv) To be tidy and smart

(v) To be able to justify the need for running umpteen diagnostic tests

From Nurses

(i) To be gentle, cheerful, helpful and friendly

(ii) To be tidy

(iii) To be able to answer simple queries pertaining to the disease To appreciate the need for privacy by the patient

From attendants

(i) To be tidy

(ii) To be cheerful

From reception personnel

(i) To be able to guide patients to respective divisions

(ii) To be well groomed and courteous

(iii) To be able to handle rush hour situations

Billing and registration personnel

(i) To be able to give a user friendly bill

(ii) To enter registration datas correctly

(iii) To have technology and procedures which are customer focused

As already mentioned earlier, patients have expectations of hospitals and hospital personnel performance. If the performance of the two is to be in accordance with the expectations of the patients, it is obvious that the suppliers of those services be the best in the field. It is also essential that hospital service providers' develop a strong and positive relationship with the suppliers of these inputs even if they have to pay a premium for it. These relationships have to be of an enduring nature since seeking and partnering new suppliers frequently would he a very expensive and time-consuming proposition. The service provider could use that time spent on supplier search and acquisition more judiciously on customer relationship building and retention. It is therefore essential that any CRM effort should first ensure a proper SRM followed by a PRM. This will automatically result in customer loyalty and retention.

Problems of Nursing Homes

Hospitals are providing health care to only those who are approaching them, there are no programs specifically designed to attract the customers. They have poor linkages with the community and the family and no feedback programs/ activities are undertaken once the patient is treated. Most of the patient complains of a great distance between the doctors and the patients. This gap has to be narrowed and seen to it that the nursing homes should-concentrate on providing personal attention and good nursing care, which is also revealed by our study as the factor the customers give due importance.

Lack of managerial training and motivation to employees, besides professional skills the owners of nursing homes also needed managerial skills to manage and market their health care services effectively. So I suggest here that management institutions should come forward and design sector specific training programs for enhancing the managerial skills. Absence of effective personnel, it has been revealed by the study that few of the owners of nursing homes are not going for further expansion and are not satisfied with the performance of their nursing homes. The reason being the non-availability of qualified and trained staff and it takes a lot of time to recruit and select qualified and experienced staff. And if the nursing home wants to build a good customer relationship than it becomes utmost necessity of nursing homes. It has been also seen that, in order to have a CRM there has to he again, concessions given to the customers in the form of revisits allowance, special cases, providing free food, laundry, etc., which requires funds, and generating funds is again a problem to the nursing homes.

The state and central governments should come out with scheme to help the nursing homes, which will certainly help in motivating the doctors and expand the base of the health care industry in India.

CRM IN BUSINESS SCHOOLS

Business schools (Mgmt Institution) are similar to other teaching institutions, in many way, i.e. infrastructure, administration, course duration and assessment. But, because of the practical nature of the subject, its academic content and faculty composition is different. The content is more extensive on projects, seminars, presentation (all practicals), placements, and the faculty is partly, full-time but largely visiting drawn from the industry, who provide students with "just-in-time' managerial inputs on practices and strategies. All teaching institutes are non-profit making bodies, but; this nomenclature has changed since the General Agreement of Trade in Services (GATS), which initiated the liberation of trade in services. GATS has classified services into 12 sectors and education is one sector, which includes primary, secondary and higher education. This service sector is believed to increase considerably, and VITO has estimated global public spending on education to be Rs 47,00,000 crores (UGC plan 2061) University Grant Commission's vision and strategy for Xth plan states. The universities and college need to be used as a focal point of activities to spread and sustain the torch of life-long learning. The vision is in consonance with the competitive scenario that is emerging because of globalisation of education which demands the use of information and communication technologies in the management of higher education. Referring to the above para, teaching institutes in general and business schools in particular are no longer charitable trusts but are "business entities" serving customer needs of Providing educational products and services.

With this analogy, it will need to face a formidable competition with other business schools (private institutes, corporate business schools, other university departments and foreign collaborations). There have been schools which have divergent management techniques (private to foreign) and these are believed to provide superior education and placements. Though we may not formally give it a business stature it can he described as serving customers (students) who have varied needs, (different educational products) demographically and psychologically varied and also a varied buying power. And to serve this divergent market, it must adopt the latest marketing tools supported by advance technology, which could give it a competitive advantage to serve larger markets. This article will explain briefly ECRM, and its application to provide business schools with information on its customers to competitively survive in future and also maintain its leadership in the current scenario.

Key E-CRM Features which can find Applications at Business Schools

(i) *Database*: One of the key requirements for customer relationship module is the customer database. The students who are the customers at institutes, (current former or ex-students) can he given a student ID (Identity Number). All the information regarding the student should be maintained according to the student's ID. The data would include name, address and other demographics, service details and also academic details, e.g., the course registered for, the attendance, the assessment and marks obtained at each semester for each subject (result description), fee payment, making for a comprehensive 'profile of the student" available at a click. The data can be stored in a centralised database server and can be accessed by other systems for retrieving or modifying the information.

(ii) *Benefit*: The 'profile of the student' can serve many valuable purposes to the institutes.

   (a) It can contribute to a "Management Information Systems (MIS); where this data can be analysed through Decision Support Systems (DSS); or data mining techniques to group students with similar profiles and education backgrounds.

   (b) Past records of customers became the precursors, for the decision maker to design future educational products.

   (c) A database comes as a handy tool to send customised messages about products to customers, or other information on new program launches and events (annual programs, felicitations, etc.)

   (d) Students who have completed the course can upgrade information of their advances in career through the ID number, and enable institutes to monitor their careers through the career advancement charts.

   (e) Unhappy Internet-enabled students can share their dissatisfaction about the courses with the institute.

   (f) Reveal hidden information and trends within the data.

   (g) Gain a complete process for identifying, targeting and responding to the needs of the most profitable customers.

   (h) Similarly a "faculty data bank' can be created to enable institutes to seek their expertise opinion at a click.

(ii) *Interactive voice response*: According to experience, a number of incoming calls at institutes can be broadly classified as:

   (a) Admission dates for various courses.

   (b) Eligibility for admission to courses.

   (c) Results announcement.

(d) Fee payment dates and amounts.

(e) Day-to-day lecture cheek and confirmation.

(f) Others.

It is generally observed that the students find it extremely difficult to get the above information for the reasons as,

(a) Non-availability of telephone operator.

(b) Not enough knowledge of the attending person.

(c) Non-availability of the correct person.

The issue can very easily be solved by using interactive voice response module in the following way: Whenever the student dials the board number, he/she would be first welcomed and asked to enter the student's ID. After entering the ID the student should be asked by the system to choose the number for accessing the required information. Even a non student can assess the information executive by choosing this option.

(iii) *Website*: Its high time for the institute to maintain their own website if not started still.' The web site should contain following major information.

(a) Brief profile- of Institute of Management, its history, ranking - countrywide and nationwide, details about the professors and faculty members, their experiences and qualifications.

(b) Details of various courses available, part time as well as full time. It should include the course period, syllabus, date of starting the course, course fees, admission procedure, the dates for entrance exams, etc.

(c) Various facilities available to the students, like library, study rooms, conference halls, presentation rooms, hostel and canteen facilities. Its location and available bus and train routes.

(d) Contact Details: Names of the concern connectable persons with phone and fax number with e-mail address and postal address. A site map of the institute.

(e) Placement: Names of reputed companies coming for the placement, their pay offerings, positions, percentage of students selected every year, through campus interviews. The views of organisations regarding quality of students.

(f) Linkages to the informative and e-learning sites from where the student can download the required knowledge data.

(iv) *Student's log in*: Existing student can log in the web site through a special window provided on the web with the log in password provided by the institute. He can view the following information:

(a) Time table, availability of lecturers, any lecture cancellation report.

(b) Schedules of the companies arriving for the campus interview.
(c) Schedules for the internal tests and test results.
(d) Last dates for submissions.
(e) Details of the events organized in the institute pertaining to his area.
(f) Formats of the various forms required in the course duration.

(v) *e-mail*: It is the simplest and easy to operate tool in the customer relationship management module. E-mail server can be configured with various other systems to send an e-mail to the student with the following major purposes.

(a) A welcome message to newly admitted student informing him the date of commencement of the course, rules and regulations of the institute.
(b) For sending the class room and examination time table.
(c) Informing test results and final examination results.
(d) Reminder for fees payment.

CRM IN TELECOM SECTOR

Telecom companies have moved quickly to adopt CRM principles. A number of issues which can challenge CRM adoption, including the vision and commitment of senior management, choosing customers, creating new value, overcoming legacy investments and developing meaningful e- CRM strategies. These issues are barriers in the telecommunications services arena, too, although not always of equal significance. The following are some of the dimensions that merit special mention in the telecom sector:

(i) Single view of the customer: Companies with a single view of the customer are able to link call centre databases, Internet orders and inquiries, customer prospect lists, accounting files, and other databases so they have but one view of the customer. They are able to update this in real time and ensure that a customer accessing the company through the Internet, for example, is treated seamlessly if they next contact the call centre. This single view is necessary before the company can consider issues such as a learning relationship, true interactivity, prediction, and creating new value with individual customers. For telecom service companies, a single and comprehensive view of the customer, while a sought after objective, is not yet in place. For several firms, there remains an opportunity to further develop the customer data warehouse and knowledge management, and deploy software to manage all inbound and outbound customer interactions.

(ii) *CRM as a series of tactics*: The full potential of CRM will not be realized until one view of the customer is in place. But, more generally, telecom service companies would do well to see CRM as more than a series of tactics to realise customer value. It is highly beneficial to send out highly targeted customer promotions and measure the ROI of these promotions. It would also be very advantageous to redefine and restate the strategy of the business as a CRM strategy.

(iii) *Businesses well known for B2B CRM:* Telecom service companies deploy sales reps to cover business-to-business accounts. These reps know their accounts well indeed, but they are less well supported by CRM technology than they right be. Opportunities exist, for example, for each salesperson to be a CRM manager, reviewing the relative importance of their business accounts, seeing computer-generated suggestions for effective behaviour management, and selecting personalised and customised communications solutions to drive this behaviour, all at a distance, on-line. Software exists to ease this task.

(iv) *Customers triaged according to their value*: Telecom companies have already assessed the value of their customers to the company and have triaged customers by this value - 'Best', 'Average' and 'Worst' or according to their profitability and potential for growth. Some telecom service companies have used this triage as a basis to organise their companies according to the value of the customer. They often have the processes in place to address each type of customer efficiently and effectively. As suggested by comments from the preceding section, there remain opportunities for some companies to more fully realise the value potential of their customers through technology, to manage customer churn, to increase the scope of services used from a single service provider, and to build a learning relationship.

(v) *Excellent use of people to respond to e-mails*: From personal experience, telecom service companies do a great job of personally responding to e-mails but might do more with technology to handle the flood of e-mail. There is not only a need to intelligently manage the flood of inbound e-mails that many companies are experiencing but to tie in a corresponding outbound management system, ideally with a single solution. Companies can do much more than simply automate the response. It is no longer acceptable to many customers to receive a timely but irrelevant or impersonal response, which has obviously been sent by an automated system. Software and service bureaus are available to manage responses, analyse content in e-mails to auto-reply in context with personalised messages. Without technology intervention, telecom service companies will have to scale up or refocus some among their human resources to meet the challenge, not quite what their shareholders have in mind.

Technology enables companies to automate, personalize and customize interactions, with minimum human intervention.. The right technology can provide an intelligent response to every customer choice on-line. Part of the challenge is to do this so it adds value to customers unobtrusively, in real-time or near real-time. An example: a customer visits MegaCDs.com adds a classical CD to their shopping cart, but then leaves without fulfilling the transaction. MegaCDs.com then automatically followsup by e-mail a few days later offering that particular CD at a reduced price, perhaps bundled with another CD also likely to appeal to the buyer.. and so on. Outbound e- mail that is customised and personalised in a manner such as this, using more than simply the name of the respondent, can generate more than 10 times the response rate of banner advertising, according to a US consultancy.

Telecom service companies want to forge close and enduring customer relationships and many have taken important steps to ensure that they do precisely this. Yet it still appears to some businesses and consumers as though additional value remains to be unlocked from the customer data the telecom companies have and the knowledge and insight they could create and use.

INTERNET IN TOURISM (E-TOURISM)

Internet has become one of the most important information sources for tourism worldwide. Global exposure through Internet has triggered off a desire to travel overseas. e-tourism sector remains the first Internet sector in terms of value. There is an increase in the number of Internet users using services to get driving directions, maps, for place to stay, for things to do, airline schedules, travel packages. A new type of user slowly but surely is appearing. According to the survey carried out by the Forrester Research Firm, the Internet has become one of the most important sources for European travel worldwide.

The predominance of the Internet as a favoured information source is such that among European Internet users, it is as much as 30 to 60% of them who use the Internet to get travel information. Online Consumer Sales at Travel U.S. Sites indicate the rapid usage of Internet for travel.

INDIAN TOURISM SECTOR

India, a land of variety and beauty, occupies a strategic position in Asia. A beautiful countryside, a land of temples, vast desert land with oasis, golden beaches, lakes and waterfalls, varied rich wild lift, mountain ranges constitute a great potential for tourism. Though tourism is the third largest foreign exchange earner for India, it is not given the right kind of importance it deserves. Tourism gains momentum when translated into a marketable product through well-planned, integrated programs. The need of the hour is a business like approach in promoting tourism. In business terms, every tourist is a prospective sales agent.

He markets tourism more than any brochure, booklet or advertisement, does. Hence, business strategy in tourism should involve attracting people of all classes, which in turn accelerates the means of bringing all the potential tourists for a quantum leap in Indian Tourism. Not only attracting the tourists is vital, but also developing goodwill is imperative. It is essential to offer services of money worth to develop goodwill.

CASE STUDY

INTRODUCTION

CRM is a set of strategies, processes, metrics, organizational culture and technology solutions that enhance an organization's ability to see the differences in its customers' and prospects' behavior and needs, track new opportunities to better serve their customers and act, instantly and profitably, on those differences and opportunities. Recently CRM has taken a center stage in the business world with businesses concentrating on saving money and increasing profits by redefining internal processes and procedures. It costs a company dramatically less to retain and grow an existing client, than it does to court new ones. It is said that "It is seven times more expensive to acquire a new customer than to keep an existing one", therefore the value of customer information and management should never be underestimated.

Customer relation management analysts say CRM is "a buzzword that's really not so new. What's new is the technology is allowing us to do what we could do at the turn of the century with the neighborhood grocer. He had few enough customers and enough brainpower to keep track of everyone's preferences. Technology has allowed us to go back to the future to this model." The aim of CRM is optimize the use of technology and human resources for the business to gain insight into the behavior of costumer.

Seeing the new market (CRM) emerge, the world's leading business software vendors have reinvented themselves to focus on CRM, and there has been a fierce competition for the dominance in this market. Technology is now an essential part of CRM nowadays but buying technology before defining CRM business goals, is a recipe for disaster. It is important to remember that technology used for CRM should be 'tailor-made' depending on the type of consumer base of the company and the business goals.

Companies need to understand CRM in relevance to customers and customers only. Technology like call center services and software's will prove helpful only if they improve the customer services and relation, otherwise all fancy technology is useless if it fails to benefit the customer.

INTRODUCTION

Aim of Customer Relationship Management is to produce Customer Equity. Three major drivers of customer equity are:

Value Equity: This measures the customer perception about benefits relative to its cost. The sub-drivers of value equity are quality, price and convenience.

Brand Equity: Customer's subjective and intangible assessment of the brand beyond the objectively perceived value. The sub-drivers are customer brand awareness, customer attitude towards the brand, customer perception of brand ethics.

Relationship Equity: Customers tendency to stick to the brand above and beyond the objective and subjective assessment of its worth. Sub-drivers of relationship equity includes loyalty programs, community building programs and knowledge building program.

EVOLUTION OF CRM IN BANKING SECTOR

Regulation and technological improvements are responsible for the vast majority of innovations in banking over the past quarter century. The introduction of personal computers and the proliferation of ATMs in the1970s captured bank management's attention. The regulatory changes in the 1980s fueled much of the industry's growth, then downsizing as bankers focused on amassing market presence which resulted in significant merger activity. Recent technological improvements are at the root of bankers' focus as well as a target for their significant investment dollars today. In fact, according to recent projections, bankers and their financial service company brethren will spend almost $7 billion this year on CRM and increase that by 14 percent each year for then next several years.

Looking at this CRM phenomenon in light of the drivers of banking innovation since the 1970s, one might wonder if CRM itself is the innovation, or (conversely) the technology, once again. Much is being written about CRM. Bankers at all points of the CRM spectrum are looking for a way to quantify their return on investment—either what it actually is or, if just starting out, what it should be and over what period of time should the value be realized. Ironically, the answer to this question may lie in a simple review of a few known quantities generated from historical innovation. Look, for example, at ATMs. What drove many bankers to invest in ATMs was the promise of reduced branch cost, since customers would use them instead of a branch to transact business. But what was discovered is that the financial impact of ATMs is a marginal increase in fee income substantrially offset by the cost of significant increases in the number of customer transactions. The value proposition, however, was a significant increase in that intangible called customer satisfaction. The increase in customer satisfaction has translated to loyalty that resulted in higher customer retention and growing franchise value.

Internet banking, a product of the 1990s, shows similar characteristics. Again, bankers invested believing that the Internet was a lower-cost delivery channel and a way to increase sales. Studies have now shown, however, that the primary value of offering Internet banking services lies in the increased retention of highly valued customer segments. Again, the intangible called customer satisfaction drives the value proposition.

Now we explore CRM. CRM is not another ATM or Internet bank. It is not a checking account, a stock or a mortgage. In fact, CRM is not anything a customer should even know about! You will never sell your customer your CRM, will you? So, one can conclude that CRM is not tangible. If it's intangible, can it be expected to produce a tangible return? Probably not, or at least not with any direct financial value exclusively linked back to the investment in CRM.

CRM is primarily driven by the innovation of technology, but unlike other technological innovations, CRM has power to help bankers quickly and directly improve customer satisfaction. CRM is an added dimension to ensure that what the customer expects is consistent with what the bank is prepared to deliver. One expert in bank CRM initiatives recently said that CRM is an approach that is less focused on providing the right services to the customer than attracting customers who are the right fit for what the bank has to offer. Further, the primary value of CRM is its potential as a customer retention tool. People are starting to measure CRM in terms of increased customer satisfaction, rather than ROI. So how much of a return can you expect from your CRM investment, and when can you expect it? Refer to your reasons for continuing to offer ATM and Internet banking services. The answer for CRM is the same.

FACTORS CONTRIBUTED TO THE RAPID DEVELOPMENT AND EVOLUTION OF CRM

Growing de-intermediation process in many industries due to advent of sophisticated computer and telecommunication technologies that allow producers to directly interact with end customers.

Databases and direct marketing tools have given the means to individualize their marketing efforts. As a result, producers do not need those functions formerly performed by the middlemen. Even consumers are willing to undertake some of the responsibilities of direct ordering, personal merchandising and the product use related services with little help from producers.

The de-intermediation process and consequent prevalence of CRM is also due to growth of service econoany. Since services are typically produced and delivered at the same institutions, it minimizes the role of middlemen. A greater emotional bond between service provider and service user also develops the need for maintaining and enhancing the relationship.

Another force driving the adoption of CRM has been the Total Quality movement. When company embraced Total Quality Management (TQM) philosophy to improve quality and reduce cost, it became necessary to involve suppliers and customers in implementing the program at all levels of value chain. This needed a close working relationship with customers, suppliers and other members of marketing infrastructure.

With the advent of digital technology and complex products, system selling approach became common. Customers liked the idea of system integration and sellers are able to sell the augmented products and services to customers. The popularity of system integration began to extend to customer packaged goods, as well as services. At the same time companies started to insist upon new purchasing approaches such as national contract and master purchasing agreement, forcing major vendors to develop key account management programs, these measures created intimacy and cooperation in the buyer-seller relationships. Instead of purchasing product or services customers were interested in buying the relationship with a vendor.

Current era of hyper competition, marketers are forced to be more concerned with customer retention and loyalty. As retaining customer is less expensive and perhaps a more sustainable competitive advantage than acquiring new ones.

In the era of dynamic environment customer expectations, cooperative and collaborative relationship with customer seem to be most prudent way to keep track with changing and appropriately influencing it.

CRM BUSINESS CYCLE

CRM

1. Understand customer's needs
2. Differentiate based on customer needs, Characteristics and behaviour
3. Develop product services Channels to meet customer's needs
4. Customize by Customer segment
5. Interact with customers and prospective customers
6. Deliver increased value to the customer
7. Acquire customers and prospective customers
8. Retain valuable customers

CHANGING APPROACH OF CRM

Traditional Approach	*Web-enabled and Integration Approach*
Customer contact Telephone, Mail, in Person	Customer Information System, Customer Data-base
Personal selling	Electronic Point of Sales Force
After sale services	Automation of customer support process
Account Management	Call Centers
Customer Care	System Integration
Customer Satisfaction	Life Time Value of Customer

Private Banking and CRM

Private Banks have traditionally viewed themselves as exceedingly 'Customer Centric' offering what they believe to be highly personalized services to the High Net Worth Customers. However, changes in the customer behaviour and accumulation of wealth are resulting in the needs of HNW customers becoming more diverse and complex in terms of the sorts of products they want, the channels through which they want to access them and the associated range of advice.

IJIJI Bank

IJIJI Bank was originally promoted in 1994 by IJIJI Limited, an Indian financial institution, and was its wholly-owned subsidiary. IJIJI's shareholding in IJIJI Bank was reduced to 46% through a public offering of shares in India in fiscal 1998, an equity offering in the form of ADRs listed on the NYSE in fiscal 2000, IJIJI Bank's acquisition of Bank of Madura Limited in an all-stock amalgamation in fiscal 2001, and secondary market sales by IJIJI to institutional investors in fiscal 2001 and fiscal 2002. IJIJI was formed in 1955 at the initiative of the World Bank, the Government of India and representatives of Indian industry. The principal objective was to create a development financial institution for providing medium-term and long-term project financing to Indian businesses. In the 1990s, IJIJI transformed its business from a development financial institution offering only project finance to a diversified.

IJIJI Bank is India's second-largest bank with total assets of Rs. 3,446.58 billion (US$ 79 billion) at March 31, 2007 and profit after tax of Rs. 31.10 billion for fiscal 2007.

IJIJI Bank is the most valuable bank in India in terms of market capitalization and is ranked third amongst all the companies listed on the Indian stock exchanges in terms of free float market capitalization.

The Bank has a network of about 950 branches and 3,300 ATMs in India and presence in 17 countries. The Bank currently has subsidiaries in the United

Kingdom, Russia and Canada, branches in Singapore, Bahrain, Hong Kong, Sri Lanka and Dubai International Finance Centre and representative offices in the United States, United Arab Emirates, China, South Africa, Bangladesh, Thailand, Malaysia and Indonesia. Our UK subsidiary has established a branch in Belgium.

IJIJI Bank's equity shares are listed in India on Bombay Stock Exchange and the National Stock Exchange of India Limited and its American Depositary Receipts (ADRs) are listed on the New York Stock Exchange (NYSE).

Based in India, IJIJI Banking Ltd. is a technology-driven virtual universal bank that delivers a wide range of corporate banking and personal finance products and services, all under one umbrella. IJIJI implement an enhanced customer relationship management solution that provided front-office staff with a single view of customers and their contact history with the organization across products and channels. This solution was a key component in IJIJI's overall strategy to deliver more value to its customers by deploying more customer centric communication technologies and improving online self-service. The platform supporting the e-business solution provided the highest levels of reliability, availability and scalability, along with simplified management.

IJIJI Bank is partnering Indian industry at every level. From customizing innovative solutions for global Indian corporates to supporting indigenous R&D and cleaner technologies. Our customers have come to rely on our in-depth expertise, value-added products, and advanced multi-channel banking facilities provided by the IJIJI to fulfil their CRM through providing more and more services to the customer.

Business Services		*Banking Made Easy*	
Transaction Banking	Rural and Agri. Banking	Internet Banking	Business Banking Card
Treasury Banking	Structured Finance	FX Online	Inquiry Card
Investment Banking	Technology Finance	Multi Pay	Payment Cards
Capital Markets		Online Trade	Phone Banking
Custodial Services		Email Statements	Mobile Banking
International Banking		Kiosk Banking	Online Tax

The Benefits

A powerful, scalable and flexible technology platform is essential for banks to manage growth and compete successfully. And Finacle provides just the right platform to IJIJI Bank thus fuelling its growth.

The bank has successfully leveraged the power of Finacle and has deployed the solution in the areas of core banking, consumer e-banking, corporate e-banking and CRM. With Finacle, IJIJI Bank has also gained the flexibility to easily develop new products targeted at specific segments such as IJIJI Bank Young Stars—a product targeting children, Women's Account addressing working women and Bank at campus targeting students.

IJIJI Bank is today recognized as a clear leader in the region and has won numerous accolades worldwide for its technology-driven initiatives. In 2003, the bank received the best multi-channel strategy award from *The Banker* magazine and this year it was rated as the 2nd best retail bank in Asia by *The Asian Banker Journal*. The bank has effectively used technology as a strategic differentiator, thus not only redefining the rules of banking in India, but also showcasing how technology can help in transforming a bank's business.

FUTURE PLANNING OF IJIJI

IJIJI Knowledge Park (IKP) nestles in a 200-acre pollution free zone in Genome Valley, Hyderabad. The master plan of the Park mirrors its objective of nurturing an environment for innovation and the expected growth in life sciences and related fields. It has a mix of ready-to-use multi-tenanted modular wet laboratory blocks (Innovation Corridors) with in-built flexibility around some common, shared facilities and support services, as well as developed land for customized R&D facilities.

Currently, the 140,000 sq. ft. Innovation Corridor 1 with 84,000 sq. ft. of wet laboratory space is operational. Around 35 acres of land has been developed with utilities for customised R&D centers.

Mission

"To create a world class centre for leading-edge business-driven research in India."

A hassle-free environment

The Operations and Maintenance of IJIJI Knowledge Park is certified by ISO 9001-2000.

IKP provides a range of support services to the resident companies to create a congenial stress-free environment and ensure customer delight. The infrastructure services include electricity, telecommunication, and refuse disposal, conference facility, meeting rooms, cafeteria and gymnasium. Professional agencies take care of common services like round-the-clock utility maintenance, IT administration, surveillance and security, doctor's services, housekeeping and landscape maintenance to ensure safe, reliable and hassle-free operations. The administrative support services include speedy customs clearance, environmental clearances, legal/patent counseling, assistance in getting venture funding, S&T advisory services, liasoning with government departments, secretarial services etc. Some key analytical facilities like a 300 MHz NMR, LCMS, HPLC, GC, FTIR and Polarimeter are available at IKP.

Issues

Some issues significant at this time includes:

How to connect this vast new pool of employees with each other;

How to share business-related information about clients, deals and ideas;

How to manage staff through the change process via communication, messages, channels and so on;

How to overcome the problems caused by staff turnover;

How to ensure that every person in the company is adequately equipped with the skills and training required for their jobs and for lifelong learning and development.

The deeper question was, quite simply, how do we create a hunger among staff to acquire and share knowledge? That is to say, how do we create the culture? The aim was to ensure that employees stayed permanently aware of the external competitive challenges of the business, and to persuade them to remain constantly open to new thoughts, ideas and ways of working.

Finacle Solutions for IJIJI Bank

Finacle CRM solution offers features tailor-made to the banking domain. The ready to deploy functionality for service requests and complaints management increases efficiencies in customer service processes significantly.

Asset origination can be streamlined through straight through account opening in Finacle core banking solution.

Customer acquisition and retention strategies can be executed through the Campaign and Opportunity management features. All these business functionalities are backed up by a very sophisticated workflow engine which allows mapping of all types of business processes from the most simple to the most complex.

They enable IJIJI bank to setup or consolidate call centres. Our native support for email obviates the need for any other Email management tool to communicate with customers. And our Interaction management framework consolidates all customer communication across channels so that bank staff have a Single View of customer interactions.

CONCLUSION

Banking can be anysterious for consumers and how they interact with their finances can be a complex matter. The challenges faced by banks and their customers are many but the trick lies in de-anystifying complex financial relationships.

Technical solutions deployed by banks today are flexible, user-friendly and meant to facilitate specific workflow and requirements in implementation processes. In order to simplify lives, banks have begun to implement end-to-end technologies through all departments with the intention of removing human error from processes. Previously existing manual environments could not have been adequate for future visions, growth plans and strategies.

In this day and age, customers enjoy complete luxury in terms of customized technical solutions and banks use the same to cement long-term, mutually-beneficial relationships.

FOOD FOR THOUGHT

Security

As banking is converting itself into e-banking to increase its customer relationships through providing them a very big add on services base but here security aspect on internet put very big question mark on it.

Infrastructure Costs

As banks are providing large number of services to its customers for CRM but it results into heavy burden of infrastructure costs on the financial sector.

Not proper Internet Services

As stated earlier that the financial sector in India is converting itself into electronic services from manual services, but it needs very good base of Internet which is not available in India at present. So, it's very big hurdle in the way of financial sectors to provide CRM easily to its customer.

STUDY-QUESTIONS

Discuss the role of CRM in the following:

(i) Hospitality;

(ii) E-tourism;

(iii) Hospitals and nursing homes; and

(iv) Financial services.

Glossary

Abandoned shopping cart Set of products a customer intended to buy, but did not ultimately purchase. Although possible in a brick-and-mortar store, the term more accurately applies to a Web site where a visitor collected one or more items in his virtual basket but never made it as far as checkout.

Acculturation: The process of learning a new culture.

Actual self A person's self-image of who he or she is.

Addressability A feature of a database wherein each customer's address is known in order to enable a marketer to address marketing communications individually on a one-on-one basis.

Adoption (of an innovation) Customer acceptance of an innovation for continued use.

Advocate sources Communication sources that have a vested point of view to advocate or promote.

Affect The feelings a person has toward an object or the emotions that object evokes for the person.

Affective choice mode (ACM) A decision mode wherein affect or liking for the brand ensues a choice based not on attribute information, but based on holistic judgments.

Affinity analysis Detecting sets of products or services purchased together. Example: Tortilla chips and salsa.

Affordability The possession of adequate economic m-sources needed to buy and use a product or service.

Aggressive personality A person who values personal accomplishment over friendship and socks power and admiration from others.

Analytical CRM Use of data originating through front- office or operational CRM to enhance customer relationships. Combined with other organisational or external data to evaluate key business measures such as customer satisfaction, customer profitability, or customer loyalty to support business decisions.

Annual purchasing agreements Agreements made by government agencies with specific suppliers, which allow the governmental entity to purchase small items routinely.

Application services provider (ASP) Company whose business is outsourcing application services for its client companies. Such applications can include both tactical systems, such as billing systems, and strategic solutions, such as CRM. (CRM ASPs currently account for over half of the ASP market.)

Approach/avoidance motivation The human desire to attain a goal-object and desire to avoid an object of negative outcomes.

Arousal-seeking motive The drive to maintain the organism's stimulation at an optimal level.

Assimilation and contrast Information within the acceptance range is assimilated and accepted; information outside of this range is contrasted and rejected.

Assortment The number of different item a store carries. Asymmetrical power one party has more power over the other.

Atmospherics The physical setting of the store that influences customer behaviour. Atomistic family unit A person living alone.

Attitude hierarchy The sequence in which the three components of attitude-cognition, atect, conation-occur.

Attitude Learned predisposition to respond to an object or class of objects in a consistently favourable or unfavourable way.

Attitude molding Forming a new attitude or changing a preexisting attitude.

Attitude persistence After initial attitudes are formed through exposure to ads, the extent to which these attitudes persist over time until the actual purchase decision is made.

Attitude strength The degree of commitment one feels toward a cognition, feeling, or action.

Attitude valance The favourableness and unfavourableness of attitudes, i.e., of thoughts, feelings and actions about an object.

Attitudinal brand loyalty A customer's consistent repurchase of a brand due to his or her preference for it.

Attraction of alternatives How attractive a customer finds alternative brands to be.

Attribution motivation Humans' innate need to assign causes to events and behaviours.

Attributions Inferences that people draw about the causes of events and behaviours.

Attrition Customer leaving to go do business with a competitor.

Authoritarian families Families where parents exercise strict authority over children; children learn to obey their elders in all matters.

Automated workflow Enabling work processes to "flow" through a company without human intervention. Workflow systems usually involve moving data through a process, such as order and fulfilment, that reaches across various systems and departments.

Automatic call distribution. Ability for call centre telephony software to balance incoming calls across agents, thereby optimizing agent productivity and minimizing customer wait times.

Autonomous decisions Decisions that are made independently by the decision maker.

Autonomy One's power to control his or her own life.

Awareness set Brands a customer is aware of.

B2B Common abbreviation for "business- to-business.'

B2C Common abbreviation for "business-to-consumer."

Back-office CRM The area of CRM that involves analysis to optimize customer-facing business processes and revenues. See also Analytical CRM.

Bargaining A method of conflict resolution, based on distributive justice for all, wherein the dissenting members negotiate a give and take.

Behavioural brand loyalty A customer's consistent repurchase of a brand.

Behavioural compatibility The degree to which an innovation requires no change in existing behaviour.

Behaviourally anchored scales Measurement scales that utilize descriptions of specific behaviours to which the respondents express their reactions.

Behaviourism theory The theory that a person develops a pattern of behavioural responses because of the rewards and punishments offered by his or her environment.

Beliefs Expectations that connect an object to an attribute or quality.

Biological determinism The belief that human behaviour is determined by biological factors such as genetics and DNA.

Borrowing power The anticipated level of income of a person (lifetime disposable income and asset accumulated through savings); a primary indicator, in addition to income and wealth, of a customer's economic condition.

Brand belief A thought about a specific property or quality associated with a brand.

Brand equity The enhancement in the perceived utility and desirability that a brand name confers on a product.

Brand loyalty A customer's commitment to buy and use a given brand repeatedly.

Brand parity The concept of how similar and mutually substitutable the brands are.

Brand valuation The financial worth of a brand name. Business A licensed entity engaged in the business of making, buying or selling products and services for profit or non-profit objectives.

Brick-and-mortar business A physical storefront or branch. Brick-and-mortar can be a company's core business or simply one of several sales channels.

Business cycle A cycle of boom and recession experienced by the business world and caused by fluctuations in the economic environment.

Business intelligence Normally describes the result of in-depth analysis of detailed business data. Includes database and application technologies, as well as analysis practices. Sometimes used synonymously with "decision support," though business intelligence is technically much broader, potentially encompassing knowledge management, enterprise resource planning, and data mining, among other practices.

Business markets Customers who buy products for use of the organisations they work for.

Business process reengineering (BPR) Redesigning core business processes to drive organizational and technological efficiencies. Term made popular by Michael Hammer and James Champy in their 1993 book Reengineering the Corporation.

Business sponsor Manager or executive who acts as visionary for the CRM program and can articulate how CRM can drive business improvements. This person establishes the "need, pain, or problem" CRM will solve, serves as a tiebreaker for issues during the project, and might actually fund some or all of CRM development.

Buyclass Type of purchase need in terms of its newness.

Buyer A person who participates in the procurement of the product.

Buyers' remorse The regret customers feel after buying a product or service because they are unsure if buying it was wise.

Buying counter All the members of a customer firm who play some role in the purchase decision.

Buy-side business models A buying organisation using Internet-based technologies to buy from contracted suppliers.

Buy-to-browse ratios The proportion of customers who come to browse on the internet concluding the browsing by buying.

Call centre automation Use of technology to facilitate communications to, within, and out of a call centre. Automatic routing of calls to specific CSRs is one example of call centre automation.

Call centre Organisation in charge of direct customer support interactions. The term "call centre" refers to the classic telephone support infrastructure and is being replaced by "contact centre" or "customer care centre," both of which imply more technological sophistication and multichannel support.

Call routing Directing customer calls to a specific agent based on a specific parameter such as that agent's expertise, geographical location, subsidiary affiliation, or other characteristic.

Campaign management Analysing data for purposes of launching a marketing campaign and then monitoring that campaign and tracking its results to determine the campaign's value.

Central processing route Message content is attended to and scrutinised actively and thoughtfully.

Change agent A person or organisation that brings about a planned social change.

Change targets People whose behaviour is sought to be altered by change agents.

Changing demographics Change in characteristics such as age, income, and geographic location of customers in a given market.

Channel optimisation Determining the best channels by which to communicate with and sell to customers, especially when they have not made these preferences clear, and making these channels available to the right customers. For example, a company might choose to use rescuers to sell a product in order to minimise its costs.

Churn Customers leaving your business to go to a competitor. Implies the customer might or might not return. "Churn reduction" is another way of saying customer retention and is a major goal of CRM. Churn is most often used in conjunction with highly competitive commodity product businesses such as communications companies, utilities, and airlines.

Classical conditioning The process in which a person learns an association between two stimuli due to their constant appearance as a pair.

Clickstream Series of page visits and associated clicks executed by a Web site visitor while navigating through the site. Analysis of clickstream data can help a company understand which products, Web site content, or screens were of most interest to a given customer.

Climate A component of the geophysical market environment, consisting of temperature, wind, humidity, and rainfall in an area that affects consumers' needs for food, clothing, and shelter.

Closed-loop campaign management Using the results of past campaigns to refine future campaigns, the goal of which is to hone customer knowledge while improving campaign response rates over time.

Cocooning The habit of staying at home rather than going out.

Cognition A thought about an object.

Cognitive consistency The principle that a person desires consistency among all his or her beliefs or thoughts.

Cognitive dissonance A tension between two opposite thoughts, typically manifested after a customer has bought something but is uncertain whether a correct choice was made.

Cognitive learning The acquisition of new information from written or oral communication.

Collaborative commerce Known as c-commerce," reflects the ability of various partners within a supply chain to share important data about products, inventory levels, and orders.

Collaborative CRM Specific functionality that enables a two-way dialogue between a company and its customers, through a variety of channels, to facilitate and improve the quality of customer interactions.

Collaborative filtering A computer program that allows the prediction of a person's preferences as a weighted sum of similar other people's preferences.

Commitment An enduring desire to continue the relationship and to work to ensure its continuance.

Communicability The extent to which an innovation is socially visible or easy to communicate about in social groups.

Compensatory model A decision rule and process where a customer arrives at a choice by considering all of the attributes and benefits of a product or service and mentally trading of the alternative's perceived weakness on one or more attributes for its perceived strength on other attributes.

Competitive procurement A government buying procedure whereby there are two approaches: invitation for bid (IFB) and request for proposal (RFP)'.

Complexity Extensiveness of effort it takes to comprehend and manage the product during its acquisition.

Complexity of an innovation The difficulty in comprehending an innovation.

Compliance Steering customer behaviour by government regulation.

Compliant A personality trait where a person acts in an agreeable number to earn others' acceptance and friendship.

Compulsive buying A chronic tendency to purchase products far in excess of one's needs and resources.

Compulsive consumption An uncontrolled and obsessive consumption of a product or service, likely to ultimately cause harm to the consumer or others.

Computer telephony integration (CTI) Combining telephone systems with computer technology such as software applications and databases to automate functions. Example: Using caller-id to provide customer information when distributing calls to CSRS.

Conation The action a person wants to take toward an object.

Concept-oriented families Families that are concerned with the growth of independent thinking and individuality in children.

Concurrent protocols A record of respondent thoughts at the rime of decision making.

Conditioned stimulus (CS) A stimulus to which a new response needs to be conditioned.

Configuration support Usually a component of sales force automation. Automates the estimation process for sizing and pricing a product, using prospect or client data as input. Companies selling complex custom products, such as computer equipment, are the main users of configuration support tools.

Configurator Common name for tool that performs configuration support. Also the brand name for Siebel's configuration support tool.

Conjunctive model A decision-making procedure wherein the customer examines all alternatives on a set of attributes or evaluative criteria in order to identify an alternative that would meet minimum cut-off levels on each attribute.

Consumer Another term for customer but in a household market.

Consumer behaviour odyssey A qualitative research project undertaken in the late 1980s in the U.S. that involved personal visits by an interdisciplinary team of academic consumer researchers to a variety of consumer sites.

Consumer socialisation The acquisition of knowledge, preferences, and skills to function in the marketplace.

Contact centre A more sophisticated version of the classic call centre, which was staffed by telephone operators. Contact centre suggests a greater degree of technological sophistication, including multimodal customer support, out- bound telemarketing, and customer self-service.

Contact management Area of sales force automation that allows salespeople to record key customer information such as names and addresses, as well as organisation charts and account activities. Prevents salespeople from having to remember who's who at each of their accounts.

Content-based filtering A recommendation for web sites based on consumer preferences for product attributes.

Control group Group of customers, usually randomly selected, whose responses to a campaign are compared to those of a specially selected customer group that is more systematically chosen. Evaluating customer responses to a specially designed communication with the responses of a control group can indicate the effectiveness of a target marketing campaign.

Convenience sampling A method wherein a group of customers are recruited based on convenient availability.

Convenience value Saving in time and effort needed to acquire the product.

Cookie Unit of text placed on someone's computer when he accesses a Web site, intended to serve as a permanent way for the site to recognise that customer when he returns. Allows the site to track various pieces of information the customer submits to the site across multiple visits.

Co-production A situation wherein customers routinely provide direct input into the making of a product or service.

Corporate image The public perception of a corporation as a whole.

Corrective advertising Advertising whose message includes a correction of a previous deception.

Country-of-origin effects Bias in customer perceptions of products and services due to the country in which they are made.

Cross-functional Description for a technology that serves more than one business function (e.g., financial analysis and sales analysis) or organisation (e.g., Human Resources and Accounts Receivable). CRM point solutions, by their definition, are not cross-functional, whereas CRM suites might be.

Cross-selling Selling a customer a product or service based on her past behaviours or purchase history. Best done when a company understands the relationship between two products and identifies which product might "pull" another.

Customer interaction centre (CIC) Evolution of the operational call centre into the locus of all inbound and out-bound customer communications, with special focus on customer satisfaction and multimodal customer access.

Customer relationship management (CRM) Infrastructure that enables delineation of and increase in customer value and the correct means by which to increase customer value and motivate valuable customers to remain loyal-indeed, to buy again.

Customer semce representative (CSR) Member of the company's customer support staff (or a third-party call centre agency) who takes. phone calls and participates in Internet live-chat sessions to answer customer questions, lodge complaints, record trouble tickets, or instruct customers on product use.

Customisation Customer's ability to tailor Web site content to her specific needs, interests, and usage preferences.

Cyberagent Software program that can guide a user's decisions and recommend potential action. Cyberagents can help customers navigate a Web site, answer frequently asked questions, and suggest next steps, and their capabilities are growing all the time. Some cyberagents are animated to appear human.

Data mart Usually refers to a physical platform on which summarised data is stored for decision support. Data marts are commonly used for specific analysis purposes by a single organisation or user group.

Data mining Advanced analysis used to determine certain patterns within data. Most often associated with predictive analysis.

Data warehouse Collection of integrated data used for decision-making. Normally the system of record for detailed customer data from heterogeneous systems across the company to provide a consistent view of the business.

Decision support Data analysis with the purpose of fuelling accurate and effective business decisions. Known by the abbreviation "DSS," for decision support systems, decision support usually involves accessing data on a data warehouse.

Deep involvement A customer's extreme interest in a product or service on an ongoing basis.

Defence Acquisition Regulations (DARS) Procurement regulations that apply to the Department of Defence.

Democratic families Families where every funfly member has an equal voice and who encourage self-expression, autonomy, and mature behaviour among children.

Democratic justice A family noun in which each family member is given a voice in family decisions.

Demographics Easily verified, objective characteristics of a group of customers.

Descriptive beliefs An association in the customer mind that links an object or person to a quality or outcome.

Detached personality A person who is independent minded, entertains no obligations, and admits little social influence on personal choices.

Diagnostic The ability to diagnose why certain attitudes are the way they are.

Diffusion process The spreading of an innovation's acceptance and use through a population.

Direct marketing Classic marketing practice of communicating directly to consumers, normally via the postal service. Has evolved to encompass a range of media, from e-mail to banner ads to wireless massaging services.

Direct purchase method A method usually adopted by the U.S. Government for orders costing up to $25,000, which entails directly contacting a few suppliers and placing an order with one of them, usually on the lowest quote basis.

Discretionary expenditures The purchase of goods and services to make life physically or psychologically more comfortable beyond sustenance.

Disguised-nonstructured technique A questionnaire design wherein the research purpose is not apparent to the consumer nor are the response categories provided.

Disguised-structured technique A questionnaire design wherein the real intent of the question is disguised, but the response categories are provided.

Disintermodiation A practice in which the customer is enabled to transact directly with a firm without any intermediaries.

Disjunctive model A decision-making procedure that entails trade-offs between aspects of choice alternatives.

Door-in-the-face strategy A strategy of eliciting a behaviour by first making a large request whose refusal is followed by a small request.

Drive An internal state of tension that produces actions purported to reduce that tension.

Ecological design A strategy of influencing behaviour by the design elements of the physical facility surrounding the customer.

Ecology Natural resources and the balance and interdependence among vegetation, animals, and humans.

Economy The state of a nation with respect to levels of employment, wages, inflation, interest rates, currency exchange rates, and aggregate household savings and disposable income.

Electronic customer relationship management (ECRM or e-CRM) Activities to sell to, support, manage, and retain customers who do business through a company's Web channel. Online personalisation is an example of ECRM.

E-marketplace Online exchange that enables buyers and sellers in a supply chain to come together, providing better information (better than they would have with classic human- intensive supply chain processes) as well as automation of key business processes.

Enterprise application integration (EAI) Integration of often disparate corporate systems that routinely exchange or share data. Facilitating this data interchange between systems increases the likelihood of consistent data.

Enterprise CRM Cross-functional CRM system used across various organisations and departments. A salesperson reviewing his customer's most recent open trouble tickets before making a sales call is an example of enterprise CRM.

Enterprise portal User interface, usually Web-based, that provides a virtual window into different data sources and subject areas. Provides a common look and feel across the company for various business data, but can nevertheless be. customised to provide user-specific information at various levels and from various sources.

Enterprise resource planning (ERP) Tying together and automating of diverse components of a company's operations, including ordering, fulfilment, staffing, and accounting. This integration is usually done using ERP software tools.

E-tailer "Internet retailer." Usually refers to a company for whom the Internet is the exclusive sales channel.

Event-based marketing Detecting a key event that triggers a tailored marketing communication or business action designed to increase customer loyalty or profitability. Example: Responding to a customer's inordinately large bank deposit with an offer for a high-interest certificate of deposit.

Exchange Company partnership that beverages spending power and critical mass to negotiate more favourable deals with suppliers. Usually specific to a single industry and often involving companies that compete as well as cooperate with each other.

External data Data acquired outside of a company's internal IT organisation. Usually entails consumer data that has been cleansed, formatted, and updated with current information, but might also include market research, demographic statistics, and business and industry information.

Extranet Secure Internet site available only to a company's internal staff and approved third-party partners. Flourishing in B2B environments where suppliers can have ready access to updated information from their business customers, and vice versa.

Field service management Optimizing processes and information around support of a company's product or service on the customer's premises. Often involves a combination of CRM applications, wireless technology, and historical customer service data.

Frequently Asked Questions (FAQs) Usually a Web page wherein the company answers basic questions for its customers, such as "How do I change my name and address online?" or "How do I make a return?" Saves live service agents from repeating the same information over and over, allowing them to focus their support efforts on more specialised issues.

Front-office CRM Customer-facing CRM capability. Usually pertains to sales force automation systems and other systems that involve direct customer interactions that can be recorded for back-office analysis.

Householding Consolidating customer data to organise individuals into the households in which they live. Grouping customers within a household allows a company to be more prudent with its communications and at the same time to more accurately profile individuals in relation to one another.

incremental development Deploying periodic releases of software such that end-users receive functionality "in chunks" and not all at once.

Inferential personalisation Using analysis and extrapolation of customer behaviours and preferences, including performing collaborative filtering and other types of data mining, to tailor Web content and dictate the optimal marketing message.

Interactive voice response (IVR) Telephony software that recognizes human voice instructions or the pressing of numbers on a keypad to route customer calls to the appropriate call centre or agent.

Iterative development Desirable CRM approach of going through small, repeatable development steps to speed up software implementation and deliver small amounts of functionality more quickly. Reduces risk and allows for adjustments, enabling technical staff to refine the development plan as they go.

Knowledge management (KM) Centralised management of a company's corporate knowledge and information assets to provide this knowledge to as many company staff members as possible and thus encourage better and more consistent decision-making.

Knowledge management system Centralises a company's knowledge assets. Much of this documentation is widely dispersed both internally and externally, enabling KM users not only to access information in the system but also to supplement it with new or additional information as it's created.

Lead management Sales force automation capability for tracking and monitoring sales prospects and a company's interactions with them, as well as enforcing sales tactics and automating key tasks. Also enables telemarketing staff to pass leads along to the appropriate sales channel.

Life-stage marketing Targeting consumers based on where they are on their life continuum. For instance, a bank might e-mail a promotion for a new credit card to a recent college graduate, but might market a home equity line of credit to a recent home buyer or financial planning to a recent retiree.

Lifetime value (LTV) modelling Applying historical customer behaviours and financial information to calculate a given customer's value throughout her relationship with a company (as opposed to at a single point in time).

List generation Automatically developing a list of customers for a marketing campaign, based on specific customer characteristics. Core feature of most CRM campaign management products.

Market-basket analysis Analysis of items purchased together during a shopping trip. Need not he retail specific but can also be applied to a bank's or telephone company's products. Classic example: Peanut butter being purchased with jelly.

Marketing service bureau Third-party ,company to which marketing campaigns and mailings are outsourced for a fee. Many companies have historically relied on marketing service bureaus due to the company's lack of complete data or mailing infrastructures.

Mass marketing Traditional practice of marketing a product to an undifferentiated group of consumers. Also known as "spray and pray" or "batch and blast.'

MCRM (mobile CRM) Communicating key information to customers or internal customer support staff via wireless technologies.

Metadata "Data about data.' Usually refers to agreed-on definitions and business rules stored in a centralised repository so business users-even those across departments and systems-use common terminology for key business terms. Can include information about data's currency, ownership, source system, derivation (e.g., profit = revenues minus costs), or usage rules. Prevents data misinterpretation and poor decision-making due to a sketchy understanding of the true meaning and use of corporate data.

Multichannel Support of more than one sales or service channel; for instance a retailer's Web site and its catalogue.

Multimodal Numerous ways a customer can interact with a company, and vice versa. A call centre that allows inbound customer interactions via fax, voice, telephone keypad, or hand-held device is providing multimodal access.

Online analytical processing (OLAP) "Drilling down" on various data dimensions to gain a more detaded view of the data. For instance, a user might begin by looking at North American sales and then drill down on regional sales, then sales by state, and then sales by major metro area. Enables a user to view different perspectives of the same data to facilitate decision-making.

Operational CRM Involves customer- facing business functions. Sales force automation and customer service are two examples. See also Front-office CRM.

Partner relationship management (PRM) Qualifying, tracking, and allocating leads to third-party sales partners (e.g., rescuers) to understand how to price, market, and compensate channel partners. In effect, advocating to the partner relationship the customer differentiation inherent to CRM.

Permission marketing A customer's implicit or explicit agreement to be communicated to or to communicate with a company. Usually implies customer perception of value in the relationship, suggesting a quid pro quo between the customer and the vendor.

Personalization Company's ability to recognize a customer or prospect as an individual and differentiate its interactions with her. Although personalisation usually means individualized content delivered on a Web site, it can also involve target marketing, tailored e-mail campaigns, or customized banner ads.

Point solution Piece of software used for a specific business purpose. Example: A product that performs only automated campaign management. Many companies decide to choose point solutions for discrete CRM functions to select the best-of-breed tool for each function (rather than relying on a CRM suite from a single vendor).

Proof of concept Software trial that allows a prospect to try out the product before buying it. Delivers a realistic slice of functionality and is often used as the foundation for the first application.

Pure play (n), pure-play (adj) Refers to a dot-com company without a brick-and- mortar presence.

Referential personalisation Using explicit customer data-such as survey responses, service requests, and satisfaction feedback-to determine the best selling strategies and marketing messages for a customer.

Relationship marketing Marketing to customers based on your knowledge of their behaviours and their relationship with your company: what they do and don't purchase, how often they buy, and how they use your support services.

Retention Company's ability to keep customers by offering products and services-and, by extension, the right messages-to keep the customers satisfied and avoid losing them to a competitor.

Return on investment (ROI) Measuring CRM's contribution to the bottom line versus its cost. Most accurately performed after CRM has been put in place and improvements can be measured. "Intangible" ROI such as increased customer satisfaction might be more difficult to measure but is nevertheless also a factor in CRM success.

Return on relationship (ROR) Applies to overall value of a relationship and how it has paid off. Can describe B2B relationships, as in measuring the uplift in sales triggered by certain partnerships, or B2C relationships, as in the increase of customer satisfaction rates. Can also imply a superset of a customer's financial value to a company, specifically in cases where a customer might refer other customers to the company.

Rules repository File or database containing business rules to ensure they are tracked and understood. Example: Each time a customer opens an account online, e-mail him a welcome letter.

Rules-based personalization Involves the coding of user-defined rules that are analysed by the specific personalisation software tool and used to create tailored customer messages.

Sales force automation (SFA) Electronic tracking and management of account activities by individual salespeople. SFA data is integrated at the corporate levelto provide a company with a rich view of its customers and prospects.

Screen pop Small window that appears on a user's workstation screen to provide contextual information. Could be a survey ("How do you have this Web site so far?") or a response to a marketing analyst's mouse click on a certain product, listing the product's specifications.

Scripting Automatic "scripts" (prepared questions or comments) generated for customer service reps based on an individual customer's segment and/or customer prolific contents. Scripts remove the guesswork from determining how to respond to a customer query or complaint, guiding reps through a dialogue with the customer and thus optimising discrete customer interactions.

Segmentation Grouping customers (or products or other business metrics) to analyse characteristics or behaviours with an aim toward target-marketing specific products and services to the group.

Self-service Customers can ask their own questions or resolve problems without the intervention of a live person. Usually performed over the Web.

Service-level agreement (SLA) Contract with a service provider-be it an internal IT organisation, an ASP, or an outsourcer-specifying discrete reliability and availability requirements for a given system. Might also include such requirements as support of certain technology standards or data volumes. Outsourcer's failure to adhere to the terms laid out in an SLA could result in financial penalties.

Skunkworks CRM Project being developed "under the radar," apart from the sanctioned CRM project that might be underway. Usually the result of unhappy political situations, skunkworks projects can jeopardize the reputation and funding of the authorised CRM project by raising questions about its value, timeliness, or planned deliverables.

Steering committee Group of managers or executives charged with planning and prioritizing CRM functionality and allocating appropriate funds for CRM development, rollout, training, and usage. Can also influence CRM adoption rates and accompanying business process changes.

Sticky Web site that grabs and keeps a visitor. Often juxtaposed with the term "eyeballs," implying that one's eyes (figuratively) stick to an effective Web site.

Suite Range of functional software modules that interact with each other. Often combines marketing, sales force automation, and analytical functions.

Supplier relationship management (SRM) Offshoot of CRM that focuses on improving relationships with vendors and rescuers. SRM includes selecting the lowest-cost supplier and matching suppliers with their optimal sales channels and product sets.

Supply chain management (SCM) Integration and optimization of a company's supply chain, usually involving automation of business processes that bring a product or service to market. Can help to tighten integration and communication between a company and its suppliers and partners.

Target marketing Dividing the sum of the customer base into discrete subsets that range from large (dividing customers based on whether or not they own a product) to small (even individual "segments of one").

Touchpoint Point of interaction when the company communicates with a customer, or vice versa. One interaction - a customer order, for instance - can involve several touchpoints: comparing products on the Web (touchpoint 1), checking inventory levels (touchpoint 2), and placing the order with the sales representative (touchpoint 3).

Trouble ticket Record of a customer's call into the call centre. Usually contains identifying features such as the reason for the customer's call, the status of the Problem, and the ultimate resolution of the call. Trouble tickets enable a company to track and monitor the superset of customer calls into the contact centre to summarise the main reasons for inbound customer contacts, whether problems, questions, or service requests.

Up-selling Motivating a customer to trade up to a more expensive or profitable product. The logic is, now that I know what this customer wants to buy, perhaps we can motivate him to buy a more profitable version or model. Example: A jeweller might convince the buyer of a diamond tennis bracelet to go for larger diamonds, at a higher price.

Vertical silo An organisation or system involving a specific and often narrow business function. Example: A financial analysis system specific to a certain car model and not the automaker's entire line. The opposite of a vertical silo is a cross-functional system.

Viral marketing Word-of-mouth on steroids. Could be positive or negative, but is definitely effective.

Waterfall development Methodical and linear approach to technical development. Although rigorous, usually implies going through an entire development life cycle before deploying functionality to end users. Possible only when exhaustive, detailed requirements are known up-front; has been known to take years. The opposite of the waterfall approach is iterative or incremental development, the ideal means of deploying regular CRM functionality.

Workforce management Usually applied to staffing the customer support centre. Deals with optimizing staffing levels in terms of both numbers and skill sets. Workforce management tools can analyse historical call types and volumes and help suggest optimal call centre staffing.

INDEX